MATERIAL STRATEGIES

Material Strategies
Dress and Gender in Historical Perspective

Edited by
Barbara Burman and
Carole Turbin

A Gender and History Special Issue

Blackwell
Publishing

© 2003 by Blackwell Publishing Ltd

First published as a special issue of Gender and History, 2002

350 Main Street, Malden, MA 02148-5018, USA
108 Cowley Road, Oxford OX4 1JF, UK
550 Swanston Street, Carlton South, Melbourne, Victoria 3053, Australia
Kurfürstendamm 57, 10707 Berlin, Germany

First published 2003 by Blackwell Publishing Ltd

Library of Congress Cataloging-in-Publication Data has been applied for

ISBN 1-4051-0906-8

A catalogue record for this title is available from the British Library.

Set by Advance Typesetting Ltd, Oxon
Printed and bound in the United Kingdom
by MPG Books Ltd, Bodmin, Cornwall

For further information on
Blackwell Publishing, visit out website:
http:/www.blackwellpublishing.com

Contents

NOTES ON CONTRIBUTORS

Christopher Breward is Professor in Historical and Cultural Studies at London College of Fashion, the London Institute. The author of *The Culture of Fashion* (Manchester University Press, 1995) and *The Hidden Consumer* (ManchesterUniversity Press, 1999), he is currently researching the history of fashion in London.

Cheryl Buckley is Reader in Design History at the University of Northumbria, Newcastle-upon-Tyne. She writes on aspects of design and gender. A new book is forthcoming (with H. Fawcett), *Fashioning the Feminine: Representation and Women's Fashions from the Fin de Siècle to the Present*. She is a founder member of the new journal *Visual Culture in Britain* (Ashgate).

Barbara Burman teaches at Winchester School of Art, University of Southampton. Her research interests lie in the cultural and social history of fashion and demotic dress and textiles from the nineteenth century to the present. She edited *The Culture of Sewing: Gender, Consumption and Home Dressmaking* (Berg, 1999). Work in progress includes a book on the social life of the sewing machine.

Jill Fields is an Assistant Professor in Twentieth-Century US Social, Cultural and Woman's History at California State University, Fresno. Her book, *The Production of Glamour: A Social History of Intimate Apparel in the Twentieth Century* is forthcoming from University of California Press.

Maria Hayward trained as a textile conservator and took her PhD, 'The Possessions of Henry VIII, a Study of Inventories', at the London School of Economics. She is a Lecturer/Head of Studies and Research at the Textile Conservation Centre, University of Southampton and one of the Associate Directors of the AHRB Research Centre for Textile Conservation and Textile Studies.

Katrina Honcyman teaches in the School of History at the University of Leeds. Her publications in recent years have focused on issues in gender and industrial history including *Women, Gender and Industrialisation in England, 1700–1870* (Macmillan, 2000) and a major study, *Well Suited: A History of the Leeds Clothing Industry 1850–1990* (Oxford University Press, 2000). She is currently researching child and family labour during the Industrial Revolution.

Andrew M. Ivaska is a doctoral candidate in History at the University of Michigan. He is currently completing a dissertation tentatively entitled 'Cultural Politics in Colonial and Postcolonial Tanzania: Urban Style, Sex and the State'.

Gabriele Mentges is a Professor in the Department of Textile Sciences at the University of Dortmund. She has researched and published in the areas of history of fashion, visual anthropology, museology and material culture. Recent publications include an edited collection, *Geschlecht und materielle Kultur* (Münster, 2000), with Ruth Mohrmann and Cornelia Foerster. She is currently working on an interdisciplinary project, 'Uniforms in Motion', on the process of uniformisation of body and dress.

Eugenia Paulicelli is Associate Professor at Queens College and the Graduate Center, City University of New York. She is author of *Word and Image: Pathways of Writing* (Florence, 1996), and has published several essays on Italian writers and poets, as well as on fashion. Her latest book is entitled *Fashion Narratives: Gender and National Identity in Italy*.

Carole Turbin is Professor Emeritus of History and Sociology at SUNY/Empire State College. She is author of *Working Women of Collar City: Gender, Class, and Community in Troy, New York, 1864–86* (University of Illinois, 1992) and numerous articles, including 'Collars and Consumers: Changing Images of American Manliness and Business', in *Beauty and Business*, ed. Phillip Scranton (Routledge, 2001.) Her research on fashion and textiles incorporates her fine arts training.

Verity Wilson is a curator in the Far Eastern Section of the Asian Department in the Victoria and Albert Museum, London, where her field of research is centred around East Asian textiles and dress. Her current work focuses on clothes and culture in twentieth-century China.

1

INTRODUCTION

Material Strategies Engendered

Barbara Burman and Carole Turbin

Clothing is one of the most consistently gendered aspects of material and visual culture. It is consumed on a daily basis. Its production is a dominant force in local, national and global economies. Because clothing is highly gendered it is often emotionally charged, and always with us, literally carried about on our backs. Judging from crowds attending dress exhibitions in museums and the popularity of historical sites such as Colonial Williamsburg in the US, re-enactment events, and films and TV dramas highlighting period dress, people are not only interested in their own clothing but are also fascinated by what was worn in the past. Yet even scholars who study people's daily lives worldwide have been slow to systematically analyse dress and visual and material culture. Some anthropologists and historians of non-western cultures have drawn attention to how clothing and textiles reveal characteristics of (and changes within) specific groups and cultures, but they have focused primarily on how material objects are used rather than materiality itself, including visual, tactile and other aspects of the physical world. Historians of western society, including social historians who are committed to interpreting working people's daily lives, have paid little attention to material culture or its visual and tactile dimensions. Historians of women and gender in the West, too, have neglected dress, despite the fact that most garments are designed exclusively for one sex or the other, and that women have been seen as preoccupied with personal appearance and consumption and disproportionately responsible for the production and maintenance of clothing.

From the late nineteenth century until the early 1980s, the study of dress in the West was largely dominated by costume historians, collectors, art historians and museum curators who contributed a rich though limited body of knowledge and detailed visual record of continual changes in garment styles and textiles. Most defined their subject as fashion, the attire of elites in western society, in contrast to ordinary people's dress or utilitarian work clothes, while others focused on examples of regional or folk dress. They developed a connoisseurial approach to techniques and materials that valorised them as decorative art, and divorced clothing and textiles from the body, from everyday life and from ideological concerns. The few social scientists, including woman's historians, who wrote on dress accepted a dichotomy of fashionable/unfashionable and explained fashion as reflecting social roles or distinctions. Their 'top down' and 'trickle down' emulation model (related to Veblen's 'conspicuous consumption') assumed that fashionable styles continually changed because elites competed with each other to display wealth and status in novel ways and to distinguish themselves from their imitators. In this model, the extent that ordinary women and men were fashionable was due to their imitation of elite styles.

A more analytical approach to dress within visual and material culture began in the early 1980s, chiefly in western Europe, North America and Australia, primarily in response to new studies of consumption. Economic historians took a fresh look at consumerism in western society, replaced the 'trickle-down' model with one recognising the rich material culture of ordinary people, and pushed the birth of consumer society back into the sixteenth century or earlier. Anthropologists like Appadurai began to define consumption broadly, emphasising that it was not only a matter of individuals or markets but also a cultural process.[1] Many turned their attention to how commodification in the West influenced other countries, especially those with a colonial past, revealing the complex, often contentious, process through which cultures and identities are constructed and/or compromised. Cloth and clothing are now more fully represented in studies of consumption and culture, including those concerned with colonial and postcolonial contexts. At the same time, some feminist scholars in Britain and North America began to rethink social and cultural meanings of stylish clothing to women. Elizabeth Wilson laid to rest simplistic social psychological interpretations of fashion, characterising it neither as language nor simple cultural expression of society or individuals, but as a form of visual and tactile communication linked to the body, self and communication. She developed the notion of fashion as paradoxical and double-edged, public and private, individual and social, adorning the surface and at the same time masking and/or revealing (sometimes unwittingly) the inner psyche.[2] Valerie Steele warned feminist scholars that those who ignore fashion, or dismiss it as oppressive to women, trivial, or the realm of the rich and famous, do so at their own peril: they contradict fundamental goals of the feminist project, revealing women's agency and their own interpretations of their lives. Thus, feminist scholars who uncritically accepted Victorian medical theories that women's dress was unhealthy neglected to ask how women themselves felt about their clothing, and missed fashion's inseparability from sexuality and the body.[3]

But let us not single out women, as is too often done by critics. After all, feminist scholars were fundamentally social historians who were slow to use visual or material sources, despite the importance of textile and garment production in the industrialising societies they studied, because their field was rooted in the written and spoken word. In the 1970s and early 1980s, social historians' innovative methods often relied on quantifiable as well as qualitative sources and stemmed from central characteristics of the industrialising West in the nineteenth century. They studied a period during which officials devised new types of written records (such as census records), reformers energetically compiled statistics and reports, public education became more widespread, popular fiction and periodicals aimed at women and working people (including artisans' trade journals) proliferated, and literacy was on the increase. Some social historians (such as industrial archaeologists) considered the significance of material objects but rarely for their visual or tactile meanings. Most who were aware of the growing photographic record of people and events used visual or material sources to illustrate text rather than to drive forward an argument, in the way that quantifiers used calculations presented in tables and graphs. Recognising this gap, Raphael Samuel called for historians to treat visual sources as rigorously and respectfully as they would other forms of evidence, not least in the quest for 'unofficial knowledge'.[4] But because the written word was so central for social historians, most missed the opportunity to incorporate insights of the 'new' art and design history of the 1980s which directly addressed gender.

The neglect of visual and material sources was remedied in the early 1990s when innovative scholars, primarily in the West, turned to material and popular culture, leisure and consumerism, revealing playful, sensual, tactile, visual, imaginative aspects of daily life. These scholars came from diverse backgrounds in social and woman's history, dress history, art and design history, economic history, anthropology and literature. They built on the work of a few pioneers of the early 1980s, recognising that clothing and textiles almost uniquely combine production and consumption and private, bodily, intimate sensation, sexuality and fantasy with public self-presentation. Fashion history leaped beyond both simplistic universalising or psychological explanations and dress historians' and curators' preoccupations with haute couture and the dress of élites, while building on their valuable detailing and recording of construction and technique. Evans and Thornton first united a study of classic haute couture and contemporary fashion design with feminist cultural discourses.[5] All these scholars have in common a focus on the material and cultural characteristics of the object and/or its wearer, either as their central concern or a touchstone for wider inquiry. They define their subject as dress, which incorporates not only fashion but also everyday dress, including specialised garments such as uniforms.[6] Because, quite simply, scholarly analysis aside, everyone everywhere wears some form of clothing every day of their lives, their inquiries reach around the globe.

Because of its subject matter, the emerging field of dress history is necessarily cross-cultural and interdisciplinary. It is cross-cultural not only because of the ubiquity of clothing but also because the production of textiles and garments is a key industry operating at intersecting local, national and global levels. It is interdisciplinary because meanings of dress and textiles are multiple, many-layered, and overlapping, concerning, for example, individuals, aesthetics, sexuality, cultures, economies, and ideologies.[7] Interdisciplinary scholarship can be analytically powerful, if it avoids the pitfall of using interpretations, sources or evidence from several disciplines uncritically, without regard for context and underlying implications. It addresses and generates questions crossing disciplines, historical periods, and/or national entities, questions that require a variety of methods and sources.

Interdisciplinary exchanges have been fruitful. Social historians have taken notice of insights about dress, and dress historians have drawn on the material approaches of 'history from below'. Since the 1980s, studies of production and consumption have become considerably more complex. Victoria De Grazia's 1995 collection *Sex of Things* finally took seriously and revised women's identification with decoration, appearance and consumption.[8] Nancy Green's *Ready-to-Wear, Ready-to-Work* (1997) revised assumptions about ready-made clothing in advanced capitalism and recast the relationship between fashion, national culture and economic change.[9] Wendy Gamber's *The Female Economy* and Barbara Burman's *The Culture of Sewing* complicated the story by looking at households, the interstices of production, documenting uneven and overlapping changes in patterns of acquiring clothing, and revealing a complex mixture of traditional and new practices.[10] Cultural historians opened up new areas of inquiry, such as textual analysis, consideration of audience, the role of ideology, and the notion of subculture and counter-culture. More recently, Diana Crane draws together visual and documentary material from nineteenth-century France, England and the US to explore dress and social identity including working-class dress.[11] Many scholars explore the influence on developing countries of the western production, marketing and consumption of garments – as, for example, in Karen Hansen's study of used clothing in Zambia.[12] Multicultural studies have influenced museum collecting and curating, which now seek to represent a wider constituency. Although big museums still court blockbuster fashion themes and designers to generate audiences, many exhibitions feature subcultures seen as outside the fashion mainstream. Examples include Barbara A. Schreier's exhibition *Becoming American Women: Clothing and the Jewish Immigrant Experience, 1880–1920,* which toured from Chicago in 1995–6 (published as a book of the same name) and, in London, the Victoria and Albert Museum's popular *Street Style* exhibition (1994–5).

Fashion and textile historians have turned especially to the work of cultural anthropologists for whom, as for historians of pre-literate cultures and periods, material objects are at least as essential as written records. Anthropologists such as Jane Schneider and Annette Wiener contribute a cultural approach to cloth. This approach has been neglected by historians, who have until recently focused mostly on the technical and economic aspects of textile production and labour, including regional or local settings, and the early modern and industrialising world.[13] Anthropologists, too, have paid more attention to the gendered implications of cloth and clothing.[14] Joanne B. Eicher uses anthropological studies to challenge common assumptions about dress in non-western societies and among minority ethnic groups residing in Britain and the US.[15] Laurel Thatcher Ulrich, whose approach has much in common with that of anthropologists, brings 'female-centred production' to the study of colonial America and links it with ways that ordinary people made sense of the world through household goods.[16] As a signal of burgeoning interest in cultural approaches to textiles, *Textiles: The Journal of Cloth and Culture* (Berg) was launched in 2003.

Historians of dress and textiles have learned to mine the meaning of material objects, visual and tactile culture, not as a substitute for verbal sources when these are unavailable, but in order to reveal dimensions of political and social transformations that cannot be discerned in observed social behaviour or verbal and written articulations. As Daniel Roche has observed, 'clothing helps to constitute the values of sensibility and mobilises the senses'.[17] As palpable material objects that communicate visually (and through tactile stimulation), the meanings of fashion and textiles both span and reflect particular times and places. Christopher Breward has pointed out that because fashion is closer to personal identity than other material objects, it reveals significant social change at several levels, and subtle links between changes in individuals and historical processes, especially with regard to gender ideologies.[18] Like the textiles that were a key means of communication in medieval Europe, the clothed and fashioned body is a visual medium that carries varied messages. For Dorothy Ko, the body itself is a form of attire which can be modified to communicate meaning to observers. Her study of the meaning of footbinding to the people who experienced it in seventeenth-century China underscores the significance of tactile, visual sources, and in the process can shed new light on contemporary western fashions such as tattooing, crash diets and exercise regimes.[19] Yet, as Wilson observes, fashion also expresses ambiguities specific of fragile modern identities, and is 'essential to the world of modernity, the world of spectacle and mass-communication. It is a kind of connective tissue of our cultural organism.' She defines fashion as 'one of the most flexible means' by which we express the ambiguities of capitalism, selfhood and art.[20]

Gender issues are interwoven into this emerging field of dress and textile history, but are not at the forefront and do not yet add up to the systematic analysis or synthesis that they deserve, considering the fundamental gendering of attire. In a relatively new interdisciplinary and cross-cultural field, scholars, overwhelmed by literature within their own discipline, are often slow to take note of analytical insights from other disciplines and countries which might enrich their own work. However, Valerie Steele's *Fashion Theory: The Journal of Dress, Body and Culture*, which gathers a variety of perspectives and approaches into one internationally distributed periodical, has become a major forum for new scholarship, as have inter-disciplinary conferences. In the UK, a major international conference, '*Dress in History: Studies and Approaches*' (1997), explored the broadening of the parameters of dress history and key issues, particularly challenges presented by the fact that the 'language and methodologies of fifty years ago are no longer adequate for modern approaches'.

This collection of essays, which we have entitled *Material Strategies*, contributes to this project by bringing together scholarship focused on geographically diverse settings – Britain, the US, Italy, Germany, China and Tanzania – and ranging chronologically from pre-industrial society to the mid-twentieth century. It pushes forward a more comprehensive analysis of clothing and textiles by combining the diverse perspectives of dress, design and textile history, economic and business history, cultural anthropology, social history and cultural and art history. The essays in this volume thus represent a new dress and textile history that incorporates multiple approaches to analysing material objects and visual representations and to exploring human agency and audiences, attempting to avoid the reductive tendencies and pitfalls of a single approach. The result is a powerful analytical perspective that sheds new light on gender history. Each essay in *Material Strategies* assumes that, like verbal and written articulations and observed behaviour, material objects and dress and textiles figure in social configurations and transformations in ideology, ethos, culture and/or institutions, whether for individuals, social entities (classes, races, ethnic groups, genders, communities), industrial sectors, or nations. Above all, because garments are identified with one sex or the other, the meaning and consequences of these material strategies are inherently gendered.

Essays in Section 1 (see Contents, pp. i–ii) reveal how people and/or institutions in pre-industrial Europe used material objects to manage self-presentation, to convey identity, or to locate themselves at a time when visual communication through garments and textiles was more important in daily life than the written word. Maria Hayward tells us that liturgical textiles in Reformation London contributed to locating individuals in gendered time and life stages, birth, marriage and death. Gabriele Mentges's essay contends that an individual's self-representation through images of himself clothed (and unclothed) represent gendered notions of the relationship of individuals to historical time.

In Section 2, essays centre on specific objects or, in the case of Katrina Honeyman, on a gendered ensemble, the men's suit, that figure in shaping gender ideologies and identities. Honeyman's essay takes analysis of production and consumption beyond the manufacture, retailing and purchasing of textiles and ready-made garments by looking at a complex mix of developments, shifts in fashion, masculine identities and consumerism, and innovations in the organisation of production in the Leeds garment trade. Carole Turbin's essay on the Arrow Man, an image advertising detachable collars in the early twentieth-century US and Cheryl Buckley's contribution in Section 3 analyse a visual dimension of production and consumption in mass-circulation magazines to provide a more complex understanding of shifts in clothing styles. Hayward's essay also looks at the interstices of the economy, production and the church as an unexplored locus of the meaning of textiles.

Two essays in Section 2, along with Breward's in the third section, are about the enthusiastic male consumer, until recently neglected by scholars who accepted the notion that in western society male attire has been austere and unchanging since the late eighteenth century. Honeyman, Turbin and Breward document subtle but complex changes in men's dress and the keen interest of many men in enhancing their personal appearance. Both Honeyman and Turbin address changing ideologies about manliness and consumerism, with Turbin's essay on the twentieth-century US contributing to understanding homoeroticism in some advertising images of men and the eroticism inherent in consumerism. Breward's essay on the Teddy Boy outfit in postwar London underscores that male types identified by dress were not new phenomena but combined British traditions and new trends and, like women's dress, were the result of continuing and uneven fashion changes. Mentges's essay in the first section also underscores a man's consciousness of the consequences of his appearance to others.

The essays by Burman, Turbin and Fields reveal gendered identities shaped by a combination of public and private dimensions: garments such as pockets, underwear and collars are both intimate and a means of managing personal appearance for the purpose of public self-presentation. These essays are about individual garments or components of clothing with a special relationship to the public and private body, showing how, as Joanne Entwistle puts it in *The Fashioned Body*, 'fashion, as discourse and practice, articulates the body, making it social and identifiable', which is 'of considerable importance to the development of modern society'.[21] Because underwear lies next to the skin, the wearer is aware of the feel of the texture and drape of fabric on and moving with or constricting her/his body, and at the same time conscious of the effect of her/his public presentation. Fields's essay on closed- and open-crotch drawers in the US from the mid-nineteenth to the early twentieth century reveals that women's undergarments are both public and private, and have two sides, eroticism and modesty, dichotomous aspects of sexuality that changed in relationship to gender ideologies over time. Turbin's essay explores the meaning of collars, borders between the private body and public presentation, for changes in ideals of white middle-class manliness. Burman's story of the placement, size and contents of pockets explores a private, hidden segment of clothing that serves to protect and/or transport objects of private or social (public) use, revealing gender ideologies embedded in pockets. Mentges's essay in the first section also touches on this theme, as Matthäus Schwarz depicted himself nude as well as clothed, showing the importance of the private, intimate sense of himself in public.

Section 3 is about varying ways in which material strategies contribute to social transformations that include subtle, or not so subtle, reconfigurations of specific subcultures or entire nations in a short period or over many decades. Both Buckley and Breward explore how dress fashioned specific group identities in twentieth-century Britain, Breward by looking closely at stylish London men, and Buckley by analysing a periodical aimed at lower-middle-class women during the World War I period. Andrew Ivaska's essay on 1960s Tanzania, Eugenia Paulicelli's study of interwar Italy, and Verity Wilson's essay on early to mid-twentieth-century China draw attention to gendered dimensions of national political change. Feminist scholars of the welfare state have revealed gendered dimensions of emerging national social and political policy, especially in western Europe, Australia and North America. Ivaska, Paulicelli and Wilson contribute to linking gender and politics by examining the history and consequences of fashion policies of political leaders seeking to forge, redirect or shore up a tattered or undeveloped national identity. Along with studies like Emma Tarlo's book on how India's political leaders used clothing during the independence movement, these essays reveal that emerging nations whose identity is shifting and contested are of special interest to historians of dress and textiles.[22] The fact that powerful leaders both recognised and used dress as a strategy to further their agendas underscores the political significance of dress on an individual and national level. Problematic situations, with all their tensions and contradictions, often reveal ideological assumptions underlying social patterns. During transformational periods, dress reveals aspects of ideologies linking individuals and societies that may be difficult to discern through other sources because dress is more closely tied to individual identity than most other material objects. This has been demonstrated elsewhere through, for example, studies of veiling in Islamic culture and antebellum African-American clothing.[23] In this section, each essay uses material objects and/or their visual representations to detail how identities of nations in widely different settings are fundamentally gendered, both changing and continuous, and often result from contentious debate and/or cooperation among groups.

Ivaska's and Paulicelli's essays, for different reasons, underscore that dress and textiles provide a window into world level transformations related to the globalisation of production and consumption. Fashion is central to understanding globalisation, firstly because many workers producing garments for western-owned companies are either immigrants from or live and work in the developing world, and secondly because, as Ivaska shows, western dress brings to developing countries not only new garments but also new ideologies and ways of life. The globalisation of fashion production is construed as both progressive (for example, in Benetton's claims to unite all the world's people) and destructive, in that it exploits and erodes distinctive national and regional cultures. Taken together, these and other studies of non-western settings underscore the inadequacy of Eurocentric scholars' approaches to the task of revealing the significance of what people wear and have worn.

Fashion and textile history is still in transition. Scholars no longer view fashion as primarily the realm of journalists or of costume and art historians, as simply involving a list of detailed characteristics, or as a monolithic look or style which is easily summed up – the Victorian S curve, the flapper, the New Look, or the Nehru suit. Scholars from diverse fields and perspectives have opened up fashion history to consider dress as central to visual and material culture for people worldwide. They seek to understand the complex influences of consumption and production and their interstices, explore the gendered dimensions of national identity and develop new ways of looking at the relationship between public and private life, the body and sexuality. The essays in this volume forge new conceptualisations through particularity: garment manufacture (Leeds), individual garments (undergarments, collars, pockets), specific times and places (post war London, mid-twentieth-century Tanzania, fascist Italy, pre-industrial London), moments of transformation (World War I Britain, unifying Italy), the emergence of modern notions of time (Renaissance Germany, Revolutionary China). In their different ways, the authors reveal previously neglected nuances and complexities, bring to light new evidence by exploring new sources, put accepted evidence to new use, challenge conventional wisdom, and replace old generalisations with new more complex insights. In short, *Material Strategies* moves scholarship on dress and textiles toward more inclusive, nuanced and multi-layered analyses of the cultural meanings and consequences of the gendered material strategies (knowing, deliberate, unwitting and/or inadvertent) of women, men, social groupings, and nations.

Notes

1. Arjun Appadurai (ed.), *The Social Life of Things: Commodities in Cultural Perspective* (Cambridge University Press, 1986).
2. Elizabeth Wilson, *Adorned in Dreams: Fashion and Modernity* (Virago Press, 1985).
3. Valerie Steele, *Fashion and Eroticism: Ideals of Feminine Beauty from the Victorian Era to the Jazz Age* (Oxford University Press, 1985).
4. Raphael Samuel, *Theatres of Memory*, vol. 1, *Past and Present in Contemporary Culture* (Verso, 1996).
5. Caroline Evans and Minna Thornton, *Women and Fashion: A New Look* (Quartet, 1989).
6. Lou Taylor, *The Study of Dress History* (Manchester University Press, 2002).
7. Stella Bruzzi and Pamela Church Gibson (eds), *Fashion Cultures: Theories, Explorations and Analysis* (Routledge, 2000); Anne Hollander, *Seeing Through Clothes* (1975; repr. University of California Press, 1993); Rozsika Parker, *The Subversive Stitch: Embroidery and the Making of the Feminine* (The Women's Press, 1984).
8. Victoria De Grazia (ed.), *The Sex of Things: Gender and Consumption in Historical Perspective* (University of California Press, 1996).
9. Nancy L. Green, *Ready-to-Wear and Ready-to-Work: A Century of Industry and Immigrants in Paris and New York* (Duke University Press, 1997).
10. Wendy Gamber, *The Female Economy: The Millinery and Dressmaking Trades, 1860–1930* (University of Illinois Press, 1997); Barbara Burman (ed.), *The Culture of Sewing: Gender, Consumption and Home Dressmaking* (Berg, 1999).
11. Diana Crane, *Fashion and Its Social Agendas: Class, Gender, and Identity in Clothing* (University of Chicago Press, 2000).
12. Karen Tranberg Hansen, *Salaula: The World of Secondhand Clothing and Zambia* (Columbia University Press, 2000).
13. Annette B. Weiner and Jane Schneider (eds), *Cloth and Human Experience* (Smithsonian Institution Press, 1989).
14. Ruth Barnes and Joanne B. Eicher (eds), *Dress and Gender: Making and Meaning* (Berg, 1992).
15. Joanne H. Eicher (ed.), *Dress and Ethnicity: Change Across Space and Time* (Berg, 1995); Joanne H. Eicher, 'The Anthropology of Dress', *Dress*, 27 (2000), pp. 59–70.
16. Laurel Thatcher Ulrich, *The Age of Homespun: Objects and Stories in the Creation of an American Myth* (Alfred Knopf, 2001).
17. Daniel Roche, *The Culture of Clothing: Dress and Fashion in the Ancien Regime* (1989; repr. Cambridge University Press, 1994), p. 33.
18. Christopher Breward, *The Culture of Fashion: A New History of Fashionable Dress* (Manchester University Press, 1995), p. 5.

19. Dorothy Ko, 'The Body as Attire: The Shifting Meanings of Footbinding in Seventeenth Century China', *Journal of Women's History*, 8 (1997), pp. 10–26.
20. Wilson, *Adorned in Dreams*, pp. 12, 15.
21. Joanne Entwistle, *The Fashioned Body: Fashion, Dress and Modern Social Theory* (Polity, 2000), p. 238.
22. Emma Tarlo, *Clothing Matters: Dress and Identity in India* (Hurst, 1996).
23. Fadwa El Guindi, *Veil: Modesty, Privacy and Resistance* (Berg, 1999); Helen Bradley Foster, *'New Raiments of Self': African American Clothing in the Antebellum South* (Berg, 1997).

2

Fashion, Time and the Consumption of a Renaissance Man in Germany: The Costume Book of Matthäus Schwarz of Augsburg, 1496–1564

Gabriele Mentges

1520. Today, 20 February 1520, I, Matthäus Schwarz of Augsburg, having just turned twenty-three years old, looked as I do in the above painting. Then I said that I have always enjoyed being with the old folk ... And among other things we came to talk of costumes and manners of attire, that is, how they dressed everyday ... This caused me to have my apparel portrayed as well, in order to see over a period of five, ten or more years what might become of it.[1]

With this preface, Matthäus Schwarz, citizen of Augsburg, announced his intention to record his personal clothing history. It has come down to us in the form of a miniature leather-bound manuscript measuring 10 x 16 cm, encompassing 137 pages of vellum, with text and painstakingly detailed hand-painted colour illustrations. It contains the pictorial representation of Schwarz's life history, told on the basis of the fashions he wore over the years, and depicting him in changing outfits within and without the walls of his home city of Augsburg.[2] The book offers present-day readers (and viewers) both a unique insight into the wardrobe of a male individual of the Renaissance period and a seemingly narcissistic glimpse of a masculine Self. Most remarkable, however, is the fact that his personal history of fashion is accompanied by the story of his life, a story indeed completed only by the final pictorial and textual entry of 1560. In fact, M. Schwarz did not originally conceive of his book as an autobiographical account. It began instead as more of an experiment, to see 'what might become of it'. It assumes its final form only with the last picture and text entry from the year 1560. I would thus like to ask to what extent fashion made a particular contribution to the conceptualisation of a masculine ego in the Renaissance. To put it more precisely, to what extent did linking his subjective history of fashion with his life story produce a singular model of a masculine self? The almost total lack of a female presence, (except for his mother and sister), whether in the form of concrete persons or environments, is characteristic of this document. One may thus regard the document as purely masculine, to the extent that 'masculinity' is understood as 'extended in the world' and 'merged in organised social relations'.[3] One may thus address the gender dimension by examining how, where and when not speaking about women becomes a constructional element of, or even a precondition for, his conception of masculinity. It is thus remarkable for the reception history of Schwarz's costume book that, while it clearly presents itself as a specific product of male self-perception, it has scarcely been studied from this perspective.

For August Fink, writing in the 1960s, gender constructions were not yet a focus of interest, and his extensive and highly detailed study pursues mainly biographical, art historical and fashion historical issues.[4] It is more surprising, however, that later biographical research has also ignored the gender issue, limiting the analysis instead to questions of the conditions and genesis of autobiographical writings in the late Middle Ages and the Renaissance.[5] The historian Heide Wunder was the first scholar to draw our attention to the clothing rituals of male socialisation in M. Schwarz's life history, and to treat the work as a contribution to a history of Renaissance masculinity.[6] Recent publications such as those by Philippe Braunstein, Pierre Monnet and Valentin Groebner presuppose this masculine attitude, but do not address it separately or question its genesis. Certainly, Philippe Braunstein explicitly explores the construction of the bourgeois self, but without taking into account its gender dimension. In contrast, Monnet writes of the male-defined life-world of the early modern city, without however examining this construction more closely. Groebner is more concerned with issues such as the relationship between the 'bookkeeping' mentality displayed in the texts, fashion and Schwarz's corporeality, and does not explicitly examine the cultural concept of Renaissance masculinity. All three approaches nevertheless indicate key aspects that helped to constitute Schwarz's masculinity: first, the dimension of corporeality and the history of the body (Braunstein); second, the significance of the city as an environment and an agent of memory (Monnet); and third, the influence of bookkeeping on Schwarz's self-image and self-understanding (Groebner).[7]

Matthäus Schwarz was born at Augsburg in 1496 and died there in 1564, four years after completing his costume book. The little book, begun when he was 19 years old, provides a retrospective view of his childhood and youth before continuing with Matthäus's present life and ending with

Figure 1: Schwarz: 'When I wanted to learn fencing', dated June 1518, when Schwarz was 21 years old. Published with the kind permission of the Herzog-Anton-Ulrich Museum, Braunschweig.

his sixty-fourth year. Valentin Groebner coined the term picture chain (*Bilderkette*) for the 137 carefully painted images in which Schwarz surveyed his life in the form of the clothes he wore.[8] On the one hand, this term refers to the book's apparent lack of coherence when approached from the modern perspective. On the other, it emphasises how closely the individual pictures or pictorial stories relate to each other both thematically and formally. Schwarz begins his account with a portrait of his parents, relates his childish pranks and experiences as a youth and then continues with descriptions of personal situations, political events, celebrations, activities such as fencing, riding, hunting and the like, and ends with the illness, old age and death he perceived in his immediate surroundings in 1560, aged 64. His picture of his parents, taken from an older portrait, is followed by depictions of scenes from his childhood showing him as the pupil of a pastor in Heidenheim, as a schoolboy and young runaway, until his entry into the service of the mercantile house of Fugger. He then notes the journeys he undertook on behalf of the Fuggers, the images of which always show him on horseback. Other pictures tell of his drinking bouts with friends, his attempts to become a hunter and his sporting activities such as fencing and archery. They show him on a wintry sleigh ride in which he crashes the sledge, they mention his falling in love with a Dutch girl (who does not appear in the picture) and portray him in his wedding attire on the occasion of his marriage at the age of 41: '20 February 1538, when I ventured to take a wife'.[9] The subjects of his narrative are events that occurred in and around Augsburg, such as the time that an epidemic of influenza (the 'English sweat')[10] was visited upon his home town, or the onset of another epidemic in Augsburg in 1535, which caused numerous deaths.[11] He also mentions his own ailments and subsequent recovery. However, very often he only describes his clothing. The way in which he refers to his clothing is consistently remarkable. Even his mother's pregnancy is interpreted in terms of his first mode of dress, and he describes his nappies as his first suit of clothes. The description of his self revolve almost exclusively around his physical person. The scenes from his childhood and later the scene of his sick-bed, which shows him amidst his children, are important exceptions, as is the picture that shows him together with his employer Jacob Fugger in his counting house.[12] Women are occasionally mentioned in the text, but are portrayed only in the retrospective pictures of childhood. The pictures present the different phases of his life with varying intensity. Some periods are documented in particular detail, for example his young manhood between the ages of 19 and 30. With increasing age, however, the intervals between the pictures grow longer. The narrative ends with a depiction of what he wore on the day of Anthony Fugger's death: '16 Sept. 1560, this was my clothing when my gracious master, Anthony Fugger of blessed memory, died on the 14th at 8 o'clock in the morning'.[13]

When he began his book at the age of 19, Matthäus was already employed as a bookkeeper to the Fugger company. He commissioned most of the pictures from the illustrator Narziss Renner, whom he knew personally. The portraits were prepared either after copies of earlier pictures of M. Schwarz or simply traced and then painted in the relevant clothing. The year is written over each portrait, along with descriptions of the subject's attire and indications of the occasion, event or activity. Underneath the picture, Schwarz's age at the time was noted tidily, down to the exact month and day. Everything was executed in a fine calligraphic hand, in late Gothic minuscule. One even occasionally encounters corrections added later by Matthäus, which suggests his spontaneity in dealing with the manuscript, and concern for the veracity of the documentation. In technical and artisanal terms, the portraits seem rather dilettantish, because the representation of physical traits is often very imprecise and clumsy, so that at times Matthäus is practically unrecognisable or appears much altered. On the one hand, these stylistic differences stem from the techniques of the various illustrators who contributed to the book after the death of Narziss Renner. On the other, they correspond to the stylistic and painterly conventions of the time, for, as recent art historical studies of the portrait have discovered, even aristocrats were frequently too impatient to spend hours sitting for artists. Portrait painters were often negligent in depicting even such important details of physiognomy as the hands.[14] In contrast, they paid enormous attention to costume, whose ornate splendour was lovingly reproduced, causing Christopher Breward to conclude that the aesthetics of fashion in those days were primarily intended for pictorial effect. After all, it was in paintings that the finely woven patterns of damasks and silks developed their full aesthetic impact.[15] Dress thus served as an essential means of social identification and consequently also played a central role in the cultural construction of masculinity.

In his constant wardrobe changes, Matthäus Schwarz also displayed a marked sense of contemporary fashionable taste and extravagance alongside his consistent concern to be on the cutting edge. The slashed fashions he wore from his youth onward permitted a particular flirtation with the fine points of dress and reveal him to have been an elegant man with a highly developed sense of his own body. With increasing age he became more reserved, favouring more sombre colours – a bow to Spanish fashion – and most pictures show him wearing a loose coat or *Schaube*, the central representative item of male costume, albeit always in an appropriately luxurious version. He rarely dispensed with an imposing biretta, occasionally wearing a close-fitting coif, which sometimes even lent him quite an exotic and foreign appearance. In his individual clothing history he thus also represents the more general history of fashion of his day. Special emphasis is placed on his slashed breeches and the particular shape of leg they created, depending upon whether they were loose or tight. The demonstratively dramatised leg poses, in which his legs are always slightly spread, gain particular significance against the background of the gendered history of fashion in the late Middle Ages. One could interpret them as an expression of the increasing dichotomy between male and female dress and, by implication, between male and female worlds, to which Schwarz alludes. Schwarz does not, to be sure, adopt the sartorial stance of the mercenary soldiers, whose elaborately slashed breeches and bag-shaped codpieces embodied the aggressive masculinity of the age. For him, the highly developed language of the body and costume, as well as his 'elaborate consumption of clothing', represented primarily an appropriate medium for expressing his social rank and position within Augsburg's elites. With his competence and taste in matters of fashion, he demonstrated at the same time his knowledge of the way of life of urban elites.[16] Slashed breeches in particular allowed for sophisticated play with patterns and fabrics. The stuffs and colours on which Matthäus laid great stress in his descriptions changed frequently and were of great preciousness – the production of dyes was a costly and technically elaborate process. The garments he mentions most often are doublets, breeches and shirts, for example a 'golden shirt'. The 'golden shirt' hints at a particular luxury for the time; it served as an important means of distinction for the demonstration[17] of luxury as well as a new standard of cleanliness. In one picture (Figure 2) he models three different types of shirt.[18] The Renaissance eye for details of costume was already trained by the stipulations of contemporary sumptuary laws, which linked social demarcations precisely to such apparently inconspicuous details as the width of sleeves, pleats and the like. Matthäus delighted in playing with exactly such details and so testing the boundaries of dress codes.

Fashion is thus frequently the actual theme of the appended text, for example when he models his fine embroidered shirts or explains the various stages of mourning and their sartorial expression. To be sure, the multiple representation of a person in the picture belongs to the formal repertoire of contemporary miniature painting, but it also seems likely that he combined his pleasure in fashion with documentary objectives. Scholars have speculated on the composition of his intended audience, but the intention of the text itself already formed part of his model of masculinity. Above all, Schwarz combined in his own person both the beholder-subject and the beheld object. He becomes an 'observed observer', who can examine and correct himself in and through the representations he commissioned. His claim to masculine hegemony arises out

Figure 2: Three views of Matthäus Schwarz, showing different types of embroidered shirt, dated June 1524. Published with the kind permission of the Herzog-Anton-Ulrich Museum, Braunschweig.

of this monopolisation of the visual discourse for the shaping of his self. Schwarz claims the authority of memory, which Monnet relates to the construct of the city, solely for the male side of his family. In this exclusively masculine connotation of pictorial space lies the key difference from other contemporary pictorial documents such as the so-called *Augsburger Monatsbilder*, which have been attributed to the painter Jörg Treu. These large-format depictions present the cultural and social life of the city of Augsburg in programmatic harmony, and the frequent female presence in urban public space is quite striking.[19] Schwarz's wife also had her portrait painted, though she is significantly excluded from the representations in the costume book, perhaps most notably from the wedding picture. Arguably therefore the costume book formulated an autonomous, particular discourse of masculinity. In terms of methodology, this suggests that we should interpret the document as a whole and not merely take account of individual noteworthy aspects.

Schwarz's discourse on masculinity is deeply embedded in the social and cultural context in which he lived. His family belonged to the urban upper classes, the so-called *Mehrern*, who formed a sort of 'merchants' chamber'. They occupied a place in the Augsburg hierarchy below the patricians and noble families (*Geschlechter*), but were gaining in influence.[20] Social mobility, both upward and downward, was not unknown in Matthäus's family. His grandfather had been executed for allegedly embezzling municipal funds. Perhaps these circumstances, along with his near death as a child, helped make Matthäus more sensitive to the experiences of historical and social change. We should, however, be cautious with such psycho-historical interpretations, associated as they often are with projections of modern personality formations backward in time. In fact, upward and downward mobility were both real and related possibilities in Matthäus Schwarz's Augsburg. His employers, the Fuggers, for instance, tried all their lives to rise to the city's uppermost stratum of aristocrats and patricians, ultimately succeeding because of their skilful matrimonial policies. Although their wealth had long since moved beyond the city's borders, to the extent that they became key financiers of more than one early modern state and they had no compunctions about occasionally violating municipal regulations, within Augsburg they remained culturally and socially dependent upon the city's elites.[21]

Schwarz maintained close professional and personal ties to the Fuggers. The gifts of clothing that he received from his employers on the occasions of their weddings are evidence of this profound connection. In the Renaissance and later, gifts represented an important component of the network of social relations. They created social connection or cemented already existing ties.[22] Gifts of clothing were generally made from the higher placed to their subordinates, and strengthened personal bonds all the more by referring directly to the body. Thus Matthäus was deeply impressed by the splendid red wedding costume presented to him by Anton Fugger, which was by far one of his most magnificent garments.[23] As head bookkeeper in the Fugger company, Schwarz not only occupied a key position, but had also proven himself as particularly skilled in the modern accounting methods of his day. He had acquired his knowledge in Italy, where bookkeeping techniques were far superior to those current in Germany. Schwarz had also made a name for himself as the author of an expanded bookkeeping system in his work on 'triple bookkeeping'. He also appears to have shared the Fuggers' open-minded and advanced economic thinking. Thus he could be understood as a sort of cultural and social go-between, who moved from the narrow horizons of his urban environment to the expansive cosmopolitan horizon of the Fuggers and circulated among the various municipal social strata. We may thus view his self-conception as an attempt at reassurance regarding his cultural and social existence in the form of a self-assigned place within the context of the various social arenas around him. To what extent, then, can Schwarz's costume book claim to be unique, and to what extent is it comparable to other documents of the period?

August Fink's conclusion that Emperor Maximilian's costume book *'der Weißkunig'*, with illustrations by Hans Burkmaier, served as a model for Schwarz's work does not withstand detailed scrutiny.[24] In terms of internal organisation, the book is more reminiscent of other Renaissance texts. Renaissance Augsburg was well known for the art of printing. A wide variety of written and pictorial documents of the urban elites around Schwarz affirm this reputation. Pictorial representations of manners of dress were among the self-evident practices of the urban elites, who used them to shape their social selves. The Fuggers, for example, pursued a veritable politics of pictures in order to demonstrate their wealth and power.[25] In a recent study Hans Belting emphasises the extent to which the portrait as a medium for burgher self-representation competed with noble coats of arms. According to Belting, both media were concerned with the body, whereby the portrait as a picture of the body referred to immediate subjective corporeality, while the coat of arms mainly referred to the body in the form of signs.[26] However, he overlooks the importance that clothing assumed in the competition between these visual media. After all, it was only apparel, or rather, fashion, that clothed the body in the era's formal language, thus rendering it culturally communicable. Individual style was less important here than categorisation within a complex set of formal visual rules. Breward speaks in this context of a veritable dictatorship of the portrait, indicating not just the formal rules governing the production of portraits, but above all the relationship between dress and the thematic layout of the picture.[27]

Particularly in the miniature portrait, it is 'the costume, not the face, [that] is privileged'.[28]

Groebner's suggestion that we should read the costume book as the product of a specific form of urban perception in the sixteenth century, which produced the framework for the masculine self, must be expanded or re-evaluated from the perspective of a cultural anthropology of dress; clothing behaviour not only trains and hones social perception, but also intervenes actively in the modelling and shaping of the cultural ego. After all, dress should be understood not as a predetermined cultural object, but rather as a primary arena of negotiation, in which the ego can articulate and express itself culturally via the body. Schwarz's book thus represents in exemplary fashion the attempt to demonstrate, by means of attire, the claim to autonomous agency within the framework of the current social norms of dress. This should be understood not just as a fiction, as Groebner suggests, but rather as real practice.[29] Schwarz himself entitled his work a *Klaydungsbüchlin*, a little book of costume or clothing, thereby clearly admitting to the dominance that he himself accorded dress. Costume gains in significance in several respects; as Schwarz's personal wardrobe, as the 'history' of contemporary fashion and as an expression of the immense consumption of clothing, that is, of fabrics, accessories and the like. Groebner compares the book to a catalogue of merchandise, with the qualification that Schwarz could not, however, be considered a fashion model for the Fugger company.[30] In fact, the text resembles domestic account books or *libri di ricordi* from the Italian Renaissance (fourteenth to sixteenth century), in which the paterfamilias noted the arrival and stocks of goods and merchandise. These books registered in colourful profusion a mixture of goods owned, key family events and other household occurrences. 'These writings testify to an increased attachment to the possession of a kind that was unprecedented at this time.'[31] Above all, according to Martha Ajmar, they document the consumer practices of the day, in which the advent of novel objects was particularly noted.[32] The costume book likewise displays similarities here to another genre as well: in its unsystematic collection of data, in which personal, political and social information mingled with annals, it resembled other ego documents of the early modern period. The far earlier 1360 *Püchel von mein Geslecht und von Abentewr* (Little Book of my Family and of Adventures) of the Nuremberg merchant Ulrich Stromer, for example, is characterised by a comparable blending of annals with information on the author's personal way of life. Like other ego documents of the Renaissance, this text lacks what Michael Sonntag has called the 'reflexive coherence of an ego'.[33] For that reason Schwarz's text resembles neither an (auto)biography nor a diary. According to the cultural anthropologist Martin Kohli, the organisation of one's personal lifetime in the form of a biography presupposes temporalisation, and with it the integration of social life into the chronometric temporal system, that is, the coincidence of social age with chronology. Chronologisation, in turn, demands the liberation of individuals from estate and local ties, that is, from 'pre-modern ways of life … [and] begins with individuals as autonomously constituted units'.[34] Kohli's definition certainly should not be applied schematically to historical epochs. Important socio-cultural preconditions appear to be necessary, however, in order to conceive of one's own life as a progression with a beginning and an end. The cultural capacity for chronological narrative demands that we incorporate the events of our own lives into a larger whole as a frame of cultural reference like historiography. It is only this precondition that permits the construction of biographical meaning, which can be accomplished through this relating of an individual history to a 'general history'. Matthäus's manner of reporting, which appears from a present-day perspective to aggregate disparate facts, including contemporary historical events, personal circumstances and stages of life, randomly and without any logical reason, without any visible coherent context, shows that he was not interested in a reflexive processing of past events and experiences in the sense of an autobiographical text. His conception of self was oriented toward the present and the future, and to that extent contained key dimensions of his era.

Thus we find some remarkable references to contemporary political events or significant municipal occurrences. Schwarz mentions the Schmalkaldic War, during which he performed guard duty, the entry of Francis, king of France, into Milan 'after the battle', and the visit of King Ferdinand. He mentions epidemics such as the influenza (*englische Schweiß*), which caused him to seek refuge outside the city for a time. Each event is connected with the written description of the costume he wore at the time, but is not itself depicted in the visual representation. Public time is invoked by the naming of the event. In this way, as the ethnologist Klaus E. Müller puts it, time is summarised, becoming a history of events that is neither linear nor cyclical.[35] In this manner, Schwarz also demonstrates his fictive participation in public, social time, with which he seeks to secure his position in the public arena of memory. His home city of Augsburg constitutes his spatial network of relations, to which almost every picture refers. With very few exceptions, the pictures do not address domestic intimacy. In most cases, representations of domestic interior space are combined with a prospective view of the surrounding city, for example when Schwarz is just about to leave the house or when he poses impressively in front of the archway to his home. The frequent emphasis on transitions signals the threshold character which they possessed for Schwarz, both spatially and symbolically, both establishing and crossing boundaries between the interior space of the house and exterior, public space. Writing of this epoch, the historian Heide Wunder notes a growing separation between the worlds of women and men, which chiefly affected the urban upper classes to which M. Schwarz belonged. In the upper strata the domestic sphere increasingly became the realm of women, while the public world became dominated by men.[36] The threshold signals transitions, while at the same time forming the point of orientation from which Schwarz organised urban space, since he began his peregrinations in the city from the door of his own house, or rather that of his familial household.

As a consequence, Schwarz's clothed appearance was always closely associated with this exterior urban space. His surroundings appear in many scenes in the form of streetscapes, houses or city walls which M. Schwarz strides along or paces off. In this way urban space becomes an extension of his bodily self. At the same time, he classifies his walks through the city according to personal data; his age and changes of costume. Thus he situates his own personal lifetime and its changes within urban space. Schwarz's urban space must be clearly distinguished from the modern urban space that de Certeau has dissected with such acuity. Schwarz's urban peregrinations provide no occasion for those 'aberrations' that, in de Certeau's view, shape the topography of the modern city.[37] Instead, in Schwarz's enterprise the dimension of time is organised in reference to urban space. In this way a spatio-time (*Raumzeit*) arose that must be clearly distinguished from the temporal space (*Zeitraum*) of our modern age. Space, after all, remains the primary yardstick, to which time must be subordinated. This is expressed in the prioritisation of the physical dimension, with Schwarz in his massive corporeality appearing to dominate the pictorial space.

The manner in which the pictorial stories are organised within the book also corresponds to this relationship between space and time: the written descriptions, which contain notes on Schwarz's personal as well as universal time, on the occasion and nature of his respective outfits, create the frame for each portrait. The pictorial contents themselves tell us far more than the written notes alone ever could. One could almost speak here of a hidden autonomy of the visual discourse, which operates with what Bourdieu called a 'surplus of meaning'. After all, Schwarz's pictures show habitus, body language and gesture; they 'speak' of the city and its environment, everyday life and celebrations. In their language of the body and gesture, they repeat themselves, to be sure – following the contemporary grammar of representation – but through their embedding in the respective pictorial surroundings, they undergo a specific contextual coding. M. Schwarz uses the visual, non-linguistic invocation of his surroundings, the depiction of the city wall, the background of the meadows during fencing or archery, as an additional definition of his clothing, and it provides the justification for a change of costume that is visible in the picture.

What happens here – and what came to assume central importance in the development of an autonomous language of fashion – is the transformation of space into a specific locality; space is appropriated and occupied in a dual sense. This occurs first through the picture itself: 'Painting united space', according to Breward,[38] and second through content and pose, which here assume the significance of a mise-en-scène. 'The body transformed into a representation is positioned in space, and this space thereby transformed into a "place".' 'Clothing is always transformed thereby into a pose, which', according to Kaja Silverman, 'is worn by the body. Everything becomes a costume here.'[39] Silverman's reflections proceed from photography, that is, they begin with the current regime of the gaze. Her assumptions can, however, be transferred quite fundamentally to costume. For the dress worn by the body forms and shapes space and thus creates the substantive connection between space and body. In so doing, it gives the body its cultural place. The pictorial references to his surroundings, particularly the intensity with which the city is incorporated, gain in significance in relation to the included texts. After all, they render the picture a means for male subjectification and the personalisation of his clothing. This helps explain, on the one hand, the exclusive concentration of the pictorial representation on the person of Schwarz, since the presence of the female 'other' would only disturb or confuse the unambiguous quality of this relationship between body and costume. The relationship between space and dress was also a concern of the sixteenth-century costume books, which assigned different types of apparel to geographical spaces such as the great commercial cities.[40] In so doing, they undertook a general cultural-geographical mapping of their world in order to provide a geopolitical and social overview. The *Klaydungsbüchlin*, in contrast, set new standards by introducing the additional dimensions of time (event and personal time), and mapped the urban universe from an exclusively male perspective.

Schwarz expressed his personal time, the biographical thread, through the history of his body, spun out from its beginnings in the womb, through birth to sickness and old age – even his apparent death is addressed. In this way, his clothing history parallels his body and his life history. The repeated changes and renewal in his clothing contrast with the biological process of the body's aging. Matthäus Schwarz's fashion history develops along and is oriented toward this personal history of the body. He speaks of his body often, consciously and extensively; for example of his remarkably trim twenty-four inch waist,[41] showing off his fashionably slender silhouette in various sporting pursuits. Later, he increasingly mentions illness and age. Nowhere is this connection more apparent, however, than in the portrayals of his honest and realistic nakedness, both from the front and behind. 'I had grown fat and portly', he comments ironically.[42] These scenes of exposure thus gain a multiple cultural weight, and they can be read in several ways. In their drastic realism and the radical portrayal of nakedness, they signal a break with medieval conceptions of the body, in which complete nudity was conceivable only as an act of self-abnegation.[43] Braunstein's claim that this was the first realistic portrayal of the human body, however, is rightly rejected by Groebner with reference to a similar picture by Albrecht Dürer. Here too, according to Groebner, we have the mise-en-scène of a self-image not uncommon for the time, which makes the male body the site of critical self-orientation.[44]

By contrast, for women such radical exposure was completely inconceivable, because female honour was directly inscribed upon the individual body.[45] The meanings of clothing were thus constructed on different levels and from different points of view for men and women. The connotations of feminine clothing arose primarily in direct relation to women's bodies, while the fields of connotation of masculinity remained oriented towards the outside world. Masculinity and the male honour associated with it were inaugurated in the first place through the incorporation of external material objects.[46] To this extent M. Schwarz, too, had to refer to the urban environment in order to imbue his clothing with meaning. This, in turn, enabled him in his nakedness to distance himself from his clothing and, with it, at the same time, from his social role. His naked body stands for Nature, which, as difference, invades the artificial history of clothing, the 'fashion time' on which the pictures report. This in turn shows that clothing fashion has emancipated itself from the history of the body in order to develop a narrative of its own. After all, in the world of commodities, the world of consumption, to which fashion belongs, natural time is eliminated: fashions in dress create their own time with its own rhythm, to which the category of aging is alien. Fashion never ages, but rather always finds itself anew in permanent change.

One can also decipher another message in the scene showing Schwarz naked. The point in time of the portrayal coincides with the death of Jacob Fugger, Schwarz's beloved and revered employer. While, at his father's death, he showed himself in various versions of mourning, he now breaks with this ritual and dispenses with clothing altogether. Regardless of the economic well-being of the Fuggers, he was not only fixated on Fugger as a person and a friend, but also participated in Fugger's economic and social power and its potential uncertainties.[47] The loss occasioned by Fugger's death may have left Schwarz feeling vulnerable and naked, both symbolically and materially – that is, economically. After all, it may have entailed a loss of financial security and with it the possibility of future investment in sartorial luxuries. It triggered this crisis in the representation of his self, since he dispensed altogether with clothing as the decisive instrument of his self-representation. The temporary representational departure from the economic-cultural sphere was motivated not only by mourning and a sense of threat, but also by the experience of the finiteness of Schwarz's own corporeal time. In this way the costume book brings the fashion discourse back to its actual beginnings and hidden prerequisites, namely the death of the individual body. At that moment the archaeological link connecting the fashion discourse with the body is revealed.

The scenes of nakedness suggest another conclusion, namely that the connection to the Fuggers had become Schwarz's central identity, affirming him not just in his capacity as a citizen, but also as a 'modern'-style merchant, who himself occupied an unconventional position in urban society. Groebner has already pointed to the close connection between Schwarz's ego-project and the idea and concept of accounting. It also becomes evident in the form and content of the book, which the temporal axis lends a clear thematic structure and cohesion and, formally speaking, a uniform frame for the various portraits. The temporal axis is composed of a combination of the chronometric calculation of time with Schwarz's own lifetime. It does not result from simple addition, however, but rather gradually forms a qualitatively new category of time. Within this category, the time of commodities, or, more precisely, of fashion, achieves a synthesis with personal and social time. A close examination of the picture showing Schwarz in the counting-house together with his employer Jacob Fugger provides the key to the construction of this concept of time. Here, for the first and only time, he relinquishes the dominance of his own pictorial self-representation. The only commanding figure here is Jacob Fugger. In the background, in the form of the names of their branch offices, appears the European mercantile world of the Fuggers, and with it the horizon and fabric of Schwarz's life-world.[48] As head bookkeeper, Schwarz occupied a key position in the Fuggers' merchant capitalist enterprise. He performed a multiplicity of monetary and commodity transactions and oversaw the work of the branch offices. The trade in commodities or, in the German parlance of the time, *die Hantierung mit Waren* in the Fugger empire was an abstract operation, which placed Schwarz in an equally abstract relationship to space and above all to time, thereby conveying a dynamic concept of time.[49] Schwarz was considered a bookkeeper of outstanding quality and rank. He not only possessed knowledge of Italian bookkeeping, the most advanced of its time, which was far superior to German methods, but with his treatises on the subject had himself set new standards in the field, which helped make economic history. Based on his Italian experiences in the Fuggers' Venice office, he had developed the concept of 'triple bookkeeping'. He was motivated here not just by economic concerns, but as he himself said, used his accounting methods above all as a memory aid. It was 'like a copyist [*Gegenschreiber*] and controller' or 'a money box … a suitable, orderly, exact, diverting, pleasant … art for merchants'.[50] It was practised as a veritable mnemonic technique for the merchant's memory, necessary in case of legal disputes, but also appreciated as a passionate game by the era's men of affairs.[51] The mercantile mentality penetrated and took hold of life practice more generally and was closely tied to the visual arts, since it promoted new forms of perception. According to Michael Baxandall, commercial arithmetic and the trade in goods were manners of describing reality that rendered it at once accessible and comprehensible.[52] The costume book arose in this economically determined cultural context: It is indeed the record of the 'credit' side of his clothing and thus evidence of his demonstrative consumption of dress.

Schwarz used the Arabic numerals that had been introduced by Italian accounting for the pagination of his costume book. His life story is organised into uniform units of text and image. The order of the numbers and the textual descriptions adhere closely to the rules of bookkeeping:[53] the chronology of the years follows the time elapsed since Schwarz's birth, which occupies the lower portion of the page. He tirelessly calculates it each time, down to the month and day: '27 years 19 weeks 1 day'. The order of the dates in the upper portion of the picture – the numerical order of society – is followed in the text by event, occasion, personal circumstances, and assigned to the appropriate depiction of clothing. The outfits are always described according to the same scheme, including the name of the garment (biretta, doublet), the fabric and colour. Herein, too, Schwarz follows the very rules that Luca Paccioli set down for bookkeeping records in his famous text of 1494: 'I possess garments of several kinds, so many of this, and so many of that sort, listing quality, colour, lining and shape.'[54] This is precisely how Schwarz proceeds.[55] 'On 2 June 1527 I was dressed thus: the doublet of satin, a sayon of camelot, biretta with velvet all around.'[56] Using bookkeeping logic and its language, he succeeds in rendering dress describable, and thus founding a first 'language of fashion'. The terms for fabrics used by Schwarz frequently contain geographical and spatial designations such as 'Spanish mantle, Genoese biretta, Lombard sayon'. The semantics of this language of fashion is indeed still replete with economic meaning, since it refers to real sites of production and trade.

By orienting himself closely to the order of bookkeeping, M. Schwarz succeeds in transforming his lifetime into a linear structure and in developing a specific coherence of his personal ego. Therein lies the achievement and uniqueness of his work. The basis for the creation of linearity was formed by his changes of costume, which he takes as units of measurement for the stages of his life. For each new picture, and thus each new temporal interval, is occasioned by the respective change of dress. Fashion

Figure 3: Schwarz in Augsburg, '27 years 19 weeks 1 day old', dated 14 June 1524. Published with the kind permission of the Herzog-Anton-Ulrich Museum, Braunschweig.

time thus becomes the standard for his subjective experience and shaping of time. He uses it to manage and structure his biographical time. It is thus what characterises the essence of Schwarz's biography, for it becomes his clock, socially, psychologically and economically speaking. Clothing thus constitutes the decisive interface in Schwarz's life story, because it represents the plane on which the order of bookkeeping could intervene in his life. At the same time, it is tailor-made to fit his body. In and through the mediating device of clothing, the natural order of the body, which resists accounting, and Schwarz's history, beginning with birth, through old age and death, become intertwined with the order of economic time.

'To see what might become of it' was the intention with which Schwarz began his book, which, following the course of his own life, demonstrated the social development of his male self through the construction of the world he lived in. His clothing served not merely as a medium for associating the outside world with his masculine self, but also became *the* instrument for structuring his life-world and organising his lifetime as a linear temporal concept. In the medium of contemporary fashion, the passing of time became objectified for him, and the historical-social process was rendered tangible and comprehensible.

The construction of the world from the masculine perspective is accomplished here in both a symbolic and a material-practical sense. For the production of the portraits, he will have placed the professional knowledge of the manufacturing and types of textiles that he had acquired in the service of the Fuggers at the disposal of the artist. After all, the procedures employed for colouring painted clothing paralleled those used for dyeing textiles. The obsession with detail and painstaking care in depicting clothing in the miniature manuscript thus also provides evidence of his knowledge and abilities as a merchant who handled the most precious stuffs on a daily basis.[57] Thus the *Klaydungsbüchlin* offers no finished product of his masculine self, but documents instead his process of coming to grips with himself and the world. Step by step, or rather picture by picture, his path of self-discovery on the way to a 'coherent' masculine ego appropriate to the time in which he lived emerges. With it, he staked his claim to establish the male line as the repository of family memory, a task he later delegated to his son Veit. And so his costume book, whose outcome he himself awaited with anticipation, may also be read as a rite of initiation into a public, masculine world of his own making.

Notes

1. '1520. Auf heut, 20 Febroario 1520, was ich Matheus Schwartz von Augspurg, krad 23 jar alt in obgemalter gestalt. Da sprich ich, das ich all mein tag gern was bey den alten. Und under anderm ward wyr etwa auch zo röd der trachtung und monier der klaydungen, wie sy

sich also teglich verkerete ... Da ursacht mich, die meyne auch zu controfaten, zu sehen uber ein zeit als 5, in 10 oder mer jarn, was doch daraus werden wölle.' Quoted in August Fink, *Die Schwarzschen Trachtenbücher* (Deutscher Verein für Kunstwissenschaft, 1963), p. 98.

2. The original manuscript is now housed in the Herzog-Anton-Ulrich-Museum in Braunschweig.

3. Robert W. Connell, *Masculinities* (Polity Press, 1995), p. 29.

4. Fink, *Trachtenbücher*.

5. See Ralph Frenken, *Kindheit und Autobiographie vom 14. bis 17. Jahrhundert: Psychohistorische Rekonstruktionen* (Oetker-Voges Verlag, 1999), pp. 362–87. See also Erhard Wiersing, 'Vormoderne Lebensformen als Thema und Herausforderung der Lebenslauf – und Biographieforschung am Beispiel des Edelherrn Bernhard zur Lippe (1140–1224)', *BIOS*, 10 (1997), pp. 161–81.

6. Heide Wunder, 'Wie wird man ein Mann: Befunde am Beginn der Frühen Neuzeit (15.–17. Jahrhundert)', in *Was sind Frauen? Was sind Männer? Geschlechterkonstruktionen im historischen Wandel*, ed. Christiane Eifert (Frankfurt a. Main, 1996), pp. 130–38 (p. 135), English trans., 'What Made a Man a Man? Sixteenth- and Seventeenth-century Findings', trans. Pamela Selwyn, in *Gender in Early Modern Germany*, ed. Lyndal Roper and Ulinka Rublack (forthcoming Cambridge University Press, 2003).

7. Pierre Monnet, 'Reale und ideale Stadt: Die oberdeutschen Städte im Spiegel autobiographischer Zeugnisse des Spätmittelalters', trans. Hermann Krapoth, in *Von der dargestellten Person zum erinnerten Ich*, ed. Kaspar von Greyerz, Hans Medick and Patrice Veit (Böhlau, 2001), pp. 395–430 (p. 430); cf. Valentin Groebner, 'Die Kleider des Körpers des Kaufmanns: Zum Trachtenbuch eines Augsburger Bürgers im 16.Jahrhundert', *Zeitschrift für Historische Forschung*, 25 (1998), pp. 323–58; and 'Inside Out: Clothes, Dissimulation and the Act of Accounting in the Autobiography of Matthäus Schwarz 1496–1574', *Representations*, 66 (1999), pp. 100–121; Philippe Braunstein, *Un Banquier mis à nu* (Gallimard, 1992).

8. Groebner, 'Die Kleider des Körpers'.

9. Pl. 113.

10. Pl. 95.

11. Pl. 111.

12. Pl. 28.

13. Quoted in Fink, *Trachtenbücher*, p. 176. See Pl. 138.

14. Claus Grimm, *Lucas Cranach: Ein Maler-Unternehmer aus Franken* (Pustet, 1994), p. 356; see also Ann Rosalind Jones and Peter Stallybrass, *Renaissance Clothing and the Materials of Memory* (Cambridge University Press, 2000), p. 34.

15. Christopher Breward, *Culture of Fashion* (Manchester University Press, 1995), p. 67.

16. On this more generally, see Jutta Zander-Seidel, *Textiler Hausrat: Kleidung und Haustextilien in Nürnberg von 1500–1650* (Deutscher Kunstverlag, 1990). On aggressive masculinity, see also Lyndal Roper, 'Stealing Manhood: Capitalism and Magic in Early Modern Germany', in her *Oedipus and the Devil: Witchcraft, Sexuality and Religion in Early Modern Europe* (Routledge, 1994), pp. 125–44.

17. Gerhard Jaritz, '"Seiden Päntel an den Knien" oder: Die Hoffart liegt im Detail', in *Ut populus ad historiam traktatur, Festgabe Herwig Ebner*, ed. Gerhard Michael Dienes (Leykam, 1988), pp. 63–74 (p. 68).

18. Pl. 70.

19. *'Kurzweil viel/ohn' Maß und Ziel': Augsburger Alltag und Festtag auf den Augsburgern Monatsbildern der Renaissance*, ed. Hartmut Boockmann, Deutsches Historisches Museum (Hirmer, 1994).

20. On the term *Mehrer* see *Augsburger Eliten des 16. Jahrhunderts: Prosopographie wirtschaftlicher und politischer Führungsgruppen 1500–1620*, ed. Wolfgang Reinhard (Akademie Verlag, 1990), p. xv. See also Götz Freiherr von Pölnitz, 'Augsburger Kaufleute und Bankherren der Renaissance', in *AUGUSTA 955–1955: Forschungen und Studien zur Kultur- und Wirtschaftsgeschichte Augsburgs* (Hermann Rinn, 1955), pp. 187–219.

21. Peter Burschel and Mark Häberlein, 'Familie und Eigennutz', in *'Kurzweil viel/ohn' Maß und Ziel'*, pp. 48–66; Olaf Mörke, 'Die Fugger im 16. Jahrhundert: Städtische Elite oder Sonderstruktur', *Archiv für Reformationsgeschichte*, 74 (1983), pp. 141–64; see also Katarina Sieh-Burens, *Oligarchie, Konfession und Politik im 16. Jahrhundert: Zur sozialen Verflechtung der Augsburger Bürgermeister und Stadtpfleger 1518–1618*, Schriften der Philosophischen Fakultät der Universität Augsburg, 29 (Voegel, 1986), p. 91.

22. Sue Vincent, 'To Fashion a Self', *Fashion Theory*, 2 (1999), pp. 197–218 (p. 209).

23. Pl. 86.

24. Fink, *Trachtenbücher*, p. 23. Cf. Braunstein, *Un Banquier mis à nu*, p. 109.

25. Groebner, 'Die Kleider des Körpers', pp. 335–6.

26. Hans Belting, *Bild-Anthropologie: Entwürfe für eine Bildwissenschaft* (Fink Verlag, 2001), pp. 115–43.

27. Breward, *Culture of Fashion*, p. 67.

28. Jones and Stallybrass, *Renaissance Clothing*, p. 35.

29. Groebner, 'Die Kleider des Körpers', p. 328.

30. Groebner , 'Die Kleider des Körpers', p. 343.

31. Martha Ajmer, 'Toys for Girls: Objects, Women and Memory in the Renaissance Household', in *Material Memories*, ed. Marius Kwint, Christopher Breward and Jeremy Aynsley (Berg Publishers, 1999), pp. 75–90 (p. 79).

32. Ajmer, 'Toys for Girls', p. 79.

33. Ulrich Stromer, *Püchel von mein geslecht und von abenteuer: Teilfaksimilie der Handschrift Hs6146 des Germanischen Nationalmuseums Nürnberg. Zur 600-Jahrfeier der Grundung der esten Papiermühle in Deutschland* (Verband Deutscher Papierfabriken, 1990). On the concept of individuality, cf. Michael Sonntag, *Das Verborgene des Herzens: Zur Geschichte der Individualität* (Rowohlt, 1999), p. 89; cf. Wiersing, 'Vormoderne Lebensformen', p. 168.

34. Martin Kohli, 'Gesellschaftszeit und Lebenszeit: Der Lebenslauf im Strukturwandel der Moderne', in Johannes Berger (ed.), *Die Moderne – Kontinuitäten und Zäsuren*, Soziale Welt, Sonderband 4 (Schwartz Verlag, 1986). Cf. the same author's 'Lebenslauf und Lebensalter als gesellschaftliche Konstruktionen: Elemente zu einem interkulturellen Vergleich', in Georg Elwert, Martin Kohli and Harald Müller (eds), *Im Lauf der Zeit: Ethnographische Studien zur gesellschaftlichen Konstruktion von Lebensaltern*, Spektrum, 25 (Breitenbach, 1990), pp. 11–32, 15 and 16.

35. Klaus E. Müller, 'Zeitkonzepte in traditionellen Kulturen', in *Historische Sinnbildung*, ed. K. E. Müller and Jörg Rüsen (Rowohlt, 1997), pp. 221–39 (p. 223).

36. Heide Wunder and Christine Vanja (eds), *Wandel der Geschlechterbeziehungen zu Beginn der Neuzeit* (Suhrkamp Verlag, 1991), pp. 12–26 (p. 23). Joan Kelly argues in a similar direction in 'Did Women have a Renaissance?', in *Women, History and Theory*, ed. J. Kelly (University of Chicago Press, 1984), pp. 19–50. Carole Turbin was kind enough to recommend Kelly's essay to me.

37. Michel de Certeau, 'Die Kunst des Handelns: Gehen in der Stadt', in *Widerspenstige Kulturen: Cultural Studies als Herausforderung*, ed. Karl H. Hörning and Rainer Winter (Suhrkamp Verlag, 1999), pp. 264–92 (p. 271). I would like to thank Barbara Burman and Carole Turbin for informing me of Certeau's stimulating essay, the original French version of which is in Certeau's *L'Invention du quotidien*, I, *Arts de faire* (Editions Gallimard, 1990), pp. 139–64.

38. Breward, *Culture of Fashion*, p. 65.

39. See Kaja Silverman, 'Dem Blickregime begegnen', trans. Natascha Noack and Roger M. Buergel, in *Privileg Blick*, ed. Christian Kravagna (Edition ID-Archiv, 1997), pp. 41–64 (p. 48).

40. Hans Doege, 'Die Trachtenbücher des 16. Jahrhunderts', in *Beiträge zur Bücherkunde und Philologie: August Wilmanns zum 25. März 1903 gewidmet* (Harrassowitz, 1903), pp. 429–44; Rolf Walther, 'Das Danziger Frauentrachtenbuch von Anton Möller und seine Vorläufer im 16. Jahrhundert', in *Studien zur Geschichte des Preussenlandes; Festschrift f. Erich Kayser*, ed. Ernst Bahr (Elwert, 1963).

41. Fink, *Trachtenbücher*, p. 123.

42. Quoted in Fink, *Trachtenbücher*, p. 145, pls 79, 80.

43. Braunstein, *Le Banquier mis à nu*, p. 112.

44. Groebner, 'Die Kleider des Körpers', p. 335; see in particular Norbert Schnitzler, 'Tugendhafte Körper und die Disziplinierung des Blicks', in *Gepeinigt, begehrt, vergessen: Symbolik und Sozialbezug des Körpers im späten Mittelalter und in der frühen Neuzeit*, ed. N. Schnitzler and Klaus Schreiner (Fink, 1992), pp. 337–63 (p. 339).

45. Lyndal Roper, '"Wille" und "Ehre": Sexualität, Sprache und Macht in Augsburger Kriminalprozessen', in Wunder and Vanja (eds), *Wandel der Geschlechterbeziehungen*, pp. 180–97 (p. 197).

46. Jean-Thierry Maertens, *Dans la peau des autres: Essai d'anthropologie des inscriptions vestimentaires*, Ritologiques, 4 (Aubier Montaigne, 1978), p. 17.

47. M. Schwarz was all too familiar with the insecurity of social status, since his own grandfather had been executed for fraud. See Groebner , 'Inside Out', pp. 111–12.

48. For an explanation of this picture from the perspective of economic history, see Balduin Penndorf, *Geschichte der Buchhaltung in Deutschland* (1913; repr. Sauer und Auvermann, 1966), p. 56.

49. See Alberto Tenenti, 'The Merchant and the Banker', in *Renaissance Characters*, ed. Eugenio Garin, trans. Lydia G. Cochrane (University of Chicago Press, 1991), pp. 154–79 (pp. 162–3). The merchant class of the Renaissance was marked by a new consciousness of time that differed from that traditionally propagated by the church; they were guided by the conviction that every instant in life was precious, and founded their fortunes on that belief.

50. Cf. Schwarz, quoted in Alfred Weitnauer, *Der venezianische Handel der Fugger: Nach der Musterbuchhaltung des Matthäus Schwarz*, Studien zur Fugger-Geschichte, 9 (Duncker und Humblot, 1931), pp. 21 and 20. The *Gegenschreiber* copied the accounts into an additional set of books for checking purposes.

51. On this, see Iris Origo's brilliant study, *The Merchant of Prato* (Jonathan Cape, 1957).

52. Michael Baxandell, *Painting and Experience in Fifteenth-Century Italy* (Clarendon Press, 1972), pp. 86–7, 94–102.

53. Luca Pacioli, *Abhandlung über die Buchhandlung 1494*, ed. Rudolf Seyffert. Translated from the Italian original of 1494. With an introduction on Italian bookkeeping in the fourteenth and fifteenth centuries and Pacioli's life and work by Balduin Penndorf, *Quellen und Studien zur Geschichte der Betriebswirtschaftslehre*, 11 (Poeschel, 1933), p. 55.

54. L. Pacciolo, *Abhandlung über die Buchhaltung*, quoted in Penndorf, *Geschichte der Buchhaltung*, p. 91.

55. Pl. 88.

56. Quoted in Fink, *Trachtenbücher*, p. 149. 'The sayon of camelot is a black jacket (*Wappenrock*) with pleated tails slit at the sides, a wide neckline and slightly bell-shaped puffed sleeves ending in conical cuffs.' Camelot was a fabric made of camel's hair.

57. Jones and Stallybrass, *Renaissance Clothing*, p. 42.

3

Reflections on Gender and Status Distinctions: An Analysis of the Liturgical Textiles Recorded in Mid-Sixteenth-Century London

Maria Hayward

London in the mid sixteenth century was a city in religious flux. The reformation of the English church, which had begun under Henry VIII (1509–47) with the king pronouncing himself head of the church, reviewing the liturgy and dissolving the monasteries, took a more radical doctrinal turn under Edward VI (1547–53). Transubstantiation was denied, with 'justification by faith' promoted in its stead. The reintroduction of the Book of Common Prayer on 1 November 1552 was significant in this process, and its impact was visual as well as liturgical. John Stow noted in his *Annales of England* that on this day Nicholas Ridley, Bishop of London, wore 'his rochet only, without cope or vestment'.[1] This rejection of liturgical textiles went beyond vestments and included the textile furnishings for the church and linen for the priest and the altars. These textiles belonged to the parish churches and they played a significant and symbolic part in the parishioners' communal and individual religious lives until 1552. After a brief resurgence under Mary, and as a consequence of royal religious policy, the role of textiles in the liturgy was radically reduced.

Prior to 1552 these textiles represented the parish communities in London. This paper explores whether, within an essentially patriarchal society, such textiles could temporarily highlight women over men, children over adults, paupers over the well-to-do. Although very few of London's pre-Reformation liturgical textiles have survived, they are still accessible via ninety-six surviving parish inventories. Much research on changing religious attitudes in the early modern period has focused on wills where individuals, often from the middle ranks and above, expressed their private beliefs.[2] However, the appurtenances of worship were highly significant in a society where literacy levels amongst the lower social groups were not high. The parish church was a semi-public environment where men and women interacted away from the domestic and commercial spheres.[3] The textiles belonging to these churches will provide a means of exploring the nature of female subordination in sixteenth-century London.

In 1550 approximately 70,000 people lived in London.[4] The capital's wealth and population placed it in a separate class from the other leading English towns like Bristol, York and Norwich. However, it is this abnormality that makes London such a good place to study. London had 107 parishes, the vast majority of which were inside the City walls.[5] This high number meant that the intra-mural parishes were small, with an average area of four acres. At the human level, according to the 1,548 chantry certificates, the mean number of communicants per parish was 310.[6] In spite of their modest size, the parishes were relatively wealthy compared to parishes elsewhere in the country.

On average, there were 115 men for every 100 women in sixteenth-century London.[7] Numerically, women were just in the minority, but legally the position of women was more ambiguous. The legal system reinforced the patriarchal nature of English society by subordinating married women and absorbing them within their husband's family.[8] A single adult woman or widow, a *femme sole*, could make a will, trade in her own name, contract debts and own, buy or sell property. Technically, a *femme couvert* or married woman was free to do none of these things, but within London there was more flexibility.[9] Distinctions between men and women would have been visible in London society. The question of belonging, or not belonging, to the London community was significant: citizens were included (adult males with membership of a livery company), aliens (from outside England) and strangers (from outside London) were excluded. Women did not enter the freedom of the city in London by purchase or patrimony but through marriage to freemen. Women's familial roles were complex and included running the home, caring for her husband, children and possibly other family members and contributing to the family income.

People were well attuned to the subtle nuances conveyed by textiles in sixteenth-century London.[10] Objects conveyed a wealth of meaning and textiles, which were both visual and tactile, did so by their colour, the cost and quality of the cloth and the type of ornament or imagery used to decorate them. The high financial value of textiles in the sixteenth century, their diversity of function and their associations with the different phases of the human life cycle make them a rich source for exploring contemporary attitudes to gender ideology and social standing.

In 1552 the parish churches of England were surveyed at the behest of Edward VI and the Council as a part of the continued reform of the church. Each parish's moveable goods were inventoried in order to make an appraisal of ecclesiastical wealth and to reduce the possibility of misappropriation prior to its sale. The resulting revenue was used to pay for modifications to the parish churches, to finance Edward's wars and to provide poor relief. The large number of sales, along with some instances of iconoclasm and theft, reflects the laity's review of the material culture associated with the church. For many people suspicion or apathy replaced devotion.[11]

The commissioners compiling the inventories, their clerks and the church wardens were all male. Their descriptions of the objects were often brief, a consequence of limited time and of familiarity with the items. Chasubles, dalmatics and tunicles were not usually listed by name but by reference to the male wearers – the priest, deacon or subdeacon. This transference of details about the male wearer on to the object also occurred when size distinctions were made for the albs and surplices worn with the vestments. They were generally described as being for men or boys rather than being large or small. The references to women or textiles used by women are limited but telling. Most of the items associated specifically with women, such as care cloths or cloths for midwives (see below), were often square or rectangular and undecorated. A number of the parishes had silk and linen textiles of this type that the clerks did not associate with a specific function. It is quite possible that the clerks consciously chose not to record the female associations of these pieces.

The church, as the promoter of official religion, was essentially a male institution within which women played a small but significant part. Vestments were worn by the male clergy as a means of distinguishing them from the laity and to emphasise their role as an intermediary between humanity and the divine (Figure 1). For some reformers, vestments represented an inequality that the Catholic church promoted amongst men, by marking out the clergy as closer to God than the male laity. While laymen could progress into the ranks of the clergy, women could play no part in the administration of the sacraments – they could only receive them. Indeed women were not supposed to touch the altar, a consequence of longstanding male concerns about women being weaker and more sinful than men. However, as recipients, women made up approximately half the congregation and in this sense women had an equal share with men in the sacraments administered by the clergy and in the vestments worn during the celebration of mass.

Vestments acted as a material manifestation of the ecclesiastical hierarchy, with the chasuble for the priest when he officiated at the mass, the dalmatic, a T-shaped, sleeved garment, for the deacon, and the tunicle,

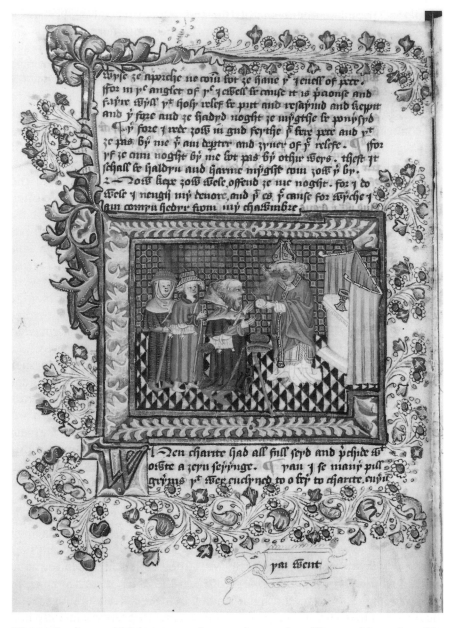

Figure 1: An archbishop, wearing a mitre and pallium, with a chasuble over a dalmatic (?) and a linen alb (with an apparel at the hem), administers the sacrament to three pilgrims. The altar is covered with a linen (?) cloth and there are hangings behind and to the sides of the altar. MS. Laud Misc. 740, fol. 25v. With permission from the Bodleian Library, University of Oxford.

similarly shaped to the dalmatic, for the subdeacon. The cope was a processional garment worn by the clergy and cantors. An analysis of the colours and fabric types used for these vestments reveals an amazing diversity. Although the entries can be frustratingly vague, twenty-eight colours and forty-two types of cloth featured in the inventory entries. White, red and green were the most commonly occurring colours, while velvet, damask and baudekyn were the most frequently used materials.[12] The clerks rarely recorded the decoration on vestments but it is very unlikely that many were plain. When details about the motifs were noted, they fall into three categories: general objects including plants and animals, artefacts and individuals with religious associations and initials, badges and heraldic devices. The number of motifs within each category are 102, ninety-five and thirty respectively. Amongst the group of the religious motifs, female saints were in the minority when compared to their male counterparts but this imbalance was offset by the popularity of images of the Virgin.

While vestments were essentially male, being items of dress restricted solely to men, this distinction becomes blurred when female images were depicted on the orphreys. Although figures of male saints and prophets were most common, female saints alternating or paired with male saints are regular occurrences on surviving pieces. In a few instances the orphreys on a set of vestments were focused around a female theme, such as the life of the Virgin (Figure 2).[13] Although Mary, Mary Magdalene and virgin saints like Margaret, the patron saint of women in childbirth, promoted models of female virtue that most living women could never attain, their representation on vestments, as images and in wall paintings ensured a strong, irreproachable female presence in most parish churches. It was not uncommon for women to favour female saints, especially their namesake. The influence of Dame Helen Branch in St Mary Abchurch parish may be seen in the depiction of St Helen and St Margaret on an altar frontal of red damask.[14]

Vestments distinguished the clergy from the laity. This division was further highlighted by the use of Latin for the liturgy and by the priest standing with his back to the congregation for the elevation of the host. In the body of the church, the congregation was segregated according to gender, marital status and social standing.[15] Men and women could be divided in two ways: either women to the north and men to the south side of the church, or with men at the front, so nearer the east end of the church and the high altar, and women behind them. Sir Thomas More sat in the choir while his wife Alice sat in the body of their parish church in Chelsea.[16] Once divided by gender, the congregation was then ranked by status. So married women and widows sat before unmarried women, and women in service and children were at the back. John Myrfyn Cowke

Figure 2: An orphrey on the Whalley Abbey dalmatic depicting the Virgin Mary, with her parents, taking her first steps. Late fourteenth/early fifteenth century. The full cycle of orphreys starts with the betrothal of Mary's parents and culminates with the flight into Egypt and the miracle of the palm (29/2). With permission from the Glasgow Museums: The Burrell Collection, Glasgow.

bought the 'tymber of the maydens Loft', a special pew for unmarried women at St Michael Queenhithe.[17] At St Mary Le Bow, servants were seated separately on three 'long settles for servants to sit upon'.[18] Such divisions reflect contemporary views that separating the sexes would help promote morality and reinforce the social hierarchy. In the same way, the ordering of individuals and groups in processions subtly observed the interaction between gender, social standing, age and marital status.[19]

Close to London was Syon Abbey, a community of Bridgettine monks and nuns that Charles Wriothesley called 'the virtues[t] house of religion that was in England'.[20] However, as a consequence of Henry VIII passing the acts dissolving the lesser and greater monasteries in 1536 and 1539 respectively, this and the twenty-three monastic houses in London were closed. By dissolving the nunneries, the government ended a way of life that had allowed English women a means of openly expressing their religiosity and a lifestyle freer of male influence than either marriage or remaining within the parental home.[21] The dissolution also removed the nun's habit from the repertoire of English women's dress.[22] It had been significant for women within holy orders or those, like Lady Margaret Beaufort, who took a vow of chastity in 1504 while still married to her fourth husband and was painted after this date wearing clothes that evoked a nun's habit.[23]

Although over fifty per cent of the London population was under twenty, young children played a very minor role in society after their public induction into parish life at their christening. While young girls were seen within the body of the church but not heard, a number of London churches had copes, surplices and albs for boy choristers to wear when they took a small but significant part in the church services. One-fifth of the parishes had eight to ten boys' copes. The average number of boys' copes was four, although most churches had just two. The majority of boys' vestments were recorded without detailing the colour (84.5 per cent) or fabric type (59 per cent), suggesting that the clerks felt less need to record information about these vestments than they did about those for the adult clergy. In part this reflects the fact that these smaller vestments were less valuable. Equally, their small size would aid identification, so reducing the need for additional information. Where extra details were given, they indicate that the boys' vestments were made of less expensive fabrics emphasising their relatively lowly position.

The boys had a distinct and subsidiary role within the church that could act as preparation for a future career in the church. Boy choristers would have participated in services throughout the liturgical year, but on one occasion each year the priest/chorister relationship was inverted. On 6 December, the feast of St Nicholas, one boy was nominated to play the role of the boy bishop until Holy Innocents (28 December). The boy bishop would process around the parish wearing vestments like 'the childe bysshope coape' at St Alban, Wood Street.[24] The boys also dressed as women during these processions.[25] The idea of inverting social relationships had a parallel at the Tudor court. A junior member of the royal household was appointed as the Lord of Misrule, who organised entertainment for his social superiors for the Christmas and New Year period.

The sacraments of baptism, marriage and extreme unction, with the latter followed by a funeral, would have punctuated the lives of the majority of the population. In turn, many of the textiles owned by the parishes related to these events, while other object types recorded within the parish inventories, such as books and plate, did not act as markers of gender or status in the same way. The birthrate in sixteenth-century London was relatively low, when compared to the overall growth rate of the city's population, because most women were in their late twenties at their first marriage. It was the steady influx of immigrants into London that ensured the population increased rapidly. Numerically women are in the majority on the Nevill altar frontal (Figure 3), yet in reality male children were valued more than female offspring, and marriage was more important for women than men. The central scene of Christ crucified flanked by the Virgin and St John is balanced by the kneeling figures of Ralph, 4th Earl of Westmoreland, and his wife, Lady Catherine Stafford. Behind Ralph knelt their seven sons and behind Catherine were their thirteen daughters.

Childbirth was a private, domestic event focusing on the mother, her female relatives and the midwife, placing it outside the sphere of the church and its male hierarchy. However, parish churches and monasteries could loan relics to protect the mother and child in return for a fee. Evidence of these relics, primarily associated with female saints, can be found in the letters of the monastic visitors, who surveyed the religious houses prior to the dissolution. On 24 August 1535 Dr Richard Layton wrote to Thomas Cromwell, who orchestrated the dissolution, stating

> I send you … Our Lady's girdle of Bruton [Abbey in Somerset], red silk, which is a solemn relic sent to women travelling, which shall not miscarry.[26]

Doubts about the validity of such relics had been raised prior to the sixteenth century. In the prologue to *The Canterbury Tales* Chaucer described the pardoner as being without comparison, 'For in his wallet he kept a pillow-slip which, he said, was/ Our Lady's veil'.[27] Concern over how the relics were used, in particular if their treatment could be interpreted as idolatry, resulted in the government condemning their use and carrying out a programme of destruction. Pregnant women with no recourse to relics often invoked St Margaret. Consequently, the church

Figure 3: Ralph Nevill with his wife Lady Catherine and their twenty children. Ralph kneels on the left, behind the Virgin, while Catherine kneels on the right behind St John. This is the opposite of the seating arrangements found in many churches where women sat on the left or north side and men sat on the right or south side. c. 1550 (T&D 35-1888). With permission from the Victoria and Albert Museum, London.

also sought to curb this practice. In the early 1540s, midwives in Worcester and Gloucester were called before the bishop's court and quizzed as to whether they still used

> any prayers, or invocations unto any saint, saving to God in Christ, for the deliverance of the woman, [or] any salt, herbs, water, wax, cloths, girdles or relics, or any such like thing.[28]

Christenings would have been a common occurrence. The significance of having a child christened shortly after birth, in a time of high infant mortality, was enhanced by the belief that an unbaptised child could not enter heaven. The textiles associated with christenings were limited primarily to font cloths. Nine font cloths were recorded within London. At St Lawrence Jewry the font cloth had three borders, while at St Andrew Undershaft there was a canopy to hang over the font. Unlike the other textiles associated with the sacraments, the font cloths were of relatively poor quality. Although three of the covers were made of silk, five were described as being either painted or stained.[29] While designs could be painted or stained onto silk grounds, the fact that the fabric was not identified suggests that a cheaper linen fabric had been used.

One possible reason for the relatively small number of font cloths was that many fonts were highly decorated, as illustrated by two surviving examples from outside London. At Weston, Suffolk, the font was carved with scenes representing the seven sacraments, while at Ufford in Suffolk, the wooden font cover was topped with a pelican in her piety.[30] Indeed, the provision of a textile canopy at St Andrew Undershaft may indicate that the font lacked a carved canopy. Like so many elements of the liturgy, lit candles were integral to the christening service, as was the 'white linen cloth to bear the taper to the font' at St Thomas the Apostle.

Christenings marked the admission of a new child into the church and the start of its religious life. However, as the parents often did not attend, relatively few church textiles were associated with the event. While the father might be present, the mother would not be. Firstly, she might not have recovered from the birth and secondly a new mother would not attend church until her official churching (see below). For all but the poorest families, the emphasis at the christening was usually on the godparents, while back at the family home the focus was on the mother and child. This was seen in its most exaggerated form in the rituals for royal christenings.[31] However, for female godparents this was an opportunity to demonstrate their faith to the wider community.

While Christianity did not require women to be purified after childbirth, the new mother went to church a month to six weeks after the birth, accompanied by her female relatives, to thank God for the child and a safe delivery.[32] At her churching, the new mother would present a candle to the Lady Altar or the image of the Virgin, make an offering of chrism (holy oil) and sit in the churching pew.[33] This had a parallel with the Purification of the Virgin celebrated at Candlemas on 2 February. A very small but significant group of textiles linked to this event were recorded in the inventories. The care cloth at St Mary le Bow was used 'to lie before women at their purification'.[34] However, in December 1553 Anne Williamson entered her parish church without having been churched and refused to offer chrism for her child.[35] Afterwards she was forced to do penance, but her defiance indicates the inherent contradiction of women being prized for their fertility and motherhood yet regarded as impure after having given birth.

One group of women that was regarded with suspicion by church and state were midwives or 'child wives'. The reason for this anxiety was twofold. Firstly, God intended women to suffer pain in childbirth after mankind's fall from grace, and midwives sought to alleviate these pains. Secondly, women often looked to midwives to terminate unwanted pregnancies. An act of parliament passed in 1512 required midwives to swear before the local bishop's court that they would avoid witchcraft. At a parish level, the presence of these textiles associated with midwives, which actively promoted their role, contradicts the official line.

The role of the midwife or child wife was acknowledged at St Ethelburga by the provision of 'two yards of coarse dornix painted which child wives to kneel over' and at St Thomas Apostle there was 'a cloth of child wives of silk'. Textiles of this type were not common, as the Kent parishes inventories indicate, for just two items were recorded: 'one towel for the child wife' at St Mary Bredne, Canterbury, and at Great Chart there was 'an old coverlet for child wives'.[36] It is telling that the midwife's role was indicated by the presence of special textiles, as she washed the new child and then 'swathith hym in clothis and cloutis', according to Bartholomaeus Anglicus.[37] As reformers came to reject the sacrament of baptism, some children were christened at the family home or at the home of the midwife.[38] Alternatively, the midwife could take the child to the parish church and act as its sponsor.

Henry VIII advocated marriage in his private life and public policy. He had the sacrament of marriage ranked along with baptism and communion in the *Bishops' Book* and the *King's Book*.[39] Even so, the London parish inventories reveal that specific textiles associated with marriage were rare and that they were more closely associated with women than with men. There was just one type – the care cloth. Care cloths (from *carré* meaning square) were placed over the head of the bride as a veil during the wedding ceremony. Only six care cloths were recorded in London and limited details on colour and fabric type were given: three were of silk, one of baudekyn; one was blue, one was green and one was changeable (the warp and weft were different colours creating a shot fabric). No references were made to any embellishment. This pattern is echoed in the inventories for Kent. Inventories survive for 136 Kent parishes and, of these, only twelve have specific wedding textiles. Six were identified as care cloths, two as bridal canopies, three as wedding cloths and, rather surprisingly, one as a cloth used for both weddings and funerals. Again additional details were minimal, with three of silk, one of damask and one of dornix. Colour was mentioned only in three cases. All of the cloths were red, including the dual-purpose cloth. The predominance of red may be accidental or it may have been chosen for its association with fertility.

A smaller group of additional textile items was used at weddings. At St Martin Vintry there were two cushions for the bride and groom to kneel on and St Michael Cornhill had a bawdrick for brides to wear. St Margaret's, the parish church of Westminster, had 'St Margaret's circlet' that prospective brides could hire for 16d.[40] While the set of marriage cushions at St Martin Vintry appears to be unique in London, most parishes owned several cushions that could be used for a variety of purposes, including weddings. However, the lack of marriage textiles within the parishes suggests that people brought their own textiles into the church for the service, indicating a change in the relationship between the family and the parish. Increasingly, families looked to their own resources and those of their extended family and friends to provide the textiles used to celebrate births and marriages.

A percentage of women never married, so marriage textiles would play no part in their lives. However, many women married more than once because of the high deathrate. Marriages were often arranged with the social and financial benefits as the main priority, and the first marriage was usually the most significant. When women considered a second marriage they had to weigh the potential advantages of financial and personal independence associated with widowhood against companionship, status and children with remarriage.[41] Four-fifths of sixteenth-century London aldermen were survived by their wives. Only one-third of the 208 widows remarried.[42] An alderman's widow had wealth, a place in society and a degree of freedom that made remarriage an unattractive option.

Death, like birth, was common to all, but the funerary textiles indicate that the ceremony attached to a funeral revealed the subtle nuances of the individual's gender, age and social standing. Funerals were a regular feature of London life because life expectancy in the city was low. It ranged from twenty to twenty-five years in the poorer areas to thirty to thirty-five years in the wealthier areas. Those who survived in London into their late twenties would live on average for an additional twenty-six and a half years. In contrast, those born in rural areas lived to be forty-six on average.[43] When the inevitable happened, the church oversaw the interment of a person's mortal remains and charged the bereaved relatives mortuary fees for doing so. The level of these charges often caused resentment in London and they were cited as evidence of clerical greed, most famously in the Hunne case.[44]

Provision for the dead within the parish inventories went beyond a hearse cloth to drape the coffin or hearse. St Bride, Fleet Street, had four coffins, and sets of trestles to rest the coffin on, along with a pickaxe and a shovel for digging the grave. The parishioners also played an important role as mourners, and women had a stronger association with funerals and mourning than men. For example, the female members of the guild of Our Lady's Assumption, Westminster, had special responsibility for the dead.[45]

Attitudes to death and the dead were to change markedly with the Reformation. In pre-Reformation England, prayers, masses for the dead and purgatory were an important part of many people's lives and deaths. These issues recurred in wills in the form of money for masses, lights (candles) and alms. Between 1500 and the 1530s, female testators (more so than their male counterparts) also gave gifts in kind, including clothing and lengths of cloth that could be converted into liturgical textiles.[46] Even so some individuals were already reacting against the traditional idea of purgatory and the prolonged suffering of the soul after death. Between 1534 and 1546, only 23 per cent of London testators left money to a priest.[47] In 1543 the *King's Book* stated that 'we should ... abstain from the name of Purgatory and no more dispute or reason thereof'.[48]

Much of the decoration of funeral textiles was suitably mournful, such as the cloth of black velvet decorated 'with dead men's skulls' at All Hallows the Great.[49] But not all. Funerals were the final opportunity for an individual to display their wealth. Several of the documented hearse cloths had coats of arms, most probably of the donor. At St Peter, Paul's Wharf, there were two hearse cloths of 'fustian of naples, orfred with red velvet and embroidered with ragged staves of gold and blue garters'.[50] Others had more traditional religious imagery, such as the cloth of 'blue velvet with borders of red satin of bridges [Brussels] with a crucifix, Mary and John and certain images and three buckles in a scutchion' as at St Martin Outwich.[51] The placement of the Virgin on Christ's right, as she undoubtedly would have been, emphasised her central role in traditional iconography. It also placed an irreproachable female figure before the parishioners at a time when many would be thinking of her role as an intercessor between God and mankind. Mary's ascension was depicted on the London Brewers' pall. The preferences for colour and cloth discussed below are borne out by this pall which combined a top panel of red cloth of gold with side panels of red velvet. Members of the various livery companies could be buried using their company's pall. This ensured that the membership of the company had a luxurious funeral that would have been beyond the means of many individuals.

Adherents of reformed religious ideas often rejected the trappings of Catholic funerals. The mid sixteenth century was a period of transition for funerary textiles, and the 1552 parish inventories record the changes in terminology and in the physical form of these textiles. Sixty-nine of the ninety-six parishes had funerary textiles, with an average of two each. Although black vestments are associated with funerals and Good Friday services, black was not always used for funerary textiles (Table 1) or vestments in the mid sixteenth century. Only 8 per cent of the London chasubles, where the colour was recorded, were black. Black, either alone or in combination with a colour, accounted for twenty-one of the funerary textiles (14.3 per cent), while sixty-six were coloured, representing 45 per cent. Turning to the choice of fabric (Table 2), cloth of gold, velvet or a

Table 1: Colours used for funerary textiles

Colour	Bier cloths	Burying cloths	Coffin cloths	Hearse cloths	Palls	Total
Black	–	1	–	10	–	**11**
Black/crimson	–	–	–	1	1	**2**
Black/gold	–	–	–	2	–	**2**
Black/red	1	–	–	3	–	**4**
Black/tawny	–	–	–	1	–	**1**
Black/white	–	–	–	–	1	**1**
Blue	–	2	–	7	–	**9**
Blue/gold	–	1	–	4	1	**6**
Blue/white	–	1	–	–	–	**1**
Copper	–	–	–	1	–	**1**
Crane	–	–	–	1	–	**1**
Crimson	–	1	–	4	–	**5**
Crimson/blue	–	–	–	2	–	**2**
Gold	–	5	1	15	–	**21**
Green	–	–	–	1	–	**1**
Green/purple	–	1	–	–	–	**1**
Lion	–	–	–	1	–	**1**
Purple	–	1	–	2	–	**3**
Red	–	–	–	5	–	**5**
Red/blue	–	–	2	2	–	**4**
Red/gold	–	–	–	2	–	**2**
Tawny	–	–	–	1	–	**1**
Unspecified/entry damaged	4	6	2	42	5	**61**
White	–	–	–	1	–	**1**
White/green	–	–	–	1	–	**1**
Total	**5**	**19**	**5**	**109**	**8**	**146**

Table 2: Fabrics used for funerary textiles

Textile type	Bier cloths	Burying cloths	Coffin cloths	Hearse cloths	Palls	Total
Baudekyn	1	2	–	4	1	8
Buckram	–	1	–	1	–	2
Camlet	–	–	–	1	–	1
Cloth	–	–	–	1	–	1
Cloth of gold	–	3	1	12	–	16
Cloth of gold/satin	–	–	–	1	–	1
Cloth of gold/velvet	–	3	–	11	1	15
Damask	–	–	–	1	2	3
Dornix	–	–	–	1	–	1
Fustian, naples	–	–	–	3	–	3
Linen	1	–	–	–	–	1
Linen/buckram	–	1	–	–	–	1
Satin	–	–	–	1	–	1
Satin, bridges	2	–	–	5	–	7
Satin, 'tinsen'	–	–	–	1	–	1
Silk	–	1	–	6	1	8
Tincel	–	–	–	3	–	3
Tissue	–	–	–	4	–	4
Unspecified/entry damaged	–	6	4	33	2	45
Velvet	–	2	–	17	1	20
Velvet/satin, bridges	–	–	–	1	–	1
Velvet, tissue	–	–	–	2	–	2
Total	**5**	**19**	**5**	**109**	**8**	**146**

combination of the two occurred most frequently. These were luxury fabrics and the frequency of use reflects in part the wealth of London. Cloth of gold, either alone or in combination with other fabrics including velvet, accounted for thirty-two entries (21.9 per cent), while velvet, alone or in combination, represented a further 15 per cent. In contrast, only 4.2 per cent of chasubles were made of cloth of gold, with 15.7 per cent made of velvet.

When distinctions are made in the inventories, it was usually a question of size differentiating between palls for adults and for children, rather than differentiations between those for men and for women. This is of particular interest as children are often even less accessible than women in the historical record. Palls for children and infants would be half the size, or less, of those used for adult burials and so could be distinguished by their size. When a parish had one hearse cloth for adults and one for children, the cloth for the children was frequently of inferior cloth to that for the adults. At All Hallows the Less they had a hearse cloth of cloth of gold for men and a cloth of black velvet for children.[52] However, in other cases provision for adults and children was the same: both made of cloth of gold at St Dionis Backchurch.[53] Only two funerary textiles were described as being used for both men and women, in comparison to four that were identified as being for men (Table 3). As none were described as being for women only, this apparent exclusion of women may be a linguistic distinction rather than a reflection of actual practice. The term 'men' may just have been used to imply that the pall was for adults. However, in the majority of instances, no indication of size or usage was given.

These textiles also express the social distinction between master and servant. Men, as father, husband or employer, often arranged the funerals of their dependants – wives, children, apprentices and servants.[54] The subtle nuances of gender, age and social standing dictated where a person was buried, but these could be overridden. The most desirable, and most expensive, place of burial was the chancel, followed by the aisles, side chapels, the body of the church, and ending outside in the churchyard. In death, while some women were named in the church wardens' accounts, for example the entry 'for covering Mother Olyver's grave', others were absorbed into the identity of the male head of the household as in the case of 'Thomas Surbot for his daughter's burial'.[55]

At St Botolph, Billingsgate, there were three hearse covers: one of cloth of gold, one of red and blue velvet with flowers and one of crane coloured (grey brown) silk for servants.[56] At St Dionis Backchurch there were four burial cloths: one of cloth of gold, one of velvet, one of cloth of gold for children and one of silk for the poor and servants.[57] Many young unmarried women were employed as domestic servants in London and if they died in service they would have been buried using these textiles. Other parish inventories reveal a similar variation in the quality of the fabrics used for their funerary textiles, suggesting the same pattern of use as above that was not recorded by the clerk. For example, at St Andrew Hubbard in 1550, they had one hearse cloth of cloth of gold and a second of red fustian of Naples. If these or similar hearse cloths were in the parish at the end of the decade, it is possible to tell from the parish wardens' accounts

Table 3: Types of funerary textiles

Designation	Bier cloths	Burying cloths	Coffin cloths	Hearse cloths	Palls	Total
For men	–	1 (5.3%)	–	3 (2.8%)	–	4 (2.8%)
For men and women	–		–	2 (1.8%)	–	2 (1.3%)
For children	–	2 (10.6%)	–	10 (9.2%)	1 (12.5%)	13 (8.9%)
For servants and/ or the poor	–	1 (5.3%)	–	1 (0.9%)	–	2 (1.3%)
Unspecified	5 (100%)	15 (78.8%)	5 (100%)	93 (85.3%)	7 (87.5%)	125 (85.7%)
Total	**5**	**19**	**5**	**109**	**8**	**146**

how they were used. In 1558 Master Wilkins paid 4d for the use of 'the hearse cloth at the burial of his man', and in the period 1558–60 'the hearse cloth' was hired twice at 12d a time.[58] The hearse cloths and the vestments discussed earlier have the highest status of the textiles considered here and it is no accident that they were associated with the mass and funerals, both of which drew the parish community together.

Before the Reformation, the interests of three groups were promoted in the parish churches – the living, the dead and the community of saints who acted as intermediaries between mankind and the divine. The role of the saints has been discussed briefly in relation to vestments but they were much more prominent in the form of statues and wall paintings. Their function was a vexed question and the Ten Articles of 1536 stated that 'we may pray to our blessed Lady and John the Baptist, the apostles or any other saint particularly as our devotion doth serve us so that it be done without any vain superstition'.[59] In 1538 Henry VIII's commissioners destroyed the shrine dedicated to the Virgin at Walsingham and sent the statue to London where it was burnt. By the time the parishes were surveyed in 1552, most of the images would have been removed.[60]

The central role of the Virgin meant that special provision was made for more female statues than male images. Small clothes were made for the images and by 1552 nineteen such garments were still listed in the London inventories. Fourteen were for female figures: eleven for the Virgin, three for Christ, two for St Katherine and one each for St Ursula, the Trinity and St Nicholas. In spite of their small size, these garments still had significance for some people in 1552. A coat for the Christ child of green (Brussels) satin bridges with flowers and one for the Virgin were sold for 3s 5d, another coat for Our Lady was bought for 2s, while 'St Tursellys coat' (Ursula) was priced at 16d.[61] In addition to the clothing, there was 'a shewe of Siluer for the rode' at St Olave, Silver Street, and 'one showe of sylver in the Image of Our Ladye' at the hospital of Elsing Spital in Cripplegate.[62]

In spite of the inevitable emphasis on the Virgin Mary and a significant minority of female saints, overall they were in the minority. This is apparent by looking at the accounts of St Andrew Hubbard that refer to Mary and two other female saints, in comparison to Christ, six male saints, the Trinity and St Spirit. This imbalance is also evident in the dedications of the London churches. In turn, this reflects the inequality between men and women in parish life being extended to the heavenly community of Christ, Our Lady and the panoply of male and female saints.

Moving from evidence relating to gender ideology/identity, the liturgical textiles also provide evidence of gendered actions. Although women were associated primarily with the home, many women took a more active role. Poor women needed to earn a living, while wealthy women often had to look after their family's interests when their menfolk were absent. Women played an important part in the small producer households that were found throughout early modern London, and church wardens' accounts, like the series at St Andrew Hubbard, make it possible to explore how liturgical textiles played a part in the working lives of London women. In 1480–82 the clerk's wife received 2d for sewing an ouch (brooch) onto the best cope, while in 1552 12d was paid to Master Sturton's clerks for recovering a cope.[63] The less skilled work required to repair albs and surplices appears to have been done by women, as in the case of the 2d paid 'to goodwife Clarke for mending surplices' in the account for 1533–35.[64] The women were described in relation to their husbands in the accounts, for example payments were made to 'Christopher Tailor's wife and Osborne's wife for mending surplices'.[65] This practice helped locate women within their families and provided an indication of their status and social role.

Women were often involved in the cleaning of linen albs and surplices. According to Goldberg, washing was an exclusively female activity, although for many women it was only a part-time occupation.[66] While washerwomen were usually only identified in taxation records by their occupational by-name (for example, *laundere*), sometimes they were named in the parish records. In the account for 1480–82 at St Andrew Hubbard, Hamelyn's wife was paid approximately 12d a quarter 'for washing and setting on the albs', while in 1492 the account was more vague, recording 4s 2d 'for the launderer for a whole year and a quarter'.[67] By carrying out this work, the women combined earning some money with caring for the parish's textiles. It is significant that women were allowed to handle and care for these textiles.

Men were heavily involved in the production, dissemination and ornamentation of textiles as weavers, merchants and embroiderers. However, women were also employed in most areas of textile production in London. Many were paid at lower rates than their male counterparts, but one small group made a decent living. London silk women produced expensive silk trimmings used by vestment makers.[68] Just as women were involved in the production of these textiles, they also purchased, donated and bequeathed some of the textiles belonging to any parish. At St Dionis Backchurch there was 'a vestment of tymsyn the gift of Mrs Gayll with the appurtenances' and 'ij old white cushions embroidered that was the gift of Mistress Digby'.[69] At St Dunstan in the West a widow took back a gift made by her late husband. A set of vestments represented a substantial gift to a church and in this transition period people often looked to recover their former property. John Whitepane, church warden, returned three suites of vestments and three copes of red velvet brodered with scallop shells of silver, gift of Mr Henry Tailor, merchant tailor, to Mistress Dacres without the consent of the parish.[70]

Women also played their part in the dispersal of the liturgical textiles between 1547 and 1552. While the monastic land was beyond the means of most people, these textiles would have been affordable for a much broader group. Twenty-one (3.2 per cent) of the 649 identifiable buyers of liturgical textiles in London, either individuals or partnerships, were female. While women formed a very small subset of the group, the sample indicates that they had less money to spend on these textiles than men (Table 4). This would support other research on female work in London that has shown that women were poorly paid. Consequently, women did not buy in bulk in the way that a few male buyers did. The women's purchases were generally small and included items that were readily converted to domestic use such as cushions, linen towels, amices and altar cloths. However, a few women also acquired chasubles and copes, probably with the intention of using the fabric to make furnishings. This may well have been the case with Lady Askew, widow of Sir Christopher Askew, mayor in 1533 and benefactor to the parish of St John the Evangelist, who spent £10 on items made of cloth of gold. While some of the female buyers were widows, others were married women, and in one instance a husband and wife both bought items independently of each other. Women would also have shared indirectly in the purchases made by their menfolk, especially if the textiles bought were for conversion to domestic use.

The 1552 parish inventories focus on a short but significant period of London history that saw a profound decrease in the variety and number of their liturgical textiles. These textiles had marked the distinction between laity and clergy, while also allowing individuals within the congregation to stand out at transitional points in their lives. This was particularly signifi-cant for women as they had fewer opportunities to do so than men.

Table 4: Male and female expenditure on liturgical textiles

Expenditure	Number of female buyers	Number of male buyers
Less than 1s	1	7
1s–4s 11d	5	79
5s–9s 11d	6	94
10s–19s 11d	2	98
£1–£4 19s 11d	4	207
£5–£9 19s 11d	–	56
£10–£49 19s 11d	2	47
£50–£99 19s 11d	–	4
£100 plus	–	1
Partnerships of two or more	–	13 (consisting of 35 individuals)
Unspecified	1	21

Private prayer in the home and public devotion within the parish church were suitable occupations for women. Numerically, women were essentially equal recipients with men of the sacraments and spiritual strength that the church had to offer in the course of their everyday lives. Equally significant are the ways in which boys were highlighted over girls and the usual boundaries of the adult/child relationship were overturned with the St Nicholas celebrations.

In view of the financial value of liturgical textiles as a whole, it is possible that the quantity and quality distribution of textiles relating to birth, purification of mothers, marriage and death, reflects the importance of these events to individuals, families and the larger community. The relative lack of value attached to textiles associated with birth, purification and marriage could indicate several not necessarily contradictory points about their significance for a study of the interrelationship of gender, family and status. Firstly, that families might have their own textiles for these ceremonies that were used by successive generations. Secondly, that clerks did not always acknowledge the specific function of these textiles in the records, so making them appear less prevalent than they actually were. Thirdly, the presence of textiles acknowledging the role of the mid-wife may reflect an appreciation of their role at ground level that was at odds with official church policy.

In contrast, the quantity and quality of the textiles in 1552 associated with burial and the transition from this life to the next reinforces the emphasis on death and purgatory in pre-Reformation religion. The painful associations with funerals meant that families were less likely to have their own hearse cover and chose to hire one from the parish, their livery company or guild. The hearse cloths in London were made of expensive materials emphasising the importance of departing this life in an appro-priate manner. Although belief in purgatory was denounced, the social significance of funerals remained, and as a consequence many churches acquired more funerary textiles in 1552 or shortly after. These textiles bring out the differences between adults and children, rich and poor, master and servant, far more effectively than those between men and women. In part this reflects the fact that the male head of the household usually arranged the funerals of his dependants.

Although many of the textiles disappeared, the issues of inclusion and exclusion that they raised still prevailed at all levels of society, and revealed much about sixteenth-century ideas on the differences, real and imagined, between men and women. Birth, marriage and death were still central to people's lives. The emphasis on the visual within the pre-Reformation Catholic church was replaced by a simpler faith rooted in the word of God and personal contemplation.

Notes

This research could not have been undertaken without grants from the University of Southampton and the British Academy, for which I am most grateful. I would also like to thank Nell Hoare, director of the Textile Conservation Centre, University of Southampton, for permission to publish this paper and Dinah Eastop for reading and commenting on an earlier draft. I am particularly grateful to Carole Turbin, Barbara Burman and the referee for their excellent editorial comment and encouragement. Thanks are also due to Melissa Dalziel, Winnie Tyrrell and Martin Durrant.

1. J. Stow, *Annales of England* (London, 1605), p. 1027.
2. For a summary of work on religion and gender, see R. Shoemaker and M. Vincent (eds), *Gender and History in Western Europe* (Arnold, 1998), pp. 229–31.
3. Also see N. Zemon Davis, 'The Sacred and the Body Social in Sixteenth-Century Lyon', *Past and Present*, 90 (1981), pp. 40–70.
4. S. Rappaport, *Worlds Within Worlds: Structures of Life in Sixteenth-Century London* (Cambridge University Press, 1989), p. 50.
5. J. Schofield, 'Saxon and Medieval Parishes in the City of London: A Review', *London and Middlesex Archaeological Society*, 45 (1994), pp. 23–146.
6. C. Burgess (ed.), *The Church Records of St Andrew Hubbard East Cheap c.1450–c.1570*, London Record Society, 36 (1999), p. x.
7. S. Rappaport, 'Social Structure and Mobility in Sixteenth-Century London: Part 1', *London Journal*, 9 (1983), p. 113.
8. S. Walby, *Theorizing Patriarchy* (Blackwell, 1990), pp. 19 20.
9. See C. M. Barron, 'Introduction: The Widow's World in Later Medieval London', in *Medieval London Widows 1300–1500*, ed. C. M. Barron and A. F. Sutton (Hambledon, 1994), pp. i–xxxiv, and Rappaport, *Worlds Within Worlds*, pp. 34–8.
10. See C. Breward, *The Culture of Fashion: A New History of Dress* (Manchester University Press, 1995), pp. 29–34.
11. E. Duffy, *The Stripping of the Altars: Traditional Religion in England 1400–1580* (Yale University Press, 1992).
12. The level of import duty charged on these fabrics indicates their relative value, e.g. 15s–25s per yard for velvet; see T. S. Willan (ed.), *Tudor Book of Rates* (Manchester University Press, 1962).
13. L. Monnas, 'Opus Anglicanum and Renaissance Velvet: The Whalley Abbey Vestments', *Textile History*, 25 (1994), pp. 3–27.
14. H. C. Walters (ed.), *London Churches at the Reformation* (Church History Society, 1939), p. 413.
15. M. Aston, 'Segregation in Church', in W. J. Sheils and D. Wood (eds), *Women in the Church*, Studies in Church History, 27 (Blackwell/Ecclesiastical History Society, 1990), pp. 242–50, 269–81; also R. Gough, *The History of Myddle* (Caliban Books, 1979), pp. 27, 56, 71, 110, 161.
16. Aston , 'Segregation in Church', pp. 241, 246.
17. Public Record Office, Kew (PRO), E117/4/85.
18. PRO E117/4/39.
19. For a review of the social hierarchy in eighteenth-century Montpellier, see R. Darnton, *The Great Cat Massacre and Other Episodes in French Cultural History* (Allen Lane, 1984), pp. 116–31.
20. D. MacCulloch, 'Henry VIII and the Reform of the Church', in *The Reign of Henry VIII: Politics, Policy and Piety*, ed. D. MacCulloch (Macmillan, 1995), p. 164.
21. See C. Paxton, 'The Nunneries of London and its Environs in the Later Middle Ages', DPhil thesis, Oxford, 1992.
22. It was similar to male monastic dress but with the addition of the wimple and veil.
23. Lady Margaret was painted wearing a wimple and a white barb with black clothing, see M. K. Jones and M. G. Underwood, *The King's Mother: Lady Margaret Beaufort, Countess of Derby and Richmond* (Cambridge University Press, 1992), pp. 188–9.

24. PRO E117/4/72.
25. N. Zemon Davis, *Society and Culture in Early Modern France* (Polity, 1987), p. 137.
26. A. G. Dickens and D. Carr (eds), *The Reformation in England to the Accession of Elizabeth I*, Documents of Modern History (Edward Arnold, 1967, 1993), p. 95.
27. G. Chaucer, *The Canterbury Tales*, prose edition by David Wright (Grafton, 1965), p. 24.
28. Quoted in C. Rawcliffe, *Medicine and Society in Later Medieval England* (Allan Sutton, 1995), p. 200.
29. See N. Mander, 'Painted Cloths: History, Craftsmen and Techniques', *Textile History*, 28 (1997), pp. 137–40.
30. See C. Platt, *The Parish Churches of Medieval England* (Secker & Warburg, 1981), pp. 136–8.
31. K. Staniland, 'Royal Entry into the World', in D. Williams (ed.), *England in the Fifteenth Century*, Proceedings of the 1986 Harlaxton Symposium (Boydell, 1987), pp. 297–313.
32. The priest greeted the new mother saying 'Enter the temple of God, adore the Son of the Holy Virgin Mary who has given you the blessing of motherhood' (R. Parker, *The Subversive Stitch: Embroidery and the Making of the Feminine* (Women's Press, 1984), p. 59).
33. J. S. Brewer, J. Gairdner, R. H. Brodie, et al., *Letters and Papers, Foreign and Domestic of the Reign of Henry VIII*, 21 vols and addenda (1862–1932), XVIII.ii, p. 196; also E. Duffy, 'Holy Maydens, Holy Wyfes: The Cult of Women Saints in Fifteenth- and Sixteenth-Century England', in W. J. Sheils and D. Wood (eds), *Women in the Church*, Studies in Church History, 27 (Blackwell / Ecclesiastical History Society, 1990), p. 302.
34. PRO E117/4/30.
35. S. Brigden, *London and the Reformation* (Clarendon, 1989), p. 567. Forty days elapsed between Christ's birth and the purification of the Virgin in the church calendar and this provided a guideline. However, Eleanor of Castile lay in for thirty days for a daughter and forty days for a son. (K. Staniland, 'Welcome, Royal Babe! The Birth of Thomas of Brotherton in 1300', *Costume*, 19 (1985), p. 13.)
36. M. E. C. Walcott, R. P. Coates and W. A. Scott Robertson, 'Inventories of Parish Church Goods in 1552', *Archaeologia Cantiana*, 8 (1872), pp. 121, 158.
37. Rawcliffe, *Medicine and Society*, p. 201. Medieval embellishments to the story of the Nativity included Mary coping without a midwife and Joseph using his hose to swaddle Christ; see S. Oosterwijk, 'The Swaddling Clothes of Christ: A Medieval Relic on Display', *Medieval Life*, 13 (2000), pp. 25–30.
38. Brigden, *London and the Reformation*, p. 601.
39. See D. McCulloch, 'Henry VIII and the Reform of the Church', in *The Reign of Henry VIII: Politics, Policy and Piety*, ed. D. MacCulloch (Macmillan, 1995), p. 178.
40. Anthony Goldsmith's wife gave the circlet to the church; see G. Rosser, *Medieval Westminster, 1200–1540* (Clarendon, 1989), p. 200.
41. See B. J. Todd, 'The Remarrying Widow: A Stereotype Reconsidered', in *Women in English Society 1500–1800*, ed. M. Prior (London and New York, 1985), pp. 54–92, and R. A. Wood, 'Poor Widows, c.1393–1415', in Barron and Sutton (eds), *London Widows*, pp. 55–67.
42. Rappaport, *Worlds Within Worlds*, p. 38.
43. Rappaport, 'Social Structure: Part 1', p. 118.
44. In 1511 Richard Hunne refused to pay a mortuary fee for the burial of his son to the priest Thomas Dryffeld. The resulting legal struggle ended with Hunne's arrest. Two days later Hunne was found dead in his cell; see G. R. Elton, *Reform and Reformation: England 1509–1558* (Edward Arnold, 1977, 1981), pp. 51–3.
45. Rosser, *Medieval Westminster*, p. 200.
46. Scarisbrick, *Reformation*, p. 3.
47. R. Whiting, *Local Responses to the English Reformation* (Macmillan, 1998), p. 24.
48. MacCulloch, *Reign of Henry VIII*, p. 177.
49. PRO E117/4/95.
50. PRO E117/4/97.
51. PRO E117/4/27.
52. PRO E117/4/44.

53. PRO E117/4/70.
54. V. Harding, '"And One More May Be Laid There": The Location of Burials in Early Modern London', *London Journal*, 14 (1989), pp. 115, 122–3.
55. Burgess, *St Andrew Hubbard*, pp. 137, 117.
56. PRO E117/4/57.
57. PRO E117/4/70.
58. Burgess, *St Andrew Hubbard*, pp. 178, 183.
59. MacCulloch, *Reign of Henry VIII*, p. 176.
60. E.g. PRO E117/4/76.
61. PRO E117/4/76, E117/4/25 and E117/4/65.
62. PRO E117/4/74.
63. Burgess, *St Andrew Hubbard*, pp. 37, 172.
64. Burgess, *St Andrew Hubbard*, p. 135
65. Burgess, *St Andrew Hubbard*, p. 109.
66. P. J. P. Goldberg, 'Women's Work, Women's Role in the Late Medieval North', in *Profit, Piety and the Professions in Later Medieval England*, ed. M. Hicks (Goucester, 1990), pp. 35, 47.
67. Burgess, *St Andrew Hubbard*, pp. 37–8, 61.
68. K. Lacey, 'The Production of '"Narrow Ware" by Silk-Women in Fourteenth and Fifteenth Century England', *Textile History*, 18 (1987), pp. 187–204.
69. PRO E117/4/70. Lady Margaret Beaufort made substantial gifts of vestments and other liturgical textiles to two Cambridge colleges.
70. PRO E117/4/37.

4

Following Suit: Men, Masculinity and Gendered Practices in the Clothing Trade in Leeds, England, 1890–1940

Katrina Honeyman

Much industrial and business history in Great Britain has been dominated by economic concerns.[1] The gendered characteristics of production, distribution and consumption have typically been ignored.[2] Conversely, fashion historians, while informed by the insights offered by several disciplines, including cultural and gender studies, have tended to neglect the potential that an economic analysis might offer to an understanding of historical transformations in dress.[3] For example, in a recent surge of interest in the man's suit, historians of fashion have focused on cultural issues to the neglect of material concerns. This paper aims to contribute to the body of literature on the man's suit by integrating economic and gender approaches. Its findings are consistent with those of Christopher Breward, whose research on male consumption of clothing has concentrated on the late nineteenth century, and Frank Mort, whose focus is on the period after the Second World War.[4] However, it differs from these important studies in two key respects. Firstly it is concerned with the supply of the garment as well as its purchase and argues that an understanding of the relationship between production and consumption is necessary to explain the ubiquity of the suit. Secondly it focuses on the early twentieth century, especially the interwar years which, so far, have been surprisingly overlooked in this context. The years between the wars were special not only in terms of developments in production and retailing, but also because the suit reached a peak of popularity among all social groups at this time and loosened its main association with the world of work.[5]

By the outbreak of the Second World War, the majority of British men of all social groups wore a suit for many occasions. The man's suit, a standard woollen two- or three-piece garment of sombre shade, was for several decades a symbol of mass male dress. It lost its universal appeal only from the late 1950s as less structured male clothing became increasingly popular and, for many, the suit became confined to 'Sunday Best' outings. This paper attempts to explain the emergence of the suit as a ubiquitous male garment by considering changes in tailoring production and retailing in their social and cultural context. The men's clothing industry during the period when the suit became standard male attire provides an instructive case in which to examine the connections between consumption and production – processes which are typically analysed separately.[6]

The three main components of the menswear trade are examined below to reveal the importance of gender. First, the emergence of the core product – the suit – and its association with a specific male identity from the later nineteenth century is investigated. The process of production, and especially the gendering of the workforce, is then examined. The gender division of labour was vital to the shape, development and long-term success of the men's outerwear trade. Finally, consideration is given to the distribution and retailing of menswear. This explores the mechanisms by which the consumer was constructed or reconstructed as male, and the way in which masculinity was sustained through the (traditionally female) act of consumption. These threads when woven together will show how the history of this particular industry and the explanation for its extraordinary success are imbued with gendered meanings.

The suit, which even today constitutes respectable and conformist male attire, became fashionable during the later nineteenth century and was ubiquitous through the 1920s and 1930s. The explanation for the replacement of more elaborate male costume by a sober and conservative suit through the nineteenth century has exercised fashion and social historians for years. The rise of the suit is often associated with industrialisation and a world in which work assumed a more central role, yet criticism of Flugel's overarching notion of a 'Great Masculine Renunciation' of elaborate clothing from the early nineteenth century suggests a more complex interpretation.[7] Colin McDowell, for example, argues that a shift to simplicity in dress pre-dated the French Revolution and represented a change to a more responsible way of life, rather than a mere alteration to clothing styles.[8] Breward also believes that the connection between industrialisation and a dark unchanging uniform is overdrawn and that the reality was much more complex,[9] while Tim Edwards argues that the spread of the suit did not anyway begin until the later nineteenth century.[10] Despite the validity of such criticisms, there is little doubt that the relatively plain, tailored suit did supersede more decorative dress among men of high social status, during the course of the nineteenth century, and eventually became a staple of the male wardrobe of lower social groups as well.

The simplicity of the suit has encouraged suggestions that it was a functional, business-oriented garment. The appearance of functionality, however, was probably more important than its reality,[11] yet its undoubtedly sensible look – in contrast to earlier forms of male dress – was relevant to the contemporary making of masculinity, the key features of which were respectability, rationality, sobriety and diligence. Appearance was paramount. Like any other garment, the suit made a statement about its wearer. In this case the sartorial message was honesty and rationality, seriousness and discipline. The suit was also important as a practical uniform of respectability.[12] Simplicity in dress indicated that a man could be trusted, that he was serious, and that he meant business.[13] It also meant that he was unlike a woman. Thus, as simplicity of men's dress implied a serious approach to the world, women's dress became even more elaborate and constrictive, in line with a more domestic and physically circumscribed role.[14]

Consistency in gender role expectations was accompanied by uniformity in dress. The new technical and organisational procedures for the making of the suit, which developed from the later nineteenth century, permitted a standardisation of the product. Thus, men came to resemble one another, which, according to Hollander, was exactly what they wanted. Although such an assertion has been contested,[15] the desire to look like other men became increasingly powerful by the early twentieth century.[16] The explanation for men's desire for conformity in dress is unclear, yet Paoletti's analysis of late nineteenth-century cartoons suggests that the popularity of the suit was associated with the fear of ridicule. Once the suit had become a symbol of a stereotypical masculine role, anything else would become the object of derision.[17]

Whatever the reason, the practice of suit wearing became widespread, suggestive of a more democratic and egalitarian society.[18] Although the tendency for men of all social groups to acquire a suit is not proof of growing equality, key menswear producers at the time were apparently motivated by the idea of promoting democracy. Indeed the Leeds multiple tailors played an essential role in widening access to a standard product, especially in the interwar years. Known as 'multiple' tailors because they distributed their products – mainly suits but also separates and sometimes raincoats – through numerous nationwide branches of their own shops, they integrated the manufacture and retailing of their product.[19] By far the largest and most enduring of such businesses was Montague Burton Ltd which owned 600 shops nationwide by the late 1930s. Close behind came Henry Price's Fifty Shilling Tailors and Hepworths, with 200–300 shops apiece.[20]

Henry Price believed that his business contributed to the revolution 'in popular tailoring',[21] and described his 'rational' tailoring as a 'social movement ... [a] movement to make Britain the best dressed nation in the world'.[22] Although Price's role should not be underestimated, there is little doubt that Montague Burton did more than any other individual to enable the man of limited means to 'dress like a gentleman'. Being committed to social justice, Burton believed strongly that dress constituted an agent of democratisation, and that access to good-quality, well-fitting suits generated a spiritual social equality.

> Come for a moment to the high street on a Saturday afternoon [he wrote in the mid 1930s]. Who are those well dressed men you see? Do they work at the bench or at a desk or round the Director's conference table? You cannot tell thanks to the tailoring evolution that Montague Burton set in motion ... today clothes no longer divide the masses from the classes. Masters and men rub shoulders in the crowd and nobody can tell one from the other. Better still nobody wants to. That is probably the most significant of the many big things Montague Burton have [done] ... By putting good clothes within the reach of all they have made democracy a living force.[23]

Burton's philosophy was informed by the principle of self-help at least as much as by notions of social justice, however, and he strongly believed that, among those of limited means, spending on clothing should take precedence over that on drinking.[24]

Montague Burton and the other Leeds multiples who manufactured measured garments on a large scale, ensured that most employed men could afford a tailored suit of reasonable quality. Such increasing availability was associated with standardisation of product, a decline in distinctions in dress – which itself is suggestive of democratisation[25] – and even what Montague Burton himself referred to as 'style monotony'.[26] In order to satisfy a wide market, the majority of tailors made available an inoffensive but inevitably unexciting garment that would have appeal to all. Standardisation made spectacular progress after the First World War as:

> The miner used to insist year in and year out on bell-bottomed trousers, vest with clerical opening, shortish jacket, usually made with cloth with a prominent blue check, now the young miner dresses exactly like the bank clerk, and the same refined designs and styles which sell freely in a fashionable south coast town are also popular in the industrial areas.[27]

Such social and geographical consistency in men's dress was crucial to the mass production, mass-marketing practices of the Leeds multiple tailors, yet at the same time, the multiple shop method of retailing itself encouraged standardisation in men's dress.

Respectable working-class and lower-middle-class men were offered the opportunity to dress like gentlemen, but this did not mean that all were regarded or appeared to be equal or equally gentlemanly. It can be argued that the visual perceptions of class differences became blurred, while such distinctions themselves remained.[28] Rather than constituting a democratic garment, even though it was brought within reach of the majority of men, the suit can be interpreted less controversially as a popular garment. Such demotic dress – and there is little doubt that the suit was the garment of choice in the years between the wars – can be seen rather to represent collective taste or collective male behaviour within a society increasingly defined by the mass.

During the interwar years, therefore, the suit was socially- as well as occasion-inclusive. Although it was neither a comfortable nor a practical garment, memories and visual sources suggest that the bulk of the male population wore suits for work and for recreation,[29] and thus it formed the basis of most male wardrobes at this time. For several decades from 1900, the suit played a social role. It provided its wearers with a sense of place in modern society. It was developed as mass masculine dress and men as a mass adopted it with enthusiasm. The popular practice of suit wearing can be seen as the outcome of a collective acceptance of the social requirement to adopt a distinct masculine identity, reflected through dress, which symbolised values of hard work and sobriety. Thus, manly ideals became less class-based and because mode of dress was part of the emerging popular culture, men of different social groups came to resemble one another in appearance.[30] These common patterns of behaviour were supported by mechanisms of production and distribution by which reasonably priced clothing for the masses was made available.[31] The process by which suit wearing became popular depended on the interaction of the economics and the gendering of production. This can nicely be illustrated through an analysis of the Leeds clothing industry which from an early stage specialised in the production of men's tailored outerwear.

The emergence of Leeds as the British centre of men's tailoring – a position consolidated in the interwar years – can be explained not only by the local tradition in textile production and marketing in which female factory labour was common, but also by the specialisation in industrial engineering and a dynamic and fluid industrial structure. Leeds had also become an important retail centre by the turn of the century, when it was known as the London of the north. None of these features alone would have been sufficient to account for the extraordinary growth of the Leeds trade from the late nineteenth century, but in concert with the operation of the multiple tailors, they gave Leeds the edge.

The organisation of the industry in Leeds was complex. It comprised businesses of varying sizes but it was the large scale of many Leeds manu-facturers, especially the multiples, who created a standard yet made-to-measure product, that distinguished the city from other producing centres. The majority of British multiple tailors were based in Leeds, where the largest six supplied about 50 per cent of the suits bought by

British men. Such an achievement derived from the integration of creative manufacturing and retailing practices. The resulting system – which operated at the intersection of production and consumption and was known as 'wholesale bespoke' – was first developed at the turn of the century but was extended and improved by Montague Burton and other Leeds multiples.[32] During the interwar period when Leeds consolidated its position as Britain's foremost producer of men's tailored outerwear, the interplay of marketing and manufacturing became tighter. The shops and the factories of the multiple tailors effectively comprised a single system. Clients were measured for a bespoke suit in one of the many nationwide retail outlets. Their measurements were conveyed to the relevant Leeds factory, where the suit was cut out and made up according to the individual's requirements.[33] Within a week, the completed garment was delivered to the shop for collection by the customer.[34]

The financing of the system – whereby the garment was partly paid for by the customer before it was produced – was important to the rapid and extensive growth of the multiples in the interwar years. Retail bespoke and other non-multiple tailors of the time, who felt their business to be threatened,[35] complained that 'the multiples conduct business on a strictly cash basis, requiring a deposit with every order'.[36] The practice of Montague Burton was formally to require a 25 per cent deposit before the order was transmitted to the factory, and 'strictly nett cash before delivery', but sales staff were instructed to extract a larger proportion if possible. This was not only to enhance cash flow but also because 'a good deposit has a steadying effect on an unreasonable customer'.[37] Salesmen were taught to 'ask if he wishes to pay for suit in full or leave a deposit of £2 or £3. This results in a good deposit.'[38] Such a practice was seen to be 'one of the great fundamentals of our business which enables us to save customers half their money', especially because it eliminated 'all bad debts which OTHER customers pay for … We buy for cash, sell for cash, and save the customers cash.'[39] The multiples also gained by dispensing with the need to carry large quantities of stock and the associated burden of financial risk.

The manufacture of men's suits among the Leeds multiples was founded on the basis of labour-intensive mass production. In the wholesale bespoke manufacturing units, each garment was cut out separately with hand-held shears according to customers' requirements, and the remaining processes were mechanised as in the large-scale ready-made trade. Such a system was possible and profitable because of the standardisation of the product, the cheapness of labour and the detailed subdivision of tasks, which also depended on the patience and resilience of the female workforce. Indeed, the key to the growth of the industry's output and productivity was the producer, but although women were integral to the long-term profitability of the industry, they were not regarded as essential workers. Women, who comprised between 70 and 80 per cent of the labour force, were constructed or confirmed as secondary workers.[40] The concentration of women in machining and other 'unskilled' operations, such as binding and buttonholing, in overcrowded conditions, undervalued their skill both symbolically and literally, and their contribution was deemed to be a simple extension of their domestic culture. Male workers, the small proportion of the total labour force, monopolised the skilled operations associated with the initial and final processes, including laying out, cutting, final pressing, and supervision, and enjoyed better conditions of work. Despite the limited history of craft tailoring in Leeds, its male clothing workers acquired craft status, even invoking tradition as they did so.[41]

Women were poorly paid and, after marriage, were expected to cease employment, thereby sustaining a particular family form in which the male was assumed to be the primary wage-earner. Through their low wages, women were constructed not simply as undervalued labour subject to intense discipline, but also as having only a secondary association with the world of work. It was alleged that women were satisfied with a low fixed standard wage, and even that they did not aspire to anything more. For example, when the tailoring trade board proposed to raise women's rate of pay to 3½d per hour, it was met with staunch employer opposition, on the grounds that, 'we have found that a very large percentage of our female labour has not the slightest desire to earn more than 12/- per week', and further that, 'It is not necessary for these girls to earn more than a sufficient wage to clothe themselves and provide some small weekly [wage] towards the support of the home.'[42] From the outset, therefore, female labour was constructed as liminal, with only a marginal commitment to the workplace. Testimony of former clothing workers, and evidence of female support for a range of strikes in the interwar years and beyond, suggest that not all women accepted such a construction. Indeed, a number were angered at the extent of gendered pay differentials. Nevertheless, it appears that, in the interwar years at least, the majority of women were resigned,[43] and rarely questioned the principle of the male breadwinner wage.[44]

Women's pay was determined by a system of piece rates through which employers influenced the degree of worker intensity. This became the main source of profitability in the later stages of the industry. Employer control of female workers in Leeds was extended by routine fines for lateness and for mistakes in their work. Until the interwar years, deductions from women's wages were made for the thread that they used, for the power that kept their machines running, for their scissors, and sometimes even for machine parts.[45] The low wages of women, combined with their greater work effort, were essential ingredients of the employers' cost containment strategy and were more important in the industry's short-term performance than the 'rationalisation' of production. Gains in efficiency, through improvements to the manufacturing process increasingly required elements of control and exploitation of the female workforce.[46] Men had more control over their wages, which in any case were calculated more generously.[47]

The construction of women as primarily associated with the home and family was also confirmed by the non-commercial activities of employers. For example, the welfare schemes of the Leeds tailoring businesses constructed men and women differently,[48] as did the operation of an implicit marriage bar. There was no rigidly enforced requirement for women in the clothing industry to leave work upon marriage, as was the case in some other occupations, yet the expectation was clear. The firm operated a dowry scheme, whereby young women under the age of 30 contributed weekly amounts, withdrawing the total plus the firm's contribution plus interest upon their marriage. If a woman did not marry, the amount, to a maximum of £100 would remain with the firm until her retirement.[49] Other activities relevant to the construction of gender identities included the frequent and gender-specific beauty contest.[50]

The feminisation of the Leeds tailoring workforce was a strategic success for menswear businesses, though the irresistible temptation to make intensive use of low-cost labour, while satisfactory in the short term, limited the options open to employers in the context of later structural changes in the industry.[51] The process by which work became gendered was important to the industry because it created a small group of skilled workers who prioritised their own interests at the expense of the lower-paid and more exploited group, who thus became vital to the profitability of the industry.

While the contribution of cheap female labour remained crucial to the growth and survival of the Leeds industry, its exceptional interwar expansion owed much to the interaction of manufacturing and marketing, to innovation in retailing, and to the role of the consumer. Although the market for men's suits was expanding, the success of the Leeds multiple tailors also depended on the making of an active male consumer. Consumption is widely accepted to be a gendered activity. Historians and sociologists draw evidence from the late nineteenth-century department store to suggest that the acquisition of goods was socially perceived to be the responsibility of women.[52] Men's relative insignificance in the process of shopping was represented by the separate male sections of the department store, which were both physically distant from the main female area, 'with separate ... entrances',[53] but also conveyed a different ethos with 'distinct and sober décor, where the task of consumption could be completed quickly and efficiently'.[54] Although women's dominant association with the act of consuming has been challenged, and a more complex analysis attempted, it is still assumed that while men may engage in consumption, they do so with less enthusiasm and more rationality than women. The image of men as reluctant, unnatural and embarrassed consumers continues to form the basis of modern sociological studies.[55]

The neglect of men's historical position in the marketplace and masculine consumption habits is beginning to be remedied.[56] A small number of studies has emerged in recent years which illuminate men's historical engagement with shopping. Breward, for example, suggests that the meanings attached to the 'task' of consuming relied very much on the nature and type of consuming taking place, and, with specific reference to menswear, argues that in the later nineteenth century some men embraced consumption.[57] Yet, the contemporary association between sartorial indulgence and homosexual tendencies inevitably deterred others.[58] By the 1950s, as Mort's study reveals, it had become commonplace for men to buy their own clothes.[59] Thus it seems likely that it was in the intervening period that male consumption habits were encouraged. The case of the Leeds tailoring business tests this possibility. By examining menswear, and its key purchasers, it is possible to determine both the extent to which the male became an active consumer, and the type of consumer he was persuaded to become. During the 1920s and 1930s demand for men's suits reached a peak. At the same time many tailors – especially the multiples – integrated the manufacture and retailing of their product. Thus, they were as concerned with the marketing of their product as with its manufacture. The unprecedented success of the multiple tailors during this period was undoubtedly founded on their ability to persuade the male person, reluctant or otherwise, to purchase their product. As will be shown below, there were other forces operating at the time which facilitated their ambition.

If the consumer were perceived as female in the retailing environment of the later nineteenth century, it appears that the consumer was repackaged during the interwar period to include the male. An inclusive construction was developed which embraced a novel culture of masculinity, in which 'real' men could shop without appearing effeminate. Evidence from contemporary advertising indicates that men were at least potential customers, and the content of interwar magazines confirms men's essential participation in the 'new consumerism' of the 1920s and 1930s.[60] Lifestyle magazines facilitated the commercial development of masculinity and suggested that male interest in fashionable clothing was the result not of vanity but of utility and practicality. Within this context, men were shown that having a suit made for them should be a pleasant and leisurely rite.[61] Thus, men were to become consumers during the interwar years, but it was recognised that gender differences in purchasing practices would persist.[62] The success of the multiple tailors was largely attributable to their own creative strategies, especially the style and organisation of their shops, but was clearly sustained by a wider context of active consumerism.

During the interwar years the retail menswear outlet became a common feature of the British high street.[63] The centre of even the smallest towns contained at least one (Leeds) multiple tailor's shop, and very often several were grouped together in close proximity.[64] The outlets of the Leeds multiple tailors conveyed a particular style, encapsulating masculine good taste. The appearance, fittings and commercial transactions of these shops 'were loaded with cultural significance'.[65] The shops constituted a space in which men would be comfortable shopping for suits. It had been noted by an informed observer in the early twentieth century that, 'with our knowledge of the masculine temperament teaching us that men as a rule hate shopping, our chief motive became to provide for our clients, salons for fitting and choosing where they would find in all the appointments ...

Figure 1: One of Burton's Leeds city centre shops, 1931. Although less minimalist than later windows, this display – consisting mainly of lengths of cloth – was relatively sparse and tasteful. The firm's claim that a '5 guinea suit to measure' could be had for 55 shillings, however, was hotly disputed by contemporary retail tailors and brought Montague Burton close to legal action.

the comfort and good taste of their club or home'.[66] An integral component of the multiple tailors' strategy, therefore, was to attract the male consumer unaccustomed to shopping by constructing the shop as an egalitarian masculine sphere, but not necessarily one in which the act of consuming appeared to predominate. Montague Burton, whose vision and command of the market established a standard to which others might aspire, placed the 'shop' at the centre of his business strategy.[67] He masterminded both the design of the shops and the code of behaviour of the sales staff. As retail outlets, Montague Burton's shops were striking, with uniform external and internal architecture. Externally the 'outstandingly handsome' stores were finished in terra cotta, empire stone, granite, bronze and other fine materials, and were 'of a quality which was immeasurably superior to any other building in the country's high streets in those days'.[68] The simple and tasteful exterior was matched by an equivalent internal décor 'of oak and gunmetal, quiet and dignified';[69] without doubt a 'manly' interior which bore little resemblance to a shop as traditionally understood. Indeed, Burton's shops operated as 'order points', since the customer selected from a pattern book or rails of cloth[70] rather than from a choice of finished articles. Although some ready-made stock, especially raincoats and sports jackets, was increasingly carried, initially Burton's shops were uncluttered, typically containing only a counter, some lengths of material and books of styles and patterns. Burton's clearly wished to convey the impression of being an old-style bespoke tailor. The inscription 'cutting room' on the door to the staff rest-room, for example, was intended to deceive. Customers were led to suppose that their suits were to be tailored on the premises and not in a unit of mass production.[71]

The masculine structure of the shops was complemented by a specific gendering of sales staff in which all employees, except the 'invisible' female cashier, were men, and by the conventional masculine demeanour required by the male sales and managerial staff. The duties, responsibilities, and codes of dress and behaviour for all involved in the selling of suits were specified in great detail in various guides which provided the basis for the six-week course of classroom instruction for apprentice tailoring salesmen.[72] Recruits to the sales staff were carefully selected. Potential apprentices 'of good appearance and education',[73] 'who [are] bright, alert, likeable, courteous, [and] smiling',[74] were sought in order that they could be trained to become 'a refined type of assistant',[75] and 'those who are not likely to make good' were dispensed with rapidly.[76] Training in 'measurement methods', 'textile technique', 'scientific selling' and 'window display'[77] was provided, together with advice on self-presentation.[78] Much of the learning, however, took place 'on the job' as the style of experienced salesmen was observed and imitated. The 'Manager's Guide', the Burton staff bible,[79] contained upwards of 700 exhortations for male employees.

Figure 2: Sales assistant F. W. Alcock poses in the spare surroundings of a typical Burton shop (in fact King Street, Huddersfield) 1937, where the lack of finished garments on display confirmed this as a tasteful, even ambiguous, masculine space.

Appearance and smartness were essential ingredients of Burton's blueprint for the creation of masculine good taste in his shops. 'Resolve to be always well groomed and suitably dressed in dark clothes', sales assistants were admonished.[80] Typically, the sales staff, from the manager to the apprentice, worked in 'black and stripe' suits over white, stiff-collared shirts.[81] Such garb, standard among lawyers and bankers, helped to create a male, non-shopping atmosphere. Courtesy and politeness were considered as crucial as 'energy, virility, sparkle and buoyancy – these are the positive [and very male] qualities to be looked for in the ideal sales assistant'.[82]

The subservient role of women in the stores of Burton and the other multiple tailors, confirmed the space as a man's world. Women were employed as poorly paid cashiers, and as such they recorded measurements and dealt with payments and accounts in a back room. The extent to which they were undervalued can be illustrated by their extremely low profile in the 'Manager's Guide'. In contrast to the carefully structured and constructive message for men, the code of conduct for women was confined to a single disrespectful sentence. 'The cashier', it read, 'should not do her knitting, sewing, novelette and magazine reading, or similar unbusinesslike performances during business hours.'[83] Invariably, 'she' was kept well out of sight, behind a hatch, both to spare the possible discomfiture of the clientele, and above all to preserve the masculinity of the place.[84]

The comfort of the male customers was thus prioritised. It was acknowledged that at this stage not all men willingly embraced their role as consumers, and they were to be enticed. 'Let Burton dress you' was emblazoned on the windows of Burton's shops and conveyed a multi-layered message, which included a hint of seduction, an element of male ignorance, but above all indicated the passive role that men were expected to play in the purchase of a suit. Burton's guide emphasised the importance of creating a rapport with potential clients. 'Make your customer feel he is welcome ... avoid the severe tone of the income tax inspector, and the smooth tongue of the fortune teller. Cultivate the dignified style of the "Quaker tea blender", which is the happy medium.'[85] The strategy was clearly to coat the undoubted hard sell with a veneer of politesse. 'The prefix [sic] "Sir" after "Good morning" or similar conventional courtesies', it was suggested, 'appeals to your average man, whether your intellectual, social, economical superior or inferior.'[86] Salesmen were also encouraged to 'cultivate the art of listening ... do not interrupt the customer';[87] and to be succinct, stick 'to a few important points – drive them in and clinch them. But tell him what he wants to know.'[88] Not all men were to be accorded the red carpet treatment, however. Indeed, unfortunate individuals with a waist or chest measurement greater than 44 inches were to be discouraged. 'Such customers are

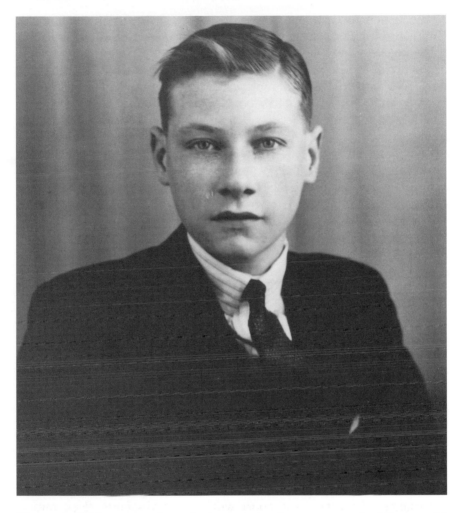

Figure 3: This portrait of immaculately presented 15-year-old R. McDonald was taken on 8 July 1935 soon after he was taken on as an apprentice tailoring salesman, in the Regent Road, Salford, branch of Burton's. In November of the same year, it was recorded that 'this lad has the makings of a good man if unforeseen events do not alter his standard of interest and enthusiasm'.

usually very faddy and difficult to fit … avoid serving a customer of over 50″ chest or waist measures if you have a reasonable excuse, such as if he enquires if his order can be made in a week, reply at least a month.'[89] Such an apparently sizist attitude was founded on simple economics. Profit margins, already tight even for the man of ideal physique, would be completely eroded by a man of corpulent proportions.

The taking of customers' measurements was a potential minefield. Unless procedures were strictly followed, especially when measuring the inside leg, the carefully rehearsed welcome could be compromised. Strict protocol was to be observed to minimise embarrassment. Burton's guides were less diffident than those of the nineteenth century described by Breward,[90] yet still emphasised tact and diplomacy. 'Before taking [outside leg] measure, notice if the top of the trousers customer is wearing is in the correct position. If you think it is too high or too low, consult him on the matter.' With respect to the thorny issue of the inside leg measurement: 'ask customer to pull his trousers well up; then using the long metal end of your tape, place it as high up in the crutch as possible and continue to the shoe heel'.[91]

The location of Burton's and other tailors' shops also featured in the successful construction of the consumer as masculine. Recognising that men were busy, and sometimes reluctant to engage in a specific shopping expedition, stores were commonly sited near workplaces with opening hours to suit. 'As we cater for men who work up to 6 o'clock', the 'Manager's Guide' stated, 'an hour in the evening is worth more than the rest of the day.'[92] As always, 'the customer should be attended to in a businesslike way. His time should not be wasted.'[93] Other aspects of the Burton strategy conversely attempted to catch the potential customer – especially the young man – at leisure. Every effort was made by the company to let surplus floor space for male recreational pursuits. Where possible, the storeys above or sometimes below the shop floor were used for billiards, or less commonly for dancing lessons, which served partly to catch the passing trade, but also to confirm the edifice as one in which respectable manly activities took place. Both offered alternatives to the drink culture that Burton disliked. As an advocate of the Temperance movement, Burton sought to encourage dancing in unlicensed premises, as a means of escape,[94] and neither drink nor women were permitted in the Billiard Halls. Within purpose-built Burton shops, 'the upper floors were designed as Billiard Saloons'; but otherwise managers and inspectors were advised to 'make a special effort to get a tennant … In case the property is large enough for billiards, please ask for Billiard Hall To Let posters.'[95] Such was the success of this strategy that it quickly became common knowledge that a game of billiards could be enjoyed 'above Burton's'. It was quite possible, therefore, to visit Burton's without necessarily aiming to make a purchase, and a diffident potential consumer could be lured to the building without being identified unambiguously as a 'shopper'.[96]

In the years between the wars, men bought suits in unprecedented numbers. Burton's and the other Leeds multiples helped to construct men as a particular type of shopper. That they were 'manly' purchasers – both rational and purposeful – was emphasised not only by the invisibility of women employed in the stores but also because 'wives or lady friends' of male customers were not encouraged until the 1950s, when they were distracted with tea and biscuits.[97] Nevertheless, if women did accompany a man in search of a suit, salesmen were encouraged to listen to their suggestions and to 'appeal to them for their opinion – they will side with you'.[98] Women as customers were discouraged; 'you are requested not to introduce that department when ladies call in connection with men's garments',[99] but if pressed or in order to expedite the sale of a man's suit, measurements for a 'costume' were taken and the making up subcontracted.[100]

The interwar growth of the Leeds multiple tailors and the spectacular success of Burton's can be attributable not only to a creative synergy of making and selling but especially to a cleverly devised retailing strategy in which shops were constructed as masculine spheres and where the male customer felt at ease. The multiples recognised that business turnover and profitability were enhanced when a masculine form of shopping environment was created. This continued a trend established at the turn of the century when 'the male parts of the department store accorded closely with received notions of the commercial masculine interior',[101] and, as a contemporary observed, 'it will be found that the business of an outfitter will increase when men's outfitting is kept quite separate'. Therefore, the annexing of male concerns into separate branches allowed for the development of a distinctively innovative and exclusively masculine form of shopping environment.[102]

Men became well suited during the interwar years, through the democratic diffusion of male clothing and by a careful, detailed construction of a masculine consumer. In mass marketing and mass production, the men's clothing industry encouraged the shopping experience of male consumers, 'who, theoretically, were assumed to stand aloof from its blandishments'.[103] Although the suit itself, a ubiquitous garment in the interwar years, turned out to be a blip in the history of demotic dress, the male as consumer of his own garb persisted for much longer.

Business history and industrial history have been relatively late among academic disciplines to incorporate 'culture' into their analyses. An important facet of the culture of a business or industry is that of gender, especially ideas about masculinity and femininity. This paper has shown how the gender of the actors within the Leeds tailoring trade had a strong impact on the shape of the industry's development. The interplay of manufacturing and marketing was critical to the sustained growth of men's tailoring between 1890 and 1940, but especially between the wars, and the key to its success lay in the relationship between the producer and the consumer. The gender of both producers and consumers was important to the business of making suits. Indeed, the industry depended on them as gendered beings. The dominance of women in the manufacturing component of the industry was integral to the cost containment strategy pursued by its entrepreneurs and provided the foundation for short-term or even medium-term profitability.[104] Of equal importance to the industry was the way in which masculinity permeated the retailing sector as both shops and consumers were constructed as male.

Gender historians with an interest in the cultural context of economic activity have provided the foundation for a dialogue between the disciplines of industrial history and feminist history. Scholars such as Joan Scott and Sonya Rose have shown how gender operates as a cultural process through which men and women make sense of economic activity, and how the pursuit of business goals is perpetuated through gendered practices.[105] In the case of the Leeds tailoring trade, there is little doubt that gendered practices existed and shaped the course of its development. Industrial history, like business history, needs more than economic analysis for its complete understanding. Gender may lack tangibility, yet it provides valuable insights into the operation of enterprise in the past.

Notes

This article is related to a larger study of the Leeds tailoring trade published as *Well Suited: A History of the Leeds Clothing Industry 1850–1990* (Oxford University Press, 2000). Many thanks to Barbara Burman, Carole Turbin and the participants in the history seminar at the University of Central Lancashire, April 2001, for very helpful comments on earlier versions of this work.

1. Recent examples include John Singleton, *Lancashire on the Scrapheap: The Cotton Industry 1945–1970* (Oxford University Press, 1991); David J. Jeremy *A Business History of Britain, 1900–1990s* (Oxford University Press, 1998). By contrast, analysis of the process of industrialisation has been less confined to the economic approach and has been usefully informed by gender. See, for example, Maxine Berg, *The Age of Manufactures: Industry, Innovation and Work in Britain 1700–1820* (Fontana, 1985), and Katrina Honeyman, *Women, Gender and Industrialisation in England 1700–1870* (Macmillan, 2000).
2. Welcome exceptions include Mary Yaeger, *Women in Business* (Edward Elgar, 1999); Robert Bennett, 'Gendering Cultures in Business and Labour History: Marriage Bars in Clerical Employment', in *Working out Gender. Perspectives from Labour History*, ed. Margaret Walsh (Ashgate, 1999), pp. 191–209.
3. Exceptions include Beverly Lemire, 'Developing Consumerism and the Ready Made Male Clothing Trade in Britain, 1750–1800', *Textile History*, 15 (1984), pp. 21–44, and Sarah Levitt, 'Cheap Mass-Produced Men's Clothing in the Nineteenth and Early Twentieth Centuries', *Textile History*, 22 (1991), pp. 179–92, but the interaction of production and consumption is rarely investigated.
4. Christopher Breward, *The Hidden Consumer: Masculinities, Fashion and City Life 1860–1914* (Manchester University Press, 1999), p. 3; Frank Mort, 'Montague Burton, the "Tailor of Taste"', in *Cultures of Consumption. Masculinities and Social Space in late Twentieth Century Britain*, ed. Frank Mort (Routledge, 1996) especially pp. 134–44.

5. Christopher Breward, *Hidden Consumer*; Daniel Roche, *The Culture of Clothing: Dress and Fashion in the Ancien Régime* (Cambridge University Press, 1994); Ben Fine and Ellen Leopold, *The World of Consumption* (Routledge, 1993); Anne Hollander, *Sex and Suits* (Alfred A. Knopf, 1994); and Colin McDowell, *Dressed to Kill: Sex, Power and Clothes* (Hutchinson, 1992).
6. Fine and Leopold, *World of Consumption*, p. 93.
7. J. C. Flugel, *The Psychology of Clothes* (Hogarth, 1930), pp. 110–12.
8. McDowell, *Dressed to Kill*, pp. 36–7.
9. Cited in Amy de la Haye and Elizabeth Wilson (eds), *Defining Dress: Dress as Object, Meaning and Identity* (Manchester University Press, 1999), p. 4.
10. Tim Edwards, *Men in the Mirror: Men's Fashion, Masculinity and Consumer Society* (Cassell, 1997), p. 19.
11. For the limitation of the tailored suit as demotic garment, see Claudia Brush Kidwell and Valerie Steele (eds), *Men and Women: Dressing the Part* (Smithsonian Institution, 1989), p. 17.
12. Edwards, *Men in the Mirror*, p. 3
13. Hollander, *Sex and Suits*, p. 91; Grant McCracken, *Culture and Consumption: New Approaches to the Symbolic Character of Consumer Goods and Activities* (Indiana University Press, 1988), p. 99.
14. This ceased to be the case from the 1920s but by then, nothing could shift the maleness of the suit.
15. See, for example, Joan Thomas, *A History of the Leeds Clothing Industry* (Hull, 1955), p. 51.
16. Hollander, *Sex and Suits*, p. 111.
17. Jo Barraclough Paoletti, 'Ridicule and Role Models as Factors in American Men's Fashion Change, 1880–1910', *Costume*, 19 (1985), pp. 121–34.
18. For US preference for ready-made men's garments, see Claudia B. Kidwell and Margaret C. Christman, *Suiting Everyone: The Democratisation of Clothing in America* (Smithsonian Institution Press, 1974), p. 115.
19. See also Katrina Honeyman, 'Tailor-Made: Mass Production, High Street Retailing, and the Leeds Menswear Multiples, 1918 to 1939', *Northern History*, 37 (2000), pp. 293–305.
20. Other large multiples included Jackson the Tailor and Alexandres. By the end of the 1930s, the Leeds multiple tailors together controlled around 1,500 stores.
21. *Men's Wear*, 5 October 1929.
22. *Men's Wear*, 22 August 1936.
23. Montague Burton, *Globe Girdling*, vol. 2 (Petty, 1937), p. 252.
24. Interview with Arnold Burton, son of Montague, 15 November 2001.
25. Fine and Leopold, *World of Consumption*, pp. 90–93
26. Montague Burton writing in *Men's Wear*, 6 February 1932.
27. Montague Burton's address to shareholders at the 1932 AGM, reported in *Men's Wear*, 30 July 1932.
28. Indeed, variations in the all-important accessories: shirts – especially collars – ties and shoes reflected status distinctions between men wearing the same suit. However, Carole Turbin, 'Collars and Consumers: Changing Images of American Manliness and Business', in Philip Scranton (ed.), *Beauty and Business: Commerce, Gender and Culture in Modern America* (Routledge, 2001), p. 97, argues that the availability of detachable collars permitted an elegant appearance even in the 'ordinary man'.
29. Jennifer Craik, *The Face of Fashion* (Routledge, 1994), p. 186.
30. Turbin, 'Collars and Consumers', p. 97.
31. Fred Davis, *Fashion, Culture and Identity* (Chicago University Press, 1992), pp. 39–40.
32. In the early stages of the system's operation, customers' measurements were taken in a tailor or drapers shop and then conveyed to a Leeds factory, of unrelated ownership for making up.
33. It was reckoned that, by the 1930s, 90 per cent of Burton's orders could be filled through stock garments with alterations to sleeves and leg lengths. ('Manager's Guide', 1932, pp. 17

and 22–3, Burton Records, item 201, West Yorkshire Archive Service (WYAS), Leeds City Archives.)

34. Katrina Honeyman, 'Montague Burton Ltd: The Creators of Well-Dressed Men', in *Leeds City Business 1893–1993: Essays Marking the Centenary of the Incorporation*, ed. John Chartres and Katrina Honeyman (Leeds University Press, 1993), pp. 186–216. For the US ready-made system, see Kidwell and Christman, *Suiting Everyone*, pp. 91–115.

35. For trade press hostility to the multiples' success, see for example *Men's Wear*, 17 October 1925, 7 November 1925, 24 June 1933, 14 April 1934, 8 June 1935, 12 October 1935, 26 December 1936.

36. *Men's Wear*, 25 June 1927.

37. 'Manager's Guide', p. 41.

38. 'Scientific Selling', 1927, p. 20, Burton Records, item 250, WYAS, Leeds City Archives.

39. 'Scientific Selling', p. 20.

40. For the relevance of the sewing machine technology in this process, see Andrew Godley, 'Singer in Britain: The Diffusion of Sewing Machine Technology and its Impact on the Clothing Industry in the United Kingdom, 1860–1905', *Textile History*, 27 (1996).

41. Katrina Honeyman, 'Gender Divisions and Industrial Divide: The Case of the Leeds Clothing Industry 1850–1970', *Textile History*, 28 (1997).

42. R. H. Tawney, *The Establishment of Minimum Rates in the Tailoring Industry under the Trade Board Acts of 1909* (Ratan Tata Foundation, 1915), p. 125.

43. Margaret Kirby, machinist at Burton from mid 1930s, then supervisor and then finally responsible for the machinists' training programme at Burton's. Interview recorded 1 June 1993 at the informant's residence.

44. A number of former clothing workers were interviewed for the larger study of which this is a part, and few seemed unhappy about their pay at this stage. Margaret Kirby, however, believed that she, a single woman with a widowed mother to support, should earn more than a young lad living in the parental home.

45. Although this was made illegal by the Trade Boards Act, a number of firms continued to cut costs in this way.

46. Honeyman, *Well Suited*, p. 153.

47. Cutters, for example, were paid by the 'log' system, a means of calculating pay that only they understood or were party to. The details were kept secret from employers and enabled cutters to control the pace of their work. The other male workers were typically paid according to a time rate, which, like the log, permitted some scope for varying the intensity of their work.

48. Burton's staff handbook referred to the company as a family, which indicated the nature of the mutual commitment. (Burton Records, item 128, WYAS, Leeds City Archives.) See also Bennett, 'Gendering Cultures', pp. 199–203.

49. *Men's Wear*, 8 September 1951. Also described in the *News Chronicle*, 4 October 1950.

50. Ronald Redmayne (ed), *Ideals in Industry: Being the Story of Montague Burton Ltd 1900–1950* (Petty, 1950), pp. 291–9.

51. Lack of investment in its human resources meant that the required flexibility in workers' skills was inadequate.

52. Such a position permeates the literature. See, for example, Rita Felski, *The Gender of Modernity*, pp. 61–2; and Colin Campbell, 'Shopping, Pleasure and the Sex War', in *The Shopping Experience*, ed. Pasi Falk and Colin Campbell (Sage, 1997), pp. 166–76.

53. William R. Leach, 'Transformations in a Culture of Consumption: Women and Department Stores, 1890–1925', *Journal of American History*, 71 (1984), p. 331.

54. Ruth Laermans, 'Learning to Consume: Early Department Stores and the Shaping of the Modern Consumer Culture (1860–1914)', *Theory, Culture and Society*, 10 (1993), pp. 80–81, 94; Laura Ugolini, 'Men, Masculinities and Menswear Advertising, c 1890–1914', in *A Nation of Shopkeepers: A History of Retailing in Britain 1550–2000*, ed. John Benson and Laura Ugolini (forthcoming).

55. Falk and Campbell (eds), *The Shopping Experience*; Peter K. Lunt and Sonia M. Livingstone, *Mass Consumption and Personal Identity: Everyday Economic Experience* (Open University Press, 1992); Rob Shields (ed.), *Lifestyle Shopping: The Subject of Consumption* (Routledge, 1992).

56. Breward, *Hidden Consumer*; Mort, *Cultures of Consumption*; Frank Mort and Peter Thompson, 'Retailing, Community Culture and Masculinity in 1950s Britain: The Case of Montague Burton, Tailor of Taste', *History Workshop Journal*, 38 (1994), pp. 106–27; Laura Ugolini, 'Clothes and the Modern Man in 1930s Oxford', *Fashion Theory*, 4 (2000), pp. 427–46.

57. Christopher Breward, 'Renouncing Consumption: Men, Fashion and Luxury, 1870–1914', in de la Haye and Wilson (eds), *Defining Dress*, pp. 51–9; Christopher Breward, 'Fashion and the Man: From Suburb to City Street: The Spaces of Masculine Consumption, 1870–1914', *New Formations*, 87 (1999).

58. Jill Greenfield, Sean O'Connell and Chris Reid, 'Gender, Consumer Culture and the Middle-Class Male, 1918–39', in *Gender, Civic Culture and Consumerism: Middle Class Identity in Britain, 1800–1940*, ed. Alan Kidd and David Nichols (Manchester University Press, 1999), p. 186.

59. Frank Mort, 'The Commercial Domain: Advertising and the Cultural Management of Demand', in *Moments of Modernity. Reconstructing Britain 1945–1964*, ed. Becky Conekin, Frank Mort, Chris Waters (Rivers Oram, 1999), pp. 55–75.

60. Greenfield et al., 'Gender', p. 183. Also compare Kenon Breazeale, 'In Spite of Women: *Esquire* Magazine and the Construction of the Male Consumer', *Signs*, 20 (1994), pp. 1–22.

61. Greenfield et al., 'Gender', pp. 186–8.

62. Gail Reekie, 'Impulsive Women, Predictable Men: Psychological Constructions of Sexual Difference In Sales Literature to 1930', *Australian Historical Studies*, 24 (1990–91), pp. 359–77.

63. See Peter Scott, 'Learning to Multiply: The Property Market and the Growth of Multiple Retailing in Britain, 1919–39', *Business History*, 39 (1994), especially pp. 1–3.

64. *Kelly's Directories of Leeds*, 1921–40, show the multiples' complete dominance of prime high street sites in the city. (Honeyman, 'Tailor-Made', pp. 302–5.)

65. Breward, *Hidden Consumer*, p. 129.

66. Bradley, in *Vogue* 1912, quoted in Breward, *Hidden Consumer*, p. 257.

67. For more detail, see Honcyman 'Montague Burton Ltd', pp. 186–216.

68. Orchard-Lisle 'Recollection', p. 6.

69. Sir J. Foster Fraser, *Goodwill in Industry: Being the Semi Jubilee Souvenir of Burtons* (privately published October 1925), p. 62, Burton Records, item 249, WYAS, Leeds City Archives.

70. Racks of cloth were placed in the lobby of Burton shops as a device to encourage the uncertain customer to enter the store. (Interview with Arnold Burton, 15 November 2001, Leeds.)

71. Interview with Arnold Burton, 15 November 2001, Leeds; also Arnold Burton, interviewed by Ray Gosling, broadcast on BBC Radio 4, 10 July 1992.

72. There were several of these, the most important being the 'Manager's Guide' and the 'Inspector's Guide'. First published in 1922, these were highly confidential documents to be kept away from competitors' eyes. (Burton Records, item 201, WYAS, Leeds City Archives.)

73. 'Manager's Guide', p. 53.

74. 'Clothing Classes Curriculum' (1935), p. 33, Burton Records, item 191, WYAS, Leeds City Archives.

75. 'Manager's Guide', p. 53.

76. 'Inspector's Guide', 1922, p. 23.

77. These were the titles of the texts which contained the core elements of the requisite knowledge. The timetable of instruction was specified in 'Clothing Classes Curriculum'.

78. Sometimes this consisted of very rudimentary tips on cleanliness of nails and hair. (Interview with Arnold Burton, 15 November 2001, Leeds.)

79.	It remained largely unchanged thereafter, although Frank Mort, who uses a later edition, appears to discuss it as a postwar document.

80.	'Manager's Guide', p. 44.

81.	Interview with Arnold Burton, 15 November 2001, Leeds.

82.	'Manager's Guide', p. 60.

83.	'Manager's Guide', p. 8.

84.	Interview with Arnold Burton, 15 November 2001, Leeds.

85.	'Manager's Guide', p. 44.

86.	'Manager's Guide', p. 44.

87.	'Clothing Classes Curriculum', p. 24.

88.	'Scientific Selling', p. 10.

89.	'Manager's Guide', p. 43.

90.	Breward, *Hidden Consumer*, p. 160.

91.	'Measuring Methods' by A Designer, 1948, p. 6, Burton Records, item 255. WYAS, Leeds City Archives.

92.	'Manager's Guide', p. 34.

93.	'Clothing Classes Curriculum', p. 24.

94.	Paul Johnson 'The Tailor who Shaped a Social Revolution', *The Director*, 1984, photocopy in the Burton Records, item 218, WYAS, Leeds City Archives. See also Ray Gosling, 'Yates Wine Lodges: Port and Sardines', *Listener*, 22 July 1982.

95.	'Manager's Guide', p. 47.

96.	This was consistent with the intention of the company, who never used the term 'shopping'. (Mort and Thompson, 'The Culture and Politics of Consumption', p. 120.)

97.	Interview with Arnold Burton, 15 November 2001, Leeds.

98.	'Scientific Selling', pp. 23 and 25.

99.	'Manager's Guide', p. 16.

100.	Interview with Arnold Burton, 15 November 2001, Leeds.

101.	Breward, p. 107.

102.	Breward, *Hidden Consumer*, p. 110.

103.	Breward, *Hidden Consumer*, p. 257.

104.	The manufacturing side of the industry declined and ultimately collapsed. See more on the causes of failure in Honeyman, *Well Suited*, ch. 11.

105.	Joan Wallach Scott, *Gender and the Politics of History* (Columbia University Press, 1988), pp. 28–50; Rose, *Limited Livelihoods*, especially pp. 1–17.

5

Pocketing the Difference: Gender and Pockets in Nineteenth-Century Britain

Barbara Burman

The artist Gwen Raverat (1885–1957) compared clothes of her adult life to those she had worn in her comfortable late nineteenth-century childhood in Cambridge, England. She found she regretted none of the changes except one.

> After writing so bitterly about the clothes of my youth, I must now be just, and admit that they had one great advantage over the clothes we wear nowadays. We had *Pockets*. What lovely hoards I kept in them: always pencils and india-rubbers and a small sketch-book and a very large pocket knife; beside string, nails, horse-chestnuts, lumps of sugar, bits of bread-and-butter, a pair of scissors, and many other useful objects. Sometimes even a handkerchief. For a year or two I also carried about a small book of Rembrandt's etchings, for purposes of worship.
>
> Why mayn't we have Pockets? Who forbids it? We have got Woman's Suffrage, but why must we still always be inferior to Men?[1]

A humdrum, often invisible object, the pocket has received scant attention in the literature of dress history. However, as Raverat suggests, pockets have not only personal histories to tell but they also echo the wider gender issues of the day. In spite of Raverat's wish for the greater male repertoire of pockets, her contemporary, J. C. Flugel, noted that, whilst he had twenty pockets in total when wearing his overcoat, men's pockets were 'by no means an unmixed blessing'.[2] Pockets still embody gender difference today, vividly evoked in a children's story in which a young boy wakes up as a girl and endures a day at school in a pink dress. Amazed by its lack of pockets, he asks himself, 'How was a person in a frock like this supposed to *survive*? … How can you *live* without pockets?'[3]

This essay offers a preliminary study of how the pocket can be situated as a significant gendered object in nineteenth-century Britain. After an introductory section, the essay takes an overview of the different forms of pockets in the dress of men and women at this time. Turning then to the functions of pockets, the next section explores male and female pockets in relation to gendered possessions and the ordering of things. The essay then moves on to argue that pockets were gendered through their reciprocity with gesture and their relation to the productive and reproductive body. The essay ends by proposing further lines of enquiry. In its assessment of the significance of pockets in both of these roles, relating to personal possessions and to gestures, the essay covers a period starting with the eighteenth-century tie pocket for women, well established by the time major changes in women's dress occurred in the 1790s and ending with new clothing conventions for women established by 1914. Using evidence from a long nineteenth century defined by women's clothing reveals that changes in pocket form and function were sometimes linked to mainstream fashion and, in the case of the continuing use of the old form of tie pocket for women, uncovers practices firmly resistant to fashion. It also reveals the outwardly more stable nature of men's pockets within the period, though many shifts occurred in the cut of men's clothing, especially in suits of all kinds.[4] However, the period registers tensions about masculinity reflected in contemporary discussion of pockets, and these are outlined later. Pockets in all their variety are artefacts in daily use, but they are also obscure and liminal and so even a preliminary picture of their use and significance during this period must draw on diverse primary sources. These include extant pockets in museums; paintings, prints, drawings and photographs; popular fiction; newspapers; etiquette and dress books, autobiographies and memoirs, sewing instruction books and fashion periodicals.

The principal elements of men and women's experience of pockets over the nineteenth century can be encapsulated as a series of changes in form accompanied by various expressions of discontent, even exasperation. As today, pockets took many forms and positions. Some are still familiar to us, such as the welt pockets on a man's waistcoat but others have disappeared from use and seem strange to the modern eye, such as the capacious tie pockets often worn in pairs under a woman's skirt. These years saw the erosion of women's use of this eighteenth-century device. Its gradual replacement by the now familiar smaller integral pockets sewn into the seams of skirts and dresses and supplemented by handbags was complete by 1914. Men of fashion had already replaced their pouches with pockets sewn into the structure of their garments by the seventeenth century.[5] For men a change of emphasis was marked by their giving up the old-style great-coat in the first half of the century. These important shifts of practice are examined in detail later in the essay. Despite some important differences remaining, notably in the number and disposition of pockets, there was eventually more parity between men and women in the acceptance of certain hands-in-pockets postures and gestures by the

end of the century. The widespread crime of pickpocketing was suffered
and perpetrated by men and women alike. These years were also marked
by dissatisfactions about pockets expressed as attacks on women's fashion
and its perceived tendency to ignore or abandon items of proven utilitarian
value such as pockets, and also as complaints about the unfair advantages
and freedoms of men's clothing in contrast to women's. There were also
difficulties for men in achieving desired levels of tailored sleekness when
they filled their pockets. Dissatisfactions with the adult female and male
pocket may also have derived precisely from its adult status and its part in
a sartorial system for the disciplining of gender, giving a certain order to
small personal possessions, deportment and gestures. Disciplinary pockets
were at odds with memories of the child's haphazard pocketfuls, so often
recalled with pleasure as tokens of the more carefree, imaginative possibilities in the child's experience of the world. A child's disorderly hoard
eventually gives way to the discipline and obligations, routines and roles
denoted by the adult's specialist pockets for watch, money, visiting cards
and handkerchief. As Raverat implied, in the passage from girlhood to
womanhood, a state partly constructed through powerlessness, a girl might
feel a special loss of identity as she relinquished her personal reservoir of
'lovely hoards' and 'useful objects'.

Central to an overview of the different forms of pockets in the dress of
men and women at this time is the female tradition of making and using
tie pockets, already well established in the eighteenth century in various
forms for women of all classes. They have been described recently as 'generous bags'.[6] They were usually made in pairs connected by a linen tape,
tied round the waist, worn with one on each side and independent of the
garments under which they were worn. Such pockets were individually
very capacious, typically between twelve and twenty inches long and
between eight and fifteen inches at the wide base, with a vertical slit for
access worn to the outside and edged to withstand wear and tear. Some
had small inner compartments stitched to the back part. There were
corresponding openings in hoops and the skirts of petticoats and gowns
to allow access through these over-garments or, when worn just under
an apron, the apron could be pulled to one side to reach them.[7] It is not
uncommon to find museum examples of single pockets and 'double
deckers' with two semi-circular slits giving access to upper and lower
compartments.[8] Sometimes tie pockets consisted of older materials
from furnishings, cut up and recycled. Many of the surviving eighteenth-
century pockets were embroidered, often signed and dated, a common
habit in the nineteenth century too when they were often made of plain
or printed sturdy cottons in the whole piece or as patchwork. There is also
firm evidence of an eighteenth-century and nineteenth-century market in
ready-made tie pockets, though little is yet known of this potentially

important trade and its effect on changing consumption habits.[9] The home-sewn tie pockets that survive are often striking in their own right as a result of their combination of needle skills, thriftiness and a happy eye for design. With only small variations, tie pockets showed a remarkable stability of form for two centuries (Figure 1). Given this substantial tradition, it is hardly surprising to find so many complaints about the smaller sewn-in pockets which came to dominate by the end of the nineteenth century. But why would women give up such efficient, convenient and often lovingly worked tie pockets without an adequate alternative?

The disavowal of tie pockets has been accounted for in the literature of dress history in two ways, both located in the material determinants of clothing's construction and style. Firstly, since pockets contain, secure and transport small personal possessions and therefore interrelate with other artefacts capable of fulfilling a similar function, it has been argued that there was a three-way interdependency between changing pocket construction, bags (held on the wrist, in the hand or hung on the belt) and the form of the skirt. Buck suggests the fashion for the reticule in

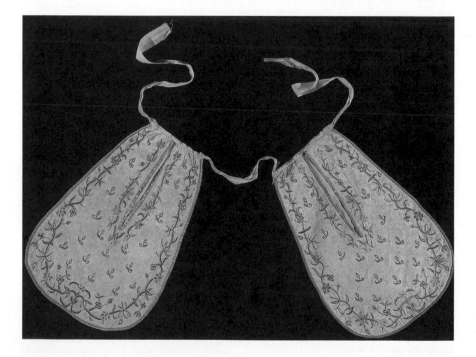

Figure 1: A pair of eighteenth-century women's tie pockets in a form which endured, with variations, for 200 years. English, 36 cm long, coloured silk embroidery on linen. T.281+A-1910. Victoria and Albert Museum. © V&A Picture Library.

the late eighteenth century and early nineteenth century was due to the fact that the slimmer neo-classical silhouettes of that time would have been 'disfigured'[10] if tie pockets had been worn underneath. But the novel reticules, so glamorously illustrated in fashion plates of the day, were valued for delicacy and ornamental charm with a fraction of the capacity of a pair of tie pockets. Buck also notes that sewn-in pockets are found 'more often' in dresses of 1845 to 1855, a period which 'probably' produced less bags. Although skirts then grew larger until the end of the 1860s, they were smoothed over the crinoline and more bags were used to compensate for the loss of sufficient folds needed to conceal a useful pocket, especially in lightweight fabrics.[11] Thus the apparent demise of tie pockets is explained by changes in the shape of fashionable garments.

Secondly, Foster suggests a change of status, so that by the time the fuller skirts with lower waistlines of the mid 1820s onwards encouraged their 'revival', the tie pockets had become 'like underwear, as something to be kept neat, white and laundered'.[12] However, whilst many surviving undecorated white tie pockets undoubtedly support this significant trend, and the old habit of embroidering tie pockets seems to have disappeared entirely, other surviving tie pockets demonstrate the use of printed cottons, heavy black and brown cottons and patchwork until late in the century. There was no doubt in *The Workwoman's Guide* of 1838 that women's pockets still came in three forms. 'Pockets are either worn tied round the waist, fastened into the petticoat, or buttoned upon the stays. When fastened into the petticoat, they are made of the same material, otherwise of dimity, calico, jean, twilled muslin, and sometimes of nankeen or brown jean.'[13] The book provided diagrams for the cutting out of these simple unadorned pockets. Whilst this comprehensive cutting out and sewing manual claimed to be largely for those who were responsible for clothing the poor or teaching them to make garments for their own use, it also offered guidance on tasks for domestic servants who would practise these for their mistresses. This leaves open the question of whether mistress or servant, or both, wore the finished pockets. The survival of mid and late nineteenth-century tie pockets in museum collections, together with pictorial evidence[14] and printed sources (including a remarkable fictional source which will be discussed later), support the argument that tie pockets, though becoming less ornate, persisted through the century in both imagination and everyday practice.

So the question of why women gave up these 'generous bags' is answered in part by evidence that many simply did not do so, signalling a resistance to fashion through both home-sewn and ready-made objects which helps inform our understanding of clothing consumption at this time. In the case of home-sewn pockets, particularly through the choice of recycled or remnant cloth, the act of making the pocket and the additional time and handicraft invested in the needlework surface decoration, a woman created an object embodying a cluster of values, including thrift. The tie pocket made in this way, to borrow from Weiner's example of an old Fijian bark cloth, could 'carry the histories of past relationships, making the cloth itself into a material archive that brings the authority of the past into the present'.[15] A tie pocket's embodiment of 'the authority of the past' was itself counter to fashion's focus on present and future. More contentiously, it can be argued that the woman's tie pocket carried a uterine symbolism in both its shape and its function. The discovery of a mid-eighteenth-century tie pocket concealed in a wall-cavity revealed within its cotton and silk 'womb-like enclosure' a cache of objects which may have had a 'protective function', including a baby's cap, coins and dried hops.[16] A lingering association with this old kind of symbolic promotion of fertility[17] or a supernatural function, combined with their embodiment of memory in handiwork, gave tie pockets a special, if shadowy, place in the repertoire of feminine material culture in the new age of industrialisation, impersonal mass production and urban anonymity. However, the many who did abandon tie pockets, or who remained in ignorance of their benefits, may help account for expressions of pocket discontent as the nineteenth century wore on.

An overview of the period shows the tie pocket lived on whilst along-side it the new trend for inset pockets in women's clothing brought a range of alternatives, such as a pocket inset into one side seam of a dress, or into a seam of the bustle area, accessed through a slit opening. Watch pockets were sometimes dropped inside the side front waist band, rather like a man's fob pocket in a trouser's waist band. Small ticket pockets could be inserted into a bodice front. As tailor-mades for women grew in popularity, the seam between the left side and centre skirt gores became a favoured site for an inset pocket. These more robust skirted suits of the 1880s and 1890s, so symbolic of the 'new woman', were never so well equipped with pockets as their male counterparts, but sometimes had outer patch pockets on the jacket, as did the coats which accompanied them. Over-garments commonly offered more pocket space as the century went on. Travelling cloaks often had a pouch pocket gathered at the top edge and set into the left front lining, a style also seen in the looser jackets of later walking suits. The long knitted sports cardigans which came into fashion at the turn of the century were amongst the first garments for women to routinely carry side patch pockets and the significance of this for women's gesture and posture is enlarged on later in the essay. Fancy aprons often had a decorative external pocket or two. Some fancy hanging pockets were worn singly outside the skirt, looped over a sash or belt.

Nevertheless, none of these alternatives had a capacity equal to the older form of tie pocket. There is evidence from the extant clothing itself, and elsewhere, that women were not able to rely on practical pockets being readily available in their clothing, whereas a man could assume his ready-made or bespoke suit or coat would be liberally provided with pockets. However, ingenious alternatives were available to women in the form of concealed pockets sewn inside hand muffs, travelling rugs and foot muffs for use in trains or later in motor cars, and travelling bags and hand-held cases designed with pockets and straps to secure small personal possessions. Travel and the accompanying fear of theft generated numerous new versions, such as coin pockets in garters or to hang round the neck beneath clothing and the old-style tie pocket worn inside a petticoat was valued in this context.[18] A variety of suspended containers were also worn externally at the waist presumably to supplement inadequate pockets. The popular aumonières and chatelaine bags of the 1870s onwards are an example of this trend.[19]

Between the 1870s and 1890s there was a kind of crisis over the position and number of women's pockets, which attracted the attention of fashion journalists:

> Her greatest difficulty is her pocket. Dressmakers take a weird delight in concealing it, and you have to search for it as long and fruitlessly as for hidden treasure. The indiscreet person who, without first extracting her purse, hires a hansom, writhes about it inside in search of her pocket, whilst the 'astral body' of the dressmaker hovers near, and almost betrays itself by its malevolent chuckle of delight.[20]

The problem was compounded if awkwardly positioned pockets contained anything more than a handkerchief. Lady Greville complained:

> The average woman is still insensible to the value of useful pockets, still carries her purse in her hand, and dives into the recesses of an impossible receptacle, situated somewhere in the back breadths of her gown, for her pocket-handkerchief, her letters, her note-book, her card-case, or her money, – the whole forming a disagreeably hard aggregation on which she patiently elects to sit.[21]

The essay now turns to the function of pockets and their role in the carrying and ordering of small possessions. This section starts with men, who had entered the nineteenth century with the same principle of multiple sewn-in pockets distributed for balance across their garments as they were to have when they entered the twentieth century. They had lost the skirted amplitude of eighteenth-century coats and during the century tailors made sleeker shapes. Men, though envied by women for having more pockets, also experienced difficulties with them. They were often inefficient, given the range of personal possessions which men of all social groupings wished to carry in them. Some or all of the following items might be owned and carried at times during the period: pocket watches, pocket knives, pocket compasses, handkerchiefs, pens and pencils,

Vesta or match cases, pipes and tobacco, cigars or cigarettes and keys. The more affluent man might also carry calling card holders, toothpick cases, napkin holders, spectacles or monocles and their respective cases, gloves and, on occasion, opera or theatre glasses and programmes, to say nothing of purses, wallets, or loose coins, cheque books and papers or notebooks. Working men may have pocketed food and drink, small tools and sundries and away from home they supplemented their pocket capacity with satchels or bags. A knee-length Sussex round smock made for a large man has two big patch pockets with button-down flaps situated on either side of the chest. Being made to be worn either way round, there are pockets to 'back' and 'front', capable of carrying substantial items, perhaps food for a day's work on the land or the necessities for attendance at market or a hiring fair. The pockets thus gave a measure of security and self-sufficiency to the agricultural worker who wore this, carrying his possessions as he laboured.[22]

The contents of men's pockets could be problematic. Nineteenth-century newspapers report the unexpected dangers which could lurk in them, causing serious accidents or death: setting clothes on fire by leaving smouldering pipes in pockets, small firearms or fireworks in pockets being set off, and injuries from open knives and even gunpowder carried in pockets. Pockets also involved women's domestic labour: the socialist reformer Edward Carpenter (1844–1929) criticised the frequent renewing of male pockets as part of the work which 'binds women down'.[23] This is confirmed by a pair of early nineteenth-century labourer's breeches made of leather-lined corduroy found in Surrey, England, in which patches inside the pockets have themselves been patched.[24]

The pocket advantage over women which was enjoyed by men had perhaps its most serious setback of the century when great-coats made way for slimmer over-garments, probably encouraged by the change from horse power to trains. Mid century, George Sala (1828–96) wrote of 'Things Departed', mourning the great-coat as yet another loss alongside numerous other services, trades and everyday objects fallen from use in the expanding, restless metropolis. Sala thought the 'host of other garments' were insufficient replacement and he situated the great-coat as a male institution sacrificed to the fashionable foibles of modern life.

> But where is the great-coat – the long, voluminous, wide-skirted garment of brown or drab broadcloth, reaching to the ankle, possessing unnumbered pockets; pockets for bottles, pockets for sandwiches, secret pouches for cash, and side-pockets for bank-notes? This venerable garment had a cape, which, in wet or snowy weather, when travelling outside the 'High-flyer' coach, you turned over your head. Your father wore it before you, and you hoped to leave it to your eldest son. Solemn repairs – careful renovation of buttons and braiding were done to it, from time to time. A new great-coat was an event – a thing to be remembered as happening once or so in a lifetime.[25]

In Sala's gendered coat the functional pockets were central to it being a kind of portable 'habitus', to use Bourdieu's term, 'a structuring structure, which organizes practices and the perception of practices'.[26] However, while the 'habitus' may be a valid analogy for all clothing during the century, new tailoring techniques, both bespoke and ready-made, could lead to physical structures at odds with other practices of male consumption.

The quality of the middle- and upper-class male consumer might be judged by the kind of possessions he carried in his pockets; the quality of his tailor might be judged by the degree to which the suit of clothes smoothly concealed them. This became more marked as the century went on and, by the 1870s, descriptions of men's wear had an 'overwhelming concern with visual tidiness'.[27] The 'right' cut and fit of men's tailored clothing were both subtle and skilled. Whilst varying in detail over the period, they continued to embody notions of gentlemanly posture and behaviour. '… everything should be sacrificed to perfect ease, as any garment which pinches or incommodes the wearer will strongly militate against the easy deportment of even the most graceful, and tend to give a contracted and constrained appearance.'[28] The size, position and number of pockets were central to the effect. Men were admonished about bulging or stretched pockets. 'If you want to ruin your coat irretrievably stuff the pockets full of things. Go for the pockets; if they are small, stretch them; fill them up, weigh them down … and in a remarkably short space of time you ought to succeed in stretching your coat out of all shape and in wearing it out.'[29] The 'sombre, dark and shapeless suits' so beloved of the middle- and upper-class male have been generally read as 'emblematic' of, or embodying, the mid-nineteenth-century gendered compartmentalisation of sexuality and power and the association of the male body with self-control.[30] We can add that the generous allowance of pockets in suits underscores the association of masculine authority with ownership of property. But the material details complexify this reading. The suits were not in fact shapeless; on the contrary, by skilled internal padding, layering, stitching and stiffening, the tailors exacted the maximum structure and shape possible from heavy suiting cloths. Mapping trends in the function of men's pockets show a tension between this moulded, external 'visual tidiness' of the suit and the tendency of used pockets to disrupt it by bulging or sagging with an abundance of portable personal possessions. Like the proverbial cat out of the bag, the disruptive male pocket then reveals just the same degree of consumerism and apparent lack of control over the world of things by which women were judged inferior. Thus a pocket, like larger elements of men's wear identified by Breward, carried 'conflicting constructions' of masculinity, 'which while remaining true to an essential differentiation from the

appearances associated with femininity ... could also carry traces of
worldliness, domesticity or display derived from the very same sources'.[31]

Turning to the function of pockets for women's possessions, we find
that this was still embedded in the earlier practice of tie pockets:

> Much better than a spinning wheel, this homely object symbolizes the obscurity,
> the versatility, and the personal nature of the housekeeping role. A woman sat at a
> wheel, but she carried her pocket with her from room to room, from house to yard,
> from yard to street ... Whether it contained cellar keys or a paper of pins, a packet
> of seeds or a baby's bib, a hank of yarn or a Testament, it characterized the social
> complexity as well as the demanding diversity of women's work.[32]

In her work on eighteenth- and early nineteenth-century sources, Amanda
Vickery has shown that the care and ordering of material household
goods, though valued for their own benefits, also represented 'more
complex responses'.[33] 'In a well-regulated household, the mistress-
housekeeper could literally itemize the physical contents of a house and
knew exactly where to lay her hands on a particular object.'[34] A woman
was not normally in a position to pass on to her family much beyond
movable goods, and her skills were 'embodied' in the household. 'Small
wonder if, in consequence, she turned to personal and household artefacts
to create a world of meanings and, ultimately, to transmit her history.'
Those meanings were likely to be gendered, and reveal on the part of
women 'a more self-conscious, emotional investment in household goods,
apparel and personal effects'.[35]

By the later nineteenth century the hands-on, working knowledge of
a household's material culture was still valued, though cast in different
terms. 'The family sense of well-being does not consist in the romantic
surroundings, or architectural beauty, or artistic furnishings of a house, so
much as in the cleanliness, the neatness, the punctuality – in a word, the
order of its interior economy.'[36] The surviving usage of tie pockets by
some women to the end of the nineteenth century may be explained
not only by their sheer capacity but also by their more robust embodiment
of women's work, and as investment in the material domestic world
which differed from the more mannered exhibition of leisured fashionable taste by means of reticules, bags and purses. The mix of things inside
these 'generous bags' was analogous with women's household life as a
bricolage of practices, skills and artefacts.

Despite their common use, few contemporary descriptions of how tie
pockets functioned in everyday life have yet come to light. However, in a
children's moralising story of 1849 by the prolific British author Anna
Maria Hall (1800–1881) we have a rare account which merits extended
quotation. In *Grandmamma's Pockets*, the form and content of the older
woman's cornucopian tie pockets are laden with meaning about the

proper roles and responsibilities of women. 'Annie always looked at these pockets with veneration: they really were venerable specimens of bygone times.'[37] Through the young granddaughter Annie's responses, rather than marginalising them as merely démodé, Hall emphasises the pockets' narrative potency. On her way to bed, Grandmamma slings them over the back of a chair and Annie contemplates them as 'majestic pockets! – so broad, and deep, and long, and strong, nothing flimsy about them ...'. Their majesty, analogous to that of the loving grandmother herself, is compared to lesser pockets. 'Let no modern lady housekeeper, who has a bag-like slip of silk inserted in the skirt of her dress – let no *demoiselle* with a three-inch pocket stitched into her pretty little apron – or a bustling country dame with a white jane pocket behind, imagine that they understand a tithe ... of the utility or comprehensiveness of GRANDMAMMA'S POCKETS!'[38]

Their 'utility' and 'comprehensiveness' are demonstrated partly through their contents. Hall takes us right inside the pockets, into their 'interior economy', into a world which was by this time 'venerable' but still common. At the midway point of the industrialising century, she charges these gendered pockets with the sense of tension between a new and an old world. The right-hand pocket contained keys 'with their parchment numbers', 'a large silver nutmeg grater, with a cunningly-devised case at one end to hold the nutmeg',[39] a snuff box,[40] 'a large pin cushion ...; then a very large "housewife" – containing every description of needle, from the Brobdignag "packing" to the graceful "darner". Then such real, actual, useful threads! ... positive flax thread of all kinds, and silks of all colours, and buttons of all sizes.' There were knives, scissors 'of every possible dimension', tweezers, bodkins, corkscrews, files, 'a most perfect, tiny, hard-headed brass hammer', tin tacks 'in a little bag'; 'a three-foot ivory rule, done up into three inches', a recipe-book, a bon-bon box, 'a little silver nut-cracker'. Hall notes that 'in fact, everything seemed to find space and place in these wonderful pockets; and, considering, they were not so *very* heavy'.[41] They also contained two small pockets-within-pockets. Utility and comprehensiveness are demonstrated again by function. The left pocket was regarded as a store place, for 'put-away-things'[42] such as the store of snuff, spare spectacles and sticking plasters in one of the little interior pockets. Grandmamma teaches Annie to appreciate the distinction between the left pocket which 'preserves' and the right pocket which 'distributes';[43] 'no matter what we *realise*; unless wo *preserve*, we shall be neither useful nor rich'. Hall reiterates the lesson. 'One typified the spirit of activity, the other of carefulness.'[44] The self-sufficiency suggested by both the contents themselves and their 'spirit' of preservation and distribution speaks directly of the role of women as household managers. Importantly, Hall's fictional pockets are not used to carry or store cash, although there are other examples of old tie pockets used to hoard money.[45] Self-sufficiency in a different sense is also indicated by the older woman, when confined to bed, calling for her pockets – 'and I will find amusement from their contents'.[46] Hall depicts a woman of this servant-keeping social class having several pairs of pockets of varying quality and status, including 'state pockets' of 'white satin, run with coloured silks to imitate natural flowers. These were put on on birth and festival days.'[47] The range of tie pockets surviving in museums supports this notion of a hierarchy of form and use.

In Hall's story, Grandmamma's tie pockets created a miniature adult world into which the child could enter, her fingers straying ever deeper inside until the desired object is grasped and consumed. The adult tie pocket was also open to the child as a site of shared work, creativity and pleasure because its informal decoration and small simple structure lent themselves easily to lessons in cutting, plain sewing and embroidery. 'I learnt to backstitch on her pockets!' says Annie of her mother's dimity pockets.[48] The home-produced tie pocket, secluded beneath layers of clothing, was one of the few opportunities for a woman or child to wear a child's work. The new style sewn-in pocket lacked this potential for the embodiment of love and labour.

If the household was at the heart of the woman's tie pocket, a man's set of integral pockets carried the prerequisites for a day spent in the public world of work. Money was at the heart of the gender difference dramatised through pockets in an American story which makes a widely applicable point about female responses to the connection between male pockets, work and power. The 'pretty little Mollie Mathewson', a 'true woman' who nevertheless wished 'heart and soul she was a man', suddenly turned into her own husband and spent the day as him. She enjoyed 'a new and delightful feeling of being *the right size*'. Pockets were amongst the numerous revelations and 'new views, strange feelings' she encountered that day. On the way to (his) work in an office, she explored them.

> Of course she had known they were there, had counted them, made fun of them, mended them, even envied them; but she never had dreamed of how it *felt* to have pockets.
>
>   Behind her newspaper she let ... that odd mingled consciousness rove from pocket to pocket, realizing the armored assurance of having all those things at hand, instantly get-at-able, ready to meet emergencies. ... the keys, pencils, letters, documents, notebook, checkbook, bill folder – all at once, with a deep rushing sense of power and pride, she felt what she had never felt before in all her life – the possession of money, of her own earned money – hers to give or to withhold; not to beg for, tease for, wheedle for – hers.[49]

In the world of later nineteenth-century fashion, with its small sewn-in pockets, the frustrations and limitations of women's access to money and ownership of property were neatly mirrored in the restricted scope of their pockets. Until the reforms culminating in the 1882 Married Women's Property Act, women were unable to own property in their own right and were legally subordinate to their husbands. For middle-class women, much shopping for goods of all kinds was achieved through the acceptance of their husband's credit-worthiness by the retailer. Abuses and failures of this system gained considerable notoriety.[50] Cash was fraught with tension right across the social spectrum. The turn from credit to cash has been described as arguably 'one of the greatest changes in nineteenth-century retailing',[51] but it remained 'culturally suspect' for wealthier women used to pledging their husband's credit.[52] For these women, pin money too was a vexed question, 'idiosyncratic' and slippery in legal terms and often disruptive in practice.[53] Whilst the developing nineteenth-century discourses of consumption sought to situate women as passive, if disruptive, spenders, outside the sphere of business and the generation of profit and income, in practice many women did continue to function in business.[54] Many women of all classes also exercised considerable decision-making powers over consumption on behalf of their households. This was well established by the nineteenth century at a local level, when dealing with small traders, 'with the shillings and pence for the immediate needs of family subsistence in their control, women seem to have been granted significant, if limited, economic responsibility'.[55] By the later nineteenth century it was a widespread working-class habit to give over part or all of the male breadwinner's wages to the wife and 'what distinguished all mothers of the poor, whether they worked or not, was their total command of the family finances in every respect, except for that money retained by a husband for his own pleasure'.[56]

What Zelizer has argued for American history in the period 1870–1930 is equally applicable to Britain: that a utilitarian theory of money is inadequate to explain how domestic money worked, because money entering the home was 'transformed' in the process, 'as it became part of the structure of social relations and the meaning system of the family'.[57] This transformation was inflected by social class in Britain. Despite variations, it is possible to argue that the resulting ambivalence and tension about money in the hands, or pockets, of women was reflected in the physical problems they described about their pockets. The ambivalence during the period concerning ownership and independence is also visible in the strange difficulties fashion illustrators seemed to have when depicting women holding handbags; repeatedly the drawings fail to make firm visual connections, showing instead limp, weak hands and small, apparently weightless bags.

If money bestowed the means for action and power, women's limited pockets, like the rest of their clothing, were ill-equipped for its enjoyment.

However, in nineteenth-century fiction, middle- and upper-class female characters enjoyed the use of their pockets for a different kind of currency, when they feature as the place in which they keep letters, often for some time, whilst they contemplate their significance. 'She hovered for an hour or two in and out of the room, conscious of the letter which she had in her pocket, and very desirous in heart of reading it'.[58] Thus the pocket offered a woman a space in which to conceal or treasure communication of a personal nature, and supplemented the few private spaces available to wives and daughters in their work boxes or baskets, portable writing cases and other small domestic nooks and crannies, prior to the emergence of handbags.

Moving on now from possessions to the gendered body itself, the interiority of pockets suggests a particular intimacy with it. Pockets offer one of the few permissible breaches of the clothed space between the private body and the public world, though subject to social regulation. The pocket is literally at the edge, it is a space attached to or enclosed by the main garment. The hand quickly learns to locate the pocket in any given garment. Once found, it is seldom forgotten and thereafter we reach into the pocket almost automatically. 'All touch traverses the boundary between interiority and externality and reciprocally returns to the agent of touching. Touch, like dizziness, is a threshold activity – a place where subject and object are quite close to each other.'[59] Through its special place close to the body, enclosing interior space and offering the hand of the wearer, and the eye of the onlooker, a conduit towards the body, the pocket signals the extent to which the clothing of men and women is open or closed to the outside world. It indicates gender by the degree to which the body beneath can explicitly draw attention to itself, and thus how much that body can inhabit, confront or command the social world. Hollander claims the 'naked male body, coherent and articulated' remains present as a 'ghostly visual image' beneath the suit.[60] The respectable female body in the nineteenth century is shown as shielded and closed off by its clothing, its power in the social world thus formally inaccessible and unknowable. In a self-fulfilling embodiment of gender difference, women's delineation and management of their own bodies in social space was limited by their lack of opportunity to touch their own bodies, by proxy, through their pockets. Instead, their hands made other gestures through the medium of dress by smoothing or arranging their clothes or through elegant turns or tasks such as pouring tea, holding fans, sewing or knitting. By the 1830s there is evidence that the tie pocket, though still worn in some quarters, was seen by others as incompatible with fashionable behaviour, and this may be due to its associated gestures. Rummaging into those deep pockets perhaps suggested housewifery or, worse still, the accumulations and fumblings of old age. In the 1831 novel

Pin Money, Mrs Lucretia is gently mocked for three simultaneous signs of age, 'conveying her *snuff-box* as she spoke through a labyrinth of *quilted petticoats* into a bottomless pit of a *pocket*'.[61] Significantly, the more modern Lady Barbara wins at the gambling table and in exhilaration 'swept her allotted handful of sovereigns' not into a pocket but a reticule.[62]

It has been noted that 'the embodiment of power does not always have to occur purely through the development of a powerful body ... It has other variants which incorporate such elements as posture, height, weight, walk, dress etc.'[63] This is evident in the way the articulation and form of the male body is emphasised by disposition of hands in pockets. It is seen, for example, in the iconic photographs of Isambard Kingdom Brunel from 1857[64] and Keir Hardie from *c*.1892,[65] and the vastly popular Victorian practice of studio photography provides innumerable instances of it. By contrast, in the photographer's studio the female hand is seldom if ever pocketed. It is usually empty or lightly holding a book or a fan, and, shown chiefly as a hand at rest, nevertheless is a hand with a message (Figure 2). Most obviously it is poised to demonstrate ease and leisure, at least momentarily. Its emptiness confers the special status of the unworldly, unencumbered and unproductive body. Such a hand also offers itself for aesthetic appreciation and for the same reading of social class and personal character as the face. The same social protocol which kept the female hand in view and prevented it being pocketed like a male hand was reinforced by frequent advice in etiquette manuals and women's magazines on how to keep hands beautiful and delicate, underlining the habitual and expectant nature of the connoisseurial gaze on the female hand. As Kowaleski-Wallace noted, certain kinds of delimited action registered femininity in the context of the development of modern consumer practices over the long eighteenth century:

> the discursive construction of business as masculine effectively relegates woman to the body. It thereby removes her from the scene of economic opportunity and positions her as the object of consumer society. For if consumption is seen metaphorically as a bodily phenomenon, then woman as body was historically viewed as ready to consume ... The management of female behaviors, gestures, and, above all, speech, were the prerequisites for women's cultural participation.[66]

To be pocketed would negate the charm of the female hand on display and disrupt its potential for certain sorts of 'cultural participation'. In the context of her exploration of the 'pervasiveness' of class and gender categories in a case study of Alfred Munby (1828–1910), the barrister, poet and diarist who maintained a secret marriage with domestic servant Hannah Cullwick (1833–1909), Davidoff notes that '*hands* take on a special significance and play a central role in both class and gender imagery ... They also carry an explicitly sexual connotation for Munby and, one

Figure 2: Located outside a modest house, this pair adhere to popular gendered conventions of pose and gesture established forty years before in the earliest days of photographic studio portraiture. She lightly holds a book with both hands on view, any pockets well hidden. He stands with his left hand in his trouser side pocket and displays the use of two further front pockets for his handkerchief and watch. Cabinet portrait photograph, English, *c*. 1890. Author's collection.

would guess, for many other Victorians as well.'[67] Exhibiting the female leisured hand reinforced the distinction in middle- and upper-class homes between employers and servants. In 1874 Hannah Cullwick remarked that her own hands, 'broad and *spread* with work', were unfitted for wearing gloves and therefore made it hard for her to pass as a lady, had she wished to do so.[68]

If male pockets created particular gestures for studio photography, it is also widely evident in fiction that male characters could signal emotions and social nuance by the positioning of their hands in their pockets. In Trollope, an angry young man confronts his rival in the latter's lodgings and, refusing a chair, stands with his hat held behind his back with his left hand, 'with his right leg forward, and the thumb of his right hand in his waist-coat pocket'.[69] The same young man signals his aggression by refusing to sit at the reading of a will, and stands 'with his hands in the pockets of his trousers, and his coat-tails over his arms'.[70] He demonstrates callous disregard for his former mistress by standing looking at her 'with his hands thrust deep into his pockets', whilst, by contrast, her gloved hands are visible and, by implication, usefully employed. 'And for this she had dressed herself with so much care, mending her gloves, and darning her little fragments of finery!'[71] Another young man, having lost all his money at the gaming table, attempts to appear indifferent by walking away from the table 'and, putting his hands in his trousers pockets, whistled as he walked away'. Nobody is deceived. 'The motion of his head, the position of his hands, the tone of his whistling, all told the tale.'[72] An anxious father 'at his wit's end' about his daughter's financial problems, 'went on walking about the room, jingling the money in his trousers-pockets, and pushing the chairs about as he chanced to meet them'.[73] Whilst Trollope's men make these emotional hand gestures by means of their pockets, in the same novel, women gesture outside their pockets: 'Lady Midlothian held up one hand in a manner that was truly imposing.'[74]

The hand in the trouser pocket, though expressive of bodily confidence and presence, was also an ambivalent stance because of its association with poor deportment, lack of restraint and degeneracy. In 1868 an English public school reportedly ruled that its scholars would no longer have 'side trousers pockets' because they 'continually had their hands in these pockets, and thereby contracted a lounging and stooping habit'.[75] By the end of the century the growing literature on adolescence, problematising it within debates about national degeneracy, included promotion of hygienic, simple clothing as a remedy for many ills. Boys' pockets did not escape attention. 'Undergarments for both sexes should be loose and well cut away, and posture, automatisms and acts that cause friction should be discouraged ... Pockets should be placed well to the side and not too deep, and should not be kept too full, while habitually keeping the hands in the pockets should be discouraged.'[76]

It can be argued that the suggestive qualities of concealed and visible pockets echoed the perceived binary division between the controlled, clean and concealed body of the respectable woman and the uncontrolled, dangerous and more visible body of the working or fallen woman. When open, the visible pocket transgresses or breaches the boundary between the body and the social world.[77] Visible patch pockets for women featured more frequently on work wear such as aprons, overalls and pinafores. For example, women gleaning grain in the harvest fields in Norfolk, England, wore aprons with 'large pockets in the front to put the short ears in'.[78] When women wore quasi-military uniforms for the first time in World War I, they acquired almost the same ration of pockets as their male counterparts, at least on their jackets. Pockets used in working clothes of all types give rise to questions about the actual and taxonomical bound-aries between clothes and tools, and therefore underline the association of certain clothes with manual labour.[79] This was suppressed by the concealed arrangement of pockets on highly fashionable clothes. When dress pocket visibility became briefly fashionable in the 1870s and 1880s, it generated a spate of fussy, ornate and awkwardly situated pockets which were emphatically without much practical function beyond the carrying of handkerchiefs, themselves the subject of discussion in fashion journalism of the day.

However, by the end of the century, there are important parallel develop-ments which merit more research. As women took up clean work in service industries, and as waged female work extended into the middle class, more substantial handbags become ubiquitous and the articulation and mobility of women's bodies were routinely represented by the placing of hands in front or side patch pockets. The new loose-fitting knitted jackets that became popular at the turn of the century suited this rapid development in the repertoire of women's gestures (Figure 3). These agile women confirm the early emergence of Hollander's notion of a more 'unified bodily experience', in which women's clothes and bodies approximated more closely to those of the male, 'as a visibly working, self-aware and unified instrument',[80] or at least in the prescient eyes of fashion illustrators.

In conclusion, it is hoped that this preliminary study of pockets can contribute to the larger challenges in dress history. It opens several lines of enquiry including the wider interaction of gesture, posture and clothing which has not been much addressed theoretically or empirically to date.[81] Pockets throw up questions about clothing in the transition from childhood to adulthood. They also reveal how little we know about the gendered everyday life of money and how it shaped self-presentation. The study argues that the form and content of pockets can be read as part of the gendering of work and consumption and that the study of details or small components of dress can offer insights not always visible with a larger lens. As Bachelard noted, 'miniature is an exercise that has metaphysical freshness'.[82] There is also a danger that fashion has been conceptualised into such a blunt and homogenising tool for historians that it is not precise

Figure 3: An anonymous illustrator stresses the advantages of knitted sports wear for women by using boldly articulated figures. Soft, loosely structured 'jackets', 'coats' and 'wraps' come in a wide range of colours and offer 'freedom of movement'. The hands shown in easily accessed patch pockets are part of an enlarged lexicon of female movement and gesture. 1914 spring and summer fashion catalogue, Harrods Ltd., London. Author's collection.

enough for understanding the full complexity of change and function in either production or consumption of clothing. Individuals have made their choices of clothing whilst living in circumstances more intricate and more fluid than fashion history has yet grasped. The common regret over the loss of pockets in the mid century which united Sala, the male journalist, and Hall, the female novelist, centred on the notion that fashion was, in Sala's words, 'a whirligig of vanity and inutility – of waste and glitter',[83] which cast aside things familiar, practical or self-sufficient. Our inventories of clothing consumption are incomplete unless they recognise that an individual, or groups of individuals, may have worn garments which lived in a present or future tense, defined by novelty and commercially generated fashion, alongside others which were imbued with more elusive functions and associations. Pockets join other marginal components such as cuffs, neckwear, hats, aprons, gloves and handkerchiefs to reveal some of the instabilities and intricacies which play over the surface of the clothed body and register the ambivalences and transformations inherent in the construction of gender.

Notes

I would like to thank Alan Bennett, Alison Carter; Anthea Jarvis; Miles Lambert; the staff of Carrow House, Norfolk Museum Service; Oriel Cullen; members of the *Gender & History* Collective; at the University of Southampton, my colleagues Dinah Eastop, Maria Hayward, Lesley Miller, Alison Matthews-David and Annie Richardson; Joyce Dawson; Ruth Gilbert and students on the MA History of Textiles and Dress.

1. Gwen Raverat, *Period Piece: A Cambridge Childhood* (Faber and Faber, 1960), p. 267.
2. J. C. Flugel, *The Psychology of Clothes* (1930; repr. International Universities Press, 1969), p. 206. Also pp. 186–7 for an extended discussion on carrying small articles about the person, including an early call for more use of the knapsack, currently achieved in a variety of forms.
3. Anne Fine, *Bill's New Frock* (Methuen, 1989), pp. 49–50.
4. Anne Hollander, *Sex and Suits: The Evolution of Modern Dress* (Alfred Knopf, 1994); Christopher Breward, *The Hidden Consumer: Masculinities, Fashion and City Life 1860–1914* (Manchester University Press, 1999).
5. Vanda Foster, *Bags and Purses* (B. T. Batsford, 1982), p. 8.
6. Linda Baumgarten and John Watson, *Costume Close-Up: Clothing Construction and Pattern 1750–1790* (Colonial Williamsburg Foundation, 1999), p. 65. Tie pockets were also in common use in America. See Yolanda Van de Krol, '"Ty'ed About My Middle, Next To My Smock": The Cultural Context Of Women's Pockets', unpublished Master's thesis (University of Delaware, 1994).
7. For example, see William Beechey, *Sir Francis Ford's Children Giving a Coin to a Beggar*, oil on canvas, 1793, Tate Gallery, London.
8. Collections of eighteenth- and nineteenth-century tie pockets consulted: Carrow House, Norfolk Museum Service; Hampshire County Museum Service; Museum of London; Gallery of Costume, Manchester City Galleries. See also Jane Tozer and Sarah Levitt, *Fabric of Society, A Century of People and their Clothes 1770–1870: Essays Inspired by the Collections at Platt Hall, The Gallery of English Costume, Manchester* (Laura Ashley, 1983).

For examples in the USA, see Linda Baumgarten, *Eighteenth-Century Clothing at Williamsburg* (Colonial Williamsburg Foundation, 1986) and Van de Krol, "'Ty'ed About My Middle'". Laurel Thatcher Ulrich notes the gender difference in the form and contents of pockets in early America in *The Age of Homespun: Objects and Stories in the Creation of an American Myth* (Alfred Knopf, 2001), p. 263.

9. Foster, *Bags and Purses*, p. 10; Van de Krol, "'Ty'ed About My Middle'", p. 39; Beverley Lemire, *Fashion's Favourite: The Cotton Trade and the Consumer in Britain 1660–1800* (Oxford University Press, 1991), p. 183. A pedlar doll of *c.* 1820 carries a ready-made pocket in its tray of wares (1922.566, Gallery of Costume, Manchester City Galleries, Manchester City Council).

10. Anne Buck, *Victorian Costume and Costume Accessories* (Ruth Bean, 1984), p. 149.

11. Buck, *Victorian Costume*, p. 150.

12. Foster, *Bags and Purses*, p. 45.

13. A Lady (Maria Wilson?), *The Workwoman's Guide, Containing Instructions etc.* (Simpkin, Marshall and Co., 1838), p. 73.

14. For example, see large linen drill tie pocket, twenty inches long, marked 'FJ 1824' (1947.1254), and tie pocket with front of silk patchwork and back of block and resist print cotton with signs of earlier gathering indicating recycled use, 1840–60 (1947.1262) (Gallery of Costume, Manchester City Galleries, Manchester City Council); tie pocket, machine-made of drab twill, marked 'E.J.Miller', *c.* 1870 (226.972.2), Carrow House, Norfolk Museum Services; tie pocket, printed cotton in green trellis pattern, two compartments one above the other, horizontal openings, *c.* 1890 (BWM 1963.163), Hampshire County Museum Service. Some paintings of the Victorian period situate plain tie pockets in bucolic scenes.

15. Annette B. Weiner, 'Why Cloth? Wealth, Gender, and Power in Oceania', in *Cloth and Human Experience*, ed. Annette B. Weiner and Jane Schneider (Smithsonian Institution Press, 1989), p. 52.

16. Dinah Eastop, 'Garments Deliberately Concealed in Buildings', in *A Permeability of Boundaries? New Approaches to the Archaeology of Art, Religion and Folklore*, ed. R. J. Wallis and K. Lymer (British Archaeology Reports Series 936, 2001), p. 80, and Kathryn Gill and Anna Harrison, 'An Eighteenth-Century Detachable Pocket and Cap, Found Concealed in a Wall Cavity. Conservation and Research', in *Textile History* (forthcoming).

17. In pre-Victorian prints and caricatures, tie pockets can be visually associated with disreputable or sexualised female behaviour, for example in the work of James Gillray (1757–1815) and Thomas Rowlandson (1756–1827). In this symbolic representation, they are plain and undecorated. See Van de Krol, "'Ty'ed About My Middle'", pp. 81–4.

18. *Queen*, 7 August 1880, p. 128.

19. Genevieve Cummins and Nerylla Taunton, *Chatelaines: Utility to Glorious Extravagance* (Antique Collectors' Club, 1994).

20. Mrs. F. Douglas, *The Gentlewoman's Book of Dress* (Henry, 1895), p. 77.

21. Lady Violet Greville, *The Gentlewoman in Society* (Henry, 1892), p. 251.

22. In Worthing Museum and Art Gallery, England, this is a rare example of a nineteenth-century *waterproofed* smock (Louise Squire, Textile Conservation Centre, University of Southampton Conservation report, 1712.2, 1996).

23. Edward Carpenter, 'Simplification of Life', in *England's Ideal* (1886; repr. 1919), p. 114.

24. Kjerstin Emilia Mackie, Textile Conservation Centre, University of Southampton (1089 – B3, unpublished Diploma report, 1988).

25. George Sala, *Gaslight and Daylight* (Chapman and Hall, 1859), p. 59.

26. Pierre Bourdieu, *Distinction: A Social Critique of the Judgement of Taste* (1979; repr. Routledge, 1986), p. 170.

27. Breward, *Hidden Consumer*, p. 31.

28. Anon., *How to Dress or Etiquette of the Toilette* (Ward and Lock, 1876) p. 13.

29. The 'Major' of *To-day*, *Clothes and the Man: Hints on the Wearing and Caring of Clothes* (Grant Richards, 1900), p. 36.

30. Leonore Davidoff, 'Regarding Some "Old Husbands' Tales": Public and Private in Feminist History', in *Worlds Between: Historical Perspectives on Gender and Class* (Polity Press, 1995), p. 236.

31. Breward, *Hidden Consumer*, p. 260.

32. Laurel Thatcher Ulrich, *Good Wives: Image and Reality in the Lives of Women in Northern New England 1650–1750* (Vintage Books, 1991), p. 34.

33. Amanda Vickery, *The Gentleman's Daughter: Women's Lives in Georgian England* (Yale University Press, 1998), p. 194.

34. Vickery, *Gentleman's Daughter*, p. 148.

35. Vickery, *Gentleman's Daughter*, p. 194.

36. Anon, *The Five Talents of Woman* (Fisher Unwin, 1890), p. 56.

37. Anna Maria Hall, *Grandmamma's Pockets* (Chambers, 1849), p. 39.

38. Hall, *Grandmamma's Pockets*, p. 36.

39. Hall, *Grandmamma's Pockets*, p. 38.

40. Hall, *Grandmamma's Pockets*, p. 43.

41. Hall, *Grandmamma's Pockets*, p. 120.

42. Hall, *Grandmamma's Pockets*, p. 119.

43. Hall, *Grandmamma's Pockets*, p. 44.

44. Hall, *Grandmamma's Pockets*, p. 39.

45. For example, a servant hoards £20 in notes, gold and silver in an old pocket under her pillow (Camilla Toulmin, *The Neglected Child* (Chambers, 1858), p. 29).

46. Hall, *Grandmamma's Pockets*, p. 119.

47. Hall, *Grandmamma's Pockets*, pp. 39–40.

48. Hall, *Grandmamma's Pockets*, p. 156.

49. Charlotte Perkins Gilman, 'If I Were a Man', in *The Yellow Wall-Paper and Other Stories* (1914; repr. Oxford University Press, 1998), p. 263.

50. Erica Rappaport, '"A Husband and His Wife's Dresses": Consumer Credit and the Debtor Family in England, 1864–1914', in *The Sex of Things: Gender and Consumption in Historical Perspective*, ed. Victoria de Grazia (University of California Press, 1996).

51. Erica Rappaport, *Shopping for Pleasure, Women in the Making of London's West End* (Princeton University Press, 2000), p. 70.

52. Rappaport, *Shopping for Pleasure*, p. 72.

53. Susan Staves, 'Pin Money', *Studies in Eighteenth-Century Culture*, American Society for Eighteenth-Century Studies, vol. 14 (1985), p. 72. The sexual politics of money in marriage were dramatised in Anon. (Catherine Gore), *Pin Money, A Novel* (Colburn and Bentley, 1831).

54. For example, Eleanor Gordon and Gwyneth Nair, 'The Economic Role of Middle-Class Women in Victorian Glasgow', *Women's History Review*, 9 (2000), pp. 791–814.

55. Edward Copeland, *Women Writing About Money: Women's Fiction in England 1790–1820* (Cambridge University Press, 1995), p. 4. Also Hoh-Cheung Mui and Lorna Mui, *Shops and Shopping in Eighteenth Century England* (Routledge, 1989).

56. C. Chinn, *They Worked All Their Lives: Women of the Urban Poor in England, 1880–1939* (Manchester University Press, 1988), p. 51.

57. Viviana A. Zelizer, 'The Social Meaning of Money: "Special Monies"', in *American Journal of Sociology*, 95 (1989), p. 370.

58. Anthony Trollope, *Can You Forgive Her?* (1864; repr. Oxford University Press, 1982), vol. 2, p. 139.

59. Susan Stewart, 'Prologue: From the Museum of Touch', in *Material Memories: Design and Evocation*, ed. Marius Kwint et al. (Berg, 1999), p. 35.

60. Anne Hollander, *Sex and Suits*, p. 113.

61. Anon. (Catherine Gore), *Pin Money, A Novel* (Colburn and Bentley, 1831), vol. 2, p. 161; italics added.

62. *Pin Money, A Novel*, vol. 2, p. 207.

63. Chris Shilling, *The Body and Social Theory* (Sage, 1993), p. 113.

64. Robert Howlett, National Portrait Gallery, London (NPG P662).
65. Arthur Weston, National Portrait Gallery, London (NPG 13173).
66. Elizabeth Kowaleski-Wallace, *Consuming Subjects: Women, Shopping and Business in the Eighteenth Century* (Columbia University Press, 1997), p. 13.
67. Leonore Davidoff, 'Class and Gender in Victorian England: The Case of Hannah Cullwick and A. J. Munby', in *Worlds Between: Historical Perspectives on Class and Gender* (1979; repr. Polity, 1995), p. 123.
68. Derek Hudson, *Munby: Man of Two Worlds* (Abacus, 1974), p. 371.
69. Trollope, *Can You Forgive Her?*, vol. 2, p. 119.
70. Trollope, *Can You Forgive Her?*, vol. 2, p. 155.
71. Trollope, *Can You Forgive Her?*, vol. 2, p. 324.
72. Trollope, *Can You Forgive Her?*, vol. 2, p. 367.
73. Trollope, *Can You Forgive Her?*, vol. 2, p. 211. Original text has extra hyphen.
74. Trollope, *Can You Forgive Her?*, vol. 2, pp. 407–8.
75. *The Times*, 6 August 1868.
76. G. Stanley Hall, *The Psychology of Adolescence* (Appleton, 1904), p. 468.
77. Karen Sayer, '"A Sufficiency of Clothing": Dress and Domesticity in Victorian Britain', *Textile History*, 33 (2002), pp. 112–22.
78. Bridget Yates, 'Rural Dress in Norfolk', *Strata of Society*, Costume Society Conference, Department of Textiles, Victoria and Albert Museum, 1974, p. 9.
79. Yates, 'Rural Dress in Norfolk', p. 9.
80. Hollander, *Sex and Suits*, p. 136.
81. There is precedent in art history, if not much in dress history, for examining gesture; for example, Arline Meyer, 'Re-Dressing Classical Statuary: the Eighteenth-Century "Hand-in-Waistcoat" Portrait', *Art Bulletin*, 77 (1995), pp. 45–63; Jan Bremmer and Herman Roodenburg (eds), *A Cultural History of Gesture from Antiquity to the Present Day* (Polity Press, 1991).
82. Gaston Bachelard, *The Poetics of Space* (1958; repr. Beacon Press, 1994), p. 161.
83. Sala, *Gaslight and Daylight*, p. 360.

6

Fashioning the American Man: The Arrow Collar Man, 1907–1931

Carole Turbin

In June 1923 New Yorkers were treated to a new musical, *Helen of Troy, New York*, whose story, inspired by the Arrow collar and Arrow Man, turned on crises of commerce and romance. Helen is a pretty young secretary to a Troy collar factory owner, Mr Yarrow, named to evoke the Arrow collar. Mr Yarrow, facing falling sales of a stiffly starched collar that consumers find uncomfortable, hires a photographer, portrayed as bohemian woman artist, to take publicity pictures. Her strikingly handsome model, Theodore, modelled on the elegant advertising image of the Arrow Man (Figure 1), demonstrates the inadequacy of comfortable cotton collars, by dipping one in water, dissolving its starch and revealing unmanly limpness. Helen, in love with the son of her boss's rival, saves the day by inventing the semi-soft collar, proving her superiority to the unscrupulous efficiency expert who pursues her affections. In the musical finale, the sons of Mr Yarrow and his rival triumphantly unite to form a new firm specialising in semi-soft collars that promises riches for all. The *New York Times* praised the show as a 'light-hearted burlesque of big business, where any man can be captain of industry … There wasn't a dry collar in the house when the audience joined in the fun with shouting and laughter.'[1]

For a 1920s theatre audience, this story recalled the real-life economic crisis and triumph of a high-profile industry, Troy, New York's manufacturers of detachable collars, a wardrobe staple for most US men and all but working-class men in Britain and Europe since the 1840s. In the first decade of the twentieth century, many young American men began to purchase informal soft collars and attached-collar shirts, rejecting their fathers' uncomfortable starched collars. The semi-soft cotton collar rescued collar companies' fortunes, thanks to the product's appeal and the power of advertising, most especially the Arrow Man. In 1907, in order

Figure 1: This 1910 Arrow collar advertisement (J. C. Leyendecker) pictures young, handsome men attired in the new loose-fitted fashions of the early twentieth century in an intimate yet cultured interior. Note the men's strong features, casual postures, and intense expressions. Photograph courtesy of the Rensselaer County Historical Society, Troy, New York.

to compete with rival companies' new soft collars and at the same time appeal to traditional tastes, Cluett, Peabody, and Co., a major Troy collar manufacturer, made advertising history. The firm introduced a new line of collars constructed of cotton rather than linen, which met older standards of formal attire while introducing new characteristics that fitted changing styles. Because, as Theodore demonstrated, traditionalists associated comfortable cotton collars with unmanliness, even spinelessness (compared to stiff collars' masculine uprightness), the company anticipated they would have to 'sell' the Arrow collar to new and old markets. In order to convince retailers to sell Arrow collars and entice consumers to buy them, Cluett, Peabody hired the firm's first advertising manager, who recruited the new advertising firm Calkins and Holden, and the noted illustrator Joseph Christian Leyendecker, to create an image representing the ideal American Man.[2] The Arrow Man's bold, elegant image, defined by crisp, precise lines and dramatic lighting, graced advertising copy from 1907 to 1931, in magazines, newspapers, billboards, public transport, and retail store displays. The Arrow Man helped make the firm the nation's foremost collar manufacturer and left an indelible mark on popular culture. Americans who have forgotten *Helen of Troy, New York* recall a line from a Cole Porter song from the 1934 Broadway musical *Anything Goes*, 'You're the top, you're an Arrow Collar'.[3] The term Arrow Man became a popular expression referring to a handsome, desirable, stylish man. Tall, well built, with broad shoulders, a strong jaw, chiselled features, and muscular hands, he was a visual representation of the New American Man and the male equivalent of the Gibson Girl who represented the New Woman.[4]

The Arrow Man and his collar were but players in a complex story of social and cultural transformations, spanning the late nineteenth to early twentieth century. Recent scholarship emphasises that, like women's dress, long synonymous with change and variety, men's fashions and physical ideals also shifted, albeit more subtly and in different ways from women's. Many men, like women, were also enthusiastic consumers and, like new modes of femininity, the new masculine ideals of the early twentieth century's first decades were tied to consumption.[5] The tale of the Arrow collar and Arrow Man are key to this story because detachable collars, mass marketed to men in the US and internationally from the 1840s, were among the earliest mass-produced consumer items. Yet the story of the Arrow Man and his collar also reveals that changing masculine ideals and physical appearance, heightened by the new visual and consumer culture, were part and parcel of broad and fundamental shifts in the US: new occupational and social class configurations and emerging American popular culture.

In an age of compelling advertising images created for enterprising manufacturers and retailers by innovative advertising agencies and talented artists such as Maxfield Parrish, why was the Arrow Man's influence so deep and wide-ranging? The Arrow Man was one of the most successful examples of a remarkable development, the proliferation of idealised visual images of people through the new mass media, which in turn heightened the significance of a long-range trend, Americans' increased awareness and preoccupation with external appearance. By the 1830s the affluent middle classes in relatively anonymous, urban settings increasingly tended to measure people encountered in public by outward appearance rather than by the personal knowledge of character typical of small, tightly knit communities.[6] At the turn of the twentieth century, films, photographs, posters, and advertising illustrations in the new mass-circulation magazines took advantage of innovations in reproduction of images, especially photography and colour lithography, and technology that increased availability and flexibility of electric lighting to dramatise personal images.[7] Owners and managers of the department stores that sprang up in cities and suburbs hired specialists trained in design and display who used colour, lighting, glass, and props to show off new fashions in clothing and other goods on shop floors and windows facing streets. Personal appearance took on new meanings, including performance and pretence, as men and women in rural and urban areas became aware of possibilities of cultivating their own external appearance through make-up, lighting, and stylish garments, which they viewed in the new media and newly designed shops. Mass-media images like the Arrow Collar Man were central to shifts in the significance of appearance because they were not only tools for marketing products nationally, but also models for individuals' presentation of self to others in public and private settings.[8]

The emerging advertising industry added another dimension to Americans' changed relationship with personal appearance. The image of the Arrow Collar Man was a novelty on the visual landscape, an early example of the advertising industry's strategy of marrying high quality art with innovations in distribution of goods, reproduction and dissemination of images, and business. Manufacturers had been using advertising since the eighteenth century, but before the 1880s most advertisements relied on words describing advantages of goods or services for sale with a few illustrations that were utilitarian, designed to provide information that supplemented the text. Advertising changed dramatically in the late nineteenth century as the goals of retailers and manufacturers shifted to selling mass-produced goods in national markets. Manufacturers and retailers sought not only to stimulate or create the desire for goods and foster product loyalty through brand-name recognition but also to legitimate profit-making strategies of business and transform commodities into cultural artefacts and icons appealing to the affluent middle class, the major market for consumer goods. Advertisers, challenged to produce more effective advertising, reinvented themselves. Art historian Michelle Bogart explains that new heads of firms enlisted art in their campaign in part to establish themselves as honest, responsible professionals, rather than misleading promoters of goods such as patent medicines. Earnest Elmo Calkins, organiser of the firm responsible for the Arrow collar advertisements, was a leader of the movement to harness to advertising goals the high-quality design, colour and form which was typical of illustration, posters and painting. Calkins, both businessman and appreciator of the arts, was convinced that visual images could communicate messages more effectively than the written word and that advertising art could be public art, a means to bring art to ordinary people.[9] Some painters rejected business interests as irreconcilable with aesthetic ideals, but many modernists who sought to imaginatively depict forms and situations of contemporary life in bold images designed to reach large numbers of people embraced advertising's goal of reaching a popular audience, and saw an affinity between public art like mural painting and new billboard advertising. When Calkins started his firm, he hired designers experienced in industry and retailing and drew into his fold prominent talented magazine illustrators, including Leyendecker, N. C. Wyeth, and Maxfield Parrish. The Arrow Man advertisements were an early example of advertising's new look in which compelling visual images dominated written copy.[10]

Leyendecker was an excellent choice. He was well known to both the general public and other artists, including his close friend Norman

Rockwell, who described him as America's 'most famous illustrator' and believed that but for unfortunate life circumstances Leyendecker's artistic status would have been greater and more enduring.[11] Leyendecker was especially admired for his depiction of masculine subjects. Connolly, Cluett, Peabody's new advertising manager, former editor of the Chicago men's apparel trade journal *Haberdasher*, was familiar with the images he created for Hart, Schaffner and Marx, Chicago's manufacturer of popular, high-quality men's clothing and a pioneer in using national advertising.[12] Leyendecker was suited to meet the needs of the new advertising industry. He began his career during the last decades of the golden age of illustration, when many talented artists created images for great literature, and he moved easily into advertising art, which self-consciously combined bold, striking images of modern art movements with natural realism that the consuming public recognised as art. He learned accurate anatomical drawing from life at the Chicago Art Institute (1889), while apprenticed to an engraving house, and then (with his equally talented brother Frank) at Paris's Académie Julien (1896–7). Leyendecker's biographer, Michael Schau, explains that, unlike the Académie Julien that disdained new trends, the young artist appreciated the potential of emerging commercial poster art and absorbed the line and colour characteristic of art nouveau masters that adorned the streets and boulevards of fin de siècle Paris.[13]

Arrow collar advertisements pioneered a strategy now taken for granted in the visual landscape. The Arrow Man campaign, which highlighted the social background and environment of the product's user, was one of the earliest to employ what was later termed a 'soft sell', a restrained, refined message in which the products' consumer was as important as images of the products themselves. Advertising agencies sought to create images with which viewers could identify, either because figures in advertisements were familiar (perhaps homey or neighbourhood) types, or admired models of stylish, knowing individuals in sophisticated settings. Because images of a product's user conveyed personal characteristics with which viewers could identify in a variety of ways, objects for sale were themselves personified or animated with personal qualities. This advertising strategy sought to convert goods for sale from utilitarian objects into a means to enhance outward personal appearance in order to manage self-presentation to others.[14]

The image of the Arrow Man was a masculine ideal that Americans could admire and/or identify with, but he was hardly a bloodless abstraction. Leyendecker used his skill and distinctive style to create a man with a distinct physical presence. Classically trained in the complexities of human anatomy, the artist skilfully indicated the physical body beneath the elegant garments without describing it blatantly or literally. The physical contours of the images are shaped with crisp lines that articulate crucial points at which the body contacts and gives shape to tailored garments.

Turns in the directions of lines that shaped the body and features are not rounded but gently angled, conveying strength and presence. Moreover, the Arrow Man was not a single individual, but a type that included salient features of various examples of white male attractiveness appealing to a variety of personal tastes. For example, a 1913 Arrow advertisement (Figure 2) shows four men of different life stages in a formal setting, a box at the theatre, observed by an attendant. Like other illustrators, Leyendecker did not rely on himself as a model but used studio models, a practice he retained even when other illustrators shifted to photographs in the early twentieth century. Many models were actors, trained to perform, convey a stance and emotions, maintain a pose, gestures, and expressions for visual artists who are astute observers. The first Arrow Man was Charles Beach, an actor who became the artist's assistant and companion, described by Rockwell as tall, powerfully built, extra-ordinarily handsome and well dressed, like 'an athlete from one of the Ivy League Colleges'.[15] The link between new film and stage stars and advert-ising images was not lost on consumers. As Americans came to associate glamour and sophistication with films, the Arrow Man became more than an advertising icon but took on the cachet of a matinée idol. Popular accounts report that fan mail for the Arrow Man, including marriage proposals and gifts on Christmas and Valentine's Day, amounted to more than that which Rudolf Valentino received at the height of his career.[16]

Appearing for twenty-three years, Arrow Man advertisements were remarkably consistent and distinctive, although they became less so as others, including Rockwell, imitated his style.[17] Earlier images were sketchier, more linear, with less bold colour and dark/light contrasts; in later years figures were more idealised and dramatically lit (although images of this sort also appeared as early as the World War I period). In the Arrow Man's last appearance in 1931 (Figure 3), figures are less detailed, with broad planes on faces and garments; contrasts in value and elegant props create drama and a romantic mood. The Arrow Man and his female companion are posed as if on a set, rather than in a specific domestic setting or place of entertainment. Interpretation of the signifi-cance of appearance is left to the viewer's imagination, imparting an air of mystery. The consistency of Leyendecker's work was double-edged, as it ensured success in advertising, but also meant less artistic development. Rockwell contends that Leyendecker lived slightly beyond his means in order to constantly produce and not linger over creations. This strategy encouraged him to rely on technique rather than depth of meaning, repeat images that had proved successful in the past and, worse, prevented him from taking jobs that paid little but could challenge him artistically and enhance his reputation. But Leyendecker was not alone. Advertising agencies began to exert more control over artists and during the Great

Figure 2: This 1913 Arrow advertisement, picturing elegant men enjoying an evening at the theatre, is one of J. C. Leyendecker's more complex images. Note the variety of male dress and types, including a young man (far left) wearing new fashions favoured by his generation. Photograph courtesy of the Rensselaer County Historical Society, Troy, New York.

Figure 3: The last Arrow advertisement (1931) is an example of a variation on J. C. Leyendecker's style. The Arrow Man and his companion are depicted more abstractly, with little detail, accompanied by elaborate yet stylised props suggesting an elegant, dramatic interior, perhaps the lobby of a theatre. Note that there is little feeling of a relationship between the two figures, and the Arrow Man's female companion has less 'life' than the Arrow Man himself. Photograph courtesy of the Rensselaer County Historical Society, Troy, New York.

Depression, businessmen, under pressure to sell products, began to reject images that drew on modern art styles in favour of those appealing to a wider public taste.[18]

The Arrow Man's compelling appearance also resonated with changes in Americans' consciousness of external appearance that varied by gender, race, and class, prescribing different sorts of outward appearance for women and men, and people of different races. In the mid nineteenth century, most white Americans evaluated both women and men in terms of moral character rather than personal appearance, and perceived physical attractiveness as an external manifestation of an individual's inner, moral qualities. Many African-American reformers, aware of racial implications of linking personal appearance with morality, questioned this notion.[19] But for white Americans, fashion, constantly changing with the vicissitudes of taste, was incompatible with beauty, which was timeless, immutable, and linked with women, not specific individuals but idealised physical types signifying inner personal characteristics tied to feminine ideals. Male beauty was also defined as universal, although rarely explicitly articulated, echoing the male silhouette of classical antiquity: broad, muscular shoulders, narrow waist, flat stomach, and long legs. By the end of the nineteenth century, as Americans' awareness of personal appearance shifted, the view that beauty was a manifestation of inner goodness and morality declined. Female beauty was increasingly linked to fashion, part of the management of self-presentation in public, and to business, including the cosmetic industry and magazines providing advice. Many respectable women took to using cosmetics and beauty-enhancing accessories.[20] Men, too, began to separate inner moral character from appearance. Contrary to popular wisdom and scholarship identifying women as the early twentieth century's quintessential consumers, men were prime targets of marketing strategies and enthusiastic consumers, albeit unlike women. Many men purchased stylish garments, especially collars, for their own use through mail order catalogues, men's furnishing shops, or at department store counters especially designed to attract and sell to the male customer.[21]

Yet, despite shifts in gender ideologies, some aspects of men and women's external appearance still invited moral judgements about the inner person, chiefly regarding sexuality. In the early decades of the twentieth century, a woman's fashionable middle-class appearance still signalled the status of a respectable 'lady', and lack of respectability could have dire consequences. A working woman who appeared unrespectable was regarded as sexually available, or a prostitute, and risked respectable woman's scorn and physical danger.[22] What was important for men was that they not appear to have external characteristics typical of women. Because Americans thought of preoccupation with fashion as a woman's realm, white middle-class men who deliberately embellished their outward appearance (beyond the purposes of health and physical fitness) risked being thought of as unmanly, effeminate, and in extreme cases suspected of homosexuality.[23]

In light of this powerful gender ideology, the Arrow Man's cachet is puzzling. If many white middle-class Americans suspected that men who embellished their appearance were unmanly, then why did the Arrow Man become a symbol of the well-dressed, fashionable, desirable man? And there is another question. A number of scholars, assuming that an artist's social perspective and response to men and women influence the content of their artistic products, read the Arrow Man's physicality and gaze as homoerotic and Leyendecker as homosexual. Martin and others observe that, in more than a few illustrations, attractive men gaze openly and even intensely at each other, suggesting an intimate, sensual relationship (Figure 2). In illustrations that depict two or more men in the company of an equally elegant woman, the Arrow Men gaze at each other rather than the woman; the woman is usually rendered with less detail (although drawn beautifully), does not regard the men, and conveys considerably less emotion. Cooper notes that in illustrations depicting the Arrow Man's full body, the crotch reveals a just noticeable bulge suggesting the fullness of genitals. Boyce points to numerous coded references to homosexuality in both images and text.[24] To twenty-first-century observers, the circumstances of Leyendecker's life support this interpretation. The artist never married, and biographical details reveal no relationships with women. Leyendecker commuted to his New York City studio from his home in New Rochelle, which he shared with his sister and his brother Frank and later also Charles Beach, who became his manager and assistant. Augusta and Frank left because of family quarrels, in 1924, but Beach stayed until Joseph's death in 1951 and inherited half the artist's estate. Yet there is no direct evidence that Leyendecker's relationship with Beach was homosexual, although Rockwell's account reveals a close emotional attachment.[25]

Another, more historical, question is more to the point. Did white middle-class men and women at the turn of the twentieth century perceive homoeroticism in Arrow Man advertisements? George Chauncey, author of *Gay New York*, says, no. Before the 1930s the gay male world was visible and diverse, but not in terms of the late twentieth-century oppositional categories of homosexuals and non-homosexuals. Men who engaged in sex with other men from time to time were not always identified as homosexual, and many homosexuals – those who identified themselves as queer – maintained their manly appearance, identifying themselves as homosexual because of their sexual orientation rather than their looks. Queers, sharing the perspective of many heterosexuals that men who obviously used artificial means to improve their looks were unmanly, took care to differentiate themselves from fairies, who lost their manly status because of their effeminate styles of dress and posture. In short, in early twentieth-century urban America, it was possible for men who had a conventionally masculine appearance to be intensely sexually active with other men but not risk stigmatisation as 'abnormal'.[26] To early twentieth-century observers, the Arrow Man was most certainly conventionally masculine.

Yet homoeroticism apparent to twenty-first century viewers of Leyendecker's images should not be dismissed out of hand. Viewed in context of the new consumer advertising, it is a window into understanding the considerable power of advertising images, and how they both tapped into and contributed to shaping ideologies of sexuality and gender. Martin suggests that Leyendecker's Arrow Man and other male images resonated with so many people a century ago because emotional, even erotic, communications between men conveyed the sexuality inherent in consumerism's message of self-gratification. Americans' new preoccupation with personal appearance was more than concern with external images, but was also rooted in the potential of gratifying deep and complex emotional and physical desires. The men who shaped the new field of advertising understood that high-quality art could resonate with these inner desires, and many talented artists were stimulated by the challenge. In the first decades of the twentieth century, people were not startled by imagery with homoerotic connotations, partly because they defined homosexuality narrowly, but also because it was already assimilated into advertising messages.[27]

It was fitting for the Arrow Man to symbolise shifts in men's perceptions of their external appearance. Cluett, Peabody, and Co. utilised innovative advertising strategies to ensure demand for a new version of a product that had been central to men's management of personal appearance for almost a century. Legend has it that the detachable collar was invented in 1827 by Hannah Lord Montague, wife of a Troy, New York, businessman, to solve a common household problem: an entire shirt had to be laundered when only its collar was soiled. Entrepreneurs who set up Troy's first collar factories in the 1840s found ready markets because of a series of interrelated changes in social class and gender ideologies. The wearing of clean white linen had long been a mark of high status for men and women.[28] In the eighteenth century and first decades of the nineteenth, elite men on both sides of the Atlantic wore shirts with stiff fronts and attached collars, often with a cravat, while working-class men typically wore collarless shirts under sturdy work-clothes, adding a muffler for warmth. (British working men continued to wear collarless shirts with mufflers well into the twentieth century.)[29] In the early nineteenth century, laundering, one of the most arduous household tasks, became even more troublesome as standards of cleanliness rose because prosperous people began to associate cleanly garments with cleanly bodies. At the same time, increasingly, newly affluent men sought to demonstrate cleanliness and taste through public display of dress, especially clean white linen.[30] These new entrepreneurs, commanders of growing commercial and industrial enterprises, sought to identify with old elites, associated with European gentility. They transformed elite gentility into a new ethos, middle-class respectability, which combined consumption, cleanliness, and genteel manners with self-discipline and economic productivity.[31] By signalling cleanliness and taste, detachable collars marked strict boundaries fundamental to Victorian social life: social position, gender, age, and situations delineated by space and time: morning, afternoon, evening, outdoors and indoors, public and private, household, schools and places of entertainment.

Linen was the fabric of choice for respectable gentlemen and imitators, but some collars were highly starched cotton and others, paper, celluloid, or rubber.[32] Figure 2 shows four examples of hundreds of collar styles, varying in height, width of opening between points, stiffness, and finishing, and characteristics of points, decoration (pleats or tucks), and fastenings. Throughout the nineteenth century, standing collars of various heights were most popular for formal wear (a low version is worn by the gentleman pictured third from the left). Informal turnover collars, constructed like twentieth-century shirt collars such as the one with long points worn by the young man on the far left, were most common in the first half of the nineteenth century. Turned-outward collars appeared in the second half. Some had turned-down tips or side edges, later termed 'wing collars', similar to that worn by the military man on the far right.[33] Collar manufacturers gave collar styles names like Hurworth, Chatley, and Warville that evoked British gentlemen, associated with civilisation and epitomised by British refinement, gentility, and political authority.[34]

In the first half of the nineteenth century, white, middle-class men's respectability also rested on ideals of manliness, conveyed in part by physical demeanour. There was not one but several interrelated and overlapping manly ideals, but the one most closely associated with economic achievement was the entrepreneur who was independent from wages – whether gentleman property-holder or owner of shop or factory. The ideal white middle-class man conveyed strength and authority through personal characteristics, self-discipline, restraint, and autonomy in private life, business, and politics, and physical appearance.[35] Yet the ideal middle-class man was not muscular and brawny – for this signified manual workers, labourers, independent farmers, and master craftsmen – but slender, refined and graceful, with erect posture, restrained gestures, and controlled demeanour. He avoided the slouching posture associated with labourers, farmers, and small tradesmen, and the downward gaze typical of servants.[36]

Detachable collars contributed to manly demeanour because of their special relationship to the body. Collars, like hats, drew attention to the head and face, often perceived as representing an individual's 'natural' state and a major focus in social relations, especially formal interaction. Faces took on new meaning in this period, as people became familiar with photographs of prominent people and film stars, and possibilities of managing appearance through make-up and lighting. Like other forms of self-presentation, face management was gendered. For women, make-up became 'dress' for the face, a second skin through which a woman represented her inner self by manipulating outward appearance.[37] For men, collars were face-enhancing because they could detract from, flatter, or neutralise the look of features, skin quality, and expression. Because collars firmly encircled the neck, they constrained the position of the head, neck, and shoulders and encouraged the wearer to sit, stand, and walk in a particular manner. At the peak of the popularity of high-standing collars in the 1890s, collars of high-ranking men (including many employers) prevented a downward gaze, differentiating them from clerks, whose low collars allowed movements required for writing.[38] To look downward, high-status men had to literally look down their noses.

Collars were about personal appearance on multiple levels, including visibility as well as guise and pretence. In the nineteenth century, collars were outer extensions of undergarments that created the appearance of bodily cleanliness by suggesting, but not revealing, what was hidden from view. Men's outer garments – waistcoat (usually high-buttoned), and jacket (often knee-length) – covered upper bodies; most collarless shirts were undergarments not meant for public display. No respectable middle-class man appeared in shirtsleeves in public, but wore a jacket, waistcoat, and cravat during his entire working day. Parts of the body not hidden by outer garments were adorned with detachable, starkly white starched linen: a 'bosom' concealed the shirtfront, and stiffly starched white collars and cuffs covered neck and wrists. The clean whiteness of these visible portions of inner garments was all the more striking because it contrasted with dark colours, typically black, of middle-class men's formal outer garments.[39] The neck, strategic because it accumulated perspiration and airborne dirt, bordered the less than cleanly private body that even most affluent men did not bathe daily. Detachable collars were strategic because they simultaneously displayed outer personal qualities and represented the private body and inner garments. A soiled collar told tales of uncleanliness elsewhere.[40]

Nineteenth-century middle-class white men's attire contrasted with working-class men's daily occupational dress. Manual workers and shopkeepers wore overalls, loose work-jackets, and work shirts with soft, attached, turned-down collars; these were dyed indigo to conceal stains, and loosely fitted to allow upper body movements necessary for physical labour without straining seams. Yet functional work clothes also had social meanings. Through occupational dress, working men displayed respectability and manhood rooted in pride in skill and success in a trade, muscularity, and physical prowess. Astute observers could distinguish manual workers and shopkeepers from gentlemen because in their own milieu working men's movements, gestures, and posture were appropriate to their occupations and garments.[41]

American middle-class manliness differed from the British model because it incorporated the contradictory double-edged ideology that simultaneously recognised the limitations of wage-earning yet celebrated opportunities for mobility. On the one hand, US class divisions were deep. Prosperous Americans pitied white-collar employees, albeit middle-class, because they were dependent on wages. Many working-class men resented humble men who imitated employers; the term white collar originated in the 1880s as 'white-collar stiffs', skilled workers' term for clerks who put on airs because they were privileged to dress like employers.[42] Yet Americans believed that US social distinctions should be fluid. Manly ideals were not entirely closed to enterprising white working-class men because apprentices in skilled crafts could become master craftsmen and entrepreneurs. New entrepreneurs represented modified manliness based not on inherited property or acquired skill but success in business, industry, or profession.[43]

Many manual workers considered themselves respectable in the middle-class sense, and emulated fashionable dress and demeanour in public, especially on Sundays. Detachable collars played a special role in working-class men's imitation of middle-class demeanour because collars were less expensive than other accoutrements of middle-class status – jackets, trousers, waistcoat, coat, and fine linen that required careful laundering to maintain a clean white appearance.[44] Until commercial laundries and indoor plumbing became common in the early twentieth century in urban areas, only the most prosperous families could afford servants necessary for daily washing, starching, and ironing white linen.[45] Detachable collars, originally signalling privilege, also required laundering, but a skilled worker who could afford a suit, coat, and shoes could purchase several collars and appear on Sundays as cleanly and respectable as a more privileged neighbour or employer.[46] In the US, unlike Europe, work clothes did not permanently define humble men's status.

The Arrow Man sold collars partly because he appeared at a moment of significant changes in the relationship between manliness and social class configurations. The demise of businesses during the severe depressions of the late nineteenth century, combined with increased consolidation and vertical and horizontal integration, convinced many middle-class families that older sources of male authority were less available to their sons. Corporate growth, the beginnings of separation of management from ownership, and scientific management produced more salaried positions. Many more young native-born white men whose fathers had looked forward to steering their economic course as entrepreneurs became white-collar workers earning a salary or wages. Increasingly, a salaried employee did not carry the stigma of a failed man. Some middle-class families still pitied white-collar workers, many of whom were still lowly office clerks, including female secretaries whose presence degraded male status and earnings.[47] But many salaried employees enjoyed new sources of authority in management and professional occupations; these did not require taking risks as entrepreneurs and sole responsibility for a firm but called for the ability to influence and work closely with others and, increasingly, for education. As middle-class families perceived that male authority no longer rested on independence from wages, and saw fewer distinctions between well-paid salaried employees and independent entrepreneurs, they abandoned the ideal of the autonomous, restrained, self-reliant, self-made man. Native-born middle-class men's manliness was also challenged by women's increased presence in public life; suffragists' stepped-up demands for political representation; immigrant men's increased control of local politics; and militant unions' efforts to control industry. The consumer culture's message of spending money and time to fulfil desires undermined older manly ideals of self-control, thrift, and restraint of emotions and sexuality.[48]

The new model for white middle-class men was less class-specific than before and more firmly rooted in American culture rather than European patterns of gentility. Many men, worried that men's refinement and women reformers' challenges weakened men and the middle class, rejected European gentility as effeminate and 'overcivilised'. The visual appearance of class distinctions between men of different backgrounds declined as white middle-class men began to perceive manly authority not only through a confident demeanour that implied internal strength but also through the outward appearance of physical prowess. Many took up spectator sports like boxing, formerly viewed as crude and unrefined when they were associated with working-class men, but increasingly considered respectable and part of American consumer culture.[49] Yet class distinctions did not vanish. White middle-class men continued to differentiate themselves from their working-class neighbours. The new man, educated and erudite, favoured a cultured, middle-class version of physical strength – physical activities already enjoyed by the affluent, like golf, tennis, bicycling, motoring, hiking, and camping – rather than the brawniness of those who did manual labour. A new term, masculinity, conveyed the new more homogeneous image of American men. Historian Gail Bederman notes that nineteenth-century manliness referred to specific attributes of the manly man, while masculine was defined as inherent in all men, usually in contrast to feminine.[50]

The Arrow Collar Man, a visual representation of the new man, captured these nuances.[51] Like the Arrow collar, he was not a radical departure; he was more physically imposing and muscular than the nineteenth-century ideal, but still classically handsome, evoking sculptures of ancient Greece, and refined, confident, and authoritative. In the informal, intimate setting depicted in Figure 1, the Arrow Man had a relaxed, easeful posture that in another context might signify subordination. Yet the room, a library, is a cultured middle-class setting, and one man reads a newspaper, a sign of concern with serious masculine matters. His shirts and collars and elegant trousers drape a tall, long-limbed body with broad chest and shoulders and muscular hands. His Arrow collar frames and draws attention to well-defined yet refined features: chiselled nose, deep-set eyes, bow lips, and a large jaw with cleft chin. His gaze is direct and reserved, not forbidding, but frank and often sensuous. Still a reserved gentleman, he is silent, cool, confident, and 'where necessary, tough'. Men like him, the white-collar man, replaced the older notion of advancement through independence with success in interpersonal relationships that involved performance, presentation of themselves to others through manners and appearance.[52]

The Arrow Man represented another new development – the mass production and systematic marketing of high-quality fashions to men of diverse backgrounds. In the mid to late nineteenth century, when the manly ideal was modelled on the English or continental gentleman, elite dress set the most visible trends, and custom tailors were undisputed arbiters of high fashion. At the turn of the twentieth century, manufacturers of ready-made garments competed with custom tailors by copying elite styles and Paris *haute couture*. But a more fundamental change was in the making. Manufacturers created their own designs that reflected popular American tastes. Custom tailors' reign waned and the centre of men's fashion trends shifted away from a small, privileged group to more diffuse sources. Retailers also actively influenced style and quality and with manufacturers used mass-circulation magazines and transportation networks to promote and distribute quality fashions nationally. Paradoxically, the ready-made clothing industry simultaneously provided an enormous variation of styles for men of differing tastes and needs and resulted in a more homogeneous look, with less clearly defined distinctions in the appearance of men of different classes and backgrounds. The new styles, part of emerging popular culture, like the Arrow Man himself, had an American flavour characterised by informality and reflecting visual images of popular personalities in the new mass media.[53]

After World War I, changes in men's fashions escalated. Trousers were softer and jackets had unpadded shoulders. High-buttoned waistcoats (but not vests) that pinched in the waist and covered most of the upper body vanished, leaving shirtfronts visible. Detachable shirtfronts became outmoded and neckwear took new forms. Cravats narrowed, evolving into bow ties or neckties (worn by the Arrow Men in Figure 2) that highlighted shirtfronts. Neckties (Figure 1) created a visible connection between shirtfront, neck, and face, and the neck no longer appeared isolated from the lower body. Because shirtfronts were now visible, no longer hidden by waistcoats, collars were less distinct from shirts and thus were a segment of a total image. Collars, cut low and shaped to fit the neck, were smaller, softer, and unstarched. Shirts became more significant outer garments, a means to display taste, status, and affluence, and were often made from soft fabrics such as linen or silk, featuring pale colours and patterns or pleats (Figure 1). After peaking in 1920, Cluett, Peabody's collar sales dropped off, plummeting during the Great Depression. As the firm began to rely on shirt sales for its profits, advertisements featured shirts as well as collars and the Arrow Man became the Arrow Shirt and Collar Man. Yet many men still wore detachable collars, and attached shirt collars were often white, their presence highlighted through colour contrast.[54]

Along with the blurring of the appearance of class distinctions came other social reconfigurations that changed the visual landscape. The nineteenth century's close-fitted fashions moved with the body, apparent only in a few places, and covered substantial inner layers that protected the body. The new more comfortable fashions constructed the body differently, encouraging more physical movement and relaxed postures; softly draped fabrics revealed hints of physicality within.[55] Many working-class men wore the new fashions, as did young affluent white men who engaged in active sports more than their fathers, taking on some aspects of manual workers' physical movements. Differences in the visual appearance of the generations sharpened, as some young men offended traditional sensibilities by ignoring older men's habit of donning distinct garments for daytime and evening, formal and informal situations, work and recreation. Along with more apparent physicality came shifts in the relationship between the private body and outward appearance. Detachable and attached shirt collars receded as signs of cleanliness and respectability partly because a cleanly body was less important as a sign of social standing: commercial laundries were more widely available and less expensive, many more people lived in homes with indoor plumbing and hot water, and more affluent households now boasted machines that washed clothing. Respectability, too, declined in importance, supplanted for many by the outward appearance of affluence, evidenced by possessions.[56]

Despite detachable collars' decline after World War I, the Arrow Man maintained his cachet throughout the 1920s, and his collar took on new and potent meanings.[57] Americans' lives had changed dramatically. Mass media, radio and illustrated magazines, the telephone, and railroads linked far-flung regions in North America. Middle-class consumers enjoyed innovations like indoor plumbing, appliances, and ready-made products that eased many of life's tasks and added pleasures promised by visual media, advertising and films. The line, 'You're the top, you're an Arrow Collar', equating Arrow collars with the most admired, the apex, evokes American sense of being the best, superior in material prosperity to Europe, which was still recovering from World War I. The name Arrow itself resonated with 1920s popular culture and American identity. The Arrow brand, which included diverse styles of collars as well as shirts, was not invented by the advertising agency, but had resulted from an 1889 merger that brought a new, aggressive salesman, Frederick Peabody, who carried with him the Arrow trademark.[58] Arrow was a fortuitous name because it conveyed American-ness – distinct from European cultured gentility – the still relatively untamed and uncivilised American West, and the authority, directness, and confidence of the New Man. In these decades, American-ness was envisioned as masculine, typified by Teddy Roosevelt's mythic rugged individuality, informality mixed with confidence and authority, and identification with untamed nature. Theodore, the photographer's model in *Helen of Troy, New York*, links rugged masculinity with the elegant, urbane Arrow Man.[59] In the 1920s some writers captured in literary terms the significance of American popular culture by linking the Arrow Man and his collar with the American Man, consumerism, and the management of personal appearance. The contrast between the culturally refined European and materially successful American was evoked by an avant-garde journal that reported in 1921 on a poor French immigrant poet who converted to American-ness by changing his external appearance. He took a job, but retreated to his Village basement apartment and grew a beard to protest against the clean-shaven faces and white collars surrounding him. Soon, however, he understood, shaved his whiskers, 'bought an Arrow collar', and 'became like an American'.[60] F. Scott Fitzgerald's 1929 story 'The Last of the Belles' linked American manhood with Leyendecker's images by describing an ideal man as having a 'Leyendecker forelock'.[61] e. e. cummings folded into the text of his 1922 poem 'Poem, Or Beauty Hurts Mr. Vinal' fragments of the song 'Of Thee I Sing' and images and phrases from advertising art, including Arrow collars, now integral to the visual landscape and American popular culture.[62]

Yet the Arrow Man and his collar did not represent unmitigated newness. Although his appearance changed little from 1907 to 1931, the transformed meaning of the garment he advertised retained references to its history. Men's collars, long associated with elites, were detached from shirts in the 1820s and came to symbolise American middle-class respectability by the mid nineteenth century. As their use declined in the early twentieth century, detachable collars gave their name to a new occupation with a specifically American connotation, the admiration of others and gratification of desire through consumerism. Nor was the Arrow Man's appeal confined to the middle class. The Arrow Man represented the stylish clothing and sophisticated surroundings available to affluent white urbanites as well as a relatively new type, the white-collar man, a salaried employee who measures manliness in terms of 'ascent through the bureaucracy'.[63] The Arrow Man, an elite representation of this new group, resonated across class and ethnic lines because he was an idealised image for those who took the opportunity ideology seriously. They hoped to ascend through bureaucracy to higher, rarefied levels or, like the young men in *Helen of Troy, New York*, to become captains of industry in big business. Over three decades, along with Americans' daily lives, shirt collars had been transformed in appearance, meaning, and function, carrying messages of gendered self-management of appearance and public performance into the early twentieth century. The transformation of multiple dimensions of the visual landscape, personal appearance and the body, advertising, and the new media, resulted in subtle and not so subtle reconfigurations of social class, gender ideologies, space and time, and generation. The Arrow Man, a potent visual image, and the Arrow collar, a material object familiar in multiple dimensions of daily existence, carried non-verbal messages that linked the imagined past with the representations of the present.

Notes

Thanks to those who commented on this essay: Barbara Burman, Shani D'Cruze, Frances Rothstein, Amy Gilman Srebnick, Wilbur R. Miller, and an anonymous *Gender & History* reader. I am grateful for permission to use ideas from my essay 'Collars and Consumers: Changing Images of American Manliness and Business', in *Beauty and Business: Commerce, Gender, and Culture in Modern America*, ed. Phillip Scranton (Routledge, 2001), pp. 87–108, and to the staff of the Rensselaer County Historical Society, especially Kathryn Sheehan.

1. *Helen of Troy, New York*, written by George S. Kaufman and Marc Connelly, music and lyrics by Bert Kalmar and Harry Rudy, opened on Broadway in June 1923. A video recording, produced by Medicine Show Theatre Ensemble (September 1986), may be viewed at the Performing Arts Library, New York Public Library, New York City. See also 'Mill Girl Heroine in New Dance Show, "Helen of Troy, N.Y." gets a Whirlwind Start at the Selwyn Theatre', *New York Times*, 20 June 1923.
2. For claims that a man who wore a cotton collar was a spineless 'slouch', see Carole Turbin, 'Collars and Consumers: Changing Images of American Manliness and Business', in *Beauty and Business*, ed. Phillip Scranton (Routledge, 2001), pp. 98–100. James Morske notes that cotton, although less costly and easier to care for than linen, was viewed as a 'debasement' of a high-status product. (Morske, 'And It All Began with One Woman', and Ken Johnson, 'Personal Investments: C. Leyendecker and the Arrow Collar Man', in *The Arrow Man: Collar City Chic*, a brochure for an exhibition at Russell Sage College Gallery, Troy, New York, 1 September–10 October 1987, especially p. 8.)

3. www.coleporter.org
4. Michael Schau, *J. C. Leyendecker* (Watson-Guptill, 1974), pp. 28–30; Richard Martin, 'J. C. Leyendecker and the Homoerotic Invention of Men's Fashion Icons, 1910–1930', *Prospects*, 21 (1996), pp. 453–70; Michele H. Bogart, *Artists, Advertising, and the Borders of Art* (University of Chicago Press, 1995), pp. 209–10, 229–30.
5. Christopher Breward, *The Hidden Consumer: Masculinities, Fashion, and City Life, 1860–1914* (Manchester University Press, 1999), ch. 1.
6. Karen Haltunnen, *Confidence Men and Painted Women: A Study of Middle Class Cultures in America, 1830–1870* (Yale University Press, 1982), especially ch. 3.
7. Christopher Breward, *The Culture of Fashion: A New History of Fashionable Dress* (Manchester University Press, 1995), pp. 182–4; Kathy Peiss, *Hope in a Jar: The Making of America's Beauty Culture* (Metropolitan Books, 1998), pp. 45–50; William Leach, 'Strategists of Display and the Production of Desire', in *Consuming Visions: Accumulation and Display of Goods in America, 1880–1920*, ed. Simon Bronner (W. W. Norton, 1989) pp. 99–103; Susan Porter Benson, *Counter Cultures: Saleswomen, Managers, and Customers in American Department Stores, 1890–1940* (University of Illinois Press, 1986), ch. 1.
8. Erving Goffman, *The Presentation of Self in Everyday Life* (Allen Lane, 1969); Georg Simmel, 'On Individuality and Social Forms', *Selected Writings* (Chicago University Press, 1971).
9. Bogart, *Artists*, 207–12; Jackson Lears, *Fables of Abundance: A Cultural History of Advertising in America* (Basic Books, 1994), pp. 295–6, 300–301; Rob Schorman, 'The Truth about Good Goods: Clothing, Advertising and the Representation of Cultural Values at the End of the Nineteenth Century', *American Studies*, 57 (1996), pp. 33–49; Ellen Gruber Garvey, *The Adman in the Parlor: Magazines and the Gendering of Consumer Culture, 1880s to 1910s* (Oxford University Press, 1996), pp. 102–5.
10. Bogart, *Artists*, ch. 5.
11. Norman Rockwell, *My Adventures as an Illustrator* (Doubleday, 1960), pp. 161–74.
12. 'Cluett, Peabody', *Fortune Magazine*, February 1937, p. 119; Morske, 'And It All Began with One Woman', p. 8; Schorman, 'Truth about Good Goods', p. 23.
13. Schau, *J. C. Leyendecker*, p. 121; Emmanuel Cooper, *The Sexual Perspective: Homosexuality and Art in the Last 100 Years in the West* (Routledge, 1986), pp. 132–3.
14. Breward, *Culture*, pp. 130; Leach, 'Strategists', pp. 99–132; Willian Leach, *Land of Desire: Merchants, Power, and the Rise of a New Culture* (Pantheon, 1993); Stephen Fox, 'The Origins of American Advertising: The Age of Lasker', *Adweek*, June 1984, pp. 26–35.
15. Rockwell, *My Adventures*, 220, 167; Schau, *J. C. Leyendecker*, pp. 30, 35.
16. Most writers on the Arrow Man cite his extraordinary fan mail, but none claim to have seen it (Martin, 'J. C. Leyendecker', p. 453). Michael Murphy ('Arrow's Eros?: Homoeroticism and J. C. Leyendecker's Arrow Collar Ads', unpublished manuscript, p. 6) cites a note in the Cluett, Peabody archives describing fan mail and comparing it to that of Valentino.
17. Thanks to Michele Bogart who pointed this out to me. Rockwell includes illustrations (Rockwell, *My Adventures*, pp. 162–5) that demonstrate Leyendecker's influence.
18. Bogart, *Artists*, pp. 51–7.
19. Peiss, *Hope in a Jar*, pp. 204–10.
20. Kathy Peiss, 'On Beauty … and the History of Business', Scranton (ed.), *Beauty and Business*, pp. 10–12; Peiss, *Hope in a Jar*, pp. 84–8; Susan Bordo, *The Male Body: A New Look at Men in Public and Private* (Farrar, Straus and Giroux, 1999), pp. 200–214.
21. Breward, *Hidden Consumer*, ch. 4; Benson, *Counter Cultures*; John Robert Harvey, *Men in Black* (Reaktion, 1995), p. 48.
22. See, for example, Christine Stansell, 'Women, Children, and the Uses of the Streets', in *Unequal Sisters*, ed. Ellen C. Dubois and Vicki Ruiz (Routledge, 1990), pp. 92–3.
23. Kathy Peiss, keynote address, Beauty and Business Conference, Hagley Museum and Library, March 1999; Bordo, *Male Body*, pp. 202–3; Hollander, *Sex and Suits*, p. 69.
24. Richard Martin, 'Gay Blades, Homoerotic Content in J. C. Leyendecker's Gillette Advertising Images', *Journal of American Culture*, 18 (1995), pp. 75–82; Cooper, *Sexual Perspective*,

pp. xv–xxi, 132–3; David B. Boyce, 'Coded Desire in 1920s Advertising', *The Gay and Lesbian Review* 7 (2000), pp. 26–30, 66; Murphy, 'Arrow's Eros?'; George Chauncey, Jr, *Gay New York: Gender, Urban Culture, and the Making of the Gay Male World, 1890–1940* (Basic Books, 1994).

25. Rockwell, *My Adventures*, pp 161–74.
26. Chauncey, *Gay New York*, pp. 12–14, 16–17, 21.
27. Martin, 'Gay Blades', pp. 75–82.
28. Carole Turbin, *Working Women of Collar City* (University of Illinois Press, 1992), ch. 1; G. Vigarello, *Concepts of Cleanliness* (Cambridge University Press, 1988), pp. 63–4.
29. Doriece Colle, *Collars, Stocks, Cravats* (White Lions Publishers Ltd, 1972), pp. 75–184; O. E. Schoeffler and William Gale, *Esquire's Encyclopedia of Twentieth Century Men's Fashions* (McGraw Hill, 1973), pp. 229–31; Christobel Williams-Mitchell, *Dressed for the Job: The Story of Occupational Costume* (Dorset, Poole, 1982), pp. 102–3.
30. Turbin, *Working Women*, 26–8.
31. Richard Bushman, *The Refinement of America* (Vintage Books, 1993), pp. 7–9; Wendy Gamber, *Female Economy: The Millinery and Dressmaking Trades, 1860–1930* (University of Illinois Press, 1997), pp. 10–11; Grant McCracken, *Culture and Consumption* (University of Indiana Press, 1990), ch. 1.
32. Turbin, 'Collars and Consumers', p. 89; Kidwell and Christman, *Suiting*, p. 20.
33. Turbin, 'Collars and Consumers', p. 89; Colle, *Collars*, pp. 11–28, 189–92; Schoeffler and Gale, *Esquire's Encyclopedia*, pp. 198–9; Arthur James Weise, *The City of Troy and Its Vicinity* (Edward Green, 1886), pp. 271–3; Horace Greeley, et al., *Great Industries of the United States* (J. B. Burr and Hyde, 1873), pp. 607–17, 1144–8.
34. Turbin, 'Collars and Consumers', p. 89; Gail Bederman, *Manliness & Civilization: A Cultural History of Gender and Race in the United States, 1880–1917* (University of Chicago Press, 1995), ch. 1, and pp. 60–67. E. Anthony Rotundo, 'Learning about Manhood: Gender Ideals and the Middle-Class Family in Nineteenth-Century America', *Manliness and Morality*, ed. J. A. Mangan and James Walvin (St Martin's Press), pp. 35–51.
35. Bederman, *Manliness*, pp. 60–67; Rotundo, 'Learning about Manhood', pp. 35–51.
36. Phillippe Perrot, *Fashioning the Bourgeoisie: A History of Clothing in the Nineteenth Century* (Princeton University Press, 1994), pp. 136–7; Bushman, *Refinement*, pp. 65–9; Herman Roodenburg, 'How to Sit, Stand or Walk: Towards a Historical Anthropology of Dutch Paintings and Prints', *Looking at Dutch Art*, ed. Wayne Franits (Cambridge University Press, 1997).
37. Peiss, *Hope in a Jar*, pp. 3–9; Susan Ingalls Lewis, 'Beyond Horatio Alger: Breaking Through Gendered Assumptions about Business "Success" in Mid-Nineteenth-Century America', *Business and Economic History*, 24 (1995), pp. 97–105; Judith L. Goldstein, 'The Female Aesthetic Community', *Poetics Today*, 14 (1993), pp. 143–63.
38. Turbin, 'Collars and Consumers', pp. 89–91; Williams-Mitchell, *Dressed*, pp. 102–3.
39. Harvey, *Men in Black*, p. 48.
40. Turbin, 'Collars and Consumers', p. 90.
41. Elliott J. Gorn, *The Manly Art: Bare Knuckle Prize Fighting in America* (Cornell University Press, 1986), pp. 132–3; Turbin, 'Collars and Consumers', p. 91.
42. Jurgen Kocka, *White Collar Workers in America, 1890–1940: A Social Political History in International Perspective* (Sage Publications, 1980), p. 88.
43. Michael Kimmel, *Manhood in America: A Cultural History* (Free Press, 1995), pp. 16–19, 26–7.
44. Kidwell and Christman, *Suiting*, p. 121.
45. Ruth Schwartz Cowan, 'The "Industrial Revolution" in the Home: Household Technology and Social Change in the Twentieth Century', *Material Culture Studies in America*, ed. Thomas J. Schlereth (American Association for State and Local History, Nashville, TN, 1982), pp. 222–36.
46. Kidwell and Christman, *Suiting*, p. 21.
47. For a humorous picture of white-collar woes, see 'White Collary', *New Republic*, 1 April 1925, pp. 154–5.
48. Bederman, *Manliness*, pp. 12–41; Kimmel, *Manhood*, ch. 4.

49. Roy Rosenzweig, *Eight Hours for What We Will: Workers and Leisure in an Industrial City, 1870–1920* (Cambridge University Press, 1983).
50. Bederman, *Manliness*, pp. 17–20.
51. Eric Segal, 'Norman Rockwell and the Fashioning of American Masculinity', *Art Bulletin*, 77 (1996), pp. 633–46, and Murphy, 'Arrow's Eros?'
52. Murphy, 'Arrow's Eros?'; 'Cluett, Peabody', *Fortune Magazine*, p. 120; Morske, 'And It All Began with One Woman', p. 8 (quote). See Erving Goffman, *Gender Advertisements* (Harper Colophon Books, 1979), 40–42, on deference and physical movements; C. W. Mills, *White Collar: The American Middle Classes* (Oxford, 1950), and William H. Whyte, *The Organization Man* (Penguin Books, 1960), on personality and appearance in white-collar work; and Clyde Griffen, 'Reconstructing Masculinity from the Evangelical Revival to the Waning of Progressivism: A Speculative Synthesis', in *Meanings for Manhood: Constructions for Manhood in Victorian America*, ed. M. C. Carnes and C. Griffen (University of Chicago Press, 1990), p. 194, on masculinity and bureaucratisation.
53. Phillip Scranton, 'The Transition from Custom to Ready-to-Wear Clothing in Philadelphia, 1890–1930', *Textile History*, 25 (1994), 246–58; Nancy Green, *Ready-to-Wear, Ready-to-Work: A Century of Industry and Immigrants in Paris and New York* (Duke University Press, 1997), p. 39; Gamber, *Female Economy*, ch. 5 and pp. 127–56, 216; *Clothing Gazette*, January 1901, p. 20, November 1901, pp. 29–38.
54. Turbin, 'Collars and Consumers', pp. 99–100; Turbin, *Working Women*, ch. 1; 'Cluett, Peabody', *Fortune Magazine*, pp. 113–16, 122; Max Phillips, 'An Unusual Layout Simplifies a Complicated Advertising Story: How the Van Heusen Checkerboard Came into Being', *Printers' Ink: A Journal for Advertising*, 125 (1923), pp. 33–6, see annual reports for Cluett, Peabody, & Co., Inc., 1917–1933 (Rensselaer County History Society, Cluett Collection); 'Arrow Advertising: A Study in Consistency', cover story of *Tide*, 13 April 1951, pp. 44–5.
55. Hollander, *Sex and Suits*, pp. 90–91; Sarah A. Gordon, 'Any Desired Length: Negotiating Gender Through Sports Clothing, 1870–1925', in Scranton (ed.), *Beauty and Business*, pp. 24–51.
56. Turbin, 'Collars and Consumers', pp. 100–101; Susan Strasser, *Never Done* (Pantheon, 1982), pp. 110–24.
57. Martin, 'J. C. Leyendecker', p. 454.
58. 'Cluett, Peabody', *Fortune Magazine*, p. 119.
59. In England, Arrow Collars typified emerging American clothing styles. See Tamsin Blanchard, 'Classic Tale from Troy: Fashion', *Independent* (London), 24 February 1996, p. 22.
60. Lears, *Fables*, pp. 303–4.
61. Cooper, *Sexual Perspective*, p. 132.
62. Cited in Lynn Dumenil, *Modern Temper: American Culture and Society in the 1920s* (Hill and Wang, 1995), p. 157.

    take it from me kiddo
    believe me
    my country, 'tis of
    you, land of the Cluett
    Shirt Boston Berber and Spearmint
    Girl with the Wrigley Eyes (of you
    land of the Arrow Ide
    and Earl & Wilson
    Collars) of you i
    sing: land of Abraham Lincoln and Lydia Pinkham,
    land above all of Just Add Hot Water and Serve –
    from every B.V.D.

    let freedom ring ...
63. Quoted in Griffen, 'Reconstructing Masculinity', p. 194.

7

Erotic Modesty: (Ad)dressing Female Sexuality and Propriety in Open and Closed Drawers, USA, 1800–1930

Jill Fields

The 1928 silent film *Our Dancing Daughters* opens with a shot of a nude female metal figurine shaped to capture a dramatic moment mid-dance. The shot dissolves as a pair of bowed white satin shoes, placed in front of a three-sided mirror, fade in and replace the figurine. White-stockinged legs, visible from mid-knee down, slowly materialise and fill the shoes. They launch into a frenetic dance, with kicking feet turning to face the mirror. The dancing ceases briefly as hands lower into view a white pair of short, closed-crotch silk drawers with a leg ruffle. These modern underpants are donned leg by leg. After a few more kicks of the heels, the scene abruptly cuts to a shot from the waist down. Now we see that the drawers are worn underneath a swinging fringed skirt. The dancing continues as a silk wraparound underskirt is placed between the fringe and the drawers to complete the ensemble, but not before hands deftly move the fringe aside to allow an unhindered look at the underwear and the legs beneath them. The final dissolve in this mirror scene reveals the full figure of Diana (top-billed actress Joan Crawford) in lavish surroundings. Now fully dressed, Diana makes some final adjustments to her clothing and hair, practises a sultry look and deeply admires her reflected image.[1]

The cinematic focus on legs in this opening scene of *Our Dancing Daughters* is visual evidence of the notorious 1920s fascination with the newly unfettered legs of women. However, the cultural preoccupation with women's legs also extends to what does or does not lie between them. This interest in legs and crotch is surely erotically fuelled. But it is also shaped, as is the erotic content itself, by social constructions of gender that prescribe distinct behaviours for men and women, and regulate access to power. These gendered distinctions are entirely apparent in the arena of dress where, in western culture since the late Middle Ages, men have worn trousers and women dresses.

This component of the gendered division of clothing characterised underwear until the nineteenth century, when women began to wear drawers constructed of two leg tubes attached to a waistband. Previously only worn by men for warmth and to protect outer garments from wearing effects of direct bodily contact, the name derived from the act of 'drawing them on'. For women to engage in this masculine act and appropriate their new garment's name from the lexicon of menswear blurred what had been a clearly marked gender boundary. Materially distinguishing female from male drawers kept that reworked boundary from shifting further. Thus, the long-held association of divided garments or trousers with masculinity, and undivided garments or skirts with femininity, influenced the design, use and implications of women's drawers. Feminised by fabric, ornamentation and open-crotch construction, the virtually separate leg sections of nineteenth-century drawers were joined only at the waistband. The open seam extended below the waistband, front to back, potentially exposing inner thighs as well as genitals. Such distinctions, and the contention that drawers advanced female modesty by adding another layer of covering to women's bodies, mediated the problematic cross-dressing implications of drawers for women[2] (Figure 1).

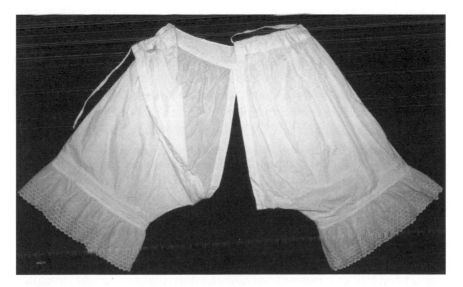

Figure 1: Early twentieth-century open-crotch drawers. Artefact 982.183.1. Courtesy Royal Ontario Museum.

Responding to a range of constraints and desires, the new female garment's design upheld gender distinctions regulated by dress that a divided
garment for women challenged, and by mid century open drawers were a
required component of respectable middle-class women's dress in the US
and industrialising western Europe. Yet despite drawers' integration within
modest Victorian female dress, open-crotch drawers also held erotic meanings, and, when Victorian ideological frameworks crumbled in the twentieth
century, became part of the struggle to establish modern boundaries of
women's sexual propriety. Most importantly, the transition from open to
closed drawers demonstrates how the duality of modesty and eroticism
operates in a shifting dialectic responsive to and productive of changes in
understanding gender difference and sexuality.

My study combines two approaches to women's fashion and sexuality.
Costume historians, who have documented changes in apparel through
analysis of costume artefacts' design, construction and visual culture,
generally hold two premises: changes in outerwear prompted the shift to
closed drawers, and open design facilitated elimination of bodily waste
made difficult because of corsets and lack of indoor plumbing. Yet they
have left the sexual meanings of open drawers unexamined, despite the
psychoanalytic theories of fashion by scholars like J. C. Flugel as early
as 1930, and more recently Valerie Steele, that explain changes in dress
styles as the result of women's desires to be sexually attractive to men.[3] In
contrast, women's historians explore sexuality by analysing texts such as
diaries, advice books, medical and legal discourses, and works of popular
culture, revealing the relationship between nineteenth-century discourses
that constructed white, middle-class women as sexually passionless, and
actual practices of men and women. As Victorian sensibilities declined,
women claimed the right to sexual desire and pleasure; female sexual
expression became more respectable but at the same time pathologised
and commercialised. Yet women's sexual identities varied by class and
race. Discourse, public policy and private censure set boundaries of middle-
class female sexual propriety by attributing erotic proclivities to female
bodies neither white nor middle class, and insisting that women with an
unseemly interest in sexuality were unworthy of respect, status and social
support accorded to white, middle-class women.[4]

Combining elements of these two sets of historical literature reveals
drawers' critical role in constructing a feminine sexuality both erotic and
modest. I argue that erotic meanings of open drawers, particularly the
ready sexual access to female bodies they provide, also served social functions. For the functions of dress, despite clothing's attachment to the body,
are not 'natural' or removed from human intervention and social structures.
Indeed, careful consideration of social understandings *about* functions of
dress related to the body reveals uninterrogated biological explanations

underlying culturally constructed gender differences, and how culture reinforces seemingly irrefutable proof of essential, biologically based gender difference. The apparently functional aspects of open drawers underscore these meanings by referencing women's biological difference, thus constructing women's bodies as different on a daily basis.[5]

Divided undergarments became part of women's fashionable dress during the early nineteenth century, a period of heightened gender differentiation, when bourgeois values replaced those of deposed aristocracies and undermined communal pre-industrial customs throughout the West. Distinctive male and female dress represented the increasingly disparate daily lives of middle-class men and women, as capricious or extravagant fashion became gendered as feminine and keyed to the newly privatised woman's sphere.[6] This was especially true for the middle class, which sought legitimacy by distinguishing itself through manners and morals from those above and below.[7] While this essay focuses on the US, gendered social relations and culture of industrialisation and class formation crossed national boundaries. US historians borrow the English term Victorian to underscore parallel moral concerns, social responses, political and economic structures, and class, race and gender identities taking shape in both countries, as well as France. While national distinctions and regional variations clearly remain significant in all areas, similarities in women's fashions provide material and visual evidence of comparable cultural concerns.[8]

Differences between nineteenth-century girls' and women's dress reveal the sexual meanings of crotch construction in women's drawers. Young girls were among the earliest members of the middle classes to wear drawers in the late eighteenth century, a transitional time in attitudes toward childhood and the construction of new distinctions based on age. The previous custom of dressing young children in smaller versions of adult clothes, maintained among working-class and poor families who required their children's labour for survival, was superseded in middle- and upper-class families by dressing girls and boys in similar clothing up to age 5. While some subtle differences in boys' and girls' dress remained, small boys as well as girls wore dresses. Gender distinction in dress was instituted as children grew. Drawers for older boys and girls transformed into short breeches and pantalettes. A rite of passage in the transition to adulthood for boys became one of donning long trousers; for girls of abandoning pantalettes.[9]

Visible drawers worn by most girls under short dresses had a closed crotch, distinct from the drawers their mothers and elder sisters were beginning to wear in the nineteenth century's early decades. This distinctive clothing encouraged girls' active play, clarifying the message of young women's shift to wearing open drawers, corsets, and other layers of underclothing. Putting on adult apparel restricted movement, and evokes 'coming-of-age' rituals that in many cultures assign the status of potential sexual partner. Donning open-crotch drawers was a signal, if not reality, to a young woman and the men in her community that she was sexually available.[10]

Drawers worn by young women during the nineteenth century's first decades extended below the dress hem in order to display their lace trim. While the exposure of girls' drawers below dress hems was condoned, this practice among young women proved controversial for moral reasons, and by 1820 drawer length receded so they were hidden when a woman was fully dressed. By the 1840s, open-crotch drawers, made of lightweight fabrics such as muslins and lawns, were worn by most women of the middle classes. Several factors coalesced to make wearing drawers possible, and subsequently required, for women during this period, including fashion's imperative of continually locating and seizing upon innovative elements. Innovations in middle-class women's fashions derived from sports, the stage, children's wear, men's wear, and working-class communities. The widespread acceptance of drawers as fashionable attire seems all too inevitable in that drawers were worn within all these arenas.[11]

When drawers were first introduced, critics characterised them as both modest and immodest because they concealed and revealed the charms of women's legs and ankles. Some male commentators welcomed erotic feelings aroused by the attention drawers brought to previously hidden lower limbs, while others mourned the loss behind yet another layer of clothing of the potential view of naked flesh afforded when long skirts were raised to avoid a dangerous step. This ambiguity suggests that the playful, decorative and erotic suggestion of drawers was an 'inoculation' for the new regime of rigidly enforced gender and sex differences. In other words, women could be allowed to wear a divided garment if feminised and sexualised, and that feminisation of the garment reassured that 'real' trousers were worn by 'real' men.[12]

The outrage fomented when drawers again briefly extended below dress hemlines in the 1850s points to social forces that perpetuated the gendered bifurcation of dress that a divided garment for women blurred. In that decade skirts took on an increasingly broad bell shape, achieved through many heavy layers of petticoats suspended from a tightly corseted waist.[13] Critics of this attire who pointed to discomfort and potential health risks or dangers of women's preoccupation with fashion, ranging from financial bankruptcy and disruption of the family to descent into prostitution and decay of the nation's moral fabric, sought to curb women's appetites with appeals to modesty and simplicity. Less conservative health reformers suggested slight modifications, such as a shorter length to avoid gathering dirt and dampness against the skin, and admonished against tight-lacing corsets. Wearing open-crotch drawers was also considered a preventive health measure, since it exposed the genitals to wholesome benefits of air.[14]

The most radical mid-century proposal for women's dress reform promoted the innovative design later known as the Bloomer Costume, that consisted of a mid-calf-length dress worn with trousers covering the legs to the ankles. Though few actually advocated and wore the short-lived Bloomer, when the costume appeared in 1851 it generated an enormous amount of published debate, ridicule and fear, exemplifying how dress serves as a powerful regulator of gender difference. Much negative attention focused on the trousers, and on the costume's links with woman's rights advocates, as many prominent activists wore the Bloomer, especially to movement events.[15] An 1851 *New York Times* editorial drew on explicitly political rhetoric to articulate fears of women in trousers, affirming that the right to wear them was constitutionally guaranteed, as with political rights, only to men. The editorial characterises women wearing masculine insignias as 'anti-masculine', rejecting femininity, and gender difference itself.[16] Magazines caricatured women dressed in Bloomer Costumes as smoking cigars and proposing marriage to timid men, or reported that prostitutes favoured the outfit.[17]

Critics of the Bloomer charged that revealing ankles was immodest and improperly erotic, and that the descriptive term 'Turkish' applied to the trousers rendered the outfit heathen. This condemnation occurred despite the fad for Turkish objects and motifs at this time, demonstrating the multiple meanings orientalist descriptors evoked, especially as some female reformers found inspiration in the dress, and stronger property protections, accorded Turkish women. The discursive strategy of linking transgressive groups, such as cross-dressers, prostitutes, colonised others, and feminists, undermined challenges to dominant authority. A middle-class woman's sexual reputation was often her only source of power in negotiating her material well-being and social standing through marriage. Thus, identifying certain acts as damaging to a woman's reputation was a persuasive means of regulating behaviour; that is, constraining her from wearing the Bloomer Costume and articulating women's rights causes they symbolised. The regulation of women in trousers was essential to defusing political claims by subjugated persons through their pathological categorisation as 'hysterical', 'deviant' or 'criminal'.[18]

The fashion industry's response to the cry for reform was the cage crinoline of the mid 1850s. It obviated the need for many heavy petticoats to produce the broadly extended skirt shape. An 1858 *Godey's Lady's Book* advertisement for Douglas & Sherwood's New Expansion Skirt noted that, 'The steel springs ... can be wound around the finger like a piece of tape, and will immediately resume their place upon being dropped ... The expansion is all in front, so that the wearer can contract or expand the skirt, without disrobing, at pleasure ... Their lightness recommends them.' Women of all classes, including agricultural and factory workers, desired to lighten their load yet remain fashionable. Deborah Gray White reports that young enslaved women wore hoops made from grapevines under special occasion and Sunday dresses. Others, like female home-steaders in the West, faced the arduous physical demands of rural life by abandoning their hoop skirts. Freed from fashionable requirements, some women took the further step of wearing a form of the Bloomer, renamed American Dress, for easier accomplishment of their many daily tasks.[19]

Women wearing hoops were no longer required to drag around pounds of clothing, but their attention was now directed to the constant adjust-ment the awkward crinoline demanded. Despite subsequent innovations, like the collapsible cage that permitted a woman to sit or to board a coach, the crinoline's stiff swinging movement regularly exposed the legs. This phenomenon solidified the consideration of drawers as a compulsory undergarment worn to protect modesty rather than to encourage eroticism. Yet because drawers had an open crotch, if a woman lost her balance completely, her lower legs might remain covered but her upper thighs and genitals might not. Despite this much remarked upon potential exposure – whether of naked flesh, or of legs and crotch shielded by fabric – a woman dressed in open drawers and crinoline conformed to contem-porary notions of propriety and modesty.[20]

The growing volume of the bell-shaped skirt silhouette from the 1840s to the 1860s stimulated further male interest in viewing the lower female body region concealed within the increasing space created by layers of petticoats and hoops. The changing fashions in drawers encouraged such interest, though drawers also protected bare legs from the direct gaze of men as long as the wearer remained upright. Two images, both titled 'A Street View' and published in the New York City newspaper the *Weekly Rake* in the 1840s, illustrate men's fascination with viewing nether regions hidden beneath women's long and full skirts. One illustration (Figure 2) shows a woman on a street who has just fallen backward and landed on her bottom, exposing legs spread apart above her in the air. She wears both stockings and drawers, but a well-dressed man standing above her gapes in horror directly between her legs. The second image shows a woman pausing to tie her shoelace on a sidewalk. To do so, she perches her leg on a doorway step, unaware that a man hides below a sidewalk grating peering up her skirt. The folds in her skirt mimic the shape of her thigh and buttocks, alluding to the presence of a powerful male gaze, held by even those men not so advantageously located, that penetrates clothing's concealment of female flesh.[21]

Figure 2: 'A Street View', *The Weekly Rake* (1842). Courtesy, American Antiquarian Society.

Changes in drawers in the 1850s and 1860s, when men's periodicals published similar images of upended women in hoops exposed to male gazes, reflected the growing potential for exposure as an event to protect oneself against and an opportunity for eliciting attraction.[77] Characterised as 'severely plain' in the 1840s, under the swinging crinolines of the next decades drawers became more ornamental. By the end of the 1860s the widespread application of frills and insertion of trim were becoming integral to the very definition of fine undergarments. A fashion magazine noted, 'If drawers are worn they should be trimmed with frills or insertion.'

Chemical dyes for undergarments, introduced in the 1860s, promoted the novelty of coloured drawers, beginning with hues of solferino red and magenta, which the ready-made clothing industry made more widely available. These frilly, richly coloured decorative drawers, designed, constructed, sold and worn with the understanding that they were meant to be seen, clarify the relationship between concealment and display essential to the dialectic of modesty and eroticism. Modesty produces eroticism not only through concealment that attracts attention to the cloaked area of the body, but also through tension generated by adhering to the discourse of modest concealment and the practice of elaborate decorative display.[23]

After the collapse of the crinoline, the fashionable silhouette of the next two decades became slimmer and straighter, except for bulges produced by the changing placement and shape of the bustle. The notorious tight-lacing of 1870s and 1880s corsets may have been caused partly by the somewhat straighter skirt shape, as a wide skirt contributes to the illusion of a smaller waistline. In this period, fine drawers were made of silk and trimmed with lace and hand embroidery, though health and hygiene enthusiasts vaunted merits of wool undergarments. Drawers in general maintained their voluminous size, contributing to the skirt's bulky outward appearance.[24]

In the nineteenth century's final decades, women's increased opportunities for education, waged work, and public activities refigured the expression and performance of modesty and eroticism in dress. The bicycle, which increased women's opportunities for spatial mobility, profoundly influenced women's relationship to divided garments. Women were granted permission to wear trousers while cycling, and in a long-in-coming victory for feminist dress reform, cycling trousers were called bloomers, surprisingly referred to in an 1894 cover illustration caption from *Harper's Bazaar*, as 'Turkish trousers'. Yet *Harper's* also names the ensemble 'Bicycle Dress', noting that 'Turkish trousers, long and ample, are made of such fullness that when standing upright the division is obliterated'. Concern about the meaning of divided garments for women shaped their design. Though cycling bloomers did not reveal the shape of legs underneath them, they inspired stares, taunts, and suggestive magazine drawings,[25] such as those found in the *Police Gazette*. One purported to depict a Chicago man who 'lashes female bicyclists who happen to wear bifurcated skirts', and another illustrated an 1895 incident when a church organist in Mason, Ohio, caused a 'sensation' because she arrived late in 'red bicycle clothes', possibly 'breaking up the congregation'. Later that year, the *Police Gazette* noted possibilities for financial exploitation of such sensational views. A San Francisco entrepreneur achieved 'a howling success' after opening 'The Bloomer Café' with 'four of the handsomest and best shaped women he could find'. A drawing portrays the bustling restaurant filled with men whose eyes happily inspect legs and buttocks of comely 'waiter girls' dressed in bloomers.[26]

While cycling bloomers declined in the early twentieth century because of public pressure, young women wore an outfit often named bloomers in the growing number of physical education classes at women's colleges and educational institutions.[27] These new athletic and intellectual opportunities for women coincided with the full flowering of luxurious, elaborate, and self-consciously erotic undergarments. The decorative ruffles, lace and flounces characterising women's underclothes from the late 1890s to about 1908 are associated with the reign of King Edward VII. Known at home and abroad for his interest in fashion and love of sensual pleasures, his reign marked the formal end of Victorian rule. Previous fashions in dress and morality would soon seem archaic, and this transition from the Victorian aesthetic led to frivolity in fashion.[28]

The image of women in frilly, erotic and expensive Edwardian lingerie contrasts sharply with the serious and purposeful Progressive-era New Woman reformer and the athletic Gibson Girl, marking the origins of the twentieth century's split between the 'pretty' and the 'practical'. These words pop up frequently in lingerie advertisements that attempt to re-solve this contradictory choice by acknowledging difficulties experienced by women selecting garments within a system that defines, constructs and represents femininity in opposition to the functional. The possibility of wearing erotic undergarments beneath serious, business-like or practical clothing fully developed during the 1980s boom of 'sexy' lingerie and 'power' suits for professional career women.[29] One could interpret such a mix in a number of ways. Because underwear is the most immediate layer of clothing next to the naked flesh, covering parts of the body often associated with sexual difference, it functions culturally to represent the body's sexualised self-awareness of gender distinctions. Highly feminised underwear can serve to reassure a woman or her intimates that under-neath it all, a 'real' woman exists at her core. However, the sensation of wearing such garments has the additional appeal of being potentially autoerotic. A mid-1910s issue of *Vogue* observed, 'Nothing caresses her to the same purring delight as a soft, silken peignoir or a fluffy matinée.'[30]

During this period of growing mobility and opportunities for women, closed-crotch drawers became more widely available, although most women still wore open drawers until the 1910s. A Butterick guide for dress-makers printed in 1911 and 1916 assumes a preference for open drawers by providing brief instructions for closed drawers at the end of the section. Knickers, a term first used around 1880, were initially distinguished from drawers by a closed crotch, though by the 1890s the term also referred to open drawers. Knickers is a diminutive of knickerbockers, drawers with either an elastic or tape back-buttoned waistband and legs gathered at the knee. Despite its popular use in Great Britain to refer to women's underpants, continuing to the present, the term originated in America. In 1809 Washington Irving published *History of New York* under the name Diedrich Knickerbocker; in 1831, knickerbocker became a popular reference to New Yorkers, especially descendants of early Dutch settlers. The link between this text and the article of clothing was an illustration in Irving's book of knee breeches worn by Dutch settlers.[31] Nineteenth-century women's knickers were usually less decorative than drawers, designed to fulfil underclothing's functional aspects of warmth and protection. Yet 'functional' requires deconstruction since open drawers' practical benefits may have included greater comfort, as closed drawers were often constructed by a wide fabric insertion or gusset that contributed to bulky material between the legs. This aspect would come into play around 1910 when the corset extended down the legs, pressing them together. Despite such potential discomfort during the Edwardian period, closed drawers became an increasing option.[32]

Because dress is both sensual and visual, an understanding of the significance of costume changes requires close textual analysis of garments as material artefacts. A 1901 mail-order catalogue from Eaton's, Canada's leading retailer, demurely indicates the closed-crotch status of the nineteen numbered drawers it illustrates for sale by a subtle visual cue, a row of short dashes which designate a closed seam. The next page hawks corset covers, drawers' complement, made of similar fabric and trim, also known as 'camisoles' and worn over corsets to cover the upper torso. These were available in a variety of necklines, denoted through descriptions of shapes such as round or square, and attributes such as high, low or décolleté. By exposing more of the body, particularly the breasts, the lower neckline emphasises the erotic aspects of this undergarment.[33]

Though drawers and camisoles were sold separately, sets of undergarments, an innovation related to development of the twentieth-century bridal trousseau, were also available. Analysis of sets illustrated in catalogues and those in costume collections suggests that the dual and competing meanings of drawers as both erotic and modest is further articulated by the material split of sets into open- and closed-crotch types. Extant undergarment sets and catalogue illustrations link the low neckline to the open crotch and the high neckline to the closed. One catalogue page of sets reveals ambivalence about a set's potential for titillation. A sleeve detail awkwardly overlays the deepest plunge of a bridal set component's décolleté neckline, allowing representation of the sleeve trim but also equivocating about presenting a full view of the garment's revealing, low neckline.[34]

Open drawer sets, including those hand-made for bridal trousseaus, further foreground the erotic aspect. Made with extremely delicate, lightweight and translucent fabrics, low-neck camisoles in the sets close (or open) at the front with only a single wisp of ribbon threaded through lace trim[35] (Figure 3). Camisoles in closed drawer sets, which often open at the centre back or front with a series of small buttons, are often longer in length than those in open-crotch sets.[36] Closed drawer sets with high-neckline camisoles frequently are simpler in decoration and made in heavier and stiffer fabric. Ornamentation is often symmetrical and orderly, unlike the flounces and ribbons of open drawer sets. The movement of these embellishments attract attention to the body, especially when the set is worn without an additional layer of clothing. Flounces hint at disarray, a long-noted heightener of erotic suggestion.[37]

The central implication of the open drawer, low-neckline sets is sexual access. These garments are flimsier and more easily removed, though sexual intercourse is possible while any pair of open drawers are worn. Their design is overtly erotic, conveying desire kindled by the implication that sexual activity could commence at any moment. A woman might choose to wear such undergarments because they make her feel sexually attractive, because she feels valued only for such attraction, or because they stimulate her own erotic feelings and seductive intentions. She might enjoy the 'caress' of the fabric, or the active declaration of sexual arousal they convey. She might, however, also be bound to a notion of femininity defining the female body as exclusively sexual or reproductive, tying her to submission in other areas of life.

An 1883 Frenchwoman's advice about the 'conjugal chemise' clarifies the erotic implications and purpose of the similarly designed open drawer, low-neckline camisole sets:

> Do not describe it to young girls … but it must be placed in their bridal trousseau. They will not wear it immediately; but after a while they will understand the value of this oriental silk or batiste, with large lace inserts, all aquiver with valenciennes flounces that embellish it at the hem. They will become accustomed to this transparent network, which in front – from the beginning of the bosom to the belt – reveals the charming graces of a young and supple bust.

Roland Barthes's concept of 'appearance-as-disappearance' also figures here. His critical question, 'Is not the most erotic portion of a body *where the garment gapes* … the intermittence of skin flashing between … articles of clothing?' explains not only effects produced by the design of such trousseau articles, but also the sexual appeal and eroticising effects of open drawers.[38]

Closed drawer sets, on the other hand, cover the body with more modesty, both in the sense of a greater area of the body clothed and in design that attracts less attention to the body. Their fabric lends a sense of the ordinary, of the everyday, as these undergarments maintain their

Figure 3: 1904 bridal trousseau open-crotch drawers and camisole set made of light, translucent fabric trimmed with a 'transparent network' of lace and ribbon inserts. Artefact 954.731a & b. Courtesy Royal Ontario Museum.

protective function of shielding outerwear from flesh and adding an additional layer for warmth. Modesty does not necessarily inhibit sexual pleasure, but these garments convey a sense of a properly restrained sexuality. The choice of modest undergarments might express discomfort with open display of sexual excitement or instead reveal a pragmatic need for undergarments that last longer and serve a wider range of purposes. A woman who wears them might not identify sexual expressiveness at the forefront of her identity, or might identify modesty as her chief allure.

The interplay of modesty and eroticism clearly generates both contradictory and consonant meanings. Yet this central dialectic of fashion structures a gendered embodiment that ultimately dissolves such distinctions and resolves their contradictions. Dress practices identified as modest complement those defined as erotic, marking female bodies as sexual whichever set of practices a woman engages in. The open or closed option furthers the meaning that each garment possesses the power to transfer, not only to the body but also to the psyche of the woman who wears it.[39]

Constructions linking modesty with concealment and eroticism with display began to change in the early twentieth century. Emerging consumerism and commercialised leisure exposed undergarments in public spaces by daylight and on theatre screens by the flickering lights of movie projectors, heightening tensions about the opposition between modesty and eroticism. The traditional practice of exhibiting the bridal trousseau to wedding guests became 'indecent' as advertising, department store displays, and film images widely disseminated knowledge of what lay hidden beneath women's outer clothing. These new sites of display altered subsequent fashion practices. Most of the hundreds of thousands of women visitors to new amusement parks experienced first-hand the entertainment value of deliberate public exposure of their drawers on attractions that featured a surprise blast of air from beneath the ground. On one Coney Island attraction this event occurred while women unknowingly walked in a darkened room across a stage in front of an unseen audience. The erotic tension generated by concealment and display was destabilised in new contexts that legitimated open display of undergarments while also attempting to retain sexual meanings of their exhibition.[40]

By 1908, both Eaton's and Sears catalogues allowed for the explicit choice of open or closed drawers in many advertised styles of drawers. Costume historians Phillis and C. Willett Cunnington note that 'closed knickers acquired more colour', and began sharing open drawers' variety of fabrics, including cotton, linen, silk, flannel, flannelette, natural and knitted wool, and silk. An undergarment introduced in the mid 1880s, the 'divided skirt', became more widely available at this time, giving the outward appearance of an underskirt, their split reality hidden behind folds of the skirt-like exterior. Some versions had a button-fastening gusset crotch, which allowed for the option of opening or closing at appropriate moments. Thus, divided skirts created a mediation for both the skirt/trouser and the open/closed-crotch dyads.[41]

After 1909 the fashionable silhouette and the undergarments required to produce it changed. Skirts narrowed, some to the extent that they were termed 'hobble skirts'. Some women wore a fetter around their calves known as a 'hobble garter' to prevent splitting their skirt while walking. In line with these changes, the volume of drawers decreased along with the number of layers of undergarments. The slimmer line of the 1910s marks the beginning of the transition toward the 1920s 'boyish' silhouette. The 'flapper' emerged as early as 1913, a bohemian version of the prevalent working-class pleasure seeker, although her style would not become mainstream until the next decade. The freer movements required by dancing or amusement-park attractions stimulated innovations in underwear, such as 'tango knickers' in 1914. The terms drawers and knickers were becoming interchangeable in this transitional period, although drawers kept their association with the underwear's older open-crotch style, while knickers continued to refer to more modern modes through the 1920s in the US and England.[42]

The growing presence of closed drawers occurred in the 1910s context of intensive public discussion of women's sexuality and women's rights. Women won their goals by agitation, organisation and persuasion, which contributed to changing views of women's proper sphere and behaviour, generated public power for women, and provided a forum for opposition to women's equal political status and reproductive self-determination. Women's activity in the birth-control and suffrage movements was comparable to women's increasing equal partnership in the public culture of commercial amusements, and presence in higher education, professional and white-collar occupations, and the labour movement. The closing of the crotch during this period had cultural ramifications, including a reversal of the meaning of the closed and open crotch. The modesty associated with the open-crotch drawer converted to wantonness, while the transgressive connotations of the closed-crotch drawer as trouser became muted. Several core issues of the suffrage movement are most directly relevant to the latter connotation, because of the link between trousers and power. As the ultimately successful campaign to decriminalise birth control involved accepting the detachment of sexual activity from procreation, women's public activism around this issue suggested an overturning of the Victorian ideology of female passionlessness, and thus also of open drawers' connotation of modesty.[43]

The movement of closed drawers from dominant choice to virtually the only option continued with the entry of the US into World War I, which provided some women with opportunities to work in a variety of traditionally male occupations, some of which necessitated wearing trousers. Thus, once again a divided garment emerged from beneath the skirt and became acceptable women's wear. Donning trousers was controversial, and was often used as a symbol both by those opposed to and in favour of women's entry into new occupations. One-piece outfits long known as overalls were called 'womanalls' to soften the impact of women performing 'manly' tasks involving risk, strength, stamina and dirt. Women's work trousers were also called bloomers to clearly demark and identify them as feminine. Ironically, a name that once caused such shock waves would now be used to assuage anxieties.[44]

Women's World War I experiences were an important step toward the later twentieth-century acceptance of women wearing a divided garment as outerwear on a daily basis. The potential for the acceptance of women wearing trousers during the war years is revealed by a Chicago manufacturer who in 1917 stated, 'a woman will wear overalls or any kind of bloomers only so long as she absolutely has to. Of course, if they prefer to wear bloomers we can make them as easily as we can skirts.' Bloomers and overalls were being sold for gardening and housework, but were considered 'too new' or improper to be used for other purposes. Upper-class women's contribution came later, when elegant lounging pyjama sets of the 1920s worn at home or beach resorts later became streetwear. Such appearances as a 'pajama-clad chorus' on a 1924 Broadway stage added to changing perceptions of women in trousers. Avant-garde American women designers, such as sartorial and political radical Elizabeth Hawes also contributed to the greater presence of women in pants. Hawes, reportedly the first woman to wear men's jeans in New York City, offered women's trousers in the 1930s and photographed models wearing them with legs boldly astride.[45] The acceptance of work trousers and pyjamas for women, whether begrudging or enthusiastic, probably contributed to the growing use of closed drawers in the late teens and 1920s. The declining rigid nineteenth-century corset, considered by most historians virtually obsolete after the war, implies less need for open drawers for simple passage of bodily waste. Yet the continuing use of twentieth-century styled corsets and girdles could present similar difficulties. The hem hikes and skimpier dresses of the postwar period that threatened exposure of the crotch were also important, but this reasoning follows the logic of modesty, ignoring eroticism.

The design of combinations, one-piece undergarments that served as both drawer and chemise, complicates analysis. Combinations made of silk and chamois leather first appeared in the 1870s, though at first they were not worn next to the skin. Dr Jaeger's 1880s woollen combinations marks the origins of what is still known as the union suit, promoted by rational-dress advocates who believed in the healthfulness, particularly warmth and comfort, of woollen or cotton bifurcated undergarments. Nineteenth-century combinations of both decorative and practical types predominantly had an open crotch, following trends for drawers and knickers. Numerous variations on the combinations concept continued to proliferate because they allowed for fewer layers of undergarments, a boon toward achieving the slimmer silhouette. By the 1910s some open-crotch combinations were referred to as 'envelope chemises' because of an attached overskirt which gave the effect of a chemise. Combinations with 'teddy bear drawers', known as teddies after the mid 1920s, had a closed crotch and open slash at the outer thigh seams. The 1917 English term 'cami-knickers' referred to combinations made of delicate fabrics rather than heavier woollens or cottons, while 1920s 'step-ins', though made of similar fabrics, were associated with comfort and modernity. Their popularity generated the use of the term to refer to contemporary short drawers, first known as 'separate step-ins'.[46]

Several 1920s variations of combinations are good examples of the transition in crotch treatment. Some had crotch pieces with buttons which, like those used in divided skirts, allowed the benefits of and provided a mediation for both the open and closed crotch. Others had a narrow piece of fabric attached to the inside centre front and back of the combination, hanging several inches below the genitals with buttons at mid-point between the legs. A more extreme version replaces this button tab with a thin ribbon. The outward appearance of these combinations is similar to a slip, except for the shorter length compared to slips of that period. The addition of the narrow tab or ribbon is puzzling in that they served no purpose, like archaic vestiges that have lost their function, such as in military uniforms; but perhaps they kept the combination from riding up if the wearer raised her arms overhead or engaged in vigorous movement.[47] Since combinations were considered to be half drawers, the tab or ribbon conferred upon the wearer the semblance of propriety that a slip worn without drawers would not. Worn during the last years of open-crotch drawers, these combinations provided the final opportunity for a woman to retain modesty while free of closed fabric between her legs.

In 1931, an Alabama observer, Matilda Kitchens, concluded that 'modesty was eventually the force that closed the door on open-seat drawers' dominance'. This observation explains the disappearance of the tab and ribbon crotch as the result of a reversal in the prevailing meanings of open- and closed-crotch drawers. The earlier connotations of modesty and propriety that an open crotch carried transformed to extreme eroticism and lascivious intent. The closed crotch, previously thought improper, unhealthy or a dangerous cross-dressing threat, came to signify modesty and propriety. These newer meanings, which hold to the present day, make clear that the crotch closed as notions about and public expression of women's sexuality changed in the first decades of the twentieth century.[48]

The last garment to retain the open crotch was the union suit, which is so similar for both men and women that it approaches gender neutrality and is desexualised. Union suits could retain an open crotch longer because, unlike most other women's undergarments, their erotic potential is muted rather than amplified. The sexual access open drawers provided could only coexist with women's propriety in the context of an ideology of female passionlessness and social structures of masculine domination. When women publicly asserted their own claims to sexual pleasure, political power and economic independence, an open crotch was no longer tolerated.[49]

Yet continuing restrictions on women's freedom to wear closed, divided garments worn previously only by men clarify that these garments remained associated with masculine power and privilege. Surely the closing of the crotch related to women's growing economic opportunities that increased control over sexual access to their bodies. A 1924 *Women's Wear Daily* advertisement for the McLoughlin's Fitz-U Bloomer suggests unfolding possibilities for greater freedom of movement and control. An ice-skating young woman in her flapper hat, sleeveless fur-trimmed sports shirt, and Fitz-U Bloomer stretches one arm out in front of her, leading her gaze and body forward, while her other arm reaches back to hold her raised bent leg at the ankle. The patented 'seamless' crotch bloomer available in double or single reinforcement sells, according to the ad copy, because it is 'stretchable and non-breakable even to the stitch. It gives every comfort and longer wear, because there is no Tension or Binding Crotch Seams. Nothing to Pull, Split or Break, as it is all Give; still the Bloomer clings beautifully to the form.' Though not meant as outerwear, the wide gusset of the bloomer's crotch allows the skater to arch her leg in the air and enjoy her body's full capabilities without fearing an unexpected revelation of her flesh or a penetrating male gaze.[50]

The skater is a young woman, however, and the closed-crotch drawers that contributed to the construction of the adolescent silhouette of the 1920s flapper evoke drawers worn by girls since the nineteenth century that allowed greater freedom of movement, but within a restricted range of activity. Women's closed-crotch divided undergarments, known as step-ins rather than drawers as the terminology for such garments also became gender specific in this decade, reassured anxieties through their association with the virginal. However, their status as pre-sexual does not entirely negate the erotic appeal of the flapper's step-ins, not only because they revealed more of the legs but also because of the seductive quality that idealised virginity holds for some individuals. In addition, in their role as a required component of postwar women's fashionable dress, step-ins were associated with pleasures accorded by freer courtship relations and recreational marital sex. Most important, these recently condoned practices and dress worn to engage in them were codified as modern in the1920s by equating Victorianism with prudery, defined as an out-dated sexual ideology exemplified by the now ridiculed abundance and weight of women's clothing from the previous era. This view helped construct the 'myth of Victorian repression' which, as historian Christina Simmons points out, 'represented a cultural adjustment of male power to women's departure from the Victorian order. It constituted a strategic modification rather than a decline of male dominance.'[51]

The commercially successful 1937 comedy *Topper*, based upon the popular 1926 novel by Thorne Smith, interprets this transformation. Closed-crotch step-in drawers are key to the film's (and novel's) narrative resolution. Mrs Topper's old-fashioned sensibilities, that demand of her husband a boring, routinised existence, endanger her marriage. A pair of lacy, closed-crotch step-ins come to symbolise in the film the sexual excitement and fun that are new requirements for the modern woman who wishes to keep her husband from straying and find acceptance among her social peers. When at the film's end she dons the step-ins, which Mrs Topper previously regarded as only worn by women of dubious reputation, it is evident she has made the needed transition from Victorianism. What is also apparent is that Cosmo Topper will now rule the roost as well as the office, as the film shows that, when Mrs Topper conforms to the new fashion in underpants, she also relinquishes her power to regulate home life and social morality.[52]

Topper makes clear that excessive indulgence in sensual pleasures is a fatal mistake, but lack of such pleasures leads to unhappiness and divorce. Fortunately, the lingerie shop is a stop on the road to marital bliss accessible to all. Wearing step-in drawers signifies women's adherence to the new codes of middle-class marital sexuality, which allow women sexual passion, but in the service of pleasing their husbands. Moreover, women must relinquish the domestic power they achieved in the Victorian era through their status as the passionless, moral superiors of men in order to conform to the redefined contours of modern, sexualised femininity.[53]

The contradictory meanings of nineteenth-century open drawers as both modest and erotic allowed white, middle-class female bodies simultaneously to conform to and defy the ideals of the cult of true white womanhood, and thus to be constructed not only as sexually accessible to male prerogative but also as sexually desirous subjects. Nonetheless, unequal access to social power and strikingly divergent understandings about male and female sexuality dominating this period meant disparate male and female experiences of sexual aspects of open drawers. Open drawers provide material evidence that female submission to gendered codes of respectability was eroticised. The dynamic interplay of modesty and eroticism not only afforded white, middle-class women space within restrictive propriety but also maintained cultural codes which constructed women in terms of sexual attractiveness and availability to men, ensuring that they demonstrated adherence to true womanhood. Open drawers also tell us that within white, middle-class men's definition of female peers as sexually passionless and thus morally superior there remained embedded an unspoken acknowledgment that they did not dispense completely with respectable women's erotic capacities. Working through a complex set of needs and desires, men could find their own sexual pleasure heightened by open drawers' eroticisation of the very modesty necessary for women to maintain social respectability in their eyes.

By 1930, short, closed-crotch drawers like those worn by cinematic modern Diana and the reformed Mrs Topper became the norm. The larger, longer and open drawers worn by proper middle-class women until the early twentieth century were viewed as hopelessly old-fashioned, prudish, and ridiculous. Turn-of-the-century changes in crotch design and meanings of women's drawers reveal how new constructions of female sexuality were enacted in a critical transitional period. Open drawers remained in vogue throughout the nineteenth century in an era when Victorian modesty for women was supposedly the predominant cultural code. Wearing these drawers marked a female body as conforming to dictates of respectable femininity, including the unspoken provision of sexual accessibility. A woman wearing a divided, closed-crotch under- or outer-garment in that period would be engaging in the sexually charged and unrespectable transgression of cross-dressing. In the early twentieth century, women increasingly wore closed-crotch drawers as they struggled and won the right to vote, to share public space with men, to assert their sexual desires, and to engage in waged labour. Significantly, the accepted sexual and moral meanings generated by open- and closed-crotch under-garments reversed along with women's changed preference in crotch construction. By the 1920s, reworked requirements of modern sexual propriety meant that reputable women who successfully incorporated claims to sexual pleasure within a new definition of respectability would only don closed-crotch step-ins. As a result, in the twentieth century open-crotch undergarments were signified as primarily erotic. Yet, the reversal only went so far. New requirements of sexually seductive dress replaced older modes. Women's new freedoms would not come unchecked, for as women levelled the playing field of sexual pleasure, they no longer could commandeer on the basis of moral superiority. The transition from open to closed drawers reveals not only the power of clothing as a medium of signification but how women's struggles for autonomy interact with resistant social forces to reconfigure gender distinctions.

Notes

I wish to acknowledge the critical assistance of Lois Banner, Steve Ross, Tania Modleski, Adrienne Hood, Carole Turbin, Barbara Burman, the anonymous *Gender & History* reader, and others who commentated on earlier versions of this essay, including presentations at the 1996 Berkshire Conference on the History of Women and Huntington Library Women's Studies Seminar. I am grateful for research support from the University of Southern California, the Veronika Gervers Research Fellowship in Textile and Costume History (Royal Ontario Museum), and the Stella Blum Research Grant (Costume Society of America).

1. *Our Dancing Daughters*, MGM, directed by Harry Beaumont, 1928; Mary Ryan, 'The Projection of a New Womanhood', in Lois Scharf and Joan M. Jensen, *Decades of Discontent* (Greenwood Press, 1983), pp. 113–30.
2. See artefact 982.183.1, Costume Collection of the Royal Ontario Museum (ROM); Rosemary Hawthorne, *Oh … Knickers!* (Bachman & Turner, 1985), p. 14. On men's drawers, see, for example, Phillis and C. Willett Cunnington, *The History of Underclothes* (Faber and Faber, 1951; rev. 1981), pp. 31–2, 42, 53, 67, 80, 90, 109, 121; Philippe Perrot, *Fashioning the Bourgeoisie* (Princeton University Press, 1994), p. 161. On women's undergarments, see, for example, Cunnington and Cunnington, *History of Underclothes*; Elizabeth Ewing, *Dress and Undress* (Drama Book Specialists, 1978); Cecil Saint Laurent, *The Great Book of Lingerie* (Vendome Press, 1986); Alison Carter, *Underwear* (Drama Book Publishers, 1992); Christine Stansell, *City of Women* (University of Illinois Press, 1982), pp. 4–5; Helen Bradley Foster, *New Raiments of Self: African American Clothing in the Antebellum South* (Berg, 1997), pp. 147–9; Deborah Gray White, *Ar'n't I a Woman?* (W. W. Norton, 1985, 1991), pp. 32–3. On women and trousers, see, for example, Lynn Hunt, *Politics, Culture and Class in the French Revolution* (University of California Press, 1984), pp. 66–7.
3. Jill Fields, 'Three Sides to Every Story: The Material Culture of Intimate Apparel', *Dress*, 23 (1996), 75–81; Farid Chenoune, *Beneath It All: A Century of French Lingerie* (Rizzoli, 1999), especially ch. 1, fn. 11, pp. 22, 25; J. C. Flugel, *The Psychology of Clothes* (Hogarth Press, 1930); James Laver, *A Concise History of Costume and Fashion* (Scribner's, 1969); Valerie Steele, *Fashion and Eroticism* (Oxford University Press, 1985), pp. 198–9; Fred Davis, *Fashion, Culture and Identity* (University of Chicago Press, 1992), ch. 3.
4. Ellen Ross and Rayna Rapp, 'Sex and Society', in *Powers of Desire*, ed. Ann Snitow, Christine Stansell and Sharon Thompson (Monthly Review Press, 1983), pp. 51–73; Nancy Cott, 'Passionlessness: An Interpretation of Victorian Sexual Ideology, 1790–1850', *Signs*, 4 (1978), pp. 219–36; Michel Foucault, *The History of Sexuality* (Pantheon Books, 1978); Carroll Smith-Rosenberg, *Disorderly Conduct* (Oxford University Press, 1985), David Kunzle, *Fashion and Fetishism* (Rowman and Littlefield, 1982).
5. *Godey's Ladies Book*, January 1872, July, 1872; *Women's Wear Daily*, 7 May 1917, p. 5; 22 May 1917, p. 5; Cunnington and Cunnington, *History of Underclothes*, pp. 124, 137, 147.
6. Flugel, *The Psychology of Clothes*; Vern Bullough and Bonnie Bullough, *Cross Dressing, Sex and Gender* (University of Pennsylvania Press, 1993), p. 175; Lois Banner, *American Beauty* (University of Chicago Press, 1983) p. 234; Steele, *Fashion and Eroticism*, p. 52; Davis, *Fashion, Culture and Identity*, pp. 33–4; James Laver, *Taste and Fashion, from the French Revolution until Today* (George G. Harrap & Co., 1937), pp. 168–70. John Harvey, *Men in Black* (University of Chicago Press, 1995); Christopher Breward, *The Hidden Consumer* (Manchester University Press, 1999).
7. Sally Helvenston, 'Popular Advice for the Well Dressed Woman in the 19th Century', *Dress*, 5 (1980), pp. 31–46.
8. Steele, *Fashion and Eroticism*, pp. 6–8; Joan Severa, *Dressed for the Photographer: Ordinary Americans and Fashion: 1840–1900* (Kent State University Press, 1995), pp. 25, 185, 292, 300, and photographs pp. 243, 260, 263, 285, 325, 451, 478, 494, 497, 507; Erna Olafson Hellerstein, Leslie Parker Hume and Karen M. Offen (eds) and Estelle B. Freedman, Barbara Charlesworth Gelpi and Marilyn Yalom (associate eds), *Victorian Women: A Documentary Account of Women's Lives in Nineteenth-Century England, France, and the United*

States (Stanford University Press, 1981); Nancy L. Green, *Ready-to-Wear and Ready-to-Work* (Duke University Press, 1997).

9. Lee Hall, *Common Threads* (Little, Brown and Company, 1992), pp. 188–99, text and photographs; Jo B. Paoletti and Carol L. Kregloh, 'The Children's Department', in *Men and Women: Dressing the Part*, ed. Claudia Brush Kidwell and Valerie Steele (Smithsonian Institution Press, 1989), pp. 22–41; *Godey's Ladies Book*, April 1857, p. 362, and July 1857, p. 78; Robert Holliday, *Unmentionables from Figleaves to Scanties* (Ray Long and Richard Smith, 1933), pp. 172–3, 179; Anne Buck, *Victorian Costume & Costume Accessories* (Ruth Bean, 1984/1961), pp. 202, 209–10, 214, ch. 20, 'Children's Costume'; Severa, *Dressed for the Photographer*, pp. 23–4, 107–8, 122–3, 129, 133, 134, 144, 146, 156, 181, 210–11, 255, 281, 220, 315–16, 363–4, 428–9, 431, 447, 483; Stella Blum (ed.), *Victorian Fashions and Costumes from Harper's Bazaar, 1867–1898* (Dover Publications, 1974), pp. 116–17, 131, 143, 154–7, 168–9, 184–5, 214–15, 222–3, 251; Michelle Perrot (ed.), *A History of Private Life* (Harvard University Press, 1990), pp. 196–219.

10. Saint-Laurent, *Great Book*, pp. 104–15; Perrot, *Fashioning*, pp. 146–8; Cunnington and Cunnington, *History of Underclothes*, p. 82, (pantalettes, 1834); *Godey's Ladies Book*, July 1855, p. 96, and July 1857, p. 554.

11. Ewing, *Dress and Undress*, pp. 56–7, 61, 166; Cunnington and Cunnington, *History of Underclothes*, p. 70, citing *Glenbervie Journals* (1811), ed. F. Bickley (1928), and p. 82; Richard Martin and Harold Koda, *Infra-Apparel* (Metropolitan Museum of Art, 1993), p. 62; Hall, *Common Threads*, p. 43; Severa, *Dressed for the Photographer*, p. 197; Diana de Marly, *Fashions for Men* (Homes & Meier, 1985), p. 97; Saint-Laurent, *Great Book*, pp. 100, 113, 145; Blum, *Victorian Fashions*, p. 77.

12. Saint-Laurent, *Great Book*, p. 222, and Steele, *Fashion and Eroticism*, p. 199, quote an 1890 French memoir cited by Pierre Dufay, *Le Pantalon féminin: un chapitre inédit de l'histoire du costume* (Charles Carrington, 1906); Cunnington and Cunnington, *History of Underclothes*, p. 99; Perrot, *Fashioning*, p. 148; Steele, *Fashion and Eroticism*, p. 86; Roland Barthes, *Mythologies* (Noonday Press, 1990), pp. 41–2.

13. Laver, *Costume and Fashion*, pp. 162–72.

14. *The Handbook of the Toilet*, cited by Cunnington and Cunnington, *History of Underclothes*, p. 94; Matilda Kitchens, *When Underwear Counted, Being the Evolution of Underclothes* (Brannon Printing Company, 1931), p. 51; see also Steele, *Fashion and Eroticism*, p. 198.

15. Sally Helvenston, 'Popular Advice for the Well Dressed Woman in the 19th Century', *Dress*, 5 (1980), pp. 31–47; Jeanette C. Lauer and Robert H. Lauer, 'The Battle of the Sexes: Fashion in 19th Century America', *Journal of Popular Culture*, 13 (1980), 581–9; Shelley Foote, 'Challenging Gender Symbols', in Kidwell and Steele (eds), *Men and Women*, pp. 144–57; 'Bloomers', *Dress*, 5 (1980), 1–12. See also 'The First of the Flappers', *Literary Digest* (13 May 1922), pp. 44–5.

16. Foote, 'Challenging Gender Symbols', pp. 149–50; Ewing, *Dress and Undress*, p. 64; Lauer and Lauer, *Battle of the Sexes*; Laver, *Costume and Fashion*, pp. 180–83.

17. Foote, 'Challenging Gender Symbols', p. 148.

18. Reina Lewis, *Gendering Orientalism* (Routledge, 1996), and Dianne Sachko Macleod, 'Cross-Cultural Cross-Dressing: Class, Gender and Modernist Sexual Identity', in Julie Codell and Dianne Macleod, *Orientalism Transposed* (Ashgate, 1998), pp. 63–85; Lauer and Lauer, *Battle of the Sexes*, p. 583.

19. *Godey's Ladies Book*, May 1858, p. 454; Stansell, *City of Women*, p. 164; Ewing, *Dress and Undress*, p. 72; Steele, *Fashion and Eroticism*, p. 75; White, *Ar'n't I a Woman?*, p. 95; Severa, *Dressed for the Photographer*, pp. 87–8, 98, 201–2, 205, 239, 278–9, 310; Hall, *Common Threads*, p. 98.

20. Ewing, *Dress and Undress*, pp. 69–76, 85; Perrot, *Fashioning*, pp. 147–8; Steele, *Fashion and Eroticism*, p. 114.

21. I am grateful to Patricia Cline Cohen for the *Weekly Rake* drawings of 9 July 1842, pp. 1, 3, American Antiquarian Society.

22. Carter, *Underwear*, p. 55; Chenoune, *Beneath It All*, p. 22; Perrot, *Fashioning*, pp. 108–9.

23. Cunnington and Cunnington, *History of Underclothes*, pp. 94, 98–9, 106; Martin and Koda, *Infra Apparel*, p. 64; Perrot, *Fashioning*, p. 101; Simon Garfield, *Mauve* (W. W. Norton & Co., 2001); Steele, *Fashion and Eroticism*, p. 86.

24. Ewing, *Dress and Undress*, p. 101; Christina Probert, *Lingerie in Vogue Since 1910* (Abbeville Press, 1981), p. 7; Carter, *Underwear*, p. 50; Holliday, *Unmentionables*, p. 208; Ewing, *Dress and Undress*, p. 85; Valerie Twelves, 'An Investigation of the Impact of the Dress Reform Movement: A Case Study of Reform Movements in the Years 1890 to 1920', MS thesis, Cornell University, 1969.

25. Ellen Garvey, *The Adman in the Parlor* (Oxford, 1996), ch. 4; Ewing, *Dress and Undress*, p. 64; Saint-Laurent, *Great Book*, p. 140; *Harper's Bazaar*, 14 April 1894, cover, reproduced in Blum, *Victorian Fashions*, p. 266; *San Francisco Chronicle*, 13 May 1894.

26. Edward Van Every, *Sins of America As 'Exposed' by the 'Police Gazette'* (Frederick A. Stokes Company, 1931), p. 180; *The Police Gazette*, ed. Gene Smith and Jayne Barry Smith (Simon and Schuster, 1972), pp. 198, 201, 202.

27. Ewing, *Dress and Undress*, p. 112; Elizabeth Wilson and Lou Taylor, *Through the Looking Glass: A History of Dress from 1860 to the Present Day* (BBC Books, 1989), p. 57; Banner, *American Beauty*, p. 149. Patricia Campbell Warner, 'Public and Private: Men's Influence on American Women's Dress for Sport and Physical Education', *Dress* (1988), 48–55, finds exercise dresses with pantaloons as early as 1832.

28. Cunnington and Cunnington, *History of Underclothes*, pp. 128–9, 133; Alison Gernsheim, *Victorian and Edwardian Fashion: A Photographic Survey* (Dover Publications, *c.* 1981), pp. 83–6; de Marly, *Fashions for Men*, pp. 97–8, 109–14.

29. Ewing, *Dress and Undress*, p. 112, citing Fray-Pruf slip advertisement, *Vogue* (July 1944), p. 12; Gary Abrams, 'Lore Caulfield: Sexy Lingerie the Antidote for Career Dressing', *Los Angeles Times*, 29 April 1983.

30. Probert, *Lingerie in Vogue*, p. 9.

31. Cunnington and Cunnington, *History of Underclothes*, pp. 108, 124; Saint-Laurent, *Great Book*, p. 115; Carter, *Underwear*, p. 152; *The Barnhardt Dictionary of Etymology* (1988), p. 568; *The Dressmaker* (Butterick Publishing Company, 1911, 1916), pp. 42–4.

32. Cunnington and Cunnington, *History of Underclothes*, p. 137.

33. *Eaton's Spring & Summer Catalogue*, 46 (1901), pp. 54–5; 1897 Sear's, Roebuck & Co. catalogue, p. 308; Carter, *Underwear*, p. 64.

34. I examined all relevant drawers and corset covers held at the costume collections of the Royal Ontario Museum, New York Metropolitan Museum, and Smithsonian Institution. See also *Eaton's Fall & Winter Catalogue*, 47 (1901–2), p. 96.

35. See artefacts 954.73.1.a and 954.73.1.b, 1904; 963.123.d and 963.123.e, 1906 (ROM), 243178.4 and 243178.7, 1902; 237724.2a and 237724.5, 1906; 58909 and 58907, 1910 (Smithsonian); and 54.51ab, 1916 (Metropolitan).

36. See early twentieth-century closed drawer set 967.175.16A and 967.175.16B; 942.27.14 and 942.27.13, 1908; 964.153A and 964.153B, 1912 (ROM), and 243102.2 and 243102.3, 1902; 212884.024 and 212884.025, 1905–1910; 273774.1 and 273774.2, 1913 (Smithsonian).

37. Cunnington and Cunnington, *History of Underclothes*, p. 38.

38. Marguerite d'Aincourt, *Études sur le costume féminin* (Paris, 1883), pp. 14–15, quoted in Perrot, *Fashioning*, p. 166; Roland Barthes, *The Pleasure of the Text* (Oxford University Press, 1990), pp. 9–10.

39. Steele, *Fashion and Eroticism*, pp. 13–17; Perrot, *Fashioning*, p. 12; Flugel, *Psychology of Clothes*, p. 16; Kathleen Canning, 'The Body as Method? Reflections on the Place of the Body in Gender History', *Gender & History*, 11 (1999), pp. 499–513.

40. Kathy Peiss, *Cheap Amusements* (Temple University Press, 1986), pp. 134–5; Perrot, *Fashioning*, p. 100; Chenoune, *Beneath It All*, p. 25.

41. 966.17.4 and 958.41, Drawer F.04.018 (ROM); Cunnington and Cunnington, *History of Underclothes*, pp. 133, 137; Wilson and Taylor, *Through the Looking Glass*, p. 52.

42. Laver, *Costume and Fashion*, p. 224; Cunnington and Cunnington, *History of Underclothes*, pp. 140, 147, citing *The Lady*; Hall, *Common Threads*, pp. 217–18; Sara Evans, *Born for*

Liberty (Free Press, 1989), pp. 161, 176; Ryan, 'Projection of a New Womanhood', p. 120, cites a 1920 *Ladies' Home Journal* article, 'Flapper is Dead'; *Women's Wear Daily*, 7 May 1917, p. 5, and 22 May 1917, p. 5.

43. Linda Gordon, *Woman's Body, Woman's Right* (Penguin, 1977), ch. 7.
44. Maureen Greenwald, *Women, War, and Work* (Cornell University Press, 1980), pp. 31, 48, 121.
45. Saint-Laurent, *Great Book*, pp. 88, 152; *Women's Wear Daily*, 25 May 1917, p. 19, and 19 September 1924, p. 24; Probert, *Lingerie in Vogue*, pp. 19, 24; Bettina Berch, *Radical by Design* (E. P. Dutton, 1988), pp. 61, 69.
46. Cunnington and Cunnington, *History of Underclothes*, pp. 111, 123, 141; Carter, *Underwear*, pp. 49, 153; Ewing, *Dress and Undress*, p. 129; *Women's Wear Daily*, 7 May 1917, p. 5; 28 May 1917, p. 5; 11 September 1924, p. 15.
47. Artefacts 989.60.8, 979.225.25, 973.272, 971.259.13, (ROM); Flugel, *Psychology of Clothes*, pp. 172–3.
48. Mary Louise Roberts, 'Samson and Delilah Revisited: The Politics of Women's Fashion in 1920s France', *American Historical Review*, 1993, p. 658; Kitchens, *When Underwear Counted*, pp. 9, 16, 51, 55.
49. Christina Simmons, 'Modern Sexuality and the Myth of Victorian Repression', in Peiss and Simmons (eds), *Passion and Power*, p. 171.
50. *Women's Wear Daily*, 23 September 1924, p. 9.
51. Simmons, 'Modern Sexuality', pp. 158, 167–70.
52. *Topper*, directed by Norman Z. McLeod for MGM, 1937.
53. Film industry censors ordered the word 'pants' deleted from the dialogue and certain scenes. See letters of Joseph Breen to Mat O'Brien, 18 and 20 March 1937; Joseph Breen to Hal Roach, 19 March 1937 and 24 June 1937; memorandum for *Topper* files from E. R. O'Neil, 19 March 1937 (Academy of Motion Picture Arts & Sciences Library Special Collections).

8

'De-Humanised Females and Amazonians': British Wartime Fashion and its Representation in *Home Chat*, 1914–1918

Cheryl Buckley

Discussion of women's fashion in Britain during the First World War has been surprisingly generalised and lacking in detailed primary research.[1] Typically characterised by a number of 'truisms'; it has been summed up thus: that uniforms were worn most of the time; that fashion was temporarily suspended; and that practical clothing predominated. Such a view has been reinforced by social historians who have interpreted the wearing of munitions clothes and uniforms by women as a further, though perhaps minor, indicator of women's progressive liberation. In such analyses, fashion comprised part of the backdrop, whilst significant change was measured in terms of employment, wage levels, or political rights.[2] Proposing an analysis which is less about measurement and more about individual experience, Susan Kingsley Kent calls for studies which reveal how war 'transformed the lives of men and women, their relationships with one another, and the cultural understandings of gender and sexuality that informed their consciousness and sense of identity'.[3] In attempting to explore such issues, this essay proposes that fashion functioned as *the* key representational site where women from the skilled working class and lower middle class in Britain began to make visible their changing consciousnesses and identities. In this respect, fashion provided a language which potentially empowered women and transgressed patriarchal codes.

Popular representations of the fashionably dressed female body between 1914 and 1918 were highly contradictory, and, as this essay will show, these were sharply delineated in *Home Chat*, one of a number of new women's magazine titles launched in Britain at the end of the nineteenth and the beginning of the twentieth century.[4] In existence from 1895 until 1956, *Home Chat* was a widely available weekly journal for the home which, at a price of one penny in 1914, was cheap enough to be bought and read by the better-off working class and the lower middle class.[5] Aiming to provide women with practical advice about all aspects of their daily lives, from the traditional concerns of fashion and beauty, marriage and children, to the more contentious issue of women's aspirations beyond the home, it exposed tensions around class and gender which were particularly evident during wartime.

Magazines such as *Home Chat* provided a crucial space during wartime in which representations of women were redefined, and fashion played a large part in this.[6] By organising leisure within an increasingly industrialised and capitalist economy, women's magazines such *Home Chat* provided a journalistic formula which structured time away from work and regulated female consumption.[7] However, it is apparent from first-hand examination of *Home Chat* just before and during the First World War, that it refused a single editorial voice, comprising instead 'a fractured rather than rigidly coherent form'.[8] The identification and representations of gender and class identities were not seamless in this magazine, and it is clear from close scrutiny that tensions emerged in *Home Chat* between the depiction of women's changing roles – in effect, their lived experiences – and idealised, essentially patriarchal, definitions of femininity which posed particular problems for the editors. These were manifested in a number of ways: in the factual reporting of what women were doing; in the fictional stories dealing with different aspects of women's lives; and importantly for the arguments in this essay, in the visual representations of femininity in fashionable clothes, photography and illustration. In the magazine's characteristic format, what it meant to be a woman was endlessly reiterated, but also subtly undermined. As this essay shows, the First World War disrupted conventional gender roles as never before, and in a magazine such as *Home Chat* the ideal of the gendered self as a fixed entity was increasingly questioned, and, in this sense, wartime issues of *Home Chat* could be simultaneously *regulatory* and *liberatory.*

Fashion, in terms both of making, buying and wearing clothes, and the representation of popular styles in women's magazines, mapped out the social and cultural boundaries of the female body in the public and the private spheres during a period of great social upheaval. At work and at home, the female body remained an aesthetic object, to be defined, refined and re-articulated, but, between 1914 and 1918, a sense of urgency underpinned the social and cultural definitions of the aestheticised, fashionable female body. As this essay shows, representations of fashion and dress in *Home Chat* were sharply polarised. Women were required to be feminine, but also serious and independent; they were to be 'womanly', but also to pull their weight in the war effort. Contradictory demands were made of women, and their bodies became a site where battle ensued. Uniforms and casual clothes were worn not merely for their practicality, but also for their fashionability – as symbols of new types of feminine identity. There was a chic stylishness about the unstructured, slightly unruly wartime looks which were also emblematic of modernity. An engagement in fashion and a knowledge of its complex language was a sign of women's entry into all areas of social and cultural life in the early years of the twentieth century, and it was also a symbol of women's relationship with modernity. Embodied in the image of the 'New Woman' wearing a masculinised cropped jacket, straw boater and shortened skirt, young working women from both the better-off working class and lower middle class had already challenged the notion that women were defined solely in relation to home and family just prior to the First World War.

The outbreak of war on 4 August 1914 drew into sharp relief those anxieties about feminine identities and women's roles which had already surfaced prior to 1914. The campaign for the right to vote was one part of a larger process of social, political and economic change which affected women from the mid nineteenth century. Work outside the home and growing participation in trade-union activity were elements in this process, as were smaller families, the Married Women's Property Acts of 1870 and 1882, the gaining of rights of custody over children in 1873, and the extension of all levels of education to women from the 1870s.[9] War, however, was initially a male experience. It offered men an escape from the routines of social, economic and sexual responsibilities; it released them from the private sphere of home – the feminine world – and propelled them into 'the domain of the masculine, the army or navy, to the world of discipline, obedience, action'.[10] The spaces of war were clearly articulated as masculine, whereas women's spaces, particularly those of middle-class women, were predominantly represented as domestic. Very soon, however, war threatened 'the collapse of those established, traditional distinctions between an "economic" world of business and a private world of sentiment' particularly for older, better-off women whose lives had not been subject to the same degree of change as that experienced by younger women from the skilled working class and lower middle class.[11] For this latter group of women, such distinctions had already been partially eroded and they were no longer sharply delineated except perhaps in the patriarchal imagination. Perhaps key to this was work as 55 per cent of single women had paid employment outside the home by 1910.[12]

When war was declared, the predominantly lower-class reader of *Home Chat* was addressed in language which was both patriarchal and class-specific, to

> keep a stiff upper lip and smiling front when things are going badly, to have a comforting word for the sad when we ourselves are almost in despair, to share our little with those who have less – these are gallant deeds which we can perform every day if we will.[13]

Women's duty, graphically depicted in *Home Chat*, was to support men in an unobtrusive fashion, and their 'gallant deeds' were to be found in the routines of everyday life rather than at the front. In this, it reinforced the upper-middle-class ideal of the 'Angel at Home'. However, the lives of many working-class and lower-middle-class women (*Home Chat*'s readership) had already undergone fairly significant change, and such depictions were at odds with their everyday experiences. Features in *Home Chat* dealing with war crèches, feeding routines for new babies, and the duties of older children reflected this. However, the erosion of boundaries between public and private, men and women, and working class and upper class which the war accelerated began to be commented on in *Home Chat*. An article in March 1916, 'How the Girl of the Period Faces War', revealed the class aspirations and orientation of *Home Chat*. Noting that under normal circumstances the 18-year-old girl would soon 'be coming out',[14] after a year of war, it was reported that instead, 'women are stepping into positions they had to fight hard for previous to July 1914'.[15] Surprise at women's resourcefulness characterised the reporting. One young woman, who gave up perfume, gloves, and sweets for the war effort before learning to drive the post van, was particularly admired as she refused payment which she claimed belonged rightfully to the man whose job she had taken. The language of duty, of self-denial, and class deference was still detectable, and occasionally the magazine's writers would remind the female readership that the war's end would return everything to 'normal'. There was a sense of foreboding that things had changed irrevocably, 'and no one can possibly foresee how it will affect HOME LIFE as well as the business of the nation'.[16] But there was an absolute certainty that 'women will not seek to do men out of their old jobs'.[17]

For those still based at home or in domestic service, it was war work which was to transform their lives, as George Wade, a writer for *Home Chat*, put it, 'She has gone into workshops, factory, office, bank and school, to keep the regular daily round going on as smoothly as possible; she has taken on jobs which women never did before to-day.'[18] Wartime offered young women greater opportunities as they took over white-collar jobs vacated by men and, as Pugh has argued, 'Their families increasingly accepted the desirability, or even necessity, of their finding some means of supporting themselves after the war … [For women] a wider and more independent personal life often appeared to be the chief gain of the war year.'[19] Registration for war work had been a haphazard affair, only gaining a sense of purpose after 1915 when state intervention initiated the reorganisation of industry and negotiations with employers and trade unions allowed the employment and training of women workers particularly in the engineering and chemical trades.[20] From 1916, working-class and middle-class women worked in many aspects of industry, in commerce, banking and finance, in the civil service, in agriculture as part of the Land Army, and as bus conductors, ticket collectors and eventually bus drivers.[21] They also volunteered for various auxiliary organisations such as the Voluntary Aid Detachment (VADs) and the Women's Army Auxiliary Corps (WAACs).[22] A direct result of these new types of work was that large numbers of young, single working-class women abandoned domestic service and sweated trades such as dress-making for factory work.[23] Although domestic service was the largest employer of women at the time, the number going into service had been falling by the end of the nineteenth century, paradoxically, as demand grew from the burgeoning middle class. Regarded by their families as respectable work, domestic service was deeply unpopular with young working-class girls.[24] Unhappy at the lack of freedom in service, many young women welcomed the opportunity to work in the new munitions factories where wages too could be significantly different.[25] For married women from the working class with a home and children to manage, factory work offered better opportunities to supplement the family income than had existed prewar when the possibility of combining work outside the home with caring for the family was very limited.[26] As Maud Pember Reeves stated, in 1913 roughly 50 per cent of adult working men in Britain earned 25 shillings or less each week.[27] To compensate for this, working-class married women had to be highly resourceful, managing woefully small amounts of money for rent, food, and clothing. Often attempting to find paid work, they then faced extra costs for childcare thus rendering the work uneconomical. At least wages for munitions work were capable of supporting some childcare even if it was heavily dependent on the goodwill of neighbours and relatives.[28] Prior to the war, middle-class married women had generally not worked outside the home. Their role was to manage the household, direct the servants, oversee the upbringing of the children, and to maintain the home as a civilised retreat for the husband. However, as the war progressed, older married middle-class women often volunteered for various public services or the Land Army, or in some cases they were prepared to work in munitions as supervisors or organisers.

Writing in *Women and Work* in 1945, Gertrude Williams reflected upon women's experience of work during the First World War, arguing that women,

> had tasted the sweets of independence; they had widened their mental and social horizons ... and they were determined not to give up lightly the control over their own lives that they gained by spending the money they earned for themselves.[29]

Defining and understanding women posed a new challenge for social commentators and for men alike. Pat Barker drew on this in 1991 in the first part of her fictional First World War trilogy, *Regeneration*, when she discussed Second-Lieutenant Billy Prior and Sarah, his working-class munitions-worker girlfriend,

> He didn't know what to make of her, but then he was out of touch with women. They seemed to have changed so much during the war, to have expanded in all kinds of ways, whereas men over the same period had shrunk into a smaller and smaller space.[30]

In discussing modernity and its implications for gender identities, Rosi Braidotti suggested that it represented 'the crisis of masculine identity in a historical period when the gender system is being challenged and restructured'.[31] One could argue that the First World War was a defining moment of modernity and in this respect it was without equal as a moment of restructuring. War loosened patriarchal control, and domestic responsibilities were necessarily redefined in ways which ruptured gender identities. Women's wartime roles differed due to obvious factors such as class, age, and marital status, but also due to the nature of the war, which saw a stark separation between the home and war fronts. Although uniformed service-men were a familiar sight on city streets and troops were highly mobile, most women did not directly confront the danger of war between 1914 and 1918.[32] They did, however, deal with the consequences of war; with the loss of their husbands, brothers, sons, friends and lovers as well as with the physical damage and psychological scarring experienced by the survivors. Most families experienced loss and anxiety, and for those women who served at the front, the experience was beyond comprehension. From this they acquired 'secret knowledge ... that transformed the consciousness, the senses, the very soul of the initiate, who was thereby ushered into a wholly different existence'.[33] As Vera Brittain put it, 'the war ... is too gigantic for the mind to grasp'.[34]

Wartime experiences also jolted women's personal lives. Spending time with other women, they discussed more openly their marriages, their sexual feelings and attitudes. Married women's relationships with their husbands were sometimes questioned as they recognised men's complacency and their own lack of fulfilment. Sexuality was a particularly highly charged issue, and Susan Kingsley Kent has argued that, partly in response to war, there was a new awareness of women's sexual needs: 'The new accent on motherhood was accompanied by a growing emphasis on the importance of sexual activity, sexual pleasure, sexual compatibility between husband and wife.'[35] Significantly, the anxieties underpinning these discourses of female sexuality frequently centred on the masculinisation of women's dress and the blurring of gender identities which came from women wearing uniforms and factory clothes. This was particularly acute during the First World War as such images clearly jarred against the dominant images of femininity which were evident before the war. Such images also recalled to popular memory the prewar struggle for women's suffrage and anti-suffrage feelings.[36] Writing in 1931 Caroline Playne remembered her perceptions of munitions workers:

> A short local train came in, drew up and disgorged, on the instant, a couple of hundred de-humanised females, Amazonian beings bereft of reason or feeling, judging by the set of their faces, bereft of all charm of appearance, clothed anyhow, skin stained a yellow-brown even to the roots of their dishevelled hair ... Were these really women?[37]

Home Chat provided a distinctive formula for being a woman which was well established and familiar. For one penny, an array of advice and information was available, mainly concentrating on the traditional concerns of the home and the family, but with some references to jobs and careers.[38] Love and marriage figured prominently in both fiction and features, and significantly women were given some practical advice in dealing with men. In June 1914 a feature asking 'Is *Any* Man Easy to Live With? A Question that Every Woman Sometimes Asks of Herself' elicited a surprisingly modern reply:

> In a condition of society where one half [of] the world is economically dependent upon the other half, the dependent half takes orders with small protest. It has to. [However] in the last twenty years women have become human beings. They have begun to reflect on their position. The fearful daughters of a past generation are to-day going their own way to work and to play.[39]

Changes in women's social and political position prior to the war clearly framed this assertion of their right '*to reflect on their position*'. Along with subsequent historians, contemporary commentators detected a difference in women's consciousness during the First World War.[40] Surprise and condescension characterised the views of the magazine's social commentator, otherwise known as 'A Man o' the World', when he wrote, 'Women are astounded at their own capacity – their own utility and value in the complex organism of ultra-modern life.'[41]

From September 1914, *Home Chat* had a new role: to map out a place for women within the conflict. The focus was initially on women's role on the domestic front, and, in an article entitled 'Householders and the War', the editors asked, 'What ought we to do? What can we do to help our country, and to defend from want and distress those for whom we are responsible?'[42] The covers of the magazine, which were particularly important in visually representing its editorial content, shifted from images of romance and the young and fashionable, to those dealing with war themes as depicted in the first issue of October 1914 which, under the headline 'Billeted: A Story of War', depicted a soldier billeted in a private home playing the piano.[43] This particular image of a smart, educated young soldier contributing to a convivial evening at home was obviously designed to reassure those who harboured anxieties about having strangers billeted in their homes. Other articles dealt in a relatively factual way with aspects of wartime.[44] In the early years of the war, magazine covers showed women crocheting, and included articles such as 'Cook – On the War: On War-time Manners' and 'How England "Mothers" Her Army'.[45] At the same time there were already efforts to provide stories dealing with other aspects of life and designed to alleviate the gloom of war, such as the short story introduced with the headline 'Nothing to do with the War!', which gave a light-hearted account of 'Dolly of the Dailies: The Surprising Adventures of a Newspaper Girl'.[46]

Alongside these, *Home Chat* ran features on the practical details of women's life that such work threw into disarray, including childcare. Dr Truby-King, the magazine's health specialist advised on 'feeding by the clock' for babies, and the advantages of the new crèches were explained next to a photograph of the London Woolwich Arsenal workers' crèche.[47] Significantly the magazine did not shy away from controversial subjects such as illegitimacy, war babies and unmarried mothers. The magazine's social observer, 'A Man o' the World', discussed the problems of war babies and illegitimacy in June 1915, pointing out that illegitimacy during wartime was not just an issue for the 'lower' classes.[48]

Interest in romantic love and marriage was underpinned by an insistence on the importance of fashion and appearance in the pages of *Home Chat*, and although it is tempting to read this as evidence of the regulatory nature of such magazines, this also drew attention to the high level of concern around representations of the female body during wartime. Wartime sharpened and intensified the experience of modernity, and women's 'practical negotiation of ... life and one's identity within a complex and fast-changing world' took on new meaning, as did their attempts to make sense of this visually through fashion.[49] *Home Chat* played a crucial part in articulating and delineating – on a weekly basis – new technologies and a vast array of consumer products for women, as well as pointing to new types of work and leisure, and personal relationships. Ostensibly about reaffirming women's traditional roles in making clothes and dressing up to meet social expectations, *Home Chat* also functioned to represent women's changing lifestyles, and although fashions could be both mundane and highly impractical, discussions of women's dress and appearance were firmly 'located' within the context of modernity.

Fashion, as both social and cultural artefact and as representational process, was increasingly discursive during the period of the First World War and it provided a highly charged space in which femininity, modernity and class identity were negotiated. The fashionable female body in particular became an interface where different values and ideologies overlapped and competed, and definitions of the female body were firmly located in the gender uncertainties which accelerated and intensified. Often living away from home, young, single women in particular began to imagine themselves differently. Even married and older women with a little more to spend could experience the pleasures of wearing new clothes. A magazine such as *Home Chat* tried to direct and inform women about fashion, but it sent out mixed messages. It attempted on the one hand to support women as they took on different responsibilities and as their approach to dress and appearance changed. But on the other hand it attempted to steer them towards images and roles which were not too contentious – practical, but at the same time feminine – often leading the magazine's editors and writers into uncertain territory.

Fashion drew attention to key aspects of women's identity, particularly sexuality and gender, but also class as it became less easy to read social status from dress. Land Girls, who took over agricultural jobs in men's absence and were largely drawn from the working class, reputedly wore their breeches off duty, whereas wealthier women apparently made a fashion out of looking shabby, thus undermining the dress codes which had previously delineated social status. Officially fashion was to be put in abeyance for the duration of the war, but it was also recognised that the country's morale required women to literally 'keep up appearances'. Their appearance was intrinsic to the war effort, but certain types of feminine images were preferred above others: those based on an upper-middle-class ideal of women as essentially decorative, idle and passive. In discussing *Home Chat* at the end of the nineteenth century, Beetham writes:

> *Home Chat* assumed that physical appearance was central to femininity and that in this respect at least women were not born but made and made themselves. Even 'the plain girl' could make herself 'as popular and charming as her Beautiful Sister'.

Central to that making was 'fashion' which was explicitly linked to the ideal of the Lady.[50]

The ideal of being a 'lady' was crucial in defining femininity in *Home Chat*, and during wartime, as class distinctions as well as gender relations were disrupted, such an ideal was especially important. Many working-class women worked in close proximity to women from the middle and upper classes; however, there were key differences in approach to dress and fashion as well as to ladylike behaviour. Whereas upper-middle- and upper-class women could enjoy the privilege of dressing up to their 'normal' social position and dressing down to demonstrate their patriotism and commitment to the war effort (by wearing uniform or shabby work clothes on the streets), for the first time, the better-off working-class and the lower-middle-class readership of *Home Chat* had access to fashionable clothes by dint of their jobs and better wages.

The contradictory nature of class and gender identities was increasingly evident in the pages of *Home Chat* as the editors and features writers avidly promoted new fashions, and fashionable looks, and offered an infinite number of fashion tips. The frivolous and the highly practical coexisted, as in September 1914, when the *Home Chat* fashion editors, Camilla and the aristocratically styled Lady Betty, advised on 'Easy to Make Fashions'. With little sense of contradiction, they wrote an article entitled 'Dress – Not Fashion' (10 October 1914), in which they argued, 'Nobody is thinking about fashion just now, but most of us will soon be thinking about a pretty blouse ... a woman's duty is to try to make herself as nice as she can.'[51] At the same time, although the magazine's letters pages were filled with complaints from women about long hours, about standing all day, and difficult journeys to work, concerns about fashion were still clearly evident as it was recognised that 'munitions work was undeniably fashionable'.[52] This extended to the wearing of khaki and uniforms on the street as these became statements of both fashion and patriotism. Significantly this new-found fashionableness was accessible to women from the lower classes as well as those from higher up the social scale, as munitions clothes, uniforms and khaki were widely available irrespective of class.

In the early twentieth century, high fashion was generally diffused in only one direction: downwards from the upper classes to the lower classes; however, the working class had 'become major consumers of the new mass media and capitalised leisure activities – publishing, the cinema, the recording industry, radio, dancing, fashion'.[53] Fashionable styles changed relatively quickly in the context of developing capitalism, and Paris led the way for fashionable women's clothes. However, women's access to fashion information widened within the context of modernity.[54] Department stores, mail order, advertising, paper patterns and women's magazines were available to more women across the country. New styles from the fashion centres were widely diffused, and it was possible to see in magazines such as *Home Chat* the increasingly simplified rectilinear outlines of Paris couturier Paul Poiret's designs, for example. Although the dominant fashionable 'looks' were still largely predicated on luxury and leisure, during the First World War other fashionable 'looks' emerged from the very different context of work; from munitions and uniforms, thus demonstrating the ways in which women's fashion could be influenced by mass as opposed to high culture.

Importantly, fashion allowed women to signal their new-found identities visually – even if it was only for the duration of the war – by wearing uniforms or garments designed for work, in the street for pleasure.[55] There was a great deal of concern at the time that war was making women more 'masculine' as they took on modes of behaviour more typical of men by becoming independent and self-reliant, working outside the home, and managing their own finances. Their clothes were practical responses to this, and although such changes were often read at the time as 'masculine', they were still highly feminised, as women's magazines show. Pretty fabrics, delicate bows and ribbons, glamorous make-up, and brightly coloured scarves were combined to 'feminise' some of the more austere wartime looks (Figure 1). As a report in the national newspaper the *Daily Mail* put it:

> the wartime business girl is to be seen any night out alone or with a friend in the moderate-priced restaurants in London. Formerly she would never have had her evening meal in town unless in the company of a man friend. But now with money and without men she is more and more beginning to dine out.[56]

Eating out is clearly interpreted as a sign of female independence here, yet some women had eaten out alone or with other women from the mid to late nineteenth century.[57] It became a necessity for some women when they were geographically isolated from their families working as munitions workers and poorly served by cooking facilities in their temporary accommodation. With little time to spare between shifts, eating out and wearing their munitions clothes on the street was inevitable.

The contradictions of identity inherent in women's fashion during wartime are summed up visually in the poster designed by Septimus Scott entitled 'These Women Are Doing Their Bit: Learn to Make Munitions', which was produced to encourage women to take up munitions work (Figure 2). In this, a young woman with her hair drawn back in a safety cap, pulls on her overall at the start of her shift. With a plain, shortened calf-length skirt and blouse, this evocative wartime

All Easy To Make.

Very, very simple patterns. Just the thing to try your hand on if you have never made your own clothes before.

By CAMILLA and LADY BETTY.

VERY few of us will have much money to spend on dress this autumn, and probably many who have never done so before may feel that they must make some of their own clothes.

One girl I know, who is an excellent amateur dressmaker, has announced that she will "help her country" by giving free lessons in dressmaking to any friends who are too hard up to pay a dressmaker, but yet don't know how to set about the work themselves. And it is really quite a good way of helping.

But it is only one instance of the help-one-another spirit that is to be found all over the country just now. Everybody is doing what they can.

People who don't know much about dressmaking want very, very simple patterns indeed, so we shall try to do our part to make things easy by providing these. The designs will be for garments easy to cut out, and easy to make so that even people who know practically nothing about dressmaking will find no difficulty in tackling them.

A tailor-made coat and skirt runs away with a lot of money, so in case you want to make your own, our first sketch shows

A SIMPLE TAILOR-MADE.
(Sketch No. 2821.)

Navy-blue serge is the medium we would suggest for this simple but smart little suit.

The skirt is absolutely plain, and the coat of simple Magyar cut, the fulness of the body part drawn into a deep waistbelt, a shaped basque concluding the scheme.

We have chosen this design because a basqued coat is so much easier to fit than any other.

A collar and revers cut in one makes a nice finish to the neck, which is sufficiently open to allow of the wearing of one of the lingerie collars that make such a delightful finish to a Navy serge coat.

Particulars as to quantities of material required will be sent with patterns.

A SIMPLE TAILOR-MADE.

(Sketch No. 2821.)—This design has been chosen because it is so much easier to fit a basqued coat than a straight up and down one. The skirt is perfectly plain, while the coat is just as simple, being Magyar style, with a wide revers collar. In Navy serge, with self-covered buttons, it would work out excellently. *Flat paper pattern, 1s. 0½d.; or tacked up, including flat, 2s. 6½d.*

A BETTERMOST BLOUSE.

(Sketch No. 2824.)—The wide flat armhole blouse is a very easy style to make. The front panel effect shown is merely two narrow folds of contrasting material laid on, and fastened in place with a row of French knots; collar and cuffs are edged with the same. *Flat paper pattern, 6½d.; or tacked up, including flat, 1s. 3½d.*

Figure 1: 'All Easy to Make', *Home Chat*, 5 September 1914. Reproduced by permission of the British Library.

Figure 2: 'These Women Are Doing Their Bit. Learn to Make Munitions', poster designed by Septimus Scott. Reproduced by permission of the Imperial War Museum, London.

image highlights the sense of purpose experienced by the independent young munitions worker temporarily loose of familial ties. Such images suggest an entirely different world to the highly regulated life typical of domestic service which was endured by large numbers of working-class girls. Similarly, contemporary photographs of munitions workers, as well as those of VADS and WAACs, although less glamorous, show a casual female body. Calf-length loose dresses and uniforms, belted at the waist, brought an informality to women's dress that was unheard of a few years earlier. Clothes such as these reveal women as subjects rather than objects; engaged in active lives outside the home and unconstrained by many of the social mores governing appropriate female behaviour. Such informality, increasingly integral to women's fashions both during and after the war, undercut the elaborate dress rituals which epitomised upper-middle-class femininity in the Edwardian era. Recruitment posters and photographs of this type sent powerful messages to young women that they could be independent and they could contribute to the war effort in a more dynamic way than knitting for the troops.

It is something of a paradox that as women's lives underwent momentous change, their personal appearance should attract such attention from the editors of *Home Chat*. Wartime practicalities were evident throughout the pages of *Home Chat*, although the editors found the lure of fashion for its own sake hard to resist. Whereas one issue might suggest, 'The reign of fashion is over for many and many a long day … The aim of fashion writers and designers to-day is to show how plainly other people are dressing, not how elaborately',[58] another issue dictated 'the narrow skirt is a thing of the past, and the new one measures sometimes as much as six yards around the hem'![59] These apparent contradictions led to the emergence of a number of representations of appropriate fashionable looks for women, as those clad in breeches and short skirts appeared in the same issues as women wearing clothes in the latest Paris styles. These were rather elongated and simplified at the outset of war, but by 1916 a clearly defined waistline was discernible. According to Camilla and Lady Betty writing in 1916, 'women are to present a more fluffy, feminine appearance than has been the case for some long while. The trend in favour of a less masculine style in dress is unmistakable.'[60] Accompanying this 'fluffy femininity' was, however, a marked casualness which differentiated women's fashions from ten years earlier, and which suggests a response to the more recent experiences of wearing clothes for wartime work. The highly corseted outline of the Edwardian era was replaced by a looser, less structured look which nonetheless required the aid of corsets. Softly gathered blouses were tucked into narrow skirts which draped and ruched at the waist rather than being panelled and gored. Feminised ties were often worn around the neck, and décolletage was open and informal. The 'easy to make' patterns included in *Home Chat* allowed women a good deal of flexibility to mix items of fashion as they desired, and recommended fabrics often included those like cotton that were hard-wearing and practical. Although the patterns were quite complex and could be difficult to follow, many women had some dress-making skills, acquired as young girls and improved upon as the demands of family life arose.[61] It is perhaps ironic that the visualisation of this new female identity depended on the continuation of such a traditional female task.[62] For those with few such skills, less time but more money, a visit to the home of a local dress-maker and the purchase of materials from the nearby draper would be sufficient to acquire a moderately priced new outfit. Drapers' shops dominated small towns and cities throughout Britain, and although they tended not to lead the way in stylistic innovation, such knowledge could be gained from the magazines and from department stores.[63] Through such mechanisms, the look of high fashion reached a wider audience.[64]

The fashion advice in *Home Chat* was supported by the inclusion of very practical information about all aspects of women's beauty and grooming. In an article entitled 'What Should a Typist Wear?', those confused about office dress codes were advised to wear 'a plainly-made serge costume. Nothing about it to date. Just plain with a stock collar and tie … And if a girl must have some sort of colour about her outdoor attire she could easily introduce it in wings on her hat.'[65] The unmistakable uniform of the 'New Woman' was described as the obvious solution to the problems facing working women. It was practical and smart, but importantly it also functioned as a symbol of emancipation and modernity. In a manner which typifies the magazine's approach of aiming to balance the traditional and the modern, the fashion editors directed women to the latest styles:

> Everyone is mad about the tango, and dresses are made specially for it. The short, slit, draped Liberty or velvet skirt, with a full tunic dropping lower behind than in front, is the most graceful thing so far, otherwise the effect of the body in movement is decidedly ungraceful. Very light and brilliant colours can be worn at a tango tea in Paris, and there is a certain tomato red which is specially named 'tango' that one sees a great deal.[66]

The dipped hemline of the dance dress and the smart practicality of the serge costume and blouse (see Figure 1) epitomised different, but related facets of modernity. Both were glamorous and chic, but a sense of movement, spectacle and performance influenced the diaphanous bodices, panniered skirts and slit or uneven hemlines of the dance dress. Dancing the tango required a type of physical flamboyance and a lack of restraint which was at odds with the prewar generation. Equally at odds, but for different reasons, was the remarkably minimal 'tailor-made' suit which epitomised the young, working woman in a man's world, albeit a 'feminised' and glamorised one. This latter image evoked most forcefully the inroads that women were making into the world of work, a process exacerbated by wartime needs. A number of 'femininities' coexisted then within women's wardrobe, and with the aid of *Home Chat* paper patterns, women could move relatively easily from one identity to the other in the peculiar circumstances that existed during wartime. The ultra 'femininity' evoked by these wide, flowing dance skirts was seemingly at odds with women's increasing confidence outside the home, yet they were part of a wardrobe which might also include a uniform, munitions wear and/or other work clothes.

As the war continued, *Home Chat* included articles that outlined suitable clothes for munitions and other types of war work. In 'Dress for War Workers' photographs showed young women workers wearing bloomers and shirts that were just below the knee, alongside an article which declared:

> It looks as if war-time work would bring about something of a revolution in women's workaday attire ... There is no doubt about it that you are HANDICAPPED if you go haymaking or harvesting or gardening or feeding the pigs in an ordinary skirt.[67]

The photographs accompanying this piece showed women wearing skirts which were just below the knee for gardening, and gaiters, a long linen coat and Panama hat for haymaking. Another article in the same month discussed the dress of the 'Lady Postmen', who looked 'very neat and business-like ... in their plain skirts and blouses, with their bags slung over their shoulder'.[68] In both articles, the discussion of suitable dress for war work was couched in the language of fashion rather than just 'dress' in order to emphasise women's duty to remain at all times within the bounds of what was considered 'feminine'. The photographs of the women gardening and haymaking were accompanied with credits which declared 'Fashions for Gardening' and 'Fashions for Haymaking', whereas the garments were clearly intended as practical work clothes. This particular article examined the background to reformed dress prior to the war, and it reminded its readers of the 'hideous and ridiculous' bloomers which were now, in the special conditions of wartime, described as practical and appropriate items of dress.[69] A few years earlier, bloomers had been tolerated for sport, but as the writer in *Home Chat* made clear, in the public mind they were associated with the suffrage movement.

For the first time, representations of fashion in *Home Chat* drew on a range of different visual codes from those used in regular fashion features. Reformed styles of work dress were unusually modelled by women doing particular jobs: the parcels lady wore a shortened skirt and three-quarter coat on her bicycle; the agricultural worker wore trousers, a shirt and straw hat as she dug in a field; and the Southampton tramway conductors wore 'short sensible skirts' just below the knee so as to run up and down the high steps of the tram.[70] The static, languidly posed images normally adopted to represent latest fashions were eschewed for photographs of women in the process of working, thus emphasising the practicality of their clothes. Two things are significant here: firstly, the juxtaposition of manual labour and fashion clearly detached fashion from its association with leisure as well as undermining any pretensions to 'ladylike' behaviour; and secondly the visual style and representational codes of the magazine diversified in response to the fragmentation of women's identities. As if in recognition of this very process, permeating the writings on fashion and dress in *Home Chat* was an attempt to provide some sort of rationale for these highly contradictory messages and images which directly addressed the reader's expectations and prejudices. An article from 1916 entitled 'How the Girl of the Period Faces War', liberally illustrated with images of women wearing breeches and uniforms, revealed the difficulties which this posed (Figure 3). Regretting 'such an old head on young shoulders', the writer admitted

Figure 3: Women farm workers wearing breeches, *Home Chat*, 18 March 1916. Reproduced by permission of the British Library.

that the modern girl is 'self-willed and full of assurance … and absolutely determined to get her own way'. At the same time, acknowledging the country's dependence on 'these fearless young women', now an important resource, the writer adds ruefully, 'well we made her ourselves. When she was in the nursery we were greatly allured by the dogma of feminine emancipation, and preached the rights of individualism for every creature.'[71] The reality for a large number of the magazine's readers was that war produced unconventional lives, and fashion was just one of a number of things that had to adapt. Women had already changed and representations of the fashionable female body in *Home Chat* undoubtedly contributed to this ongoing process.

From this study, it is clear that representations of women's fashion in *Home Chat* provided an important arena for defining and renegotiating women's gender and class identities between 1914 and 1918. As one of a growing number of relatively new women's magazines which addressed the needs of an expanding skilled working-class and lower-middle-class female readership, *Home Chat* was uniquely placed to delineate shifting gender and class relations. These shifts were especially acute during the First World War as women's lives became more complex and more demands were made on them, but it was also the case that women's lives had already undergone considerable change due to social, economic and political factors. *Home Chat* contributed to these changes by offering a lively formula of articles which depicted the range of experiences and ambitions of women. It revealed the complexities and the discontinuities in women's lives by examining a number of aspects of their experience, including home and work, love and sex, fashion and appearance, as well as their attitudes to war and their roles in it. Arguably, in its pages there emerged a 'dissonance' between women's 'lived experiences' and the visual representations of femininity in fashion, which could be especially acute in particular issues of the magazine, but in such representations it is clear that women's fashion and appearance constituted a 'feminised' space in which gender identities were renegotiated and contested, but also in some ways reaffirmed. Widespread participation in the workforce, particularly by younger women from the skilled working class and lower middle class was the catalyst for this crisis in representation which significantly focused on fashion and personal appearance. Fashioning the female body involved women in the process of 'becoming' feminine, thus highlighting the contingent nature of femininity. As this study of fashion in *Home Chat* makes clear, dressing to tango, dressing for the munitions factory and dressing to drive an ambulance in France involved women in representing themselves as female when the precarious and transitory nature of gender identities was being acknowledged, albeit reluctantly at times.

Notes

1. I am thinking here of survey texts of fashion history such as Lou Taylor, and Elizabeth Wilson, *Through the Looking Glass: A History of Dress from 1860 to the Present Day* (BBC, 1989), and Elizabeth Wilson, *Adorned in Dreams: Fashion and Modernity* (Virago, 1985).
2. This point is debated by Susan Kingsley Kent in *Making Peace: The Reconstruction of Gender in Interwar Britain* (Princeton University Press, 1993), p. 3.
3. Kingsley Kent, *Making Peace*, p. 3.
4. Other new magazines included *Home Notes* (1894), *My Weekly* (1910) and *Woman's Weekly* (1911).
5. See Margaret Beetham, *A Magazine of Her Own, Domesticity and Desire in the Women's Magazine 1800–1914* (Routledge, 1996).
6. For further information on women's magazines in addition to Beetham cited above, see Ros Ballaster et al. (eds), *Women's Worlds: Ideology, Femininity and the Woman's Magazine* (Macmillan, 1991); Marjorie Ferguson, *Forever Feminine: Women's Magazines and the Cult of Femininity* (Heinemann, 1983); Ellen McCracken, *Decoding Women's Magazines* (Macmillan, 1993); Cynthia White, *Women's Magazines, 1693–1968* (Michael Joseph, 1970); Janice Winship, *Inside Women's Magazines* (Pandora Press, 1987).
7. See Beetham, *A Magazine of Her Own* for further discussion of these ideas.
8. Beetham, *A Magazine of Her Own*, p. 12. Drawing on the ideas of other cultural critics, Beetham discusses the proposition that the fragmentation of women's magazines made them potentially subversive of men's cultural codes in a number of ways.
9. The birthrate fell from 35 per thousand in 1870 to 29 by 1899, to 24 by 1913. See Martin Pugh, *Women and the Women's Movement in Britain 1914–1959* (Macmillan, 1992), p. 1.
10. Kingsley Kent, *Making Peace*, pp. 12–13.
11. Kingsley Kent, *Making Peace*, p. 14.
12. This point is made by Pugh, *Women and the Women's Movement*, p. 2. Pugh cites a particularly buoyant British economy as a key factor.
13. 'They Also Serve', *Home Chat*, LXXVIII/1016, p. 436.
14. This is the process by which the daughters of the upper echelons of British society would be presented at court and then effectively displayed at dances, parties and the theatre, in order to attract an appropriate suitor. It was an annual ritual for the well-connected and the well-off.
15. 'How the Girl of the Period Faces War', *Home Chat*, LXXXIV/1096, p. 480.
16. 'Open Doors for Women Workers: Wonderful Changes' by George A. Wade, *Home Chat*, LXXXI/1051, p. 227.
17. 'Open Doors for Women Workers', p. 228.
18. 'Open Doors for Women Workers', p. 228.
19. Pugh, *Women and the Women's Movement in Britain*, p. 22.
20. This was undertaken by Lloyd George after he gained office in May 1915. A voluntary arrangement known as the Treasury Agreement was negotiated. This enabled unskilled women to take over some skilled men's jobs or aspects of them. By July 1916 the figures for women in the various metal and engineering industries (representing those industries producing munitions and equipment) had risen from 212,000 in July 1914 to 520,000. See Arthur Marwick, *Woman at War 1914–1918* (Fontana, 1977), p. 73, and 'Open Doors for Women Workers', *Home Chat*, LXXXI/1051, p. 227.
21. In July 1914 there were 3,276,000 women in industry, by April 1918 there were 4,808,000 – an increase of almost 1½ million. The biggest increase was in the chemical and engineering trades which included munitions. See Gail Braybon and Penny Summerfield, *Out of the Cage: Women's Experiences in Two World Wars* (Pandora, 1987), pp. 38–9.
22. By November 1918 there were 40,000 in these services largely in the VADs and WAACs. See Braybon and Summerfield, *Out of the Cage*, p. 44.
23. At the start of war, the numbers of women in domestic service stood at 1,658,000, but by 1918 the number was 1,258,000. (Pugh, *Women and The Women's Movement*, pp. 19–20.)
24. Braybon and Summerfield, *Out of the Cage*, p. 16.

25. Whereas a housemaid could earn a paltry 5s a week, a munitions worker could earn £3 a week (possibly £4 with overtime). (Braybon and Summerfield, *Out of the Cage*, p. 58.)

26. Except in a few areas of the Midlands and the north of England (the Potteries and the Lancashire cotton mills were examples), working-class women were expected to stop work after marriage; however, those in desperate circumstances worked at home taking in sewing or washing.

27. Maud Pember Reeves, *Round About a Pound a Week* (1913; repr. Virago, 1994), p. 213.

28. See Braybon and Summerfield, *Out of the Cage*, pp. 105–7, for a discussion of childcare.

29. Gertrude Williams, *The New Democracy: Women and Work* (Nicholson & Watson, 1945), p. 57.

30. Pat Barker, *Regeneration* (Viking, London, 1991), p. 90.

31. Rosi Braidotti, *Nomadic Subjects: Embodiment and Sexual Difference in Contemporary Feminist Theory* (Columbia University Press, 1994), p. 239.

32. In contrast to the Second World War when war was 'at the doorstep', and large numbers of women were killed during the blitz. Of 130,000 civilians killed during the blitz, 63,000 were women. (Pugh, *Women and the Women's Movement in Britain*, p. 264.)

33. Kingsley Kent, *Making Peace*, p. 52.

34. Kingsley Kent , *Making Peace* (from Vera Brittain's *War Diary*, October 1915), p. 53.

35. Kingsley Kent, *Making Peace*, p. 108.

36. See Jenny Gould, 'Women's Military Services in First World War Britain', in *Behind the Lines: Gender and the Two World Wars*, ed. Margaret Randolph Higonnet and Jane Jenson (Yale University Press, 1987).

37. Kingsley Kent, *Making Peace*, p. 37.

38. See 'Shall I Go in for Nursing', *Home Chat*, LXXVI/981, p. 5; 'The Playbox' and 'Gladys Owen's Tea Parties', *Home Chat*, LXXVI/981, pp. 23 and 35; 'The Playbox' and 'Gladys Owen, If You Came to Dinner on Thursday', *Home Chat*, LXXVI/983, pp. 119 and 131.

39. *Home Chat*, LXXVII/1004, p. 561.

40. See, for example, Pugh, *Women and the Women's Movement in Britain*; Kingsley Kent, *Making Peace*; and Braybon and Summerfield, *Out of the Cage*.

41. *Home Chat*, LXXXII/1059, p. 15.

42. *Home Chat,* LXXVIII/1017, p. 490.

43. *Home Chat*, LXXVIII/1020.

44. For example, one described 'Life in the Army', and another showed Sir John French, Commander of the British Army, on the cover. (*Home Chat*, LXXVIII/1021, pp. 41–2; and *Home Chat*, LXXX/1036.)

45. *Home Chat*, LXXX/1035, 1036, 1044, cover, pp. 125, 441.

46. *Home Chat*, LXXX/1021, pp. 45–51.

47. *Home Chat*, LXXXI/1048, p. 119, *Home Chat*, LXXXII/1067, p. 323.

48. *Home Chat*, LXXXI/1055, p. 395.

49. Mica Nava and Alan O'Shea, *Modern Times: Reflections on a Century of English Modernity* (Routledge, 1996), p. 11.

50. Beetham, *A Magazine of Her Own*, p. 195.

51. 'Easy to Make Fashions', *Home Chat*, LXXVIII/1016, pp. 443–4, and 'Dress Not Fashion', *Home Chat*, LXXIX/1021, p. 53.

52. Braybon and Summerfield, *Out of the Cage,* p. 62.

53. Anthony O'Shea, 'English Subjects of Modernity', in Nava and O'Shea, *Modern Times: Reflections on a Century of English Modernity*, p. 29.

54. The best discussion of this remains, in my view, Wilson, *Adorned in Dreams*.

55. See Braybon and Summerfield, *Out of the Cage*, p. 75.

56. Marwick, *Women at War*, p. 127.

57. See Lynne Walker, 'Vistas of Pleasure', in Clarissa Campbell Orr, *Women in the Victorian Art World* (Manchester University Press, 1995), pp. 70–85.

58. *Home Chat*, LXXXI/1057, p. 473.

59. *Home Chat*, LXXX/1044, p. 455.

60. *Home Chat*, LXXVI/983, p. 109.
61. See Barbara Burman, *The Culture of Sewing: Gender, Consumption and Home Dressmaking* (Berg, 1999).
62. I am grateful to the editors, Carole Turbin and Barbara Burman, for this point.
63. See James B. Jefferys, *Retail Trading in Britain 1850–1950* (Cambridge University Press, 1954).
64. See Erika D. Rappaport, '"A New Era of Shopping": The Promotion of Women's Pleasure in London's West End, 1909–1914', in *Cinema and the Invention of Modern Life*, ed. Leo Charney and Vanessa R. Schwartz (University of California Press, 1995) and Erika D. Rappaport, *Shopping for Pleasure: Women and the Making of London's West End* (Princeton University Press, 2000).
65. *Home Chat*, LXXVI/982, p. 65.
66. *Home Chat*, LXXVI/981, p. 44.
67. *Home Chat*, LXXXII/1061, p. 81.
68. *Home Chat*, LXXXII/1061, p. 171.
69. *Home Chat*, LXXXII/1061, p. 81.
70. *Home Chat*, LXXXIV/1096, p. 491.
71. *Home Chat*, LXXXIV/1096, p. 491.

9

Fashion, the Politics of Style and National Identity in Pre-Fascist and Fascist Italy

Eugenia Paulicelli

An *Istituto Luce* documentary entitled *La Grande adunata delle forze femminili* (Great parade of female forces) illustrates the ambivalent policy of the fascist regime towards the roles and images of women and reveals links between fashion, the policy that governed it and political culture during the fascist regime.[1] The documentary describes a rally that took place in Rome on 28 May 1939, chronicling a massive female parade organised by Mussolini himself. This national gathering of women from all over Italy that celebrated the twentieth anniversary of the founding of the *Fasci giovanili di combattimento* was an occasion to display women as an integral part of the national body politic through their uniforms, and their roles in the family and society. The film shows women from the Red Cross, students, athletes from the Orvieto Academy representing a wide range of sports, women from the countryside and others, all gathered at the Circo Massimo before going on to parade to Piazza Venezia for the welcome salute and speech by Mussolini and other *gerarchi*. Three distinct moments of the documentary juxtapose shots of women wearing sports uniforms with shots of the women from the countryside wearing regional costumes. These stills (Figures 1, 2 and 3) illustrate the sharp contrast between the military-like uniformity of the athletes and the women in traditional regional costumes, but also the differences in dress within the latter group of women. Those in regional costume wear accessories such as necklaces, earrings, shawls, lace collars, ornaments and headgear. Their body postures differ from the women wearing the regime-sponsored or sports uniforms: they look as if they are out taking a walk rather than marching. For the majority of these women, the differences in ornamentation were signs of their sense of belonging to strong local traditions of fine artisan craftsmanship, something that

Figure 1: 'Massaie Rurali, Great Parade of Female Forces', Rome, 28 May 1939. Reproduced by permission of 'Istituto Luce', Rome.

Figure 2: 'Women Rowers, Great Parade of Female Forces', Rome, 28 May 1939. Reproduced by permission of 'Istituto Luce', Rome.

Figure 3: 'Massaie Rurali, Great Parade of Female Forces', Rome, 28 May 1939. Reproduced by permission of 'Istituto Luce', Rome.

continues to characterise and distinguish the Italian style even today in the twenty-first century.

What we find illustrated in the documentary footage is a visual confirmation of the two-sided, indeed ambivalent, nature of the fascist attempt to include every single woman of the Italian peninsula in its purview. In this way, the regime could show off its 'good face' in tolerating and appearing to exalt at one and the same time the modern woman wearing the military uniform and local time-honoured traditions. This is especially striking in the perfectly symmetrical and geometric space occupied by the women dressed in uniforms seen against the more disorganised and scattered space occupied by the women in regional costumes.

Victoria De Grazia has described the contrast between the two female components seen in the documentary as a 'shift from military to fashion' and attributes to the women dressed in their regional costumes a rebellious individualism at odds with the massive presence of military uniforms.[2] However, because in this section of her article De Grazia relies not on the documentary itself, but on a written report of the parade, she misreads the meaning of the women's local costumes which, far from being a transgression of the dress codes prescribed by fascism, fell squarely within those codes. We must not be misled by the apparent contrast between uniformity and individualism that seems to be displayed in this popular spectacle. In fact, according to fascist regulations, the women from the countryside, the *massaie rurali*, were encouraged to wear their local costumes in order to highlight the nation's rich and diversified traditions as well as to display the beautiful embroidery that they themselves had created. Dress historian Patrizia Ribuoli in her essay 'Le Uniformi civili nel Regime Fascista' (Civil uniforms under the fascist regime) affirms, in fact, that wearing regional costumes 'instead of the official uniforms' for the *massaie rurali* was 'perfectly in line with fascist ideology' insofar as it maintained and emphasised traditions of which the whole peninsula could be proud.[3] This, of course, does not undermine De Grazia's challenge to the extent of women's consent to fascism, a thesis supported by other important scholarship. But a closer examination reveals that neither fascist policy on fashion (which allowed space for the cohabitation of both military uniforms and local costumes) nor attempts to circumvent that policy (which De Grazia erroneously attributes to the *massaie*) are simple, univocal questions. Indeed, despite extensive study of how fascism manifested its two unmatchable ambivalent souls in the construction of the so-called 'new Italian woman', there is no serious work on the role that fashion and its apparatus of diffusion played in the project of nationalising women or in the creation of a recognisable 'national style'. Neither have serious attempts been made to gauge the extent to which its policies were successful. My aim here is to offer an in-depth analysis of the political dimension of fashion under fascism, and how and why fashion became a concern of the fascist state to the point of giving rise to a specially created government institution.

By way of introduction, let me mention a number of steps taken by the fascist regime in the field of fashion in order to create the context in which the spectacle of the women's parade and its bearing on the fascist representation of women is best interpreted. The emphasis given to local costume had an immediate link to the massive initiatives undertaken by the regime in this regard in the 1930s. In 1932 Mussolini founded a government institution called the *Ente autonomo per la mostra permanente nazionale della moda* (Autonomous body for the permanent national fashion exhibition, EAMPNM). To this was delegated the task of overseeing the complete cycle of creativity and production of fashion by way of two major biannual exhibitions and fashion shows held in Turin, the body's headquarters. Later, in 1934, the name of the institution was simplified to *Ente nazionale della moda* (National fashion body, ENM). The ENM aimed at organising and promoting the Italian fashion industry and made various attempts to regulate women's dress. Since one of the credos of the ENM was to persuade female consumers and dress-makers to seek inspiration in Italy's domestic roots, the organisation emphasised regional customs as a form of true *italianità*. Not only fashion but also related domestic traditions were recruited with the aim of boosting patriotism and national pride. One of the tasks of the regime was to promote sectors of the handicraft industry most closely linked to fashion, such as embroidery, lace, coral and straw, by creating another body, the *Ente nazionale artigianato e piccole industrie* (National body for crafts and small industries). To rally support for this policy, one of the members of the Italian royal family, the Princess of Piedmont, Maria José, was photographed in 1933 in the fashion magazine *La Donna* wearing a regional costume. On the same pages of the magazine, we find juxtaposed drawings of evening gowns designed by Brunetta Mateldi, inspired by regional costumes (Figures 4 and 5). The space given to local costumes in the fascist rally is a sign, then, neither of women's dissent nor of their individualism, but is an expression of the official policy of exalting nationalism through the inclusion of regional differences, a policy which had a key influence on fashion. The subtext to these photos was to use the Savoy princess's royal image to convince well-off women and aristocrats not to go to Paris to purchase their dresses but to remain instead within the national boundaries.

Fascist fashion policy regarding the promotion of and emphasis on regional dress as a source of inspiration for Italian dress design had several tangled threads. Within the fashion world, fascist policies did not

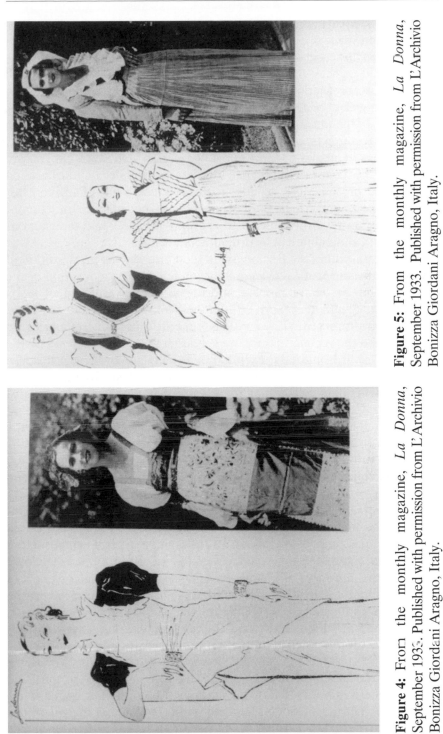

Figure 5: From the monthly magazine, *La Donna*, September 1933. Published with permission from L'Archivio Bonizza Giordani Aragno, Italy.

Figure 4: From the monthly magazine, *La Donna*, September 1933. Published with permission from L'Archivio Bonizza Giordani Aragno, Italy.

meet with complete approval. Not everybody agreed that folkloric dresses could be an always valid and single source of inspiration. Brunetta's drawings published in the pages of *La Donna*, set alongside the photographs of the princess in local costume, bear only a vague similarity to the clothes worn by Maria José. The tension between these diametrically opposed modes of conceptualising fashion is conveyed by the ambiguous expression of the models' eyes that betray a subtle sarcasm as they direct their gaze towards the costumes worn by Her Highness. The models in the drawings seem almost to whisper, 'We understand that what you are wearing is the dictate of the regime, but it is we who decide what fashion we like the most.'[4] Most striking in these pages is the sharp contrast between the country look of the queen – a sort of populist attempt suggesting that royals were close to ordinary people – and the glamour and sophistication hinted at in Brunetta's drawings.

The tension within the fashion world illustrated by the juxtaposition of images in the pages of *La Donna*, between the fascist valorisation of the local and the desire for more glamorous designs, is but one of many tensions that undercut and ultimately destabilised fascist policies. Another was represented by conflicts between the fascist emphasis on the local and the regime's policy of repressing regionalism, including the campaign towards a standardised national language over local dialects. In 1936 the ENM published the *Commentario dizionario Italiano della moda* (Commentary and Italian dictionary of fashion) by the journalist and writer Cesare Meano, whose aim was to purge the language of fashion of all foreign terminology. Meano's text is a great example of the formation of a fashion discourse in the cultural politics of fascism. It strove to uniform the social body and appearance in dress, but also and no less to create a national character that would fit fascist ideology and gender representation.

By encouraging standardisation of dress, the fascist regime also sought to erase the numerous differences of class, geography and culture that were characteristic of 1920s and 1930s Italy, and to a great extent still are today. One example of this was the massive use of civil uniforms. Some photographs show newborn babies wearing a fez, the headgear typical of fascist militants. To foster standardisation, the regime invested in the creation of a national textile and apparel industry. This policy was driven, above all, by the desire to wrestle Italian fashion away from what was perceived as the pernicious influence of French fashion, which, in the West, was seen as the indisputable world leader. The attempts to create the industrial bases for domestically produced fashion were part and parcel of the regime's attempts to homogenise a stratified social body, divided by gender and class. These initiatives, which recruited the mass media (newspapers, magazines, Luce newsreels, cinema, parades, public exhibitions, etc.) to unite the Italian population in a single sense of national identity, were successful only at the level of display and spectacle and did little or nothing to change the underlying structures of society.

In a similar vein, the *massaie rurali* seen in the newsreel are presented as if they were participants in the regime's achievements in the field of textile production. They are thus rendered protagonists in the life of the fascist state at the same level as the urban and urbane middle-class women with slender and fashionable bodies who were consumers of make-up and trendy clothes. Artificially classed together, these two sets of women actually had little in common in terms of geography, class, consumer habits and power. This approach coincided with another tenet of fascist ideology, that of persuading social subjects who were weaker either on account of their gender or class – women and workers – to believe they were agents and protagonists of history.[5] This same intent underlies the order to wear civil uniforms and so give the illusion of a sense of order and discipline, but above all to suggest a belonging to the fatherland and to Il Duce.

In the world of fascist fashion policy there was room, albeit with considerable tension, for both the local and the national, the traditional and the modern, the prolific mother and the Orvieto academist: opposite figures who turn out to be two sides of the same coin, two products of the same ideology that aimed at controlling women in the same breath as it put their differences on display. Nevertheless, difference, especially in terms of resistance to the strict codes, was not to disappear even in the dream of the fascist totalitarian state. Despite the regime's attempt to coagulate and control the social body in a centrifugal mode, influencing the masses, their costumes, social habits and language, an opposite, centripetal force was always at work almost side by side with it. Paradoxically, the very same institutions whose task it was to standardise and control also became the site for the construction of several niches of individual creativity. Indeed, as concerns both production and consumption, no field illustrates this complex two-fold process better than fashion. Fashion on the one hand assisted in the alignment of the regime's policies, while, on the other, producing from within its system visible forms of individualism and creativity that went against fascist policy.

In the crucial years between the two World Wars, fashion acts as an essential tool for the study of the social transformations of various components of Italian society. The following section discusses how fashion discourse and the policies and politics produced under fascism illustrate the hegemonic mechanisms recognised by Antonio Gramsci as determining factors in the formation of a historical bloc. At the same time, however, I would like to underline how such an analysis reveals that the inherent complexity of cultural phenomena characterised by creativity and individualism cannot be contained by a single hegemonic discourse.[6] In this way, we can also explain why neither individual and creative uses of fashion, nor the style of specific designers, can be understood under a single unifying discourse. These are all elements that are not always controllable, and which can ultimately help in the crumbling and transformation of sedimented hegemonic political ideologies, cultures and styles.[7]

It would be a mistake to think that fascist policy on fashion was produced in an ahistorical vacuum. Much of fascist policy, especially the nationalistic intent that inspired the creation of national bodies, is rooted in the debates in and around fashion that took place in Italy in the pre-fascist liberal years. Indeed, there is a strong line of continuity in the role ascribed to fashion that stretches from the early years of the twentieth century up to and into the fascist period. The two periods share the assumption that fashion is to have first and foremost a role in the forming and cementing of national identity. Focusing on these two periods shows that, in the pre-fascist years, Italian fashion was already characterised by the high degree of creativity that would enable it to emerge on the world scene at the end of World War II and gradually impose its presence on a massive scale in today's global market. In this respect, my study differs from Nicola White's examination of the post-World War II years. Italian fashion was not born in the period of reconstruction, as White leads one to believe. The great strides forward that the Italian fashion industry took in the years following 1945, which White accurately chronicles, were posited on what the industry had already achieved in the prewar period. My examination of fashion before and under fascism complements White's study because it shows how the seeds of the postwar emergence of Italian fashion as a major player on the international stage were sown.[8]

Any style of dress or ornamentation linked to a particular country, its people, its culture, and what constitutes its national character, has a long history that is intimately connected with the development of fashion. White is certainly right when she affirms that the expression 'easeful grace', used as early as 1951, has become increasingly synonymous with 'Italian style'. Nevertheless, the concept of mixing elegance and ease, as in the case of 'bella figura' – looking good – and natural ease – grace – both have a long history in Italian culture. In fact, the ultimate point of reference for much Italian fashion, whether it be pre- or postwar, was the Renaissance. As early as the beginning of the sixteenth century, Baldassarre Castiglione's *The Book of the Courtier* (1528) first identified Italian style in language, manners and dress, with the concept of *sprezzatura* (a well-constructed easeful or 'natural' grace).[9] As we shall see, references to the Italian Renaissance are legion in the world of fashion, either as a moment of national grandeur to be recovered, or as a moment when a national style was at its zenith. Fittingly, when Giovanbattista Giorgini organised his famous fashion show in his family palace on 14 February 1951, at which the best of Italian designers showed off their designs to US buyers (opening the way for the massive and lucrative influx of Italian creations on the US market), he did so in Florence, the quintessential Renaissance city, underlining the continuity between the achievements of that period and those of the contemporary designers, heirs apparent to that glory.

Fascist policies on fashion were complex and multi-layered in another way. Not only did they valorise simultaneously the old and the new but they also reflected the social, political and cultural transformations of classes and individuals resulting from the process of modernisation that gathered steam in the latter fascist years.

If, on the one hand, Italy was entrapped by the exasperated nationalism of a totalitarian regime, on the other, the nation also sought to keep up with the modernising pace of other western capitalist countries. The process of modernisation, begun in the prewar years, never stopped, but went ahead at an incredible speed in the postwar period. In this, the influence of the US, and all it stood for in those years, cannot be underestimated. Since the 1920s, the US ready-to-wear industry had been gradually improving and expanding both nationally and on the European market. At the same time, the culture industry, through Hollywood films, popular, female magazines and department stores, targeted a growing number of Italian consumers whose modes and responses helped to shape a new form of popular culture, now more open than ever before to embracing US goods and entertainment.[10] Fascist Italy, despite the politics of self-sufficiency during its autarchic phase, turned out not to be completely immune – in common with other European countries – from a gradual transformation of the social body, as well as from a process of 'Americanisation'. Hollywood films played a key role in this, but so did the visits made to North America by industrialists, economists and others, including Olivetti and Pirelli, Ferragamo and Emilio Pucci, who were destined to have leadership roles in the development of Italian accessories and fashion.

As we shall see, fascism's inability to escape from its entrapment between two opposing and contradictory forces, tradition and modernism, was reproduced in its fashion policies. The twin figures of the prolific mother and the athletic woman with her dynamic body, both figures that were promoted by the regime, reveal this internal dichotomy. Just as importantly, fascist attempts to control strictly the appearance of the social body were destined to fail, since fashion is by definition nourished by the constant drive for the new which is inherent in its transient nature, its erotic appeal and its strong hold on imagination and creativity.

In order to understand the continuity of the debate on nationalism, fashion and the search for a national style leading into the fascist period, let us take a step back and consider the most prominent figures in the battle for an 'Italian fashion' in the years preceding the advent of fascism.

Rosa Genoni, one of the pioneers and most fervent advocates of efforts to wrestle Italian fashion away from its subalternity to France, clearly represents continuity between the two periods.[11] Genoni was, indeed, a remarkable figure whose important role in the history of fashion has not been sufficiently acknowledged.[12] She firmly believed that it was important for Italians working in the field of fashion to discover and develop an autonomous style that was recognised as Italian and not a mere copy of French fashion. Born in 1867, in the midst of the Italian unification process, Genoni was determined and courageous. The first dress-maker to become a writer, teacher and political activist, she was also the first to attempt a historical account of Italian costume. She never tired of pointing out both the limits of Italian fashion and the potential it possessed for becoming independent from foreign models. Genoni understood that the Renaissance was an important inspiration for the Italian tradition in creativity and art in the field of fashion. Thus, she studied the paintings, fashion plates and sketches of the period in which the 'Italian' style first spread to the major courts of Europe, particularly the role played by powerful women such as Beatrice and Isabella D'Este. She saw the vestiges of the Renaissance tradition in the wealth of creativity and design in Italian local craftsmanship and the sewing skills of many tailors and dress-makers. To give new blood to this patrimony, she proposed strategies for organising Italy's almost anarchic field of fashion. These ranged from providing better theoretical and practical training in professional schools to establishing formal links among various branches of the sector, like fashion houses, workers and 'case di confezione'. Some of her proposals, for example the formation of a state-controlled institution (later to be called ENM) charged with organising the clothing and textile industry, were later to be taken up by the fascist regime.

The two-year period in which Genoni worked as a première in a Parisian atelier was fundamental to the elaboration of her ideas. In Paris, she studied history of art and costume, as well as technical and artistic drawing, and realised that the production of a dress resulted from collaboration between the dress-maker and a group of experts in the decorative arts. She also realised that some materials used in French dress-making were imported from Italy, but that, even if Italy possessed the raw materials for a fashion industry, something important was lacking. French fashion was famous even beyond the nation's boundaries. In fact, for the wealthy buyers who could afford them, French clothes were synonymous with what was chic, simply by virtue of being French. One of the effects of this in the US, as well as in Italy, was that French-sounding labels were put on domestically designed and produced garments.[13] As far as Genoni was concerned, French couture and design were the enemy to be defeated, in part for political and geographical reasons. Paris had long been considered the world capital of fashion and was the centre from which emanated the entire fashion industry. There was no such centre in Italy. Rather, Italy boasted several centres of art and culture, and diverse craft and culinary traditions. Italy was a de-centred nation, with a weak sense of the nation as a united entity. An article in the May 1919 issue of *Lidel*, that drew on one of Genoni's earlier proposals to set up a government institution to oversee and coordinate the fashion industry, revealed the internal rivalry between cities that hindered the creation of a national fashion industry strong enough to challenge France.[14]

The major lesson Genoni learned from her Parisian experience was that the setting-up of professional fashion schools was key for the development of an autonomous style. She was also convinced that people working in the apparel industry lacked a sense of who and what Italy was and had been, especially in the arts and culture. For this reason, a vital plank in her project to organise and launch the Italian decorative arts and fashion involved turning back to the past in order to find the sense of identity, conspicuously absent in the present, that could be promoted both domestically and abroad.

Genoni never passed up an opportunity to point out that Italian decoration, fabric and other raw materials were often acquired by French couturiers at a low price and then found their way back to the Italian market as French-produced clothes and were sold at extortionate prices. This kind of exploitation, she wrote, had to be stopped. She was in a perfect position to observe the backwardness of Italy in terms of organisation and lack of proper schools. She denounced this situation in a paper she gave at the *Primo congresso delle donne italiane* (First congress of Italian women), held in Rome in 1908, at which Genoni participated as a member of the Socialist delegation. She points out that technology – as we would call it today – and art are not separate, but work side by side. In addition, and no less importantly, she hints at a more accessible notion of art, one that does not see it solely in terms of museum objects or works of art jealously kept in private houses and salons for the privileged few to admire. She advocated the idea of a less elitist concept of art that is visible in objects on display in everyday life, on the street: in the form of architecture, the decorations of buildings, statues, and clothing. She stresses the strong Italian tradition for popular, public art appreciated by ordinary people, harking back to the Middle Ages and the Renaissance. However, she wanted Italian dress designs to use the Italian Renaissance not to reproduce passively the nation's past glories, but rather as a source of artistic inspiration to incorporate traditions into new concepts of style and beauty that would express the pulse of modern times.

At the *Prima conferenza nazionale delle donne italiane* Genoni presented a motion in favour of a national fashion approved by the majority present. Her proposal stressed the vital role that could be played by an organised and strengthened official body that would bring together the female crafts of lace, embroidery and the decorative arts, which represented a source of wealth in the Italian peninsula's female economy.[15] Genoni also emphasised that the French style of elaborate decoration was not always suitable for the Italian woman and her lifestyle; and that the ready-made clothing industry could produce more affordable garments styled for Italian women's tastes and needs. Her observations about differences between highly priced couture and the more democratic version of fashion foresaw the future of fashion in Italy.

Genoni's approach to the history of Italian fashion had political, cultural and aesthetic implications.[16] Indeed, Genoni's role was not limited to her insight into the economic importance fashion could play in Italian life and her desire to recoup Italy's Renaissance traditions. She was also acutely aware of fashion's close links to women's issues and feminism. She insisted that feminism should in no way consider fashion and style as diminishing women's political claims. Because women have consistently expressed themselves through fashion and legions of women worked in the clothing industry, feminism would do well not to under-estimate the impact of fashion on women's lives. In sensing that aesthetics is part and parcel of fashion, and in seeing it as a strength, not as a belittling of women's intellectual ability, Genoni was a pioneer in articulating issues that have come to the fore only recently in the fields of feminism, history of fashion and fashion theory.[17]

In sum, Genoni was a leading light in the debate on key issues: the return to the Renaissance as a moment of inspiration and pride; the need to update the institutions governing Italy's fashion industry; and the urgency of freeing Italian fashion from French hegemony. Her ideas were part of pre-World War I thinking about patriotism and nationalism. The clothing and fashion industry fostered the definition of a national character and boosted national pride, and also contributed to the modern economy. Constructive and non-elitist, Genoni's project is characterised by its sensitivity to workers' rights and the attention she pays to women both as workers in the industry and as consumers.

For other participants, however, in pre-World War I debate on culture and the arts, fashion was the terrain that represented a rupture between past and present. In this context, Genoni represents a voice of moderation when compared to the Futurists, who were far more radical in their ideas. The experiments and creations of painters like Giacomo Balla, and others such as Fortunato Depero, and Ernesto Thayant who designed for Madeleine Vionnet, although they did not become part of mainstream fashion at that time, represented a far more elitist form of rupture and transgression. These were taken up in France, where couture drew inspiration from Futurist design, as is illustrated by many of the exhibits at the *Exposition internationale des arts decoratifs et industriels modernes* held in Paris in 1925.[18]

Even if they did not meet with much enthusiasm in Italy, Balla's designs of clothing and accessories, from hats, scarves and shoes to handbags, still remain an important historical document, a source of inspiration for new ideas regarding shape and colours and experimentation in both male and female clothing. The Futurist project aimed at revolutionising society and individuals. This project had personal implications insofar as it required the redesigning of clothes to suit the revolutionary spirit. Futurist clothing design represented deep ruptures in the symmetry of the cut of clothes in order to allow the wearer more movement and dynamism, and eliminated the bourgeois dark and 'neutral' colours of male clothing. The Futurists were amongst the most vociferous proponents of war, and associated nationalism and militarism with dress.

Although the Futurists stressed clothing as inherently political and communicative and linked it to the debate on intervention in the war, their nationalism never took the form of a policy that aimed at creating conditions for the emergence of the kind of national fashion for which they argued. The patriotism animating Genoni's project of creating an autonomous Italian fashion was, in the years before and immediately after World War I, light years away from the kind of bellicose and expansionist nationalism of sectors of Italian cultural and intellectual debate. The war, however, was going to profoundly influence the social and political transformation taking place in Italy and the rest of Europe, and was to bring to women's lives new forms of agency and subjectivity.

World War I brought drastic changes to society, the economy and the organisation of the family. Many women whose husbands, fathers, brothers and sons were at war took positions of command in the many sectors of the economy left vacant by men called to fight in the war. New problems arose when men returned from the front and, as in other countries, in Italy women were pushed out of the industrial workplace. However, the new political situation and the growing sense of unease and instability following World War I, did not erase some of the benefits that the tragedy of the war had paradoxically brought women, even in fascist Italy. Because many women proved they were capable of doing men's jobs in addition to being care-givers and house-makers, some gained greater freedom and power within and outside their homes. In addition, the gradual shift toward an industrial economy and the influence of Hollywood cinema and US commodities led to an increase in consumption of mass-produced goods. Most advertising was now directed at middle-class female consumers, many of whom managed the household budget.[19] Because of the growing demand for goods aimed specifically at women, a number of periodicals oriented towards a female audience came into being, grew in number and continued to increase from the beginning of the century and throughout the 1930s.[20]

The magazine *Lidel*, founded in 1919 and aimed at a female bourgeois audience with spending power, was among the most important because of its focus on fashion and other activities including work, and its mission to transmit a sense of *italianità*, of Italian national identity and nationhood. Named for Lydia Dosio De Liguoro, but also for *Letture, illustrazioni, disegni, eleganze, lavori* (Readings, illustrations, drawings, elegance, works), *Lidel* was highly sophisticated in design and appearance, and featured contributions from well-known writers and artists such as Grazia Deledda, Luigi Pirandello (both later to be awarded the Nobel prize for literature), Ada Negri, Carola Prosperi, Sibilla Aleramo, Amalia Guglielminetti, Goffredo Bellonci, Matilde Serao, Eugenio Treves and others. *Lidel*'s mission was a tall order. In a variety of fields a sense of nation seemed to be in tatters. Yet, using fashion as a major vehicle for the development of its cultural, aesthetic, political and economic project, *Lidel* strenuously promoted a modern Italy and a sense of pride and belonging among its people.

One of the central pillars proposed to counteract French hegemony in fashion was the centralisation of Italian fashion policy, delegating its enactment to a state-run body. In her articles, De Liguoro reaffirmed that such a centralised governmental institution would not only organise the clothing and textile industries, including tailors' and dress-makers' shops, but also promote better professional education for people working in the field. Many of the proposals put forward by Genoni and De Liguoro mirror each other, and differences between them came to the fore only once the fascist regime came to power. Unlike Genoni, who had no sympathy for fascism and Mussolini, De Liguoro belonged to the female *ardite* from Milan, pre-fascists dissatisfied with the outcome of World War I who identified with conservative nationalists' belief that at the Treaty of Versailles Italy had been cheated out of territories promised by its war allies.

Thus, it was partly out of national political sentiments that De Liguoro exhorted wealthy Italian women not to buy dresses in Paris, and reflected on the prejudices discouraging them from patronising Italian fashion houses. Yet the practical details of her project were similar to that of Genoni. De Liguoro complains that a very fine dress, created by a Milanese fashion house and called 'Villa D'Este', was refused by clients as it had an Italian label. Later the outfit was labelled 'Ville d'Orléans', and presented as the creation of a made up Parisian house called K.Y. (two letters that do not belong to the Italian alphabet) and was sold immediately, a successful strategy that continued for the whole season. Like Genoni, De Liguoro stressed that fabric from Como and Florence, purchased at a low price and then used to create French models, came back to Italy to be sold at high prices.[21] Using patriotic language and emphasising the potential of Italian artisans and artists for the development of an Italian style, she mentions several ways to boost local craftsmanship in lace and embroidery in a number of Italian cities and regions.

The history of fascist fashion policy is one of continuities rather than ruptures. Especially in the regime's first nationalist phase, fascism's strategies in the field of fashion drew on the cultural ferments and proposals originated in the world of fashion in liberal Italy. In fact, the foundation of fascist fashion policy was in line with the project envisaged by Genoni and De Liguoro, but co-opted and turned to the regime's own overtly nationalistic end.

The construction of a new Italy and new Italians, for men, women and children alike, was a vital plank in the fascist regime's political and cultural project. The subtext of much of the intellectual debate of these years is the question of how to rescue and render great the recently born Italian nation: how to awaken it from the state of slumber into which it had slipped, and how to produce a new national subject, no longer prey to the character deficiencies that had led Italy into its current state of near crisis. Fashion played an important role in this process both in the pre-fascist years and in the years of the regime itself. During fascism, De Liguoro continued to be one of the strongest voices arguing for the need to build a national, efficient fashion industry able to compete and counteract the hegemony of French fashion. But now her voice took on much more decidedly fascist overtones. Believing that the key to a successful domestic fashion industry was demand from within Italy itself, she argued, long before the regime's autarchic phase, that the fashion industry, working in conjunction with the regime and its press, needed to create a form of consensus among Italian upper-bourgeois women and

encourage them to direct their vanity towards domestic products. Nevertheless, De Liguoro's articles notwithstanding, not a great deal of
attention seems to have been paid by fascist authorities to the economic
and cultural benefits that could accrue to the nation through a more
energetic promotion and organisation of fashion. It was not uncommon,
in fact, for Italian couturiers to complain of the lack of effectiveness of the
ENM in the coordination of initiatives to promote Italian fashion
abroad. One recurrent problem was that collections were presented in
the very season for which they were intended – winter clothes in winter,
for example – and so not enough time was allowed for the production
and launch of the models outside Italy.[22]

Some of these problems were never to be completely resolved, even
with the inception of the ENM. Divisions still persisted among various
cities like Milan, Rome and Turin, all of whose distinct regional traditions
in craftsmanship and industry hindered the development of a univocal
direction for fashion policy. Milan, especially through Montano's
initiatives and leadership, tended more towards the development of an
Italian-style haute couture, which had been missing in Italy. Frictions,
then, persisted between the artisan tailors and an industrial sector that
was more directed towards mass production.[23]

We should remember, however, that De Liguoro's thoughts on fashion
policies under fascism were not at odds with fascist ideology on women.
Indeed, her articles often betray fascism's reactionary and classist
vision of women. Moreover, De Liguoro carried out her lobbying from
the columns of the *Popolo d'Italia*, the fascist daily newspaper, endorsing
Il Duce's pronouncements on fashion: 'An Italian fashion in furniture, in
decoration and in dress does not yet exist: it is possible to create it, it
must be created.' In the same article she reveals the paternalistic
ideology underlying her writing in the fascist years, when she states that
women working for the clothing industry would be much happier
working at home instead of 'tiring out their brains' working at their desks
in an office.[24] This, of course, is firmly in line with fascist policy, which
was not to give women the same opportunity as males in clerical and
professional work. It was also a policy dictated by the fear that in time of
crisis and unemployment women would steal men's jobs. As a result, it
seemed easier to control women's lives while they were working from
home and receiving low wages, but at the same time producing goods of
the highest quality for their patrons.

The consolidation of the regime's policy on fashion was part and
parcel of a more general move to consolidate control in other areas of
Italian life. In the 1930s several government institutions were set up to
ensure fascist control over areas like sport and leisure time. Along with
fashion the regime used the cinema and sport to convey and solidify

its message of modernity, discipline, order and amusement. Sport and cinema, in fact, thanks to institutions such as the *Organizzazione nazionale dopolavoro* (National after-work organisation, hereafter OND) presided over a consistent part of the Italian lower-middle and working class's free time. However, it would be wrong to think that these activities were completely under the thumb of fascist control. For many Italians, fashion, sport and cinema offered a chance, even momentarily, to escape the grip and greyness of a totalitarian regime.

Fashion, sport and cinema were interrelated in many ways because they drew on the visual power inherent in spectacles displaying dynamism and modernity. Thus, cinema, sport and fashion were linked in the diffusion and the creation of national models and physical bodies with which women of all classes could identify or fantasise. Movie-going became one of the most popular pastimes. Especially in less urban parts of the country, where fashion magazines were a luxury item, films inspired ordinary women and dress-makers, who often copied the fashionable items they saw on the screen. The diffusion of sport influenced women's fashion a great deal, simplifying lines without sacrificing elegance. A number of pictures in these fashion magazines, as well as the photographs of women attending the Female Academy in Orvieto, confirm this, showing snugly fitting, yet comfortable, clothing and suits, composed of different interchangeable pieces, as well as shirts and skirts showing slender and attractive bodies.[25] This fashion was intensified during World War II when, despite the lack of material and fabrics, the magazine *Bellezza* continued to offer new ideas for women's fashion. The emphasis was given to clothing, coats, raincoats and accessories that showed a casual elegance and which were made out of autarchic (domestically produced) fabrics.[26] For example, gloves were made out of fabric because of the lack of leather, and the designer Ferragamo made platform shoes constructed from readily available cork and transparent plastic, using bright colours and an avant-garde design. *Bellezza* also showed a series of pictures called 'Sport and Fashion', emphasising the relationship between the two, which had gradually changed women's lives as well as their self and public images. The women in these pictures wear dresses, deconstructed suits and cardigans in wool mixed with *fiocco* (an artificial fibre); their raincoats are lined with fabric in bright colours and are worn over simple yet stylish dresses.[27] This relaxed elegance suggests that the relationship between sport and fashion would eventually lead to experiments in the design of clothes for the modern woman who works and has a busy life outside the domestic walls. In fact, the Italian designer Emilio Pucci, who became one of the icons of success during the Italian economic boom of the late 1950s, made sportswear his trademark.[28]

Stricter policies emerged from the ENM after 1935, following the fascist invasion of Ethiopia and the subsequent sanctions applied against Italy by the League of Nations. The economic hardship that had been intensified by foreign sanctions required a new set of regulations and led to the development of autarchic fabrics and fashion, so that the economy could become self-sufficient and not rely on foreign imports of raw materials. In these years, the textile industry was engaged in the production of the so-called '*tessuti-tipo*' that were to be approved and recognised as Italian by the ENM and to be used both for clothing, interior design and furnishing. In fact, artificial fibres domestically produced – such as rayon and *lanital* and others – became one of the successes in the autarchic phase of the regime.[29] To control and guarantee domestic production, the ENM introduced a label – called a *marca di garanzia* – for models and fabrics that now could be recognised as 'Italian' creations and products. At the same time, the ENM also established the percentage of Italianness – first 35 per cent, later 50 per cent – for fabric, models, or any production relating to fashion, accessories and textile. As the extant documents testify, the initiatives of the regime had a major influence on promoting the domestic production of textiles and fabrics. However, some of the well-known artists such as Marcello Dudovich and Ester Sormani did not waste any opportunity to express their dissatisfaction with the autarchic policies of the regime. They maintained that in order to create new models they needed the constant nourishment of new ideas and inspiration. This implies an openness towards other cultures and artistic experiments and their readaptation within the original design.[30] Here the artists meant that neither uniforms nor Italian regional costumes could be the only source of inspiration for fashion and that a culture closed in its nationalistic, totalitarian and autarchic modes was anathema to the creativity and change inherent in fashion.

During World War II, when Italy was occupied by two foreign armies – one fighting alongside Italian partisans against the Nazis, the other fighting with the Nazis' Italian allies from Mussolini's puppet regime – the fashion industry and single designers were not paralysed. For example, the Fontana sisters, one of Italy's leading postwar fashion houses, established itself in Rome in 1944 as soon as the Germans left the city, vacating the aristocratic building they had been occupying. Micol Fontana remembers that she was able to get the fabric she needed from Jewish retailers who had hidden their goods in their basements; she exchanged it for potatoes and other vegetables from her parents' farm outside Rome. Here, she recalls, they also helped to hide a Jewish refugee.[31] Despite adverse circumstances, many industrious, creative and resilient people working in the different branches of fashion prepared the terrain for the future success of Italian fashion in the post-World War II period. Indeed, as we have seen, the history of fascist fashion policy is one of continuities rather than ruptures. It was on the basis of the debate on nationalism that took place in the pre-fascist liberal period, as well as on the proposals put forward by Genoni, that many of the foundations for the postwar boom were laid. Mussolini was a beneficiary of this. His regime understood the political, economic and cultural potential of a national fashion. But, rather than invent fashion, fascism took advantage of it.

Notes

This essay is dedicated to the memory of my father, Nunzio Paulicelli (1918–2002), who was the first to teach me anti-fascism.

1. The Cinegiornale Luce of the rally is a 25-minute documentary held at the Istituto Luce Archive in Cinecittà, Rome.
2. Victoria De Grazia, 'Nationalizing Women: The Competition between Fascist and Commercial Cultural Models in Mussolini's Italy', in *The Sex of Things: Gender and Consumption in Historical Perspective*, ed. De Grazia and Ellen Furlough (University of California Press, 1996), pp. 337–58.
3. See Patrizia Ribuoli, 'Le Uniformi civili nel Regime Fascista', in *1922–1943: Vent'anni di moda italiana*, ed. Grazietta Butazzi (Florence, Centro Di, 1980).
4. See *La Donna*, September 1933.
5. See Patrizia Dogliani, 'Donne e partito', in *L'Italia Fascista: 1922–1940* (Sansoni, 1999).
6. In fact, the protectionism practised by the regime, a policy that to differing degrees was also adopted in the US and other European countries, had the effect of laying the foundations for an autonomous fashion industry and the sense of self that ensued.
7. It is interesting that, even in the use of fascist civil uniforms, people found various personal ways of self-adaptation to the norms. See Ribuoli, 'Le Uniformi civili', pp. 35–6.
8. Nicola White, *Reconstructing Italian Fashion: America and the Development of the Italian Fashion Industry* (Berg, 2000). The reference to fashion in fascist Italy is at pp. 76–7. See also the reference to the formation of the GFT group in 1932. This is a detail worthy of further study, see pp. 68–9.
9. I analyse these issues in depth in my forthcoming book: *Fashion Narratives: Gender and National Identity in Italy*, from which the present material is taken and where I dedicate two chapters to the Renaissance and the role of fashion in the creation of the public image, national character and identity. In sixteenth-century Italy the debate on style, literary and non, and its political valence was lively in a variety of texts by both female and male authors. See also E. Paulicelli, 'Performing the Gendered Self in Castiglione's *The Book of the Courtier*, and the Discourse on Fashion', in *Annalecta Husserliana*, ed. A. T. Tymieniecka, vol. 71, pp. 237–48.
10. Kathy Peiss, *Hope in a Jar: The Making of America's Beauty Culture* (Henry Holt and Company, 1998).
11. Antonietta Maria Bessone Aureli, 'Il Costume popolare in Italia', in *La Donna italiana*, 11 (1934), pp. 614–16.
12. For Rosa Genoni, see Aurora Fiorentini, 'L'Ornamento di "pura arte italiana": La Moda di Rosa Genoni', in the catalogue of the exhibition at the Galleria del Costume di Palazzo Pitti in Florence, *Abiti in Festa: L'Ornamento e la sartoria italiana. Florence, March 30–December 31, 1996* (Sillabe). The entry on Genoni is by A. Fiorentini Capitani, in *Dizionario della moda*, ed. G. Vergani (Baldini & Castoldi, 1999); the entry on Genoni in *Dizionario biografico delle donne lombarde*, ed. R. Farina (Milan, 1968), p. 568.

13. See Nancy L. Greene, *Ready-to-Wear and Ready-to-Work: A Century of Industry and Immigrants in Paris and New York* (Duke University Press, 1997), p. 112. I learned this in the course of the interviews I conducted with the couturiers Micol Fontana and Fernada Gattinoni, who worked for the atelier Ventura, one of the most prestigious fashion houses in the 1930s, with branches in Rome and Milan.

14. Fortunato Albanese, *Il Perché del Primo Congresso Nazionale per le industrie dell'abbigliamento* (Tipografia Colombo, 1918), pp. 9–10.

15. A comprehensive history of the Italian tradition in the decorative arts that also sheds light on the role women from different classes had, has yet to be written. For the US history on the topic see Carole Turbin, *Working Women of Collar City: Gender, Class, and Community in Troy, 1864–86* (University of Illinois Press, 1992); Wendy Gamber, *The Female Economy. The Millinery and Dressmaking Trades, 1860–1930* (University of Illinois Press, 1997), and for the British history, see Barbara Burman (ed.), *The Culture of Sewing* (Berg, 2000). In the arts of embroidery and lace, a local tradition linked to the social and economic history of a determined city and region existed. Usually aristocratic ladies had the role of supporting workshops of skilled women, most of them of modest origin, who produced wonderful crafts and decorations for dress and home. In the sixteenth and seventeenth centuries, several pattern books for lace and embroidery were published in Italy and Europe. This is the subject of Alessandra Mottola Molfino, 'Nobili, Sagge e Virtuose Donne: Libri di Modelli per Merletti e Organizzazione del Lavoro femminile tra Cinquecento e Seicento', in *La Famiglia e la Vita Quotidiana in Europa dal 400 al 600: Fonti e Problemi. Atti del Convegno Internazionale, Milan, 1–4 December 1986* (Ministero per i Beni Culturali e Ambientali, Pubblicazioni degli Archivi di Stato, Rome, 1986), pp. 276–93. According to Molfino, the pattern books for lace and embroidery, popular in the sixteenth and seventeenth centuries, reappear in the late nineteenth and twentieth centuries when ladies from the upper bourgeoisie and aristocratic classes, in order to preserve handicrafts, helped to organise female crafts workshops. See also Marina Carmignani et al., *Ricami e Merletti nelle chiese e nei monasteri di Prato dal XVI al XIX secolo* (Prato, 1985).

16. See catalogue of the exhibition held at the Galleria del Costume di Palazzo Pitti, Florence, *Abiti in festa. L'ornamento e la sartoria italiana*.

17. The prejudices Genoni is addressing in her article have been dispelled only with the appearance of new approaches to gender studies and history in the late 1980s. For further reading on these issues, as linked to fashion and feminism, see C. Evans and Minna Thornton, *Women & Fashion: A New Look* (Quartet Books, 1989); Elizabeth Wilson, *Adorned in Dreams. Fashion and Modernity* (Virago, 1985); Valerie Steele, *Fashion and Eroticism: Ideals of Feminine Beauty from the Victorian Era to the Jazz Age* (Oxford University Press, 1985). I have also addressed the relationship between women, fashion and agency related to Italian feminism, in 'Fashion as a Text: Talking about Femininity and Feminism', in *Feminine Feminists: Cultural Practice in Italy*, ed. G. Miceli Jeffries (University of Minnesota Press, 1994).

18. Enrico Crispolti, *Il Futurismo e la moda, Balla e gli altri* (Marsilio, 1986). See the introduction, 'La Moda e il Futurismo', and the references to the articles and interviews of Giacomo Balla that appeared in 1925 following the Paris Exhibition. In fact, Balla, visiting the exhibition and noticing so many objects and even the ceiling decoration of the salon of fashion, remarked: 'Questo è un *ballabile* bello e buono! Ma che ci sia un Balla anche quaggiù?' (p. 12).

19. See Victoria De Grazia, 'The Arts of Purchase: How American Publicity Subverted the European Poster, 1920–40', in *Remaking History*, ed. B. Kruger and P. Mariani (Bay Press, 1989); Victoria De Grazia, 'La sfida dello Star System: L'Americanismo nella formazione della cultura di massa in Europa 1920–1965', *Quaderni storici*, 58 (20), pp. 95–133; Karen Pinkus, *Bodily Regimes: Italian Advertising under Fascism* (University of Minnesota Press, 1995); Adam Arvidson, 'Between Fascism and the American Dream: Advertising in Interwar Italy', in *Social Science History*, 25 (2001), pp. 151–86.

20. Italy shared some similarities with other European countries in the proliferation of periodicals oriented towards a female audience. See Fiona Hackney, 'Making Modern

Women, Stitch by Stitch: Dressmaking and Women's Magazines in Britain 1919–39', in Burman, *The Culture of Sewing*.

21. Lydia De Liguoro, *Le Battaglie della moda: 1919–1933* (Luzzati, 1934), p. 41.
22. See Gabriella De Bosdari Di Robilant, 'Possibilità di affermazione dell'alta moda italiana all'estero', in *Congresso Nazionale Abbigliamento e Autarchia* (ENM, 1940), pp. 145–7.
23. Butazzi, *1922–1943*, p. 16.
24. De Liguoro, 'Verso una moda italiana', in *Le Battaglie della moda*, pp. 89–94.
25. See Lucia Motti and Marilena Rossi Caponeri (eds), *Accademiste a Orvieto: Donne ed educazione fisica nell'Italia fascista, 1932–1943* (Quattroemme, 1996); see also Patrizia Dogliani, 'Sport and Fascism', in *Journal of Modern Italian Studies*, 5 (2000), pp. 326–43.
26. *Bellezza*, September 1942.
27. *Bellezza*, September 1942.
28. For the importance of Pucci in the postwar, see Nicola White, *Reconstructing Italian Fashion: America and the Development of the Italian Fashion Industry* (Berg, 2000).
29. Maura Garofoli, *Le Fibre intelligenti: Un Secolo di storia e cinquant'anni di moda* (Electa, 1991); Bonizza Giordani Aragno, 'Le Avanguardie della moda dal 1930 a oggi', in Garofoli, *Le Fibre intelligenti*.
30. See Marcello Dudovich, 'Azione collaborativa del disegnatore di modelli per l'autarchia nell'abbigliamento'; Ester Sormani, 'Azione collaborativa del disegnatore di modelli per l'autarchia dell'abbigliamento', in *Congresso Nazionale Abbigliamento e Autarchia*, pp. 133–9.
31. My interview with Micol Fontana of June 2000 is to be published as an appendix in my forthcoming study, *Fashion Narratives*.

10

Style and Subversion: Postwar Poses and the Neo-Edwardian Suit in Mid-Twentieth-Century Britain

Christopher Breward

The young man ... dresses, when in London, in a neat dark suit, with well-pressed narrow trousers, cuffs to the sleeves of his jacket and possibly lapels to his waistcoat ... he would feel uncomfortable in anything other than a hard collar and a bowler hat. His more daring companions may flourish a flowered waistcoat and a velvet-collared coat; but if I mention too eccentric examples I may frighten the reader out of my argument. Let us agree ... that the average young man of position tries to give an air of substance without being stodgy: of having time for the niceties of life.[1]

In 1954 London couturier Hardy Amies captured the wistful and undeniably elitist tone of mid-twentieth-century British fashion commentary. Amies belonged to a generation of designers who progressed from the duties of work on the wartime Utility scheme to a more glamorous postwar incarnation under the auspices of the Incorporated Society of London Fashion Designers (ISLFD). Through its combination of traditional references (function-specific formal garments) with an ostensibly more utopian, democratic direction (new synthetic fabrics and an expansion of diffusion lines), their work was in tune with the dialectical tendencies of cultural production in 1950s Britain, which waxed nostalgically for prewar certainties whilst setting its sights firmly on the testing concerns of national reconstruction. With his fellow designers Norman Hartnell, Peter Russell, Charles Creed, Digby Morton, Michael Sherard, Victor Stiebel and John Cavanagh (the ISLFD was a clubby, all-male coterie), Amies tailored an Anglo-Saxon variation on the New Look, transporting the romantic escapism of Dior's Paris confections from the Seine to the Thames. ISLFD photographic shoots featured models whose imperious demeanour hinted at an Albion unbowed by years of bombs and rationing. Typically, they graced the spaces of a seemingly unchanged capital city in the corsets and petticoats which announced an end to frugality. The patrician façades of Horse Guards Parade, Trafalgar Square and St James's formed the backdrop for an astonishing display of female dandyism.

This juxtaposition of imperial London's 'manly' topography with the silk and netting of the couturier's salon is an intriguing one, for, as Amies's opening comments reveal and as this chapter will go on to argue, it was in the arena of men's rather than women's fashion that the most significant postwar developments would take place. The distinctive framing of the New Look on London's streets was perhaps suggestive of underlying concerns that the coming of an American-influenced mass-consumer culture, associated with feminine interests and desires, would further weaken London's diminishing reputation as a political and economic centre of empire. Contemporary fashion promotions therefore presented the city as a contested landscape in which the gendered practices of production and consumption competed for prominence. Indeed, whilst the fortunes of the home textile and luxury goods industries were increasingly reliant on the patronage of middle-class women in the department stores of the capital – even as the docks and other traces of traditional masculine labour declined and the markets of the former colonies disappeared – London's enduring status as the spiritual home to the gentleman appears if anything to have been strengthened during this transitional period. Such processes clearly demand a reorientation by the historian away from the usual concentration on women as innovators of fashionable style towards a consideration of the role of men in the operation of the fashion system.

Amies's reflections on masculine clothing were inspired by his recent appointment as consultant for the tailoring firm Hepworth's. His description of the dress-code of the aspirant young man is far more redolent of a long-established code for London life than the synthetic drafting of Parisian style on to the London scene that characterised the self-consciously patriotic activities of the ISLFD. The coordinates of what had become known as the Neo-Edwardian look are sketched out in Amies's prose. This was a 'revivalist' style of dressing that is confidently displayed in Norman Parkinson's 1950 photograph of a group of aristocratic Englishmen conversing in Savile Row. Tightly kitted-out in the products of that street, they have rejected the capacious hang of the Utility and Demob clothing that served their purpose in the drab circumstances of the recent past, opting for the panache of early twentieth-century sartorial styles – styles that in their original versions paid conscious homage to the Regency London of Beau Brummell. Bowler hats, polished shoes and rolled umbrellas hint at the glamour of the regimental parade ground, a space which had always provided important inspiration for the London dandy, while velvet collars, embellished waistcoats, ticket pockets, covered buttons and turned-back cuffs recall the ostentation of the Edwardian race track and music hall. In its adherence to the accepted rules of dressing, its sentimental nostalgia, and its sharp sense of modernity, the look captured in Parkinson's image also evoked dandyism's dual capacity for conservatism and innovation. The rewriting of the dandy's lexicon along revised class and territorial lines in the transformed and transforming London of the 1950s thus lent men's fashion a heightened significance as a marker of change. This chapter aims to assess the consequences of this process for the formation of sartorial stereotypes which challenged gendered and class-based expectations, and to test its subsequent interpretation in ongoing accounts of the development of fashionable style in the capital.

As a city of concrete spaces and intangible atmospheres, postwar London figured as a crucible for such stylistic reinvention, but in the context of continuity. Roy Porter alludes to the period as an Indian Summer, with all the cosy possibilities that the phrase suggests: 'the trams sailed majestically through pea-soupers; East Enders had their knees-up at the pub and went hop-picking in August; contented commuters ... tended their herbaceous borders ... variety enjoyed its swansong at the Hackney and Deptford Empires ... The coronation of Elizabeth II in 1953, when ... neighbourhood parties were staged in bunting festooned streets, was the high spot of London as a prosperous, well-integrated, secure ... city.'[2] Yet as the fifties progressed, premonitions of an unsettling modernity were more keenly felt. As tower blocks began to shadow church spires, new moral codes infiltrated the stuffiness of an official culture still run on Victorian lines, leading to 'a rare alliance between youth culture and commerce, aristocratic style and a new populism'. This was felt keenly in the changes affecting men's clothing. Popular historian Harry Hopkins, writing ten years later, pinpointed the social ramifications of a masculine style revival, whose expressive appeal seemed as rooted in the postwar cityscape as the new architectural grammar of plate-glass and steel which jostled for space with 'the time-honoured observances of cornice and moulding, pediment and column':

> And thus it came about that a ... discreet fashion revival among young men ... in the West End in 1948 ... a very tentative riposte to the women's 'New Look' ... crossed the River and, exaggerated – almost consciously guyed – became the defiant uniform of what the newspapers were soon calling the 'New Edwardians'. But most significant perhaps, was the Teddy outfit's function as the badge of a half-formed, inarticulate radicalism ... A sort of half-conscious thumbing-of-the-nose, it was designed to establish that the lower orders could be as arrogant and as to-the-manor-born as the toffee-nosed ones across the River ... The uniform's most important features lay, firstly, in the fact that ... it was, in origin, English class-based,

Figure 1: 'Savile Row', Norman Parkinson, 1950. Courtesy of the Norman Parkinson Estate.

secondly in its cost which … might exceed £100 … The Teddy costume conquered district after district in those years, making the fortunes of many a little corner tailor – and hairdresser – astute enough to 'humour the kids'. But, finally … the uniform gave way before the … gentler, more civilised, immensely variegated Italian and Continental styles which seemed to confirm and usher the opening society. And in England, where male fashions had always been one of those 'understood' things – essentially aristocratic, fear-edged, inhibition inlaid – nothing, it seemed, could ever be the same again.[3]

Hopkins's account of the rise of the teddy style, which traces its origins as a whim of upper-class Mayfair playboys, its migration to the deprived boroughs of south and east London, its importance as a mode of social resistance, and its rapid commercialisation at the hands of a growing retail sector adapted to the desires of the teenager, has become an oft-repeated mantra of sociologists and historians of popular culture. In the unprepossessing frame of the newly fashion-conscious postwar adolescent, journalists and academics have been able to inscribe a range of narratives that position the teddy boy at the centre of debates whose subjects have been as various as the collapse of older working-class ideals, the inevitability of crime in times of affluence, the homogenising effects of American culture, and the impact of new forms of teenage con-sumption on all of the above. The teddy boy was indeed a significant actor on the postwar social scene, his features and actions almost immediately taken up for analysis by columnists, photographers, film-makers, and criminologists.

The post-mortems ensued before the teddy-boy style was announced dead by the novelist and chronicler of youth cultures Colin MacInnes, who stated in 1965 that, 'though caricaturists (who really ought to start looking a bit – even the best of them) still draw dated Ted stereotypes, the style, in its authentic pure absurdity, is now only to be found in outlying holes and corners (I last saw it in a caff at Goring-on-Thames)'.[4] Sociologist T. R. Fyvel produced the first classic account of the mode in 1961. Noting their transference from Mayfair to Lambeth in the early 1950s, he identified in the dress codes of south London gang members a rejection of 'respectability' in preference for the easy attractions of a life passed on the borders between the legal and the illicit.[5] For Fyvel this signification bore material consequences which linked the Tony Curtis hairstyles, 'slim jim' ties and crepe-soled creepers adopted by the hoodlums who terrorised his own north London habitat to a generalised deterioration of the physical environment of the inner city, and the passing of 'traditional' family values for a selfish celebration of short-term pleasure:

Each Saturday and Sunday … I could see the small dark figures of boys and half-grown youths … wearing the identical Teddy boy suits … I sometimes thought that one could see the social wasteland through which they wandered in actual visual terms ... Row upon row of squat nineteenth-century slum streets ... stood condemned and so were harshly degraded, like a whole way of life ... together with memories of worn doorsteps ... mother at the sink and father shirt-sleeved in the kitchen with his newspaper ... To the young ... it did not matter that in its back streets this was a dispiriting region of blank warehouses, untidy street markets and sleazy lodging houses. In the main streets at any rate, the young felt surrounded by a full tide of confident life ... reflected in the ultra-modern layout of the chainstores; in shop windows crammed with radios, television sets, record players ... This London, offering its pleasures freely to those with money, spoke with the only voice of authority that mattered.[6]

Fyvel proceeded to illustrate the destructive tendencies of urban modernity, and of capitalism in particular, through recourse to detailed case-studies of those 'delinquent' young men whose pleasures disturbed his world view. He listed their expenditure on clothing, graded their leisure haunts and analysed their social prejudices. His was a cynical mode of investigation that thrilled to the otherness of the life which it aimed to describe whilst reserving a palpable disdain for the material evidence that constituted the style itself (which was clearly assumed to be lacking in taste). Thus the trappings of working-class dandyism, though spectacular in their expense and visual effects, symbolised little more than a naïve trust in the power of consumerism to transform humdrum realities. Furthermore, this false consciousness was seemingly so pandemic that Fyvel felt it necessary to show how its consequences could be felt globally from the Soviet Union through to the United States. London was simply one amongst many examples of a local culture in retreat from a coarsening vulgarity.

Later academic interpretations, predicated on an understanding of 'culture' as a mediated practice, rather than a universalising instrument of value-laden comparisons, have taken a less totalising view of the teddy-boy phenomenon. Texts including Paul Rock and Stanley Cohen's essay of 1970 have been more sympathetic to the idea that clothing and material culture might aid a negotiated sense of self-identification rather than disguise some older notion of authenticity.[7] Yet in their clear celebration of the romantic ideal of the working-class rebel, Rock and Cohen came close to supplanting one skewed version of reality with another. Their concern was to highlight the way in which the trajectory of the teddy boy was as much a process of journalistic misrepresentation, as it was a sequence of commercial and social transactions which placed the sartorial choices of slum dwellers on a par with those of West End socialites. Theirs is a discourse based on a premise of ownership, both of the image of delinquency as it was propounded by reactionary journalists, and of an attitude which Rock and Cohen felt found its most compelling incarnation on the streets of Lambeth rather than in the bars of Mayfair.

Dick Hebdige in his influential deconstruction of British subcultural styles, published in 1979, took a similarly proprietorial tone in relation to a selective trajectory of musical and fashion-related trends. In the most successful, elements of 'authentic' black street culture had been appropriated by white male working-class pioneers to forge radical new identities. For Hebdige, the 'uncompromisingly proletarian and xenophobic' teddy boy represented little more than a retrograde denial of the 'real' roots of rock and roll.[8]

Historian Geoffrey Pearson punctured this residual understanding that subcultural activities can in any meaningful way be coopted to particular political and moral ends by their investigators. Such caricatures, he stated, 'have offered a convenient metaphor of social change ... The entrance of the dazzling war babies in their ted suits, understood as harbingers of irresponsible affluence and rootless materialism, seemed to fit the bill precisely.'[9] However:

> What was and is totally submerged in the conventional understanding of the Teddy Boys was that their style and demeanour was by no means unprecedented. Their rough fighting, territorial edginess, for example, is better understood as a continuation of earlier forms of gang-life in working-class neighbourhoods – rather than a sudden departure from tradition. So, too, the Teds had borrowed large parts of their supposedly unprecedented cultural equipment from earlier youth cultures ... It is clear that the conventional picture of the sudden and unrivalled appearance of the 'affluent' and 'Americanised' Teddy Boys ... must be seen as a gross distortion of the actual events.[10]

The phrase 'territorial edginess' stands out in Pearson's account as the most suggestive route by which further investigation of the teddy-boy phenomenon might proceed. For in a geographical and temporal, as well as in a more conceptual sense, it is his location at the borders between north and south, central and inner, respectable and dangerous London, his emergence on the cusp of pre- and postwar social attitudes, and the manner in which he floats across the racial, sexual and class-based divisions of the capital that still make the teddy boy such a beguiling metropolitan figure. At the time of his notoriety, bohemian writers and artists as diverse as MacInnes, Denton Welch, John Minton and the young Joe Orton were fascinated by the possibilities which the bomb sites of working-class London held for erotic adventure and artistic inspiration.[11] The proletarian dandy emerged as a 'romantic' hero of those spaces – an attractive focus for various desires that have persisted as a form of urban folk legend. A denizen of the edge, the teddy boy's shifting characteristics are so contingent on these imaginative and spatial specificities that it is imperative for the historian to locate the broader contexts in which his identity was formed before attempting any more ambitious an interpretation of his elusive energies.

In all of the above explanations of the teddy boy's significance, the working-class milieu of south London is cited as an important influence on the honing of subcultural identities. In attempting to show how these expressions of selfhood were more complex than the classic accounts have suggested, this section aims to interrogate the manner in which representations of the teddy boy overlapped with loaded descriptions of his environment, contributing to the construction of powerful sartorial myths and actual social practices. When director Karel Reisz and photographer Walter Lassally produced their essay on the lives of members of a south London youth club in the film *We are the Lambeth Boys* in 1958, they were attempting to portray their subjects in a manner which avoided the value judgements of the sociologist or the cultural critic. They strove to stimulate a visual and emotional liveliness through the 'un-mediated' directness of their technique, inspiring personal expression from subject and audience by their recognition of the poetic significance of the 'everyday'.[12] Reisz's tender evocation of a week's work and pleasure amongst the self-consciously fashionable working-class teenagers of Kennington (a district of Lambeth) provides a glimpse of a society in transition between the familial duties and work expectations of an older generation and the more fluid networks of friendship and pleasure which the modern city offered. Most startlingly the film is a snapshot of late Neo-Edwardianism as it affected living consumers. These are not the shadowy and threatening figures of Fyvel's nightmares or the partisan hooligans of Hebdige's thesis; instead they engage in a game of back-yard cricket, exchange flirtatious banter with female members of the club, discuss the cost of modern tailoring, pose on the edges of the dance-floor, and wheel their bicycles towards school assembly or first jobs. Reisz's teddy boys, resplendent in the narrow ties and pointed shoes of their cult and choreographed against a (slightly incongruous) soundtrack of modern jazz, represent a mode of citizenship with far more positive overtones.

Other competing representations of the south London mise-en-scène were not so complimentary. Ten years before, in one of several social and economic surveys of post-blitz London commissioned in the late forties, Harry Williams had portrayed a district bedevilled by a grim sense of ennui. 'Ugliness', he stated, 'was the dominant impression of our visit, tiredness the next. The white drawn faces of the women shoppers, picking over the rubbish on sale with dispirited fingers, the unnatural quietness of the children, the sullen brooding withdrawal of the men spoke of a state of affairs never approached during the worst moments of the war.'[13] This is a rhetoric of poverty inherited from the dehumanising accounts of the East End poor which had characterised touristic and philanthropic writings of the late nineteenth century. Williams relied on the same dismissive terminology that had been employed by his forebears to describe the cheap offerings of the countless street markets which marked the territory for outsiders.[14] Money, he implies, was not necessarily in short supply, though a 'tawdry' choice of goods and the lack of a will to spend compromised the desire to consume in any manner that would have made sense to a visiting middle-class journalist. More shocking still was the apparent lack of self-respect evidenced by the bodies of the locals: 'Taken all in all they are a poor lot. Some of the young girls are fine and upstanding – the women are notably better than the men – and a handful of athletic young men may catch the eye, but look closer at the herd. Bowed shoulders, spindly legs, concave chests, weak eyes … bad teeth … small frames … grey faces … Look for yourself and see.'[15] Though damning and unsympathetic, Williams's repulsion sheds some light on the sense of threat which the 'alien' figure of the teddy boy aroused in observers who had perhaps come to expect only grey submission from the sad streets across the Thames. His topography of dingy markets and dowdy local shops maps a scenario in which working-class dandies might find copious and adaptable retail outlets for the purchase of their wardrobes together with a ready-made 'outdoor' theatre for their eventual display. Here was a longstanding culture of the street

Figure 2: 'Gambling Group, Southam Street, North Kensington', Roger Mayne, 1958. Courtesy of Roger Mayne.

corner and the crowd, a gritty setting for shameless acts of sartorial delinquency.

Delinquency was a subject which concerned the respondents of a Mass Observation report of the same year (1949) who aimed to record the habits of 'problem' juveniles in similar inner-London slum districts. The language of the report had not yet picked up on the teddy-boy terminology favoured by the newspapers, so that descriptions of the clothing adopted by young gang-members were free of the familiar references to aristocratic or West End modes of dressing, preferring instead to cite the influence of Hollywood or more localised sartorial characterisations as the source of a collective look. Bored and pointless acts of destructive energy were bracketed with transgressive sartorial tastes, making sense of a blitzed and jagged urban landscape in which the presence of violence was constantly referenced:[16]

> Two youths, ages about 18, are standing outside a dairy. They pick up between them a large crate of empty milk bottles and throw them in the road, breaking all of them … they run across the road and join a gang of youths numbering about 15 or 16. Most of them are dressed very flashily – striped flannels and 'house coat' style of belted jacket; large, loosely knotted, plain coloured ties; and several of them are wearing the wide-brimmed American style of trilby. Long 'side-boards' are a prominent feature with the majority of them.[17]

The wardrobe of these young men, with its belted jacket, loose flannels, bright tie and extravagant hat, paid homage to the enduring style of the gangster film, a source of inspiration to British adolescents since well before the war and not especially linked to London.[18] Certainly it was a look which lent some force to the swaggering demeanour of the dance-hall habitués noted by the Mass Observers, its loose and flapping layers well-adapted to a slouching, street corner posture.[19] More specific to the circumstances of working-class London was the choice of the epithets 'Spiv' and 'Dago' to describe a flaunting of garish accessories, a combination of formal and casual items and what was interpreted as an 'effeminate' obsession with the hair:

> Three youths of a 'spiv' type have sauntered in. They are all wearing grey pin-striped flannels and the 'house coat' style of jacket. Two of them are wearing white shirts with a vivid paisley tie, whilst the other is in a brilliant open-necked sports shirt. All these have carefully cared for hair – long with artificial waves, and a heavily greased 'Boston slash back' in two cases.[20]

The 'spiv' was a figure rooted in the realm of caricature, but whose extreme characteristics bore that sense of familiarity encouraged by an acquaintance with real versions on the street. Ubiquitous during the war years, his delineation provided a precedent for later descriptions of the teddy boy. Harry Hopkins recalled his presence in the life of the nation as 'an abstraction'. The spiv was 'a figure in a modern morality play. The convention was rapidly established by the pocket cartoonists ... peaked shoulders, the wasp waist, the dazzle tie, the hoarse behind-the-hand whisper "Nylons".'[21] In the developing Welfare State the spiv's flouting of the rules (circumnavigating the restrictions of rationing with a ready supply of black-market luxuries) positioned his conspicuous delight in

Figure 3: 'Charing Cross Road Shop Window', Henry Grant, 1951. Courtesy of the Museum of London.

display as a taboo. Like the teddy boy, he established his patch in the backstreets of London's poorer districts and marked out his distinctive identity through excessive grooming. But whilst the spiv adopted the sleek glamour of the Latin crooner in front of his bathroom mirror (good looks aiding his professional role as a swindler), the teddy boy called on a more extensive battery of styling techniques that placed his prouder narcissism firmly in the public sphere. As T. R. Fyvel remarked, hairstyles 'were a source of particular pride and attention to their wearers and were acquired by appointments with special barbers, which involved the use of dryers and hairnets and cost between 7s 6d and 15s for a setting, a considerable outlay for young wage earners'.[22]

Thus by 1949, though Mass Observation doesn't name him as such, the figure of the teddy boy was rapidly emerging as a particular working-class London type; Anglo-Irish or 'cockney' in his associations in contrast to the continental and American preferences of London's sizeable Italian and Maltese gang members. Though he drew some inspiration from the 'spivvy' style for which Colin MacInnes coined the term 'American Drape' – a style that 'hit Charing Cross Road in the late forties and constituted the first underground revolt against wartime uniforms and sackcloth and the whole *Men's Wear* conception of English male attire' – his look was far more negotiated, deliberately differentiated and consequently more subversive than that.[23] Rather than lift an idea of sharp respectability straight from the movies or steal it wholesale from memories of GI magnificence, the working-class version of Neo-Edwardianism located its referents closer to home, in the greyness of the inner suburbs, amongst the stilted hair-cut photographs and pots of brilliantine that gathered dust in the windows of barber shops, or the tailors' notices which announced the ease with which trousers could be tapered to the latest width.[24] Almost parochial in their styled outrages against the accepted way of being, the young of Lambeth engaged in a struggle which ironically bound them closer to home. Local historian Mary Chamberlain demonstrates how working-class cultures south of the Thames positively encouraged this attention to surfaces, those proofs of selfhood which the teddy boy's uniform so effectively communicated. Such details demonstrate the need to locate fashion practices within and against their local contexts, revealing nuances which contemporary and subsequent observers might well have overlooked:

> Those dreamy acres were far ... from monolithic. They were the battleground where a war of class and status was fought ... It mattered if you took in washing, visited the pawn shop, if shoes were unpolished and clothing torn ... It mattered because in those finer rituals ... lay a definition of self ... a way of circumventing and resisting the threat of destitution which lurked forever round every corner of working-class neighbourhoods.[25]

Journalist Douglas Sutherland claimed to have encountered as despondent a sartorial scene on returning to London's West End in 1945 as Harry Williams had stumbled across in Lambeth. The indignities of clothes rationing seemed designed to embarrass any pretender who sought re-entry into London's postwar social throng. Sutherland was only able to pass muster through his skilful adaptation of some cast-offs formerly belonging to a show-business acquaintance:

> The two suits I took, not without some diffidence, to that most elegant of all tailoring establishments, Messrs Kilgour, French and Stanbury, in Dover Street. So it came about that, in shabby suited London, I suddenly blossomed into one of the best dressed men-about-town ... It was also quite fun, when envious acquaintances used to inquire the secret of my ... magnificence, to flash at them the label sewn on my inside jacket pocket which still bore the name of Mr Oscar Hammerstein.[26]

This confident approximation of style gained through the author's privileged access to elite tailoring provision and his surreptitious borrowing from the shabby-genteel world of bohemia, is as good a summary as any of the circumstances pertaining in 'fashionable' late forties London which contributed towards the success of the Edwardian look and its variants in both 'upper-class' and avant-garde circles. The combination of constrained means, a rather 'raffish' relaxation of moral and social codes, together with a nostalgic yearning for leisured prewar lifestyles dictated a dress code which was by turns tightly controlled, impossibly presumptuous, often misleading and rather sentimental in its effects. Sutherland's passage through the louche mews pubs of Kensington and Chelsea, the patrician afternoon drinking dens of Mayfair's Shepherd Market and the exclusive clubs of Fitzrovia in the final years of the decade furnished him with a gallery of aristocratic rogues whose singular appearance set the context for a look which never strayed far from the theatrical or the deceptive. The Star Tavern, behind Belgrave Square was a typical Knightsbridge destination, home to:

> a collection of undoubtedly rich, if reckless, spenders of their inheritances [and] others whose financial backgrounds were less impressive but who nonetheless were eager to be regarded as young men-about-town of good social background ... what they had in common was a certain vagueness about their social background coupled with an insistence that they had enjoyed a public school education. They also shared a liking for Savile Row suits, and such ostentatiously displayed gee-gaws as Cartier watches, gold cigarette lighters and recently hyphenated surnames.[27]

Savile Row, whose well-crafted products finally made their way (by one means or other) onto the backs of Sutherland's privileged voluptuaries, maintained a distanced froideur as the focus for a more respectable renaissance. This famous street of tailors located in the triangle between Regent Street, Piccadilly and Old Bond Street, had enjoyed a prominence as the source of bespoke clothing for the aristocracy since the mid eighteenth century. Its fortunes had, however, experienced a levelling off in the interwar years owing to competition from manufacturers of mass-produced suits and the popularity of a more relaxed American mode of dressing. Immediately before the war the environs of Old Bond Street had witnessed the maturing of a home-grown couture industry whose opulence almost rivalled Paris. Fashion journalist Francis Marshall described what was left in 1944, noting that 'the most famous salons are nearly all within a small area of the West End, many being in Bruton Street and Grosvenor Street. They range from elaborately decorated salons with the most modern decor of mirrors, glistening chandeliers, stuffed satin upholstery and baroque ornaments, to the dress shop which is little more than a small flat on a top floor of Brook Street.'[28] Hardy Amies's move to Savile Row and the foundation of the ISLFD after the war continued the discreet glamorisation of this quarter of the West End, and though the focus was predominantly on the marketing of a very English and aristocratic version of femininity, the rising importance of men's wear had some impact on the tenor of its streets. This can be measured through the demonstrable influence of classic tailoring techniques on the style of London couture, and also through the co-option of the reticent business culture associated with the world of the bespoke tailor by a wider constituency of West End retailers. In 1953 the British Travel and Holiday Association produced a guide to shopping in the capital which asserted that 'Bond Street is to London what the Rue de la Paix is to Paris, but with this difference; whereas the Rue de la Paix is a broad and pretentious street that carries its distinctions with an ... air of self importance, Bond Street seems to be concerned only with self-effacement'.[29] The good manners of the Savile Row suit thus lent a quiet restraint to the district and, though the profound luxury of its finish was never in question, the parading of those qualities would have seemed impossibly rude.

As a symbol of tradition the Savile Row suit still maintained a powerful grip on definitions of Britishness in the postwar era. A. W. Allon of the tailoring trade press stated in 1949 that 'in an age of tremendous industrialisation it is good to know that one craft at least retains its position in the general scheme of things – as solidly important as ever. Indeed the craft of tailoring has become more than just the means of making a living: it has become a fundamental part of the British way of life.'[30] In the context of a sartorial sense of Britishness, London tastes played a distinctive role. An R. J. Pescod writing in the same tailoring compendium as Allon paid appropriate homage to the superiority of 'West End' cutting techniques which in the nineteenth century distinguished the clothing of the 'upper ten' from the provincial styles of the middle classes. A combination of factors, including a well-judged sharpness in the making-up of seams, creases and darts, high-quality textiles and a relaxed ease of wear, identified the Savile Row pedigree of a suit and whilst distinctions had since become less easy to spot, to the trained eye of the artisan or the discerning consumer there was 'a difference – difficult as it is to define. There is a subtle quality about the suit which emanates from the West End today which sets its seal upon the place of its origin as the indisputable mecca of good tailoring.'[31] Pescod attempted to delineate precisely what that quality constituted in terms of a specific style, though clear definitions were elusive in a system of meaning that protected its adherents from 'vulgar' emulation through the circulation of deliberately vague and socially exclusive codes. The single-breasted waistcoat boasted 'narrow shoulders, deep armholes, and rather long points'. The single-breasted lounge jacket was marked by its 'gracefulness of outline' and 'comfort'. 'The waist is moderately defined and the hips are fairly close. A medium amount of drape is provided.' Finally, in the evening dress coat, Savile Row saw its finest product. 'In no other garment … is there such scope for the cutter's skill … many of the finest examples of evening dress wear have come from houses in the West End; and London is proud of such work. The long sweeping lapels, the tapering skirt – these are the main points of style that should be noted.'[32]

Though essentially conservative and locked into a long tradition of understatement, it is clear that the components of the Savile Row suit in 1949 were adaptable to the subtle exaggerations that would constitute the Neo-Edwardian style. The editorials and letters pages of the trade journal *Men's Wear* traced the ways in which its flamboyance was a combative response both to the deprivations of textile shortages, and to a desire for distinction and display amongst those who sat at the edges of the establishment or in the demi-monde which was as powerful as that felt by young working-class men across the Waterloo Bridge or along the Mile End Road.[33] In 1947 the frustrations of austerity were causing concern. Under the shocking header 'Burlington Arcade had pyjamas at 11s' a correspondent reported:

> 'The East End has come to the West End'. In these words a representative of Noble Jones, hosiers and shirtmakers in London's exclusive Burlington Arcade, W1, described the appearance of considerably cheaper than usual lines in West End hosiers' windows. A *Men's Wear* reporter saw utility pyjamas at 11s, ties at 4s 6d and shirts at 9s 11d in the famous shopping thoroughfare … 'We can't get much else' a leading hosier said … 'It is a complete stalemate' he went on. 'People with taste just won't buy this stuff, and yet it is the only type of thing we get these days.'[34]

Five years later, as the spectre of clothes rationing faded, London's resurgent social calendar clearly dictated a greater degree of formality and an attention to self-presentation amongst men which bordered on the extravagant. In April 1952 the headline boasted '"Men now Dress-Clothes Conscious at West End Restaurants" says Berkley West, Men's Wear Style Critic.' The article continued:

Eighteen months ago London's Savoy Hotel put a ban on admittance ... unless one wore dinner jacket ... or tails. Within six months the ban was lifted. The attempt to restore pre-war sartorial standards failed ... partly because it was made too soon after the end of clothes rationing; and partly because it was impractical to enforce the rule on foreign visitors ... Only a few of London's ... restaurants and clubs now demand tenir-rigeur. Perhaps it is for this very reason that men now, quite voluntarily dress for dinner in the West End ... At private parties too, men's styles are attracting ... more attention than women's gowns. When the ... Marquis Pardo de Santayana gave a party recently at his Hyde Park Gate flat, men's styles were so outstanding that they were commented on by several consumer newspapers. Reason, on this occasion, was the array of coloured and embroidered waistcoats worn with single breasted dinner-jacket suits.[35]

Throughout the coronation year *Men's Wear* journalists continued to hail the return of formal styles of dress. Features like the embroidered waistcoat or the turned-back cuff were at first associated by commentators with 'the top end of the trade', although the wider take-up of the trend was gathering pace. In October 'a Pathé pictorial film in Technicolor, featuring the clothes worn by sporting, stage and radio stars', was released with great anticipation. As *Men's Wear* proclaimed, 'the four minute feature, entitled "Man About Town" ... will focus the attention of millions of cinema goers on men's clothes ... designed and styled both for comfort and appearance, and not just produced to standard patterns ... Filmed at the Victoria and Albert Museum, among the treasures of the past, the picture suggests ... that the colourful male costumes of bygone days have not given place completely to body covering which has no creative genius, but, rather, that they have been succeeded in this age by a new and modern conception of styling.'[36] The lubricating effects of show-business played a crucial role in both popularising and to an extent neutralising a masculine look that veered dangerously towards the stagey, for in its theatrical incarnation the Neo-Edwardian style was increasingly read as sexually subversive or 'camp'. In their most extreme variations the contrived bodies of Savile Row's more prominent followers paid allegiance to a dandified philosophy of life in which elegant repose and a certain withdrawal from the humdrum bother of modern living could be summed up in the placing of a button-hole. Cecil Beaton and Kenneth Tynan celebrated the arch 'Edwardian' outlook in their publication *Persona Grata* of 1953. As an apt example, the theatrical entrepreneur Hugh 'Binkie' Beaumont sprawled in profile on a chaise longue across one of Beaton's photographs. Tynan's acerbic prose described the effect:

His social manner is flawless, twinkling without smugness, shining without slickness; the gestures are soft and self-effacing, inducing a gentle hipnosis [sic] ... as he talks

he smokes, insatiably but smoothly … His trick of holding his cigarette between the
middle two fingers while wearing a monogrammed signet ring on the little one,
represents his only homage to dandyism. [He] … favour[s] a lazy, glazed, leaning
tenor, which irons out its sentences as if they were so many silk shirts. 'Terrible' is
the universal epithet.[37]

Ultimately it was Beaumont's body, as much as his clothing, which
marked him out as a dandy, the softness of his voice deputising for the
luxury of silk shirts. But perhaps this was the logical destination for an
elite sartorial practice which lost its visible potency at a moment when
refinement, modernity, outrage and all those other dandified preserves
were opened up to a teenage market on an unprecedented commercial
scale. In such a context distinction could only be marked *by* rather than *on*
the body. As pop journalist Nik Cohn stated almost twenty years later,
'the Edwardian look … lasted 'til about 1954, by which time it had been
taken up and caricatured by the teddy boys, who made it so disreputable
that even homosexuals were embarrassed to wear it. Nothing could have
been more ironic: having started as an upper-class defence, Edwardiana
now formed the basis for the first great detonation of male working-class
fashion.'[38] Giving credence to Cohn's retrospective analysis, *Men's Wear*
anxiously attempted to retrieve from the hands of 'degenerates' and
hooligans what had been a tailoring godsend, even as Beaumont drew
gracefully on his cigarette. In an extended article of October 1953 the
debate was a semantic one, aiming to differentiate the sartorial slang of
south London thugs from the received pronunciation of Savile Row. In
July of that year a stabbing case on Clapham Common had aroused the
interest of the press, largely on account of the dress of the perpetrators.
During the trial the *Daily Mirror* reported of the ringleader that:

he took great pains to look like a dandy. Like most of his companions, nearly all his
money went on flashy clothes and just before the murder he borrowed twelve
pounds from his uncle to buy a suit … This man was a born coward beneath his …
gay dog clothes.[39]

Though the words teddy boy were not used by the newspapers at this
stage, *Men's Wear* both recognised and tried to refute a connection:

Mention of Edwardian-suited youths in the recent … trial … at the Old Bailey has
created the impression … that this style has been adopted generally by that section
of young men who parade in groups around the streets. Inquiries I have made reveal
that nothing could be further from the truth. The broad shouldered, draped jacket
suit, usually in gaberdine remains the mode. Those who chose Edwardian suits for
their visits to Clapham Common did so because they wanted to be different from the
rest, whose main concern is to dress like their favourite screen tough guys.[40]

The article went on to note how tailors and outfitters close to the
Common either expressed indignation at the suggestion that they

specialised in 'spiv' clothes, or freely admitted that they catered for local teenage tastes. Mr Leonard Rose, the manager of tailoring chain Maxwell's defended his customers, claiming that 'the general run of lads in Clapham are no worse than anywhere else. They believe in colour and appearance.' And Mr Harry Avoner who traded on Clapham High Street confirmed that this parochial taste for 'colourful apparel' fell short of *Men's Wear*'s definition of the Edwardian: 'We notice that a few of our younger customers drift to shops outside the locality which specialise in "more fashionable" styles, but the phase soon passes and they come back.' It was the Edwardian look's expensive reliance on a perfect fit that protected its direct appropriation by 'undesirable' constituencies, though even the bespoke trade could not retain copyright in Mayfair for ever. During the same year the ready-made industry was beginning to respond to the inevitable shift in taste that followed such events as the International Wool Secretariat's show of men's apparel at the Festival Hall in May 1952 and the aforementioned Pathé documentary. *Men's Wear* noticed some hesitation on the part of mass-manufacturers to jettison the more standardised drape coat for the intricate sizing demanded by Edwardian lines, but the potential for renewal hidden in the new style, its bridging of modernity and tradition, positioned its clean silhouette as a symbol for London's returning confidence.[41] As Berkley West announced, '1953 was the turning-point in reviving clothes-consciousness':

> At the beginning of last year, the influence of the original Edwardian outfits was beginning to be felt in every section of the trade ... Criticism of Edwardian styles from the magisterial bench, which suggested that such styles symbolised the juvenile delinquents, came too late to have adverse effect on the influence of Edwardian trends. This trend was the greatest single factor in re awakening style-consciousness in men, because it had repercussions in every branch of the industry. An American style shirt or a jazzy tie could not be worn with an Edwardian suit. Result has been that even in the case of those who confined their Edwardianism to narrow trousers and natural shoulders to the jacket, it was necessary for appropriate accessories to be purchased. A slow return to formality in all forms of men's apparel was evident, even in such things as leisure wear and beach wear.[42]

The tense juxtapositions of elite display and street-violence which echoed the dual meanings of Mayfair hauteur and Lambeth bravado were perhaps not as unexpected or shocking as *Men's Wear* journalists liked to claim. The playing out of London's social ferment in the leisure and entertainment scene of the 1950s encouraged a degree of fluidity and sartorial exchange, promoting scenarios whereby players from both worlds could rub shoulders and borrow some of the glamour that attached itself equally to aristocratic profligacy and underworld criminality. Alan Markham's 1959 guide for visiting roués revealed a sparkling night-time map of burlesque bars, casinos and dance halls which traced those streets that during daylight hours gave themselves over to the sartorial trades:

> London now has many more … entertainments and cabaret shows to offer the visitor than has Paris … The man … responsible for this change of front is Percival Murray … proprietor of the world famous Murray's Cabaret Club. His … lead in the 'glamour plus' type of floor show has been very ably followed by many of his colleagues … Edmundo Ros, for instance, the celebrated band leader … welcomes visitors to his exclusive club in Regent Street. Bob and Alf Barnett control the highly successful and lush Embassy Club in Bond Street – established there since the early 1920's and Jimmy O'Brien is personally responsible for the destiny of that gay spot with its delectable show the 'Eve' in Regent Street.[43]

Plush interior spaces like these provided a platform for display well removed from the grey austerity which marked open-air London. In the gilt and candlelight of the nightclub the elegance of Berkley West's 'new formality' could be shown off to greatest advantage, whether the wearer hailed from Park Lane or Peckham.

Part of the attraction was clearly sexual, drawing on the established reputation of the West End as an adult playground which dated back to the Regency adventures of Tom and Jerry and beyond.[44] Douglas Sutherland recalled how 'the years immediately after the war saw the heyday of London as the vice capital of Europe … In the West End, when the lights went up again, the prostitutes lined the streets.'[45] In this context Cohn's comments on the status of Neo-Edwardianism as a transitory trend that passed from SW1 playboys to 'homosexuals' to petty criminals takes on a heightened resonance, though it is likely that the style transference which he claims as a linear and socially declining one was in effect more simultaneous, cutting across class constituencies in a dangerous and exhilarating manner.[46] Frank Mort has provided a detailed analysis of the years preceding the Wolfenden Report, when the nature of vice in the West End (both hetero- and homosexual) penetrated the rigid structures of London life, linking the political and the cultural in a radical metropolitan network of barely suppressed desires.[47] In a material form these connections manifested themselves in examples such as the pornographer John S. Barrington's easy movement between social groups and photographic genres, facilitating his priapic and professional adventures along the length of the Charing Cross Road and encouraging a relish in self-reinvention that saw him adopting a series of outrageous sartorial disguises ranging from the bohemian to the dandified.[48] Similarly on tin-pan alley, Jon Savage has shown how the manufactured personas of early English pop stars such as Adam Faith, Tommy Steele and Cliff Richard played on the gold-lamé camp of 'revue culture' and an eroticisation of the working-class lad – transactions which were the daily bread and butter of the Savile Row clad impresarios whose financial clout and underworld connections re-formed the sprawling pleasure-zone south of Oxford Street.[49] In other words, illicit carnal activity had something of a lubricating effect on the social relationships of postwar London, forging, behind a thin façade of respectability, channels through which new fashionable identities could emerge. The attendant frisson of life 'Up West' acted as an incentive for the gang members of south and east London to chance their arm in more glamorous territory, their own engagement with the centre bolstering its edgy reputation. Mass Observation singled out Jack, the son of a bookmaker and a shoplifter, as a typical denizen:

> Jack, aged seventeen … has never had a job since he left school … His clothes are made for him by an expensive West End tailor, and he also wears hand-made shoes. His mother meets these bills and invites more. 'About time you got yourself some new clobber, ain't it Jack?' she has said almost every time I have met her. In spite of his almost dandyish appearance he has no respect for these clothes and is quite frequently involved in typical West End 'rough and tumbles' … His days are spent lounging about the West End back streets with the 'boys', evenings in pubs and cheap West End clubs.[50]

The mythical streets of Soho formed the epicentre for aimless boys like Jack, though Daniel Farson's homage to the bohemian credentials of the district suggests that the attractions for young libertines were hollow: 'the few places to go in Soho were wholesome to the point of boredom with a whiffle of skiffle on the washboard and a hiss of frothy coffee from a clean machine'.[51] Furthermore, within its courts and alleys the opportunities for social mixing were more constrained in practice than they were in legend. It is notable that for all his bespoke polish, Mass Observation's Jack confined his rambles to the cheaper clubs, suggesting that access to particular venues was still carefully policed. Certainly the familiar mythology of Soho appears to favour its reputation as a haunt for public school drop-outs, slowly pickling their artistic and literary talents in smoky upstairs drinking dens and fiercely exclusive members' clubs. The brash and commercial concerns which fronted its pavements may have added local colour, but largely signified only 'vulgarity' to its self-appointed chroniclers.

In 1966 Frank Norman and Jeffrey Bernard could cite the 2i's coffee bar in Old Compton Street as a fairly longstanding feature of the Soho scene, though their sense of alienation at its fashionable 'show-biz' surfaces is clear.[52] Run by ex-stunt man Tom Littlewood and ex-wrestlers Paul Lincoln and Ray Hunter, the café launched the career of Tommy Steele and touted all the credentials of criminal connections, a well-defined 'pop ambience' (capitalised upon by the makers of the television music show *Six Five Special* who used its downstairs dance floor as a location) and a reputation as a meeting place for resting rent-boys, necessary to qualify as a significant influence on the emergence of a recognisable, if highly romanticised, London 'youth style'. It was perhaps in spaces like these that the geographical, social and mythical overlap of masculine styles forged new and challenging identities. Yet the impact of such venues has arguably been written out of histories which aim to produce a spuriously 'authentic' version of Soho's 'bohemian' past. Even Dick Hebdige seems to favour an analysis which annexes the 'materialist' gratifications of music, fashion and sex that drew the teddy boys across the bridges:

> subcultures were in fact literally worlds apart. The college campuses and dimly lit coffee bars and pubs of Soho and Chelsea were bus rides away from the teddy boy haunts deep in the traditionally working-class areas of south and east London. While the beatnik grew out of a literate, verbal culture … and affected a bemused cosmopolitan air of bohemian tolerance, the ted was uncompromisingly proletarian and xenophobic.[53]

In his more astringent study of entrepreneurship and working-class style in the East End, historian Dick Hobbs presents the most convincing account of the haphazard ways in which the collision of classes and attitudes in the West End of the 1950s resulted in those bizarre new codes of cultural and sartorial behaviour that marked the following decade. These were codes which were also locked into older patterns of consumption and social habit that raise the context and status of the Neo-Edwardian suit and its wearers above the narrow and reductive connotations of posthumous interpretations. As Hobbs states:

> Important in the formation of style was the cultural overlap of the East and West Ends of London that occurred … as a result of alterations in gambling laws, the resultant indiscreet manifestations of East End villains in West End clubs, and the fashionable 1960s notion of classlessness. Conversely show-business personalities and members of the aristocracy flirted with East End pubs and drinking clubs, and a cockney accent became de rigeur for acceptance into bourgeois society as pop stars, hairdressers, and photographers rediscovered their humble roots. For young East Enders, this opened up a privileged and exotic domain.[54]

It was this potential for personal reinvention that invested the neon lights of Soho with such promise, drawing acolytes from both ends of the social spectrum. Hobbs quotes former criminal John McVicar, who in his autobiography recalls his fascination with the actors in this twilight scenario of billiard hall, coffee bar and public house:

> their rakishness, their flamboyant clothes, their tough, self-reliant manners, their rejection of conventional attitudes to sex and money … I unconsciously modelled myself on the more successful representatives of this new society.[55]

This productive crossing of boundaries between the respectable and the dissolute, the bespoke and the commercial, the elite and the popular, the

East and the West Ends clearly fuelled the emergence of a highly loaded and varied register of London-specific masculine styles which dominated the fashion scene between the end of the war and the beginnings of 'the affluent society' that defined the cultural tenor of the 1960s. The complex patterns of its formation endorse Angela Partington's recent call for a fashion history of the period which rejects the simple logic of 'trickle down' theory for an understanding that 'post war culture is not one in which distinctions and hierarchies collapse, but a "horizontalized" one in which differences multiply'.[56] And its chameleon-like character made possible Colin MacInnes's 1966 observation that:

> a vogue for camp, rather too pretty garments ... has also spread from shoplets in north west Soho into the most unlikely places. And the pop-drainpipe line of Spitalfields is suddenly echoed, Chelsea-wards, by fawn 'cavalry' twill slacks you have to amputate both feet to get into ... As has often been noted by dress sociologists, 'top' and 'pop' clothing are usually closer in style (and influence each other more) than either is to the wide intermediate ranges of bourgeois and petty bourgeois dress.[57]

Most importantly, we should recognise that the seemingly conflicted beginnings of this 'menswear revolution', as represented by Hardy Amies and his ilk, led inexorably through Mayfair, Soho and Lambeth to a cultural moment which Roy Porter sees as one of London's finest:

> A culture materialised that was irreverent, offbeat, creative, novel. Politically idealistic and undogmatically left-wing, it broke through class-barriers and captured and transformed many of the better elements of traditional London: its cosmopolitanism and openness, its village quality, its closeness, its cocktail of talent, wealth and eccentricity. There was a rare alliance between youth culture and commerce, aristocratic style and a new populism. It was a breath of fresh air.[58]

The association of Neo-Edwardianism with a reactionary and elitist Mayfair clique, a West End sexual subculture and inner-city recidivism seemed at the outset to hold few such promises, but their distinctive patterns and blurred edges demonstrate the need to consider the progress of fashionable style both as part of a longer continuum, bound up with the ongoing formation of social positions, cultural identities and spatial networks, and as a channel through which new and differentiated manifestations of sexuality, class and taste are engendered.

Notes

1. Hardy Amies, *Just So Far* (Collins, 1954), p. 245.
2. Roy Porter, *London: A Social History* (Hamish Hamilton, 1994), p. 344.
3. Harry Hopkins, *The New Look: A Social History of the Forties and Fifties* (Secker & Warburg, 1964), pp. 427–8.

4. Colin MacInnes, *England, Half English: A Polyphoto of the Fifties* (Penguin, 1966), p. 151.
5. T. R. Fyvel, *The Insecure Offenders: Rebellious Youth in the Welfare State* (Chatto & Windus, 1961), pp. 48–51.
6. Fyvel, *Insecure Offenders*, pp. 14–15.
7. Paul Rock and Stanley Cohen, 'The Teddy Boy', in *The Age of Affluence*, ed. Vernon Bogdanor and Robert Skidelsky (Macmillan, 1970).
8. Dick Hebdige, *Subculture: The Meaning of Style* (Routledge, 1979), p. 51.
9. Geoffrey Pearson, *Hooligan: A History of Respectable Fears* (Macmillan, 1983), p. 20.
10. Pearson, *Hooligan*, p. 22.
11. Michael De-La-Noy (ed.), *The Journals of Denton Welch* (Allison & Busby, 1984); Frances Spalding, *Dance till the Stars Come Down: A Biography of John Minton* (Hodder & Stoughton, 1991); John Lahr (ed.), *The Orton Diaries* (Methuen, 1986).
12. *We are the Lambeth Boys* was the most enduring of a series of films produced by Reisz and other young film-makers as part of the experimental project 'Free Cinema'.
13. Harry Williams, *South London* (Robert Hale, 1949), p. 331.
14. Henry Mayhew, *London Labour and the London Poor* (1851; repr. Dover, 1968); Walter Besant, *East London* (Chatto & Windus, 1901); Charles Booth, *Life and Labour of the London Poor* (Williams & Norgate, 1889).
15. Williams, *South London*, p. 320
16. David Mellor (ed.), *A Paradise Lost: The Neo Romantic Imagination in Britain 1935–55* (Barbican Art Gallery, 1987).
17. H. D. Willcock, *Mass Observation Report on Juvenile Delinquency* (Falcon Press, 1949), p. 41.
18. Andrew Davies, *Leisure, Gender and Poverty: Working Class Culture in Salford and Manchester 1900–1939* (Open University Press, 1992), p. 105.
19. Willcock, *Mass Observation*, pp. 50–51.
20. Willcock, *Mass Observation*, p. 50.
21. Hopkins, *New Look*, pp. 98–9.
22. Fyvel, *Insecure Offenders*, p. 52.
23. MacInnes, *England, Half English*, p. 150.
24. I am grateful to Madeleine Ginsburg of the Daks Simpson Archive for sharing her memory of these notices with me.
25. Mary Chamberlain, *Growing Up in Lambeth* (Virago, 1989), pp. 78–9.
26. Douglas Sutherland, *Portrait of a Decade: London Life 1945–1955* (Harrap, 1988), pp. 49–50.
27. Sutherland, *Portrait*, p. 124.
28. Francis Marshall, *London West* (The Studio, 1944), p. 58.
29. The British Travel and Holiday Association, *Shopping in London* (1953), p. 27.
30. A. A. Whife (ed.), *The Modern Tailor, Outfitter & Clothier* (Caxton, 1949), p. 8.
31. Whife, *Modern Tailor*, pp. 262.
32. Whife, *Modern Tailor*, pp. 265–71.
33. *Men's Wear* was a London-based trade periodical oriented towards the needs of the outfitter, the hosier and the high-street retailer of ready-made suits. Established in the late nineteenth century, its content was more concerned with innovation and directional fashion than that of the more conservative *Tailor and Cutter* which concentrated on issues of professional education and manufacture.
34. *Men's Wear*, 25 January 1947, p. 19.
35. *Men's Wear*, 19 April 1952, p. 26.
36. *Men's Wear*, 27 September 1952, p. 18.
37. Cecil Beaton and Kenneth Tynan, *Persona Grata* (Alan Wingate, 1953), pp. 15–16.
38. Nik Cohn, *Today There Are No Gentlemen* (Weidenfeld & Nicolson, 1971), p. 27.
39. Rock and Cohen, 'Teddy Boy', p. 291.
40. *Men's Wear*, 3 October 1953, p. 34.
41. *Men's Wear*, 25 April 1953, p. 19.

42. *Men's Wear*, 9 January 1954, p. 18.
43. Alan Markham, *Shop Ahoy: Your Shopping and Entertainment Guide to London* (Newman Neame, 1959), p. 61.
44. Pierce Egan, *Life in London* (Jerwood, Neely & Jones, 1821).
45. Sutherland, *Portrait*, p. 67.
46. Cohn, *Today*, p.27.
47. Frank Mort, 'Mapping Sexual London: The Wolfenden Committee on Homosexual Offences and Prostitutes 1954–57', *New Formations*, 37 (1999).
48. Rupert Smith, *Physique: The Life of John S. Barrington* (Serpent's Tail, 1997).
49. John Savage, 'Tainted Love: The Influence of Male Homosexuality and Sexual Divergence on Pop Music and Culture since the War', in *Consumption, Identity and Style: Marketing, Meanings and the Packaging of Pleasure*, ed. Alan Tomlinson (Comedia, 1990).
50. Willcock, *Mass Observation*, p. 75.
51. Daniel Farson, *Soho in the Fifties* (Michael Joseph, 1987), p. 151.
52. Frank Norman and Jeffrey Barnard, *Soho Night and Day* (Secker & Warburg, 1966), pp. 14–16.
53. Hebdige, *Subculture*, p. 51.
54. Dick Hobbs, *Doing the Business: Entrepreneurship, the Working Class and Detectives in the East End of London* (Clarendon Press, 1988), p. 122.
55. John McVicar, *McVicar by Himself* (Arrow Books, 1979), p. 179.
56. Jim Fyrth (ed.), *Labour's Promised Land? Culture and Society in Labour Britain 1945–51* (Lawrence & Wishart, 1995), p. 254.
57. MacInnes, *England, Half English*, p. 156.
58. Porter, *London*, p. 363.

11

'Anti-Mini Militants Meet Modern Misses':[1] Urban Style, Gender and the Politics of 'National Culture' in 1960s Dar es Salaam, Tanzania

Andrew M. Ivaska

Here in town clothes make the man.

J. A. K. Leslie, *A Survey of Dar es Salaam* (1963)

On Thursday, 3 October 1968, residents of Dar es Salaam awoke to front-page newspaper headlines announcing a bold new declaration by the Youth League of Tanzania's ruling party, TANU. As the *Standard* put it, 'TANU Youths Ban "Minis": Sijaona announces "Operation Vijana".'[2] Announced by the General Council of the TANU Youth League (TYL), this action prohibited the use of a range of items – mini-skirts, wigs, skin-lightening creams, tight pants or dresses, and short shorts – as 'indecent', 'decadent' and antithetical to Tanzania's 'national culture'. The ban was to take effect on New Year's Day, 1969, and would be enforced by members of the male-dominated TYL. The ambiguity of the 'operation's' code name, *Vijana* (youth, but with the frequent connotation of young men), lent it a striking economy. For not only did it name 'youth' as both the targets *and* the enforcers of the campaign, but it also hinted at what would be the gendered nature of the ban's enforcement – an all-male affair directed primarily against female 'offenders'.[3]

Although they were just one set of a raft of resolutions announced at the conclusion of the three-day-long TYL General Council meeting, it was these 'Cultural Resolutions' that grabbed the intense attention of the press. Nor did this attention prove fleeting, as Operation Vijana dominated public debate during the three months between its announce-ment and its launch. Even as Dar es Salaam's newspaper editors weighed in on the issue, their offices were flooded with letters and poems from readers articulating a range of positions on the ban. From October 1968 through January 1969, the opinion pages of *Ngurumo*, the *Standard*, *Uhuru* and the *Nationalist*, the country's four leading dailies, produced a complex, multi-layered debate that was extraordinary in its scope and intensity. Debating Operation Vijana meant debating issues ranging from national culture, authenticity, gender roles and sex, to concepts such as *heshima* (respectability), *uhuni* (indecency, immorality, vagrancy), youth and the modern. All told, between 3 October 1968 and 1 February 1969, over 150 letters, sixteen poems and nineteen editorials – not to mention the over fifty news items – concerning Operation Vijana appeared in Tanzania's press.

Engagement with Operation Vijana was not, however, confined to the press. Within four days of TYL's announcement, Tanzania's Field Force Unit, or riot police, were called to the Kariakoo bus station (one of Dar es Salaam's main transport nodes) to control 'gangs of [male] youths' who were 'harassing all girls wearing mini-skirts or tight dresses'.[4] These young men – some of whom were witnessed boarding buses and pulling 'indecently dressed' young women off for beatings – were eventually dispersed with tear gas.[5] Denying that TYL members took part in this violence, which came months before the ban was to take effect, a TYL spokesperson said he was not surprised 'if the youth found the deadline too far away for them'.[6] As the deadline approached, after weeks that saw several attacks on 'indecently dressed' women reported, posters appeared around the capital depicting models of proper and improper dress for women and men. The TYL, which had organised the canvassing, also held a press conference at which top leaders of the League displayed more examples – stylised, sketched portraits this time – of 'decent' and 'indecent' apparel (see Figure 1).[7] On New Year's Day, 1969, Operation Vijana was launched in Dar, with 500 male Youth League members selected as the enforcers of the ban. Outfitted with walkie-talkies to communicate with TYL headquarters and thirty centres for the operation across the capital, the cadres patrolled streets and offices on the lookout for offenders.[8] By the second week of January the campaign was being heralded as a success by TYL leaders and supporters, but this 'success' appears to have been, at most, short-lived: within the year, 'indecent dress' was back on the streets of Dar es Salaam, provoking at least two more campaigns to ban it (in its ever-mutating forms) in the early 1970s.[9]

In this paper, following a brief engagement with relevant literature in the field, I sketch out a number of historical contexts within which

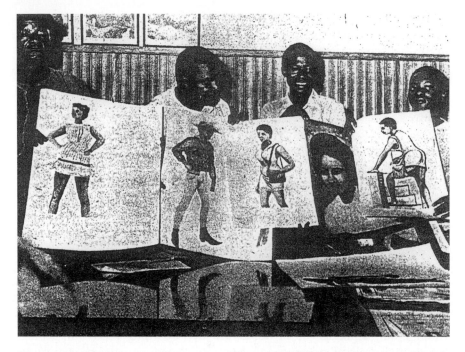

Figure 1: On the eve of Operation Vijana, TANU Youth League officials display for the press some examples of 'indecent' dress. From left to right are Brigadier Rajabu Diwani, Minister L. N. Sijaona (TYL Chairman), Joseph Nyerere (TYL Secretary-General), and Moses Nyauye (TYL Deputy Secretary-General). Unidentified photographer, *Standard*, 30 December 1968.

I find it productive to situate the events and debates surrounding Operation Vijana. Keeping these intersecting contexts in mind, I then proceed to tell two overlapping stories of Operation Vijana. In the first, I consider the campaign in the context of TANU's project of 'national culture' and explore ways in which some fundamental terms of this project – in particular, notions of the 'modern' – were contested by Tanzanians opposing Operation Vijana. In the second story, I situate the controversy over the ban at the intersection of anxieties over women's work and mobility in urban space, and the politics of sex in Dar es Salaam. Arguing throughout that 'the city' – both as an imagined space and as the site of particular social struggles – was central to Operation Vijana, I chart attempts to fashion viable urban personas and the limits of these attempts. Each of the two 'stories', I argue, captures something essential about Operation Vijana. For, if the ban was conceived within a framework of national cultural planning, its social life was quite another matter. On the streets and in the press, this campaign quickly became a site both for challenges to 'national culture' and for the battling out of social conflicts (most prominently around gender) in which far more than national culture was at stake.

In foregrounding the complex articulations involved in Tanzanians' consumption of 'western' fashion, Operation Vijana raises issues that have long been marginalised – both in academic work on Africa and in the literature on fashion in Euro-American contexts. On the one hand, Africanist scholarship has until recently been characterised by a reluctance to consider seriously the broad domain of African popular culture that involves the consumption of objects, signs and images originating in the western mass culture industries.[10] On the other hand, many of the key studies on fashion focus exclusively on its Euro-American dynamics; when the postcolonial world is mentioned, it is either as the site of production of multinational corporate clothing, or, somewhat more frequently, as the powerless recipient of an imposed and total hegemony of western styles.[11] One body of literature that has been important in challenging these marginalisations is the work on 'globalisation' and 'transnational culture'.[12] Highlighting local appropriations of global cultural forms – and insisting upon the multiple nature of modernity in contemporary times – such scholarship has worked to displace notions of a singular Euro-American modernity that spreads across the globe leaving only cultural homogenisation in its wake. While this intervention has been crucial – not least in informing my analysis of Operation Vijana – it has often been accompanied by an easy reliance upon a poorly analysed concept of 'globalisation', a ubiquitous term that increasingly obscures more than it illuminates.[13]

One antidote to this latter trend is a rigorous concentration upon situating the social lives of 'global' cultural forms in particular, local socio-historical contexts and along specific, bounded paths of movement; indeed, this has been the aim of a small but growing group of scholars working in recent years on the diverse cultural practices surrounding such products as Hindi and Hollywood films, toiletries, and used clothing in various African contexts.[14] Similarly, as I examine how the controversy surrounding Operation Vijana operated within specific discourses and struggles in Dar es Salaam in the late 1960s – concerns over women and urban space intersecting with a state project of 'national culture' – I aim to make an intervention in the literatures on urban space, gender and state power in postcolonial Africa. If interconnections between these three domains have been addressed only circumstantially in Africanist historiography, discourse surrounding Operation Vijana suggests a powerful relationship between constructions of gender and deeply held notions about the city.[15] Among others, the work of Judith Walkowitz on the ways anxieties about women's mobility, masculinity and the Victorian city were all bound up together in tales of sexual danger in late nineteenth-century Britain, sets a profound example in this regard.[16] Furthermore, while there is much work by non-historians on the postcolonial Tanzanian state (historians have only just begun to consider the postcolonial period), most of it follows the state's own emphasis on the rural scene, and virtually none of it considers the cultural dimension of the state's national project – a dimension which was intimately connected with deep official ambivalence toward the city, and which was highly visible to urban dwellers in 1960s Tanzania.[17] Far from the material weakness of the state rendering its rhetoric unimportant for under-standing the lives of everyday Tanzanians, I suggest that TANU's 'cultural initiatives' became touch points through which a variety of struggles – over urban gender relations as well as party constructions of the model citizen – were waged.

Prior to the end of World War II, migration in the British mandate territory of Tanganyika, while substantial in numbers, was primarily rural–rural in nature. This migration was driven largely by opportunities for wage labour in agriculture – particularly on sisal plantations – and the urban population of Tanganyika only increased at a relatively low rate, not much faster than the population's natural growth rate. In the 1950s, however, this pattern began to change. While rural–rural migration continued apace throughout this last decade of colonial rule, it began to decline steeply a couple of years before independence (achieved in 1961), slowing to a trickle by 1965. In contrast, migration to Tanganyika's urban areas shot upward in the early 1950s, beginning a boom that was to last for decades. Dar es Salaam received a disproportionate number of those heading for town: in less than twenty years its population nearly quadrupled, from 69,200 in 1948 to 272,821 in 1967.[18] Jobs, housing and social services, however, lagged far behind this exponential population growth, under both colonial and postcolonial states. Although wage employment in Dar es Salaam doubled during the 1960s, it failed to keep pace with the population boom and the expansion of primary schooling that also occurred during that decade.[19] Official efforts to construct housing and provide infrastructural support to new neighbourhoods were minimal and consistently benefited the wealthy. Dar's new migrants gathered in the city's burgeoning shantytowns that spread further and further out from the city centre.[20]

In the colonial period, even during the 1950s boom of rural–urban migration, those coming to Tanzania's towns were primarily men. But the 1960s saw a sharp rise in the proportion of women among migrants, a trend that significantly changed the demographic character of urban areas. In the 1950s, about two-thirds of migrants to town were men; by 1971, women constituted a majority (54 per cent) of new arrivals. Between 1948 and 1967, Dar es Salaam's male majority declined from 141 to 123 men for every 100 women.[21] There is growing historical evidence, both from Tanzania and from research in other African contexts, to suggest that motives, expectations and outcomes of rural–urban migration differed considerably for women and men. New arrivals in town were overwhelmingly young, regardless of gender, and scholars have long suggested that a primary motivation for migrating involved circumventing the control that elders in rural areas held over marriage options. But if for young, migrant men the dream was to quickly earn a cash dowry and return, respected and admired, to the village to marry on one's own terms, for many young women, 'migration [was] seen as an end in itself': an attempt to take more permanent advantage of the opportunities for autonomous accumulation that the city seemed to offer.[22]

Indeed, despite high unemployment in Dar es Salaam, the capital did present young women migrants with opportunities for increased economic and social autonomy, relative both to the lives they had left in the village and, importantly, to young men's fortunes in the city. From the late 1950s on, the proportion of women migrants who were unmarried upon arrival in town grew steadily, reaching 33 per cent in 1970. Many of these women had taken advantage of the educational opportunities for girls, which had expanded faster than those for men.[23] And while the overall percentage of town-dwelling women in formal wage employment remained small (13 per cent in 1970),[24] particular kinds of formal sector work – secretarial work, for instance – were opening up to women in ways that were nonexistent during the colonial period.[25] Furthermore, women could own property in town (even if few had the means to do so), and Dar's opportunities for informal work for women were many: street hawking, small trade, beer brewing, domestic employment and sex work engaged the energies of many of the capital's women.[26] The city also presented opportunities for a range of relationships with men – including sex work, provision of the 'comforts of home' to regular clients, non-marital cohabitation, and the cultivation of multiple lovers who helped pay the rent – all of which offered young women a greater degree of social and economic autonomy than could be gained through formal marriage. Such non-marital relationships appear to have been the norm in Dar es Salaam, a fact that was thought to have 'raised the bargaining position of women in the town'.[27]

This is not to suggest that most women in Dar es Salaam were well off, or earning a wage, or were building futures free from social controls. To be certain, men retained a privileged position in the social and economic life of Tanzania's capital, and the city's chronic shortages of jobs, housing and social services affected women as well as men. What I do suggest is that, if one compares the aims, expectations and outcomes of rural–urban migration for men and women, urban life afforded relative gains for young women that it did not afford for their male counterparts. J. A. K. Leslie, the author of an extensive, qualitative survey of Dar es Salaam in 1957, described the 'frustration' of the young, male migrant in town:

> His aim in coming to town has been to get cash; yet he finds that he is poor (whereas in the country, with far less money, he was not): yet being poor he is surrounded by tempting things which can be had only for money; all the glamour which helped draw him to town – dances, women, drink, clothes, cinemas, taxis, require money before he can enjoy them; they are so near yet out of his reach ... there is always somebody to be seen enjoying the things he cannot get ... To get cash he needs work, yet the Government, whose duty he believes it is to provide work for all, does not give him work ...[28]

If women's aims in moving to town often involved hopes of achieving a measure of socio-economic autonomy, Dar es Salaam may well have fulfilled this goal better than it did those of men. It is women's experiences of the city *in relation* to those of men to which I draw attention here.

The above quotation from Leslie also hints at the centrality of clothing to practices of self-fashioning in Dar es Salaam. Scholars have long recognised the importance of clothes as markers of social status in colonial East Africa, and a few have noted the ways in which appropriations of stylistic codes inspired by British officials or Muslim traders were key to the performance of such status.[29] Dar es Salaam of the 1950s and 1960s was a nodal point for the circulation of cosmopolitan forms of music, fashion and film, and these forms, particularly clothes, became material for self-styling. In the case of the cowboy subculture of the 1950s and early 1960s, fashion fed off the Hollywood westerns playing in Dar's several cinemas.[30] For young migrants eager 'to make a splash' in town, observed Leslie of late fifties Dar, 'how better than to buy clothes, fine clothes, bright, unusual clothes, and wear them through the streets?'[31] Indeed, in a city that seemed to promise much but deliver little to many migrants (particularly young men), fashion was one means by which one could perform a degree of success beyond one's financial situation. Of course, as Leslie noted, 'there is always scope for more display, more expensive clothes, a firmer stamp of success'.[32]

How did the state – both colonial and postcolonial – respond to the extensive changes experienced by a rapidly expanding Dar es Salaam? Wary of what they regarded as the dangers of allowing Africans to become 'detribalised', British colonial officials across Africa had long discouraged 'natives' from settling in town, justifying this policy with reference to theories of the unsuitability of Africans to urban life. In the 1950s, as the extent of Dar es Salaam's population boom became clear, the government pursued a dual strategy, paralleling British colonial policy toward urban labour across Africa: it tried to create a 'stable' and 'respectable' urban class of Africans, while using a variety of forceful methods in a failed attempt to 'repatriate' jobless 'undesirables'. Despite occasionally opposing such forced relocations in the late 1950s, the nationalist elite shared colonial officials' vision for developing a modern and orderly capital, and upon taking power in 1961 they continued campaigns against Dar es Salaam's 'unproductive' *'wahuni'*.[33] Such campaigns only escalated after the Arusha Declaration of February 1967, which, aside from enacting a series of major 'socialist' policies, also upheld the rural as the appropriate sphere for development and the performance of Tanzanian citizenship.[34]

The developments of the 1960s regarding migration, work and official urban policy were contemporaneous – and, I argue, intersected in important ways – with another state project: the development and promotion of 'national culture'. In December 1962, one year after independence, President Julius K. Nyerere launched this project with the establishment of the Ministry for National Culture and Youth charged with 'seek[ing] out the best of the traditions and customs of all our tribes and mak[ing] them a part of our national culture'.[35] But this mandate to nationalise tribal tradition coexisted in uneasy tension with another imperative: the production of a self-consciously 'modern' culture as a tool for national development. These two conceptions of national culture were both embedded within the project from the beginning, but if the former (national culture as a collection of tribal 'traditions and customs') dominated the early years of the project, the late 1960s saw a modern developmentalism gain increasing prominence as a litmus test for what could be counted as 'national culture'.[36] According to this latter agenda, outlined in a key ministerial memo in 1966, the central task of Tanzania's official culture brokers was 'to sift and purify [traditions] in order to remove or lessen elements that are inappropriate in that they are shameful or disgusting for a condition of civility and modern development in general'.[37]

This emphasis on purging Tanzanian culture of 'inappropriate' elements was manifested in a series of campaigns against a range of 'shameful' cultural practices – the Others against which 'national culture' was increasingly constituted. In addition to the fashions targeted in Operation Vijana, soul music, beauty contests, pornography, and Maasai 'traditional' dress were all subject to successive bans (which, in the end, were mostly unsuccessful). In many cases, such as Operation Vijana, these campaigns dovetailed with the cultivation of the vigilante masculinity of the Youth League. They were also characterised by a coding of rural and urban space that illustrated the connectedness of the national cultural project with the gendered histories of migration and work outlined above. Events like the first National Youth Festival, held in Dar es Salaam in early 1968, just eight months before the launch of Operation Vijana, featured an iconography of oppositions characteristic of post-Arusha Declaration national cultural discourse: a rural land-scape, valorised as the heart and soul of the nation, was to be the recipient of an austere vanguard of male, youthful strength embodied in the TYL cadre; the city, in contrast, was portrayed as the site of spoiled femininity and decadent consumption, a ruined space that young cadres were encouraged to evacuate[38] (Figure 2). It was this 'decadent' city that was the target of nearly all of TANU's 'cultural initiatives', which, in an era of an *ujamaa* ideology celebrating the rural, had the effect of pro-ducing the ugly foil against which a countryside of boundless productivity could be conjured up.

The historical dynamics sketched out above – booming migration, shifting job opportunities, women coming to the capital and claiming public space in new ways, an energetic state initiative to construct urban ills as cultural ones – all portray a Dar es Salaam that in the late 1960s was in the midst of considerable social change. If this was the context within which Operation Vijana was launched in October 1968, then the heated debate over the campaign showcases the way that fashion encapsulated and became a battleground for the social struggles brewing in the city. The TYL sought to portray the ban as a matter of national culture. But in the debate that gripped the capital, significant challenges

Figure 2: Young 'Green Guards' bearing jembes (hoes) march in formation at the 1968 National Youth Festival. Unidentified photographer, *Standard*, 6 February 1968.

to dominant notions of national culture emerged, even as discourse on the operation spilled out beyond TYL's framing of the campaign to engage issues of urban respectability and sexual politics in Dar es Salaam. I now turn to examine this complicated debate, focusing first on the ban's contested framing as a matter of 'national culture'.

From the moment of its official announcement, TYL leaders sought to portray Operation Vijana as a measure 'aimed at defending Tanzania's culture'.[39] But as debate over the ban heated up in the letters-to-the-editor pages and editorial columns of Dar's press, this portrayal was repeatedly challenged. The *Standard*, Dar's semi-independent, English-language daily with a readership estimated at 51,000 in 1967, received 111 letters concerning Operation Vijana in a mere sixteen days before the editor closed the correspondence – only fourteen of these supported the ban.[40] Much more than was the case in the Kiswahili press, which we will consider below, the debate in the *Standard* did indeed focus to a great degree on national culture. But if the *Standard*'s correspondents largely debated the campaign as the TYL had framed it – as a national cultural matter – their debate featured important challenges to notions of the 'modern' and 'youth', categories that were central to TANU's project of socialist modernisation.

TYL leaders and ban supporters often based their charge that fashions like mini-skirts, tight trousers and wigs were undermining Tanzania's culture on the contention that such items were foreign in origin. Opponents of the ban contested this logic, suggesting that it was futile to attempt to condemn banned fashion as 'imitation' of foreign culture, as all mass-produced commodities (including many that were upheld by TANU itself as good and useful) were originally 'foreign'. As 'Peter' put it, 'Unless they [the TYL] want to see Tanzanians going naked, they should believe me that we have no fashion in Tanzania which is acceptable as originating from this country ... Whatever we choose as our national dress, we shall be deceiving ourselves.'[41] Several letter-writers took jabs at the types of dress displayed at state spectacles, with some correspondents arguing that some 'traditional' costumes featured in the national dancing troupes were just as revealing as mini-skirts, and others suggesting that the TANU elite themselves increasingly favoured a 'foreign'-inspired sartorial style epitomised by what was popularly known as the 'Chou-en-Lai' suit.[42] But what drew the most comment on the perceived official hypocrisy was the comparison of Operation Vijana with 'Operation Dress-Up', a TANU campaign held earlier in the year to mandate 'modern dress' for Tanzania's Maasai.[43] As one letter-writer, R. N. Okonkwu, argued,

> If they want us to preserve our culture why don't we put on 'Rubega' and go half naked as our great grandfathers used to do. Because all the clothes we are putting

on now is [*sic*] foreign culture. Moreover, if they want to preserve our culture why are they telling the Masai tribesmen to stop going half naked and put on modern dress like trousers?[44]

Juxtapositions of Operation Vijana with Operation Dress-Up are important to consider closely, for they shed light on the criteria upon which the state's cultural policy-makers were evaluating dress, and the ironic continuities of such criteria with earlier colonial and missionary initiatives in Tanganyika.[45] Official discourse surrounding Operation Dress-Up consistently decried the 'unhygienic', 'uncivilised' and 'out-dated' nature of the Maasai 'traditional' dress and body-care, seen as an affront to Tanzania's 'modern development'. As an editorial in *Nchi Yetu*, a government journal, declared at the height of the campaign, 'Walking around half naked and smearing oneself with mud and ghee, carrying a club and a spear are not at all part of the development plan.'[46] Indeed, Maasai wearing 'traditional' dress and women in mini-skirts were often described in strikingly similar terms: 'roaming half-naked', the Maasai with their 'buttocks uncovered', the mini-skirted women with their 'thighs exposed'.[47] If in one sense, then, as many of Operation Vijana's opponents noted, the two campaigns were strangely paradoxical, they were also both driven by a single aesthetic ideal of 'modern decency' that had its roots, in part, in the mission-school culture within which Tanzania's political elite of the 1960s had largely come of age. Conceived in the heady wake of the Arusha Declaration, campaigns such as Operations Dress-Up and Vijana were part of the modernisationist face of the national cultural project, and not of a 'back-to-tradition' endeavour. In an editorial in the party press backing Operation Vijana, Okwudiba Nnoli, a political scientist working at the University of Dar es Salaam, put it in no uncertain terms: 'Tanzania's goal is to create, in the least possible time, a modern African society.'[48]

The premium placed on the 'modern' was by no means confined to the discourses of Operation Vijana's supporters. Indeed, letters by opponents of the ban were full of references to the desirability of keeping up with the 'modern changes' in a world that 'as time passes … improves and becomes sophisticated'.[49] 'We are Tanzanians of 1968 and not Tanzanians of 8000 B.C.', declared one Peter Tweedy.[50] Correspondents' satirical challenges to TYL leaders to enforce a 'return' to 'bark-cloth' if they were really serious about ridding the country of foreign influences, depended upon the assumption that no one really wanted to see Tanzanians walking the streets of Dar es Salaam dressed in such clothing, which was widely seen as a remnant of the past at odds with city life in a modern Tanzania.

But if the supreme desirability of 'being modern' in 1968 Dar es Salaam was common sense, securely in the realm of the hegemonic, the debate over Operation Vijana reveals just how unstable and contested was the notion of the 'modern' itself. In sharp contrast to those con-demning mini-skirts, tight trousers, cosmetics and wigs as affronts to 'modern decency', many opposing the campaign insisted that such fashions were eminently 'modern'. J. N. Mbussa, a TYL member dis-appointed with the ban, commented, 'Most slender men prefer slimline trousers to big and loose trousers (bombos) simply because they look smart in them ... Girls also prefer mini-skirts to long gowns, just because they look more modern, attractive and beautiful.'[51] Another letter-writer echoed this: 'Nowadays almost everybody has developed the attitude of preferring tight-fitting clothes to others because we look smarter in them.'[52] While TANU imagined a model citizenry committed to 'modern' nation-building along socialist lines, letter-writers opposing Operation Vijana articulated a notion of 'being modern' linked, rather differently, to an imagined network of 'international fashion' and (differ-ently) 'revolutionary' youth styles associated with the happenings of 1968. Issac T. Ngomuo, a high-school student, declared, 'The current youth is well aware of the fashion revolution taking place in many countries ... What is widely practiced by many other peoples is also good for us.'[53] Many letter-writers explicitly extolled the virtues of 'keeping up' with the latest styles, with the comings and goings of 'this ... fashion age'.[54] 'Django', for instance, complained, 'Why then has the Youth League suggested its unwanted styles of dress. Usually people prefer the latest models of everything. This is the century for minis, slack trousers, Texas costume, etc. ... Not many people will like to put on gowns, wide trousers, etc. in this day. Such fashion has lapsed.'[55]

In statements such as these, a vocabulary extolling modern progress became unmoored from its associations with the national, state-centred vision of development through 'hard work' laid out in the Arusha Declaration – and instead was attached to international cultures of self-fashioning through body-adornment and consumption that the state was keen to label 'decadent'. The responses of TYL leaders and Operation Vijana's most ardent supporters to this semantic challenge (a challenge to what was arguably the central category for the legitimacy of the developmentalist state, not to mention TANU's national cultural project) suggest that they took the challenge seriously indeed. Architects and promoters of Operation Vijana were at pains to repeatedly argue that the claims to 'being modern' made by those displaying banned fashion were patently false. Andrew Shija, the TYL branch leader at the Uni-versity of Dar es Salaam, declared that indecent dress was being paraded 'under the cover of modernism', a characterisation echoed by another supporter, who called banned fashion remnants of a 'false imperialist modernism'.[56] But the point was made most forcefully by Okwudiba Nnoli in an editorial to TANU's *Nationalist*. Titling his piece 'There is nothing modern about mini-skirts', Nnoli wrote, 'The problem as far as the controversy is concerned is the nature of a modern society especially as those who wear mini skirts tend to assume that by doing so they are modern.'[57] Far from describing a particular social formation or condition, I argue that modernity here is best regarded as an idiom through which Tanzanians were articulating and defending particular kinds of social selves and political claims.

The identities being articulated – and indeed embodied, on the streets of Dar – by opponents of Operation Vijana were all the more disturbing to the state, I argue, because embedded within them was the performance of a young, urban style that suggested relationships between youth and both the city and the state that were at odds with those envisioned by TANU and its Youth League. Mocking TYL leaders as 'old gentle-men who pretend to be youths', letter-writers identified themselves with new vocabularies – 'teenagers', 'real youths', 'unaged youth' – thereby reappropriating youth as an oppositional, and not a TYL-vanguardist, category. In contrast to a model citizen-youth embodied by the TYL cadre evacuating the capital for a new calling in healthy, rural production, Dar's new 'teenagers' claimed a 'right' to fashion selves out of the very signs of leisure and display through which official discourse defined the city as a problematic and ideologically suspect space.

This struggle over the ability to define urban space and personas only begins to hint at the centrality of the city to the Operation Vijana episode. As we turn our focus to the patterns of gendered discourse and violence that erupted in the wake of the campaign's announcement, we will see that, in some quarters, struggle over the ban focused less on 'national culture' and rather more on questions of gender relations and sex across a charged urban landscape. Like the debate in the *Standard*, however, discourse in Dar's Kiswahili press – and particularly in the semi-independent daily, *Ngurumo* – illustrates the way in which people targeted by Operation Vijana's assault upon particular (life)styles exploited openings in official discourse to renegotiate and sustain identities and lives in the city.

Reminiscing in 1984 about Operation Vijana, veteran Tanzanian journalist Hadji Konde recalled that while the ban had generated much debate in the country's letters-to-the-editor pages, *Ngurumo* had published 'only three' letters on the campaign.[58] If he was correct about one thing – that the debate in *Ngurumo* was markedly different from the one hosted by, say, the *Standard* – Konde was overlooking the dozens of letters, poems, editorials and cartoons engaging the controversy over dress that appeared in *Ngurumo* in the weeks and months following the announcement of Operation Vijana. Few of these interventions – and of those published in the Kiswahili press more generally – featured explicit

debate over 'national culture' or 'foreign' influence. Instead, correspondents used Operation Vijana and the attendant focus on women's
bodies and clothing, as an opportunity to air profound anxieties about
women, sex, work and mobility in Dar es Salaam. While similar anxieties
were longstanding, they were taking on new inflections with the changing
face of Tanzania's capital in the late 1960s.

Banned fashion – and particularly women's 'indecent' dress – was a
sign that had long stood for the city. But in the late 1960s, with the
Arusha Declaration's inscription of town and country life into a narrative
of the battle between the virtuous and the fallen, certain new elements
to this association emerged. Several supporters of Operation Vijana
connected banned fashion to a perceived crisis of rural–urban migration.
Mohamed Jeuri, for instance, argued that instead of 'coming to the city
in search of entertainment', fans of *'nguo za kihuni'* (immoral or indecent
clothing) should be 'back' in the villages working the land.

> Can a person like that really become a revolutionary? If she is told to return to the
> *shamba* [farm] to build the Nation, even if only for a day, will she agree? ... Where
> will she put those wigs, fingernails and tight dresses? ...
>   And not only that ... if a woman or man wears so-called modern clothing and goes
> home to the *shamba*, without a doubt s/he will tempt his or her friends and family
> greatly, make them regard the *shamba* as not a good place for life; and then they
> in turn will come to the city to look for that very life. Without knowing it they find
> themselves extremely oppressed by such a little thing: 'Taiti.' In this way, women sell
> their bodies and men find themselves with the job of ambushing people at night ...
> so they can get at least one pair of tight trousers to show off to those they left back
> on the *shamba*.[59]

As the controversy over Operation Vijana raged, the official press began
to supplement its coverage with short stories that focused on the
seductive dangers of town and highlighted the role of fashion in accom-
plishing the seduction. One such story, titled 'I'll never stay in town again',
told the tale of Kamili, a young country lad plagued with *'tamaa ya kufika
Dar'* (the (very visceral) desire to reach Dar es Salaam). He ends up
making the journey to the capital only to be seduced by a fashionably
dressed woman who takes all his money. 'What a catastrophe!' cries
Kamili, as he recites the moral of the story: 'I'd better head back up-
country, begin farming in an ujamaa village, and start being self-reliant!'[60]
The ease and economy with which a mini-skirted woman could visually
conjure up the relationship between a city of decadent, feminised
consumption and a countryside of national productivity is made even
more clear in a cartoon published in *Ngurumo* in the late 1960s or early
1970s. It portrayed a woman carrying a handbag and wearing a short dress
decorated with *jembes* (hoes), smiling and saying, *'Jembe!* I can wear it,
but I won't wield it!'[61]

In addition to being closely associated with the city, banned fashion also conjured up specific urban characters, particularly female ones. Chief among these was the prostitute. *Ngurumo*'s main page-one story, describing the first two days of Operation Vijana's official enforcement, proclaimed, 'Whores and Undesirables Mind Their Manners.'[62] One letter-writing supporter of the campaign asserted that the ban had been imposed by TYL 'to mark their anger at the prostitution being installed by some young ladies who are also members of UWT' (TANU's women's wing), and that TYL cadres 'must be prepared to cut out the minis not only from Kariakoo but even from the hotels where many are harbored'. The letter concluded, 'We cannot import culture by promoting prostitution.'[63] 'Barmaids', generally thought to be engaged in sex work, were a common target of dress-code attacks, even before Operation Vijana was announced. In March 1968, for instance, the press reported the 'stoning' of a barmaid on her way to work by a 'mob [of] youngsters' who were 'apparently incensed at the shortness and tight fit of her mini-skirt'.[64]

This association of 'indecent' fashion with the figure of the prostitute also had a long history in Tanzania. What Operation Vijana reveals, however, are the ways in which this association was being complicated in the context of a late 1960s Dar es Salaam marked by a shifting political economy of gender and work (outlined early in this paper). For in discourse around the ban and the ensuing physical attacks on women in Dar, the mini-skirt/*taiti* also stood for other urban 'types' and tropes: the secretary, the schoolgirl, the girlfriend of the 'sugar daddy'. These were ambiguous figures, which, while often conflated with that of the prostitute, were also subject to struggles to define new and viable – sometimes even respectable – urban identities for women.

If one maps out the numerous reports of physical attacks on, and discursive condemnation of, women accused of wearing banned dress in the months between Operation Vijana's announcement and its official launch, a patterned geography emerges, focused on specific spaces and sites: hotels and bars (as we have already seen), but also buses and bus stations, downtown streets and offices, and the university. In an editorial on the ban, *Ngurumo* asserted that the 'problem' of banned dress manifested itself 'especially [among] girls who are working in offices, and a few others … who are in various income-earning positions'.[65] For its part, the University of Dar es Salaam was a major site for confrontation over Operation Vijana, witnessing a clash between a demonstration supporting Operation Vijana staged by the campus TYL branch, and a 'counter-protest' of female students defiantly sporting banned clothing out in front of their residence hall. The all-male TYL demonstration had targeted the women's dormitory, and, alongside banners condemning 'indecent' dress in national cultural terms ('Minis for decadent Europe', for example), the marchers held aloft placards apparently threatening specific women: one read, 'Two devils in Hall 3, your days are numbered.'[66] But in the geography of confrontation over Operation Vijana, bus routes, bus stations, and downtown streets were particularly, and violently, charged. The attacks on women and girls alighting from buses at Kariakoo may have been the first and biggest of the collective attacks (the *Standard*'s reporter dubbed it the 'Dar riot'), but several similar scenes – of young women being pulled from buses, or chased down a city-centre street and stripped by a group of young men and boys – were reported in the press as the debate over the operation raged. Of the stories of physical attacks reported between September and February, nearly every single one featured the urban, workers' commute as its setting.

These spaces, sites, and associated 'types' all represented female accumulation, mobility and autonomy, and it was a geography that was the focus of a great deal of anxiety on the part of many of Dar es Salaam's young men. In the midst of the controversy over the campaign, one S. S. Tofiki of Dar published a poem pointing to demographic statistics as cause for his alarm over women's mobility in town. Referring to women who 'roam about' instead of 'staying inside', he wrote,

> The census came around, and they increased in numbers,
> I started thinking, and crunched the numbers,
> How have you all gone wrong, failing to stay inside?
> What defect do you have, for your husbands to refuse you?[67]

Another letter-writer, 'Socialist', explicitly interpreted the attack on women's dress as anxiety about women's work and autonomous consumption. 'Inside the minis and under the wigs', s/he wrote, 'are people with education and intelligence, able to hold down good jobs (sometimes in competition with men), with money of their own to spend, and their own ideas of how to spend it.'[68]

But particular kinds of clothes were not only the signs of particular women's accumulation and consumption, mobility and autonomy – banned fashion was also regarded as a catalyst for these phenomena, which many young men in Dar saw as socio-economic 'exploitation' of men by women. As one D. Chokunegela complained in a poem published in *Uhuru*,

> You'll see Bibi Siti, with her basket in her hand,
> Her body clothed in a *taiti*, seeking *Uzunguni* [the wealthy, formerly white area of Dar],
> Pulling cash, from John and Damian,
> As for me, I congratulate the Resolution of the Youth.[69]

This accusation, that those who wore mini-skirts/*taiti* were doing so in order to gain access to men and their money, was a charge that was levelled frequently and angrily by young men in the debate. As one letter-writer put it, 'I must condemn the minis from start to end. Ladies have to be guided as these young girls surely love the minis for gaining market; one dressing thus will win everybody.'[70] Echoing this vocabulary, one letter to the *Nationalist* complained, 'our young girls become crazy and the happiest when putting on such kind of dress because they are gaining a market'.[71]

Anxieties over young women 'gaining market' – an idiom with connotations of capitalist accumulation and illicit gain that were particularly charged in the wake of the Arusha Declaration's declared war on 'all types of exploitation'[72] – were particularly professed by, and ascribed to, male TYL members and male university students. (Indeed, these two categories of people appear to have been the ban's staunchest supporters.) One opponent of the ban charged that TYL leaders and their cadres were jealous, for they 'are the very ones who desire the taiti-wearers, and as soon as they fail to get them, they look for an underhanded way to take out their anger by forbidding them from wearing [these things]'.[73] As for the students, we have already seen that the struggle on campus over Operation Vijana featured male students making angry threats against particular women. I suggest that this anger, and the campus politics surrounding Operation Vijana, related directly to what was perceived by male students as intense competition between themselves and wealthier, older men for sexual relationships with female students on campus – competition in which the male students saw themselves as being at a tremendous, economic disadvantage to these 'sugar daddies'.[74]

Thus, the office worker, the female undergraduate and the girlfriend of the 'sugar daddy', as figures conjured up in public discourse by the sign of banned fashion, were all consistently conflated with the figure of the prostitute. All were represented as being in positions particularly ripe with possibilities for gaining access to men and their money through sex. But in the context of changes in demography and work in Dar es Salaam, this conflation was also an unstable one. Indeed, public discourse around Operation Vijana featured attempts by some women to reclaim figures linked with banned fashion as viable urban identities. Some of these attempts followed a UWT line that sought to celebrate women's entrance into formal wage-labour as a sign of Tanzania's modern progress, while condemning practices like the wearing of mini-skirts in much the same terms as the TYL: as 'indecent' assaults on respectability under the guise of modern fashion.[75] In an instalment of a women's advice column called 'Bibi Mapinduzi Asema' ('Mrs. Revolution Says') (which was tellingly

Figure 3: Cartoon portraying a woman being scolded by an older man, against the backdrop of the city, on the eve of Operation Vijana. The original caption read, 'Asha, what kind of Shameful dress are you wearing? I swear, you'll regret it when that date [Operation Vijana's launch] comes!!' 'Aaaa … step aside old man. Don't bring me any trouble, four eyes.' Artist unknown, *Nchi Yetu*, November 1968.

inaugurated in *Ngurumo* during the Operation Vijana controversy and featured exhortations against banned fashion), Bibi Mapinduzi herself attempted to distinguish the office-working woman from the prostitute. Taking readers on a virtual tour of downtown Dar es Salaam in which she mapped out a geography of burgeoning women's formal sector work, Bibi Mapinduzi marvelled at the 'beautiful image of our ... well-dressed girls emerging from offices with their purses', and continued, 'I didn't know that we have this many women working in government and company offices.' Writing pointedly that the majority of these women were 'very well-dressed and moved respectably', Bibi Mapinduzi also lamented that their reputations were being tarnished by 'certain women who were [recently] arrested for roaming the streets, in hotels and in bars for reasons best known to themselves'. These latter women, she said, 'don't like real work', and should be forced 'to leave town, to stop stealing people's husbands, and to go back to the *shamba* to farm'[76] (Figure 3).

If the UWT leadership, and other prominent women in high political office, took a position promoting public roles and work for women while attacking banned dress,[77] some young women (and a few men)[78] sought to reconcile the two. In October 1968, at the height of the debate over Operation Vijana, the vice-president of UWT met with a group of 'girls' – non-UWT members – at their Dar es Salaam hostel to discuss their concerns. In the 'heated discussion' that ensued, the 'girls' not only 'said it was unfair that a body of men should sit down and decide what women should wear', but they also explicitly justified the wearing of 'shorter dresses'. 'Modern style dresses were cheap and suited to town living', the young women told their distinguished visitor. According to the *Standard*, 'One girl said that as a secretary she had to do a lot of walking about and shorter dresses made this easier. She said that if she wore long national dress she would not be able to push her way on to crowded buses which she had to do every day.'[79]

Statements like these illustrate attempts by working women to subtly reclaim banned fashion by reinscribing it as practical, appropriate and respectable for new patterns of work and movement in new urban spaces. More difficult to perform in a public discourse dominated by deep suspicion of female sexuality, were attempts by women to celebrate banned fashion as a site of female pleasure. One woman referred, rather obliquely, to the capability of fashion to heighten 'womanish feelings' that Tanzanian women, 'like any other women', had.[80] Another quoted a saying she had 'once read somewhere' that 'a woman's dress is like a garden-gate, which protects the property without blocking the view', even as she framed her enjoyment of banned fashion safely within the bounds of her marriage and her husband's gaze.[81]

Attempts like these to de-link banned fashion from its association with female accumulation through sex faced, in Operation Vijana, an attempt to re-conflate the figure of the prostitute with figures like the secretary that challenged its stigmatisation of particular body-markings. For many of Dar's young men failing to gain the access to resources (and women) that fantasies of city life promised, Operation Vijana promised to eliminate what was seen as a central tool of women who placed themselves out of their material reach. For those participating in attacks on women and even in the TYL-led enforcement of the ban, the campaign provided an opportunity to enact sexualised performances of power over those women in the very spaces that were deemed to provide the conditions of possibility for female accumulation, mobility and occasional autonomy. In this way, the young, male rage generated around what was ostensibly a national cultural issue was intimately related to intersecting anxieties about women in urban space and the politics of sex in a post-Arusha Declaration Dar es Salaam.

Operation Vijana was launched as one of the first of what would be several national cultural campaigns targeting urban 'popular' cultures in Tanzania in the late 1960s and early 1970s. And yet, in the way it was seized upon, enforced and debated by residents of Dar es Salaam, two things happened. First, some fundamental assumptions and vocabularies upon and through which 'national culture' was constituted became contested, albeit within limits that demonstrate just how hegemonic were certain hierarchies of value. If the supreme value ascribed to 'being modern' was one such hegemonic notion, rooted firmly in the realm of the common-sensical, its conceptual content was far from stable; and the 'modern' of the state that underwrote TANU's nation-building projects was challenged by another 'modern', one defined through non national associations quite different from TANU's own invocations of socialist internationalism. Secondly, Operation Vijana tapped into anxieties among many of Dar's (often jobless) male youth about new patterns of women's work, sexuality and mobility in urban space. Such anxieties not only coincided with, and reinforced, the uneasy position of the city – depicted as a disturbing site of decadent consumption and femininity – within a state ideology that valorised the rural as the site of austere hard work; they also fuelled the enforcement of the ban, with all its attendant rage and violence against Dar's 'new women'.

Operation Vijana and, I suggest, other national cultural banning campaigns that, like it, targeted urban areas – cannot be understood simply in a national cultural frame, without considering various 'struggles for the city'[82] that were fundamental to the directions these campaigns took. Conversely, Operation Vijana (and, quite possibly, other similar campaigns) were appropriated as important sites upon which such urban social struggles – in our case, around gender and generation – could be fought out. As visual signs, fashions like the mini-skirt in late sixties Tanzania were extraordinary indices of social conflict, registering debates over national culture and 'modern development', the construction and crises of new femininities and masculinities, generational conflicts over resources, and contests over public space in a postcolonial capital. Moreover, what makes fashion such a powerful lens through which to view these struggles is that it highlights intersections between them, making it impossible to regard them as unconnected, discrete dynamics.

Notes

Funding for the research project on which this article is based was provided by the International Dissertation Field Research Program of the Social Science Research Council (with funds from the Andrew W. Mellon Foundation), and a US Department of Education Fulbright-Hays Doctoral Dissertation Research Abroad Fellowship. The project has benefited immensely from discussions with Nancy Rose Hunt, Frederick Cooper, David William Cohen, Kelly Askew, Delphine Mauger, Jim Brennan, Andrew Burton, Leander Schneider and Ned Bertz. I gratefully acknowledge the further assistance of Carole Turbin, Shani D'Cruze and an anonymous *Gender & History* reader. All shortcomings remain the author's alone.

1. *Standard*, 17 October 1968.
2. *Standard*, 3 October 1968.
3. *Uhuru*, 3 October 1968; *Ngurumo*, 3 October 1968; *Standard*, 3 October 1968; *Nationalist*, 3 October 1968. All translations from Kiswahili are the author's own.
4. *Standard*, 8 October 1968.
5. *Standard*, 8 October and 24 October 1968; *Ngurumo*, 9 October 1968; *Uhuru*, 9 October 1968.
6. *Standard*, 8 October 1968.
7. *Standard*, 29 and 30 December 1968; *Nationalist*, 30 December 1968. 'Decent' dress included modest collared shirts and slightly baggy trousers, 'maxi' dresses, socialist-style suits inspired by Mao, Chou-en-Lai and Kaunda, and dress common in coastal Dar, such as the Islamic-inspired *kanzu* and *bui-bui*, and the *khanga*. 'Indecent' dress included, for men, tight 'drain-pipe' trousers and cowboy-inspired outfits ('Texas costume'), and, for women, tight 'slim-line' dresses and, most notoriously, the mini-skirt.
8. *Standard*, 2 January 1969; *Nationalist*, 2 January 1969.
9. *Standard*, 5, 8, 10 January 1969; *Nationalist*, 3 January 1969; *Nchi Yetu*, April 1981. Campaigns against 'indecent' dress were also launched in the late 1960s and early 1970s in Zanzibar, which together with mainland Tanganyika made up the United Republic of Tanzania. For a forthcoming analysis of the Zanzibari campaigns, see Thomas Burgess, 'Cinema, Bell bottoms and Miniskirts: Struggles over Youth and Citizenship in Revolutionary Zanzibar', *International Journal of African Historical Studies*, forthcoming.
10. Karin Barber (ed.), *Readings in African Popular Culture* (Indiana University Press, 1997).
11. See, for instance, Shari Benstock and Suzanne Ferris (eds), *On Fashion* (Rutgers University Press, 1994); Alexandra Warwick and Dani Cavallaro, *Fashioning the Frame: Boundaries, Dress and the Body* (Berg, 1998); Benstock and Ferris (eds), *Footnotes: On Shoes* (Rutgers University Press, 2001).
12. Arjun Appadurai, *Modernity at Large* (University of Minnesota Press, 1996); Ulf Hannerz, *Transnational Connections* (Routledge, 1996).
13. Frederick Cooper, 'What is the Concept of Globalization Good For?: An African Historian's Perspective', *African Affairs*, 100 (2001), pp. 189–213.

14. Minou Fugelsang, *Veils and Videos: Female Youth Culture on the Kenyan Coast* (Stockholm University, 1994); Brian Larkin, 'Indian Films and Nigerian Lovers: Media and the Creation of Parallel Modernities', *Africa*, 67 (1997), pp. 406–40; Rob Nixon, *Homelands, Harlem and Hollywood: South African Culture and the World Beyond* (Routledge, 1994); Ch. Didier Gondola, 'Dream and Drama: The Search for Elegance among Congolese Youth', *African Studies Review*, 42 (1999), pp. 23–48; Phyllis Martin, 'Contesting Clothes in Colonial Brazzaville', *Journal of African History*, 35 (1994), pp. 401–26; Johanna Schoss, '"Dressed to Shine": Work, Leisure, and Style in Malindi, Kenya', in *Clothing and Difference: Embodied Identities in Colonial and Postcolonial Africa*, ed. Hildi Hendrickson (Duke University Press, 1998), pp. 157–88; Timothy Burke, *Lifebuoy Men, Lux Women: Commodification, Consumption and Cleanliness in Modern Zimbabwe* (Duke University Press, 1996); Karen Tranberg Hansen, *Salaula: The World of Secondhand Clothing and Zambia* (University of Chicago Press, 2000).

15. One recent exception is Emmanuel Akyeampong, '"*Wo pe tam won pe ba*" ("You like cloth but you don't want children"): Urbanization, Individualism and Gender Relations in Colonial Ghana, c. 1900–39', in *Africa's Urban Past*, ed. David Anderson and Richard Rathbone (Heinemann, 2000), pp. 222–34. For a critical review of work on gender in African history, see Nancy Rose Hunt, Introduction, in *Gendered Colonialisms in African History*, ed. Hunt, Tessie R. Liu and Jean Quataert (Blackwell, 1997), pp. 1–15.

16. Judith Walkowitz, *City of Dreadful Delight: Narratives of Sexual Danger in Late-Victorian London* (University of Chicago Press, 1992). See also Elizabeth Wilson, *The Sphinx in the City: Urban Life, the Control of Disorder, and Women* (Virago, 1991).

17. On the Tanzanian state, see Issa Shivji, *Class Struggles in Tanzania* (Monthly Review Press, 1976), and Andrew Coulson, *Tanzania: A Political Economy* (Clarendon Press, 1982). On the state as a cultural form, see George Steinmetz (ed.), *State/Culture: State Formation after the Cultural Turn* (Cornell University Press, 1999).

18. R. H. Sabot, *Economic Development and Urban Migration: Tanzania, 1900–1971* (Clarendon Press, 1979), pp. 43–50.

19. Sabot, *Economic*, pp. 71, 142.

20. John Campbell, 'The State, Urban Development and Housing', in *Capitalism, Socialism and the Development Crisis in Tanzania*, ed. Norman O'Neill and Kemal Mustafa (Avebury, 1990), pp. 152–76.

21. Sabot, *Economic*, p. 90.

22. Kenneth Little, *African Women in Town: An Aspect of Africa's Social Revolution* (Cambridge University Press, 1973), p. 28. See also J. A. K. Leslie, *A Survey of Dar es Salaam* (Oxford University Press, 1963); Susan Geiger, *TANU Women: Gender and Culture in the Making of Tanganyikan Nationalism, 1955–1965* (Heinemann, 1997), pp. 37–8; Akyeampong, 'Urbanization'; Christine Obbo, *African Women: Their Struggle for Economic Independence* (Zed Press, 1980).

23. Sabot, *Economic*, pp. 94–5.

24. Sabot, *Economic*, p. 92.

25. P. S. Maro and W. I. F. Mlay, 'People, Population Distribution and Employment', *Tanzania Notes and Records*, 83 (1976), pp. 1–20; see also Josef Gugler, 'The Second Sex in Town', Audrey Wipper, 'African Women, Fashion, and Scapegoating', both in *Canadian Journal of African Studies*, 6 (1972), pp. 289–302, 329–50.

26. Geiger, *TANU Women*, pp. 31–8.

27. Leslie, *Survey*, p. 4; also see Luise White, *The Comforts of Home: Prostitution in Colonial Nairobi* (University of Chicago Press, 1990), for an insightful perspective on the diversity of sexual relationships in an East African colonial city.

28. Leslie, *Survey*, p. 4.

29. Laura Fair, 'Dressing Up: Clothing, Class and Gender in Post-Abolition Zanzibar', *Journal of African History*, 39 (1998), pp. 63–94; Terrance Ranger, *Dance and Society in Eastern Africa, 1890–1970* (University of California Press, 1975).

30. Leslie, *Survey*, p. 112–13. Also see Andrew Burton, 'Urchins, Loafers, and the Cult of the Cowboy: Urbanization and Delinquency in Dar es Salaam, 1919–1961', *Journal of African History*, 42 (2001), pp. 199–216.

31. Leslie, *Survey*, p. 110.

32. Leslie, *Survey*, p. 112.

33. Andrew Burton, 'The "Haven of Peace" Purged: Tackling the Undesirable and Unproductive Poor in Dar es Salaam, *c*. 1954–85', in *The Emperor's New Clothes?: Rhetoric and Reality in Late-Colonial and Post-Colonial East Africa*, ed. Andrew Burton and Michael Jennings (James Currey, forthcoming); James R. Brennan, 'Nation, Race and Urbanization in Dar es Salaam, Tanzania, 1916–1976' (PhD dissertation, Northwestern University, 2002); Campbell, 'State'.

34. TANU Publicity Section, *The Arusha Declaration and TANU's Policy on Self-Reliance* (Government Printer, 1967).

35. J. K. Nyerere, *Cultural Revolution in Tanzania* (Ministry of National Culture and Youth, 1974?), p. 4.

36. For an ethnographic perspective on musical performance as it related to Tanzanian cultural policy, see Kelly Askew, *Performing the Nation: Swahili Music and Cultural Politics in Tanzania* (Chicago, forthcoming 2002).

37. E. R. Munseri, 'Kusitawisha na Kuhifadhi Utamaduni Wetu', Tanzania National Archives 540/CD/CR/46.

38. See coverage of the National Youth Festival in the TANU press, *Nationalist*, 30 January–6 February 1968.

39. 'TANU Youths Ban "Minis"', *Standard*, 3 October 1968.

40. *Standard*, 25 October 1968. For circulation figures, see John C. Condon, 'Nation Building and Image Building in the Tanzanian Press', *Journal of Modern African Studies*, 5 (1967), pp. 335–54.

41. 'Peter', letter to *Standard*, 17 October 1968.

42. See letters by Ukaka Mpwenku (14 October), Zainabu (14 October), Augustine Moshi (16 October), 'Regular Reader' (22 October), J. N. Lohay (23 October), 'Revolutionary Youth' (23 October), John C. R. Mpate (24 October), M. Sheya (10 October), and R. N. Okonkwu (14 October), all in *Standard*, 1968.

43. For an insightful analysis of Operation Dress-Up, see Leander Schneider, 'Developmentalism and Its Failings: An Exploration of Tanzanian Development Politics, 1961–1979' (PhD dissertation, Columbia University, 2002).

44. R. N. Okonkwu, letter to *Standard*, 14 October 1968.

45. For colonial and missionary efforts to enforce dress codes elsewhere in East Africa, see Atieno Odhiambo, 'From Warriors to *Jonanga*: The Struggle over Nakedness by the Luo of Kenya', in *Sokomoko: Popular Culture in East Africa*, ed. Werner Graebner (Rodopi, 1992), pp. 11–25.

46. 'Maendeleo ya Wamasai', *Nchi Yetu*, March 1968.

47. *Nationalist*, 9, 10, 12, 14 and 19 February 1968; Kilua J., letter to *Nationalist*, 25 October 1968; letters by Karim Hirji (8 October), Chake Mussa (23 October), 'Supporter' (25 October), all in *Standard*, 1968.

48. Okwudiba Nnoli, 'There is nothing modern about mini-skirts', *Nationalist*, 21 October 1968.

49. 'Sadru', letter to *Standard*, 25 October 1968.

50. Peter Tweedy, letter to *Standard*, 17 October 1968.

51. J. N. Mbussa, letter to *Standard*, 10 October 1968.

52. Issac T. Ngomuo, letter to *Standard*, 16 October 1968.

53. Ngomuo, letter to *Standard*, 16 October 1968.

54. M. S. Sulemanjee, letter to *Standard*, 12 October 1968. See also the letters by Abu Abdallah (4 October), M. W. Kibani (9 October), M. Sheya (10 October), Ernestos S. Lyimo (11 October), Pakilo P. Patitu (11 October), 'Django' (11 October), R. M. Okonkwu (14 October), Ngomuo (16 October), 'Concerned' (17 October), Sr Mberwa Sleepwell (22 October), Y. Makwillo (23 October), 'Unconcerned' (24 October), all in *Standard*, 1968.

55. 'Django', letter to *Standard*, 11 October 1968.
56. Andrew Shija, quoted in *Standard*, 17 October 1968.
57. Okwudiba Nnoli, *Nationalist*, 21 October 1968.
58. Hadji Konde, *Freedom of the Press in Tanzania* (East Africa Publications, 1984), p. 208.
59. Mohamedi Jeuri, letter to *Uhuru*, 22 October 1968.
60. Thomas Changa, 'Sikai Tena Mjini', *Nchi Yetu*, February 1969.
61. Cartoon reprinted in G. Kamenju and F. Topan, *Mashairi ya Azimio la Arusha* (Longman Tanzania, 1971), p. 48. Artist unknown.
62. *Ngurumo*, 2 January 1969.
63. 'Supporter', letter to *Standard*, 25 October 1968.
64. *Standard*, 18 March 1968.
65. *Ngurumo*, 14 October 1968.
66. 'Anti-Mini Militants Meet Modern Misses', 17 October 1968.
67. S. S. Tofiki, 'Kina Mama Nambieni', *Ngurumo*, 1 November 1968.
68. 'Socialist', letter to *Standard*, 23 October 1968.
69. D. Chokunegela, 'Nami Natoa Pongezi', *Uhuru*, 17 October 1968.
70. 'Supporter', letter to *Standard*, 25 October 1968.
71. Kilua J., letter to *Nationalist*, 25 October 1968.
72. TANU Publicity Section, *Arusha Declaration* (1967), p. 2. A 1970 cartoon, subtitled 'I don't want the mini's exploitation anymore', condemned mini-skirts in these very terms (*Nchi Yetu*, February 1970).
73. De Leone, letter to *Ngurumo*, 24 October 1968.
74. For a fictionalised portrayal of campus sexual politics, see Austin Bukenya, *The People's Bachelor* (East African Publishing House, 1972).
75. For UWT statements on the issue of 'indecent dress', see *Nationalist*, 14 and 15 October 1968; *Uhuru*, 14, 15, and 21 October 1968.
76. 'Bibi Mapinduzi Asema: Mabibi Viwandani', *Ngurumo*, 14 December 1968.
77. See, for instance, Lucy Lameck's letter, 'Minis Lower the Dignity of Women', *Nationalist*, 29 October 1968, a particularly virulent attack on 'derogatory' dress.
78. See, for instance, the letter by T. K. Malendeja in *Standard*, 24 October 1968.
79. 'Mini ban "surprise" to U.W.T.', *Standard*, 14 October 1968.
80. 'Freedom Lover (Miss)', letter to *Standard*, 18 October 1968.
81. 'Mrs Freedom Lover', letter to *Standard*, 23 October 1968.
82. I borrow this phrase from Frederick Cooper, 'Urban Space, Industrial Time and Wage Labor in Africa', in *Struggle for the City: Migrant Labor, Capital, and the State in Urban Africa*, ed. Frederick Cooper (Sage Publications, 1983), pp. 7–50.

12

Dressing for Leadership in China: Wives and Husbands in an Age of Revolutions (1911–1976)

Verity Wilson

The intertwining histories of Chinese dress and politics are registered by the way successive twentieth-century leaders, who in a still intensely patriarchal society were almost uniformly male, chose to present themselves. The appearance of these leaders' spouses, moreover, offers up further insights into the prevailing microtechniques of power and extends our knowledge of the experience of Chinese women in an era where personal and national identities were in an almost continuous state of potentially revolutionary renegotiation. With the address to gender as an integral part of history, the sartorial practices of three specific marriage partnerships give us a more nuanced understanding of the counterbalance of female and male roles played out in the public gaze through the great turns of Chinese history in the twentieth century.

Sun Yat-sen (1866–1925), briefly China's first president following on the events of 1911 which lead to the overthrow of the emperor, is lionised as the father of the Republican revolution.[1] Chiang Kai-shek (1888–1975) set up a Nationalist government in 1928 and over the next twenty years opposed warlords and the Japanese only to lose control of China to his third adversary, the Communists. The forces of the iconic Mao Zedong (1893–1976) claimed victory over Chiang, and the People's Republic of China was proclaimed in 1949. The female players in this game of dressing the part are these men's spouses, crucial personalities, remembered, revered or vilified as passionately as their marriage partners, each one alive to the impact of public image. The social title 'Madame', derived from international diplomatic politesse, was the common western way of address for these women, but Madame Sun, Madame

Chiang and Madame Mao were not just appendages of their husbands, despite this appellation. It is not a Chinese style of address and within China they used their own names, Song Qingling (1892–1981), her sister, Song Meiling (b. 1897), and Jiang Qing (1914–91). Given the continuing restrictions placed on women at this time, it is unlikely that any of these three would have been prominent in national politics had they not married famous politicians but, having done so, each of them carved out a very particular public role for herself, a role defined in no small measure by dress. For their male partners also, regimes of clothing contributed to a politics of the symbolic in which a newly gendered virile masculinity stood for new forms of national and class identity.[2]

In the western mind, one of the compelling images of modern China is that of Chairman Mao dressed in the utilitarian, high-buttoned jacket and matching trousers known in the West as a Mao suit. Jiang Qing, his wife, also wore it. Its close identification with Mao Zedong in the eyes of the world may not have had such exact reverberations in China itself, where the suit and its forebears have links with the other leaders who also, at times, held the fate of this vast Asian country in their hands. Chiang Kai-shek sometimes chose to wear this suit but neither he nor Mao takes the credit for its creation. Traditionally, this honour is accorded their predecessor, Sun Yat-sen, although the suit was not, in fact, 'invented' either by Sun or by any one individual. Another name for this suit is *Zhongshan zhuang* (Zhongshan suit) after Dr Sun Yat-sen, whose name in Mandarin Chinese is Sun Zhongshan.

An example of this suit is preserved today in the People's Republic in a museum that was Sun's Shanghai home between 1918 and 1924. It was supposedly worn by him and it is a smart, well-tailored affair in pale grey. All the distinguishing features are there – neat, turned down collar, inset sleeves and four buttoned pockets with the breast ones smaller than the ones at the waist, which are characteristically expandable. The preservation of the dead leader's outfit at all is a clue to the importance of clothes in the formation and the semiotics of state. The choice of this particular style of suit for posterity within Communist China sets out to legitimise Mao's political lineage. Mao eventually won the battle to lead China in 1949 but, from Sun Yat-sen's early death in 1925, the leadership had been contested by Chiang Kai-shek who also took care to project himself as Sun's heir and, likewise, wore this kind of suit. As we shall see, while Jiang Qing, Mao's wife, was seen as an honorary man and conformed to male dress codes, the Song sisters did not demonstrate a historical allegiance to other leaders. Dress and politics were differently inflected according to gender.

In the realm of appearances, however, Sun Yat-sen was far from consistent and there is a dichotomy between what Sun actually wore and how he is remembered. Surviving photographic images reveal his clothing conduct to be varied, suggesting that he often fell in with the accepted dress codes of the country or group he was visiting; he mostly lived outside China until 1912. We might expect him to have worn the fully fledged *Zhongshan zhuang* or Sun Yat-sen suit, as preserved in the museum, more often than he appears to have done. He did not invariably wear its possible precursor, the *xuesheng zhuang* (student suit), either. The student suit seems to have derived, via Japanese college uniform, from a European, probably Prussian, prototype in the last years of the nineteenth century and early years of the twentieth. The student jacket, fastened down the centre with flat or semi-spherical buttons and buttonholes, had a stand-up collar, and variations in the design centred around the number of pockets, if any, and their style, as well as the overall fit. A less familiar name for this suit is *qiling wenzhuang*, which proclaims the style's most prominent feature, the stand-up collar (*qiling*), as well as passing judgement on its modernity (in an early Republican context, *wen* can be translated as 'modern', 'civilised'). Maybe this term was used to designate one variation of the student suit or maybe the nomenclature redefined the object.

Despite having made the supremely significant gesture of cutting off his queue, the long braid of hair down the back and symbol of Manchu imperial authority, when he arrived in exile in Japan in 1895, Sun Yat-sen was late in taking up the modern or student suit already favoured by Chinese ideologues there as representing a break with the traditions of the past. He seems to have adopted a lightweight version of this high-buttoned suit in the clammy climate of Southeast Asia and by 1912 he was wearing a woollen type. Portraits from this time confirm that a western-style suit, with a lapel jacket worn with collar and tie, was perhaps the more usual formal garb for the person today perceived as the national figurehead.[3] We should note that the Republican dress rules laid down in 1912 did not include anything resembling a modern or student suit.[4] After only forty-five days as president, he would never lead the Chinese state again, but would play several different marginal roles and dress accordingly. In 1917, Sun made his way to Guangzhou (Canton) with the Chinese navy and attempted to form a military government with himself as grand marshal. The nature of the post ordained the dress. The official portrait of the time presents him in overblown military garb replete with epaulettes, gold braid, white gloves and a plumed hat. He is indistinguishable from local warlords saturated with stripes, pips and cockades. It is an unfamiliar representation now and evokes a sense of unease, but it is commensurate with one strand of clothing conduct, that of the militarised and uniformed body, prevalent in China throughout this period and not wholly limited to the male gender.[5] In 1918, Sun

Yat-sen reverted to wearing a Chinese long gown with asymmetric fastenings. Several of Sun's supporters in the Guangzhou parliament began to be assassinated and he himself was forced to retire to Shanghai, where he took time out to think, write and revise his speeches for publication. The image of a traditionally attired Sun at his desk is cognate with the age-old one of the government official withdrawing from public life to take up scholarly pursuits but, against this observation, we should be cautious about viewing this mode of dress as unfashionable or politically unsound in the twentieth century's first two or even three decades. While being different from the patterned dragon robes worn by bureaucrats of dynastic China, the plain Republican robe was, after all, quintessentially Chinese and as such had much to recommend it at this time of self-conscious nation building in the wake of imperial collapse in 1911.

In 1915, the 49-year-old Sun Yat-sen married Song Qingling. She was one of a trio of American-educated sisters from a wealthy, influential family who were scandalised by the liaison. Sun's marriage publicly acknowledged his liaison with Qingling even though Lu Muzhen (1867–1952), his first wife in an arranged marriage of his youth, was still alive. The secret ceremony in Tokyo seems not to have been chronicled, but a photograph, today sometimes ascribed as their wedding photograph, shows their outfits to be smart but not extravagant. Because we know so little about this event, the photograph and the clothes of the bride and groom become important for our understanding of this personal union which was soon to become very public. Neither wears Chinese dress, though we should remember that from the point of view of this revolutionary couple at this particular stage, western dress, taken up earlier in Japan than China, still represented revolutionary ideals.[6] Song Qingling's neat two-piece, of a kind worn by fashionable Japanese and western women, has a short jacket left open to reveal a ruched blouse with a lace collar and a pendant necklace. Her picture hat adorned with feathers is the only clue that this might perhaps be the sort of costume suited to a celebratory occasion. Sun has on a smartly tailored three-piece suit with white shirt and tie.[7]

This stormy wedding episode marks a watershed between public and private. It was some time before the disapproval abated, but from 1917 Sun Yat-sen's image is often associated with that of Song Qingling. She was frequently photographed by his side, by no means a standard practice for wives of prominent figures in China in the early years of the twentieth century, and this greater feminine exposure became central to the theme of Republican modernity. The female citizen was a new type of subject position exemplified by the short hair and unbound feet of university students and nationalist activists. They occupied a prominent position in the cultural imaginary of the period even if their actual numbers were tiny in comparison with those of women who remained constrained by traditional patriarchal ideology. After he married Song Qingling, a greater number of informal pictures were taken of Sun Yat-sen than was the case before, foreshadowing, perhaps, the public's appetite for 'at home' shots negotiated largely through the female sphere (Figure 1). Both of them frequently turned away from European dress, perhaps mindful that their heightened profiles required a clothing strategy that was perceived as Chinese at this crucial and fragile stage of republicanism and, by this time, there were clothes, whatever their origins, that in some measure fitted the description 'Chinese' as well as 'modern'. It was only after exposure to western clothes that a definition of what was Chinese could be formulated. A smiling Song Qingling stands next to Sun Yat-sen in these images and they reveal him at his most relaxed. Song Qingling herself, while not totally abandoning the American clothes she grew accustomed to while a student in the United States, now often donned reworked Chinese dress in the form of a short, high-necked jacket, fastening to one side across the collarbone, and a calf-length skirt, the sort of ensemble that was favoured by modernising young women in the urban centres. The dress of this couple surely determines, in part, an interpretation of these photographs as redolent signifiers of an incipient new society, uniquely Chinese, in which companionate marriage was axiomatic. China's greatest twentieth-century writer, Lu Xun (1881–1936), addressed the harsh realities of the issues in such stories as 'A Happy Family', and these informal images of the leader and his wife went some way to efface the censure surrounding the clandestine wedding.[8] Arguably Sun Yat-sen and Song Qingling together provided a model for the new society that each alone could not have achieved.

Did Sun Yat-sen, then, ever wear the evolved type of suit, today known in the West as a Mao suit, that now hangs in Sun's memorial museum? Full-length photographs of Sun Yat-sen from 1923 corroborate that he did indeed don this four patch-pocket style, rather different from the student suit, and 1923 is the date given by some contemporary commentators as the time that Sun himself designed the suit along with help from his tailor. One of the photographs in question shows him meeting the press in Shanghai. Perhaps such a staged occasion provided a good opportunity to give the suit its first airing but this and the attribution of its creator remain speculative. What we can say without doubt is that, by this date, Sun had returned to the fray of revolution and, bent on taking control of a unified China, was accepting aid from Soviet Russia via Comintern agents who dressed in what was fast becoming the international style of Communist revolution.[9] This was none other than

Figure 1: Song Qingling and Sun Yat-sen in the garden of their Shanghai home, *c*.1917. From Cao Feng (ed.), *Song Qingling zai Shanghai* (Song Qingling in Shanghai) (*Shanghai renmin chubanshe*, Shanghai People's Publishing House, Shanghai, 1992), p. 35, pl. 48. With permission from the Sun Yat-sen and Song Qingling History Relic Management Institute.

the suit with four pockets and a turned-down small collar linked with Lenin (1870–1924), the head of the first Soviet government, and worn by his Soviet and Chinese successors, Stalin (1879–1953), and Mao. Lenin's death in 1924 was announced during the First Congress of the Nationalist Party in Guangzhou when Soviet advisers were present, and Sun Yat-sen, who was himself to die of cancer a year later, interrupted the proceedings to deliver a eulogy. Lenin was embalmed wearing this classic suit and an effigy marking the tomb of Sun Yat-sen also depicts him in one. That the stone image was clothed in a Sun Yat-sen suit is confirmation of a desire to associate the outfit in the public discourse of the Republican period and beyond with China's lost leader, and it is significant that in 1929, when Sun's body was finally laid to rest, the Nationalist government ruled that all civil servants should wear the Sun Yat-sen suit as official dress, thus mirroring the appearance of their revolutionary 'father'.

After the death of Sun Yat-sen, Song Qingling broke with the new regime of her brother-in-law, Chiang Kai-shek, and lived in exile for some years. In Moscow, she dressed in European clothes and reportedly was embarrassed by how short the skirts seemed after Chinese dress.[10] She returned to China occasionally and in 1929 attended her deceased husband's internment at Zijinshan (Purple Gold Mountain) in Nanjing. Her own dress for the ceremony on that occasion was a simple, dark cotton gown and, set against the Nationalist pageantry of the Chiang Kai-shek regime, this signalled both her continuing disassociation from that government and her untouchable status as the widow of the now hugely venerated Sun Yat-sen. Subsequently, she lived in Shanghai and, in marked contrast to that cosmopolitan city's reputation for fast living and high fashion during the 1930s and 1940s, Song Qingling seems to have lived out those difficult years comparatively quietly. Edgar Snow, the ardent supporter and reporter of the Communist cause, remarked in 1931 on her perfect grooming and the subdued colours of her 'gowns of youthful style'.[11] With Mao Zedong's victory, Song Qingling, never a member of the Chinese Communist Party, was honoured with the title of vice-president and lent a certain dignified grace to the stiff ceremonial line-ups of the Beijing Politburo.

Sisterly affection and communication were not entirely obliterated by the political agenda during the Nationalist ascendancy. A united sorority in the face of the suffering of ordinary Chinese during the Japanese invasion is seen in a photograph taken in 1940 in a bombed-out district of Chongqing. The three Song sisters – Qingling, Meiling, and their older sister, Ailing – pick their way through the rubble in what, in practical terms, seems to be inappropriate dress for such an occasion.[12] In political terms, however, the famous Chinese women's dress, known as the cheongsam, or *qipao* in Mandarin Chinese, that all three wear was seen as the dress in which nationalism itself resided. This side-closing, high-necked, one-piece dress began to replace the skirt and jacket in the late

1920s. Revealing both the female form, via a close fit, and feminine flesh, due to shorter sleeves and a hemline with vertical slits at each side, the cheongsam style played out a modernity that chimed with the urban aesthetic of the period. While symbolic of female progress in that it signalled women's emancipation in the bodily sense, and, by extension, in the political and social one too, it could also be a provocative garment and was exploited as such by advertisers in Shanghai who depicted women posing in the dress in attitudes that seemed to suggest sexual availability.[13]

It was to be the youngest Song sister, Meiling, who used the cheongsam as the staple to wield the disruptive power of feminine charm and rally support for the Nationalists led by her husband. When Song Meiling returned to China after her United States college education in 1917, like her sister, she continued to wear American-style dresses. These were criticised as extravagant and unpatriotic and, on her wedding day in December 1927, both the red marriage outfit of traditional China and the incipient cheongsam were discarded in favour of a white and silver georgette dress with a draped skirt and long, silver-embroidered train. A white Chantilly lace veil, silver shoes and a bouquet of pink carnations completed the ensemble. This international style of white bridal dressing was gaining popularity in many rich urban centres at this period. It was perceived by some in China as modern despite many of its manifestations being based on European fashions of earlier centuries.[14] Chiang Kai-shek, Song Meiling's groom, wore a black cutaway coat with tails, a wing-collared white shirt and tie, striped trousers and spats. These ostentatious nuptials were in sharp contrast to those of the other Song sister, Qingling, and Sun Yat-sen, but the two couples' situations were not dissimilar. Chiang, like Sun, was still married, and his wife, Chen Jieru, continued to style herself as Madame Chiang Kai-shek. When the impending union between the youngest Song sister and the leader of the Nationalists was announced a few months prior to the wedding date, the headline in the *New York Times* of 17 September 1927 signalled the interaction of political and private lives with the headline 'Chiang Will Wed Madame Sun's Sister'. To his widow's lifelong regret, reference to Sun Yat-sen was to become the leitmotif of the Chiangs' unpalatable and fascist-leaning credo for China. During their marriage ceremony, they solemnly bowed to a portrait of Sun, the father figure, clad in his famous suit and although, at this stage, Chiang did not wear the outfit named for Sun, he would later do so, fully aware of its capabilities as a rallying point for support. His alliance with Sun's name was a calculated and enormously fortuitous move. But his bride brought much more to the marriage than a talismanic name.

Song Meiling was to be a charming and charmed ambassadress for her husband's cause. Right from the start of her marriage, her white wedding dress in the Christian tradition had bridged a cultural divide between China and the West. Her command of English was of enormous benefit to a China seeking to woo America's help against Japanese aggression, but her appearance was paramount in this courtship between East and West. The way she used the language of clothes to structure the effect of what she actually said lies at the heart of her subsequent choice of the cheongsam; she carefully posed in the dress to be attractive, even seductive, but was never languid or sexually inviting. When she became Madame Chiang, and, in turn, First Lady of China, Song Meiling followed her older sister's example and hugely exploited her photogenic potential to boost the Nationalist line (Figure 2). Neither she nor her husband were universally popular within China and her good looks and elegant dress sense may have helped ameliorate this. She posed beside her husband, as her sister had done, but frequently faced the cameras alone. Her triumphant tour of North American cities in 1943, without her husband, is one of the defining moments in the perception of China by foreigners. She was seen by a quarter of a million Americans, and newspapers across the land carried photographs of her and were much taken up with their charismatic Chinese visitor's clothes and looks as commentators followed Madame Chiang's progress from Washington to New York, Chicago, San Francisco and Los Angeles.[15] For both male and female reporters, whether they were social columnists or political journalists, her sartorial good taste hardly ever eluded them. The front page of the *Chicago Daily Tribune* of 20 March 1943, for example, noted the navy blue, embroidered Chinese dress and her 'scarlet-tipped nails' as well as other points regarding her appearance. The sight of her made 'brave men go limp'. A reception held in her honour in the Palm Court of Chicago's grand limestone, lake-front Drake Hotel was reported on page 10 of the same issue. The split skirt of her ruby sequin-edged black velvet cheongsam revealed 'eminently occidental pumps, open-toed and open-heeled'. The *Chicago Daily News* too reported the reception scene on the same day, this time on their society pages, with the headline 'Madame Chiang Even Lovelier Than Her Pictures Show, Guests At Reception Find'. Images of Madame Chiang captured in other photographs at this time give us a clue as to how appearances worked in her favour to become hallmarks of her campaign. The spectacle of 'Christian Miss Soong', as she was called by Henry R. Luce, the media mogul and sponsor of her tour, shaped the affection many American people came to feel for China. In February 1943, the first great set-piece of Madame Chiang's tour occurred. She addressed Congress standing on a raised central podium, the Stars and Stripes unfurled behind her. An archival photograph records the scene with Congress members, a phalanx of maleness in identically styled dark suits (there seem to be only

Figure 2: Chiang Kai-shek, Song Meiling and the American General Stilwell, April, 1942, Hulton Archive.

two other women present), standing away from the camera but facing towards the lady from China in a cheongsam. Beside these 'ripened politicians', as *Vogue* was to call them, 'she looked like a steel sword'.[16] She has her hair sleeked back into a bun at the nape of her neck, for she never bobbed her hair as others did; she thus avoided the massive controversy provoked by the cutting of women's long hair in the early twentieth-century years.[17] Instead, it was her adoption of the cheongsam that signalled her modernity and, at the same time, gave her an instant look of 'Chineseness'.

It seems apposite at this point to refer to a meeting between the Chiangs and two foreigners that took place in China in 1938. It explains much about the differing degrees of appeal between the two spouses. W. H. Auden and Christopher Isherwood, poet and writer respectively whose travel diary about China has a certain eccentric off-centredness about it, comment on Song Meiling's perfume, 'the most delicious either of us have ever smelt', as well as her 'terrifying charm and poise'. The impression Chiang Kai-shek made on them was perceptive as regards leaders' appearances:

> We should hardly have recognised in this bald, mild-looking, brown-eyed man, the cloaked, poker-stiff figure of the news-reels. In public and on official occasions, Chiang is an almost sinister presence; he has the fragile impassivity of a spectre. Here in private he seemed gentle and shy. Madame led him onto the balcony to pose, arm-in-arm, for yet another photograph. Under the camera's eye he stiffened visibly, like a schoolboy who is warned to hold himself upright.[18]

Chiang rarely wore western civilian clothes, a notable exception being on his wedding day. Prior to his withdrawal to Taiwan in 1949, an army uniform of one sort or another was his preferred public mode of dressing. He had been nurtured in military academies from youth and was to continue in that vein in his quest to unify China that, since Sun's death, had become so fragmented there was a fear that it might disappear altogether as a nation. The army style he adopted was really a Sun Yat-sen suit in khaki (Figure 2). This soldierly tunic was sometimes teamed with a leather belt and cross-wise holster-strap over one shoulder and variously worn with jodhpurs, straight-cut trousers, tall boots, or puttees and shoes. From the beginning of the 1930s, having overthrown several warlords in preposterous uniforms, Chiang himself began to dress self-importantly, as noted in the Auden and Isherwood diary. At first, he took to white gloves, dark glasses and that most flamboyant of articles, the cloak, and then he positively sparkled in a confection of a full-dress uniform awash with stars and plum blossoms and with epaulettes seemingly the width of his head. That a military mien held sway should not surprise us, for China was continuously at war, either with itself or with foreign powers, from 1911 to 1949.

Chiang's exaltation of the military way was, on occasion, tempered by a change of style. He was sometimes seen in a long gown. Chinese men who had been born in the decades either side of 1900 had grown up wearing it and all three male leaders we are discussing here were photographed in their youth dressed in it. They and others of their generation continued to give the style their allegiance to a greater or lesser degree partly because of its familiarity and comfort, and it remained formal attire for Nationalist party members under the same 1929 government edict that required civil servants to don the Sun Yat-sen suit. Chiang wore it to receive guests, as when he welcomed the

Swedish adventurer and Nazi sympathiser Sven Hedin (1865–1952) into his home in 1935.[19] He was also seen in a gown on more public occasions. He chose this more traditional form of dress to meet India's Gandhi (1869–1948) in 1942. To shake hands with this scantily clad figure, of slender physical but enormous metaphorical stature, while dressed in army uniform might seem an affront to Gandhi's nonviolent message. Furthermore, it could be seen as a gesture in recognition of the great Indian Nationalist leader's *khadi* movement. The Chinese Nationalists were also promoting home-produced cloth by wearing gowns made from silk, the quintessential Chinese fabric, instead of suits of foreign wool. Chiang sometimes favoured a gown around the time he was advocating the New Life Movement (1934–7), whose creed, gleaned from Christianity, Fascism and Confucianism, was designed to control people's moral behaviour. Against a background of defeat by the Communists in 1949, in the months before he decamped to Taiwan, Chiang Kai-shek again turned to this form of dress. He distanced himself from the increasingly visible Communist leadership by wearing different attire. His long gown can be seen as a wordless declaration of his allegiance to the ethics of China's past.[20]

There were times prior to his flight that he donned the Sun Yat-sen suit. Like Sun before him he wore it to meet the press. In 1939, he received Nehru (1889–1964), the president of the Indian National Congress and future prime minister, in such a suit. He signed the United Nations Charter in China's wartime capital, Chongqing, dressed that way and he broadcast the news of Japan's surrender at the end of the Second World War similarly suited. All these would be times when Chiang wished to play down any suggestion of the bellicose, and project China as a nation working towards peace. This suit was to play a big part in his public life, perhaps bigger than either military or traditional dress, after 1949 when he was prepared to assume Sun Yat-sen's mantle, both figuratively and literally. Once he had made his escape from Communist-dominated China, although he never entirely gave up other styles, Chiang Kai-shek opted for beige and light brown Sun Yat-sen suits, accessorised with a velour fedora and walking cane.[21] He thus mirrored his spouse Song Meiling's unwavering allegiance to the cheongsam, a dress style she has never relinquished.

The Communist leader, Mao Zedong, presided in person over Tiananmen Square in Beijing at the founding of the People's Republic of China in 1949. He began his long term of office wearing a Mao suit and deviated from that style only when he shed the jacket to reveal a white shirt in summer or to put on army uniform. It was not a new style for him; he had been wearing a more rough and ready version of it through long years of shortages and warfare during the 1930s and 1940s in some of China's remotest regions. This must have given him a familiarity with its convenience – the expandable pockets, apparently, were much to his liking for stowing things he constantly needed – which he was loath to give up when the political tide turned in his favour. Shabby and rather shapeless, creased and patched, the cotton suit served him well through the setting up of the Communist cells in isolated, inhospitable regions. It saw him through the Long March (1934–5), Communism's greatest narrative of courageous endurance, which took Mao's women and men 6,000 miles to poverty-stricken Shaanxi province. The suit endured the years in mountainous Yan'an, which was the Chinese Communist Party's base from 1936 to 1945. It can be argued that, despite the Sun Yat-sen suit's possible western lineage, as worn by Mao it nonetheless retained echoes of Chinese peasant indigo-dyed tops and trousers, common to both sexes, making it an acceptable garb in keeping with the particular ideals of post-1949 China. The style's debt to China's Communist parent, the Soviet Union, sanctioned it as well.

Whatever the worker and peasant connotations of the Sun Yat-sen suit might be, there is no doubt that in certain manifestations it could be a highly presentable and, indeed, dapper, article of clothing. That some thought went into the presentation of the leader of China's Communist regime is, of course, self-evident in a country where all images were subject to censoring scrutiny. As the government stabilised its position as legitimate after 1949, so China's ruler underwent a sartorial meta-morphosis from the rebel days of the Yan'an cave headquarters to his demise and embalming in 1976.

Tailor to Mao was Tian Atong, a man very much alive to the messages of dress. In 1989, from the then state-run Hongdu ('Red Capital') Fashion Company in Beijing, he reminisced about clothing China's rulers and mused how different clothes said different things. He concluded that 'we need them all', his own versatility with shears and needle ensuring him a full order book whatever the political climate. In 1956, the peasant-born craftsman first met Mao when he was taken clandestinely to Zhongnanhai, the Beijing enclave where the government elite lived. Tian Atong's part in sustaining the correct image of the leader was not, of course, revealed at the time but, in order not to make Mao look too fat, he tailored the suits with a wider neck, narrower lapels and no pleats on the pockets. His distinctive and refined rendering of what could have been a rather drab style lives on in the 1957 portrait of the Chairman in the Forbidden City and, within a crystal sarcophagus nearby, another of Mr Tian's suits shrouds the breathless corpse of the former ruler.[22]

While some Chinese caught a glimpse of their leader at gatherings, parades and rallies, most did not see Mao for themselves. The propaganda machine of the state, however, ensured that all 800 million people, the estimated total population during the 1970s, recognised him and imbibed his appearance so that it was utterly familiar. His clothing habits contributed to people's instant acquaintance with Mao's inescapable image and, furthermore, these images could be manipulated to produce emotions favoured by the Party, as instanced by the saviour-like oil portrait of a young Mao in a long gown, reproductions of which were distributed by the multi-million in the Cultural Revolution.[23]

It is a common perception that the overabundant visual records of the Communist leadership are remarkable for a greater absence of spouses than the previous regime. The spotlighting of partners who shared their lives with those in political power, in this argument, was not a feature of the People's Republic of China. However, further research in more recently available material may ultimately lead to a revision of this perceived situation.[24] Be that as it may, Jiang Qing, three times married herself and third wife of Mao, was, at first, allowed almost no part in public life, but was later to become an increasingly familiar figure. The daughter of a rural carpenter, she became an actress in Shanghai and wore middle-class western dress styles and the cheongsam at a time when some of her contemporaries were taking up proletarian workers' clothing as a political gesture. Her transformation to revolutionary when it came, following on the Japanese attack on Shanghai in 1937 and her marriage to Mao the following year, required a change of costume. Her acting credentials perhaps prepared her for this and, although she discarded her sophisticated Shanghai clothes, she seems to have retained a flair for dressing in a way that marked her out from others. Commentators have noticed how, from the early Yan'an days on, she belted her suit jacket or coat with a certain panache, wound a scarf over the top of her cadre cap and maintained an attractive appearance in 'a high-authority suit with a touch of colour at the throat, and the maximum possible beauty of her hair'.[25] However, we should set all this against images, perhaps less well remembered in the light of Jiang Qing's subsequent notoriety, of other Communist women who also seem to have dressed with discernment. In 1950, Jiang was assigned the task of formally bidding farewell to Song Qingling, who was returning to Shanghai after the inauguration ceremonies of the People's Republic in Beijing. Song Qingling's aide remembered Mao's wife wearing blue woollen trousers teamed with a blue and white striped blouse and a blue peaked cap. Six years later, the same aide recalled Jiang Qing looking neat and slender in a Sun Yat-sen jacket at a reception given by Sun's widow. After the low-profile 1950s, the next decade marked a shift of register for Jiang Qing. Roderick MacFarquhar pinpoints the 1962 visit of Madame Hartini Sukarno, spouse of the president of Indonesia, as seminal in Jiang Qing's visibility

within China's carefully contested hierarchies (Figure 3). Always a
significant pointer as to those in favour with the leadership at a given
time, the arrival of foreign dignitaries in the People's Republic provided
an opportunity for internal power jostling to be resolved, often in visual
terms. On this occasion, Jiang Qing was accorded a place on the front
page of China's national paper, the *People's Daily*, along with Mao and
their Indonesian guest. It represented several triumphs for the trim,
trouser-suited Jiang. It was her first photographic appearance in this

Figure 3: Jiang Qing, in a rare photograph together with Mao Zedong,
on the occasion of the visit to China of Madame Sukarno of Indonesia,
29 September 1962, Hulton Archive

nation-wide daily, the first officially released picture of her and Mao together, and it marked her ascendancy over another wife, Wang Guangmei (b. 1922), married to Liu Shaoqi (1898–1969), a possible but doomed successor to Mao. Wang Guangmei, dressed in a cheongsam, appeared on the second page of the newspaper with her husband and Madame Sukarno.[26]

Although Jiang Qing and Mao rarely appeared as a couple, she was increasingly included in the leadership line-ups as she positioned herself more prominently in politics. As Mao himself needed support against rival factions, she urged a purification of the revolutionary vision, along with a group of Shanghai radicals. During the Cultural Revolution, the dates of which are now enshrined as 1966–76, she urged greater party control over the arts and personally reformed Peking opera so that class lines became clear-cut. Workers and peasants were the main protagonists on the side of revolutionary right. Jiang Qing was thus returning to her early association with the theatre with all the concomitant staginess. We might suppose that she would dress more dramatically than she appears to have done. In public at least, during the disorderly times of the 1960s, she was frequently seen in a drab military-style suit or greatcoat with an army cap to the back of her head. In the next decade, she reverted to tailored trouser suits. In 1972, when the United States President, Richard Nixon (1913–94) opened up a new stage in American Cold War diplomacy by his dramatic visit to China, Jiang Qing escorted him to a performance of her model ballet, *The Red Detachment of Women.* She looked smart in a dark jacket with turned-back lapels revealing a shirt buttoned to the neck. In the same year, she posed for the *People's Daily* with Roxane Witke, an American academic uniquely granted a series of interviews with Jiang Qing, in a waisted, light-coloured Sun Yat-sen suit. With Mao away from Beijing for eight months in 1974, Jiang Qing was the name that appeared at the top of the list of leaders attending government functions, and these business-like suits befitted her new stature. In other pictures published in Roxane Witke's much-remarked study of Jiang Qing, Jiang chose to allow herself to be photographed in a silk shirt-waister dress with short sleeves and gathered skirt. This was a form of clothing in which she had never hitherto been presented to a mass Chinese audience through media within the People's Republic because, as an equal to men, she was required to assimilate to male norms and therefore had to look the same as them. Gendered dressing was, at times, a highly charged issue in Maoist China, but a 'normal' person remained a man, while women like Jiang Qing were singled out by the term *nü* ('woman') marked next to their names in the Politburo members' lists. A further garment associated very closely with the name of Jiang Qing is the enigmatic 'Jiang Qing dress'. This V-necked, tailored dress, evidence for which survives in the form of oral history and at least one actual example in a museum outside China, remains to be more fully investigated but is, at any rate, proof that in the eyes of her enemies, and possibly of the woman herself, clothing and the presentation of self played an important part.[27]

The various dress choices described above, although made at specific historic moments, can profitably be viewed within a framework of interconnected themes. All three marriages were made when the male partners already had a title to fame. The set-piece wedding of the Chiangs, with its show of lavish finery, asserted the political and financial prestige Song Meiling was bringing to the marriage, and set the tone for her future performance as the president's wife. Song Qingling's much more low-key outfits, in some measure, foretold her clothing conduct too. Photographs taken around the time of Jiang Qing's marriage to Mao show a youthful Jiang Qing, bandit-like in the bare landscape of the Communist rebel hideout. These glamorous pictures were publicly disseminated and privately circulated by Jiang Qing herself in the 1970s, a measure of how the originary moment of the relationship was seen as still possessing symbolic force more than thirty years later.[28]

Song Qingling and Song Meiling stepped into the spotlight at times of unprecedented media activity. The superabundance of illustrated newspapers and magazines of popular appeal cast politicians alongside film stars as celebrities, and clothes, put on in private but raised to an incredible pitch of public scrutiny, were one of the ways by which people were judged. The Chinese imperial age had its rituals of emperorship, and the autocratic style of rule lent itself to a dress code that was formalised into an hierarchical ordering that left little room for differing interpretations. Moreover, with the exception of the last empress dowager, Cixi (1835–1908), who was photographed and who cautiously opened up court life to outsiders, no reigning emperor nor his family, whether female or male, ever appeared in public. Twentieth-century leaders, denied the seclusion afforded the imperial clan, were constantly on show, as were their spouses. In the case of the sisters, Song Qingling and Song Meiling, their heightened visibility turned a brighter beam onto their male partners, whose private lives did not feature significantly in their public persona before their respective marriages. This suggests that the feminine and the domestic were resources to be deployed in opening up the personal. We have already noted a more informal side of Sun Yat-sen revealed through his wife, Song Qingling. Song Meiling, too, moderated the rather unyielding image of her husband and, when visiting front-line hospitals or makeshift orphanages, she might don an apron, roll up her sleeves or put on protective headwear. In dressing this way, she sent out messages, which touched on issues of mothering and nurturing, but there was always an artistry in the way she wore these practical clothes. Whereas women in traditional China had led separate lives from their marriage partners, the Song sisters were now being seen alongside their husbands. As one half of a couple, this exposed them as signifiers of male power, as *politicians' wives*, with their own interests subsumed under those of men. Following on the Communist victory, Song Meiling and Chiang Kai-shek retreated to the ready-prepared island fastness of Taiwan where, until recently, Nationalist troop indoctrination stressed the retaking of the motherland. In Taiwan, Song Meiling frequently posed with her husband until his death in 1975, she in a cheongsam, he in a Sun Yat-sen suit, waiting to return and resume the onward march of Republican modernity 'temporarily' interrupted by Communist insurgency. Until that moment, history and dress history alike stand still.

Mao Zedong's wife, Jiang Qing, was hardly ever seen or photographed with the Chairman for the entire duration of the marriage and, in the 1950s, the stringently controlled media were deliberately kept away from her. She was not, at first, prominent in any role at all, either domestic or political, perhaps signifying a different kind of marriage from those of the Song sisters. We can conclude that in the beginning, unlike the Song sisters, she was not seen as bringing anything positive to the marriage and, during the 1950s, a time when she suffered ill-health, no suitable public activity could be found for her. She was not prepared to be a submissive housewife, a situation to which many Communist women were assigned, despite the rhetoric about equality. There was a profound ambivalence at the heart of the Communist project as regards gender roles and this ambivalence was particularly fraught in the fifties.[29] Jiang Qing's entrée into the Communist hierarchy was publicly signalled with a press photograph, as we have seen. From that time on, she increasingly and dramatically wielded power, professing to be in line with her husband's revolutionary beliefs but still not often appearing with him.

While few photographs of Song Qingling during her ten years of marriage have come to light showing her on her own, her long years of widowhood gave her a degree of leverage in determining issues relating to the presentation of the image of her deceased husband, the lamented 'Father of the Nation' (*guofu*) as he was styled after his demise. Her role as keeper of the flame can perhaps be most clearly seen in her intervention at the planning stage of Sun Yat-sen's mausoleum some years after his actual death. Although she does not appear to have been amongst those officially listed as on the steering committee in its earlier stages, she, nonetheless, seems to have contributed her views over the figure sculptures, an innovation for Chinese memorials at this time.[30] They proved to be the subject of some controversy and it was the question of dress that caused the committee to split into two factions, with Sun's widow favouring the revolutionary look. Other statues elsewhere at this pilgrimage site show a differently clad Sun Yat-sen, suggesting a com-promise solution, but his widow's choice, which was used over the tomb itself, seems to have been paramount in constructing Sun as a national icon. From this time, portraits of Sun Yat-sen, wearing versions of the suit that came to be so associated with him, were hung in public spaces and his visage looked out from banknotes, coins and stamps.

Song Qingling, separated by death from her husband, perforce acted alone. Jiang Qing, under different circumstances, did so as well. In making a solo tour of America, Song Meiling acted as an emollient between her notoriously rebarbative husband and the outside world by representing China as something special. Her huge popularity there arguably would have been diminished if her appearance had not been so carefully stage-managed. It was her entire demeanour, heightened by the elegant cheongsam she wore, that made her such an effective lobbyist for her country.

We can only speculate what direct influence each spouse brought to bear on the other over clothing choices; we must not assume that it was always the women who took the lead over such concerns. Although all our protagonists here were seriously involved with their self-disclosure through dress, this does not mean that the messages they meant to convey were successfully or uncritically received. With regard to the women in particular, dress formed a focus of critique for vilification by their political opponents. Song Qingling – the intelligent secretary to a husband whose mythologised status both shielded her from criticism and perhaps, without totally engulfing her in the rigours of state coercion under Communism, limited her to certain options as regards visibility – remained a revered and uncontested figure. By contrast, Song Meiling and Jiang Qing came in for a barrage of negative criticism that, in some instances, was a covert way of attacking their husbands. What concerns us here, especially, is the form this critique took. It often impinged on the world of appearances and it manifested itself in the form of rumours and hearsay. The story of Song Meiling's diamond-encrusted high-heeled shoes, a snub to the sacrifices of wartime China, is one of several unsubstantiated but often-repeated narratives. Jiang Qing's flouting of dress etiquette at the memorial service of Premier Zhou Enlai (1899–1976) is another. In the same connection, we should note that very many cartoons drawn at the time of Jiang Qing's downfall depict her in a voluminous-skirted dress.[31] Jiang Qing's faction lost out in the coup d'état following Mao's death in 1976 and she was put on trial and imprisoned. In the context of rigorous state control, one aspect of destructive criticism was to show that she was a woman and that the state itself had reserves of misogyny to draw on. Such representations invoke an unambiguous link between gender, clothes and transgression, a link that has been ritualised in many cultures and periods. Dress tells the woman's story but may equally tell the man's. The women of these three marriage unions negotiated the disparities with flair and insight and, although initially they attained their pre-eminent positions by marrying the men they did, the way they then chose to present themselves cast them as equivalent actors in a single drama.

Notes

1. See Marie-Claire Bergère, *Sun Yat-sen*, trans. Janet Lloyd (Stanford University Press, 1998), for a critical assessment of Sun Yat-sen's life.
2. See Frank Dikötter, *Sex, Culture and Modernity in China: Medical Science and the Construction of Sexual Identities in the Early Modern Period* (Hurst & Company, 1995); Harriet Evans, *Women and Sexuality in China: Dominant Discourses of Female Sexuality and Gender Since 1949* (Polity Press, 1997), for discussions on Chinese gender perceptions.
3. Shanghai Museum of Sun Yat-sen's Former Residence, *Sun Zhongshan: jinian Sun Zhongshan xiansheng danchen 130 zhounian* (Sun Yat-sen: In Commemoration of the 130th Anniversary of Dr Sun's Birth) (*Shanghai renmin chubanshe*, Shanghai People's Publishing House, 1996), p. 27, pl. 2/19, p. 32, pl. 2/29, 30, p. 58, pl. 3/12, p. 123, pl. 5/12, p. 135, pl. 5/40; Cao Feng (ed.), *Song Qingling zai Shanghai* (Song Qingling in Shanghai) (*Shanghai renmin chubanshe*, Shanghai People's Publishing House, 1992), p. 29, pl. 36.
4. Henrietta Harrison, *The Making of the Republican Citizen: Political Ceremonies and Symbols in China, 1911–1929* (Oxford University Press, 2000), pp. 58–60 and pp. 190–92, discusses the dress laws of both 1912 and 1929 and the implications of these laws for the indigenous silk industry.
5. Antonia Finnane, 'Military Culture and Chinese Dress in the Early Twentieth Century', in *China Chic: East Meets West,* ed. Valerie Steele and John S. Major (Yale University Press, 1999), pp. 118–31.
6. Henrietta Harrison, *The Making of the Republican Citizen*, pp. 49, 54–7.
7. *Sun Zhongshan: jinian Sun Zhongshan xiansheng danchen 130 zhounian*, p. 126, pl. 5/19, p. 127, pl. 5/21,22.
8. *Selected Stories of Lu Xun*, trans. Yang Hsien-yi and Gladys Yang (Foreign Languages Press, 3rd edn, 1972), pp. 156–63.
9. *A Pictorial History of the Republic of China: Its Founding and Development* (Modern China Press, 1981), vol. 1, p. 247, pl. 3; *Sun Zhongshan: jinian Sun Zhongshan xiansheng danchen 130 zhounian*, p. 178, pl. 6–37.
10. Vincent Sheean, *Personal History* (Houghton Mifflin, 1969), p. 268.
11. Stuart Gelder, *The Chinese Communists* (Victor Gollanz Ltd., 1946), pp. xi–xiii, for one of several interviews Song Qingling gave distancing herself from the Nationalists; *Liangyou huabao* (The Young Companion) (July 1929), p. 3, for pictures of Song Qingling at the internment ceremony; Edgar Snow, *Journey to the Beginning* (Victor Gollanz Ltd., 1959), p. 91, for the observation about her gowns.
12. Emily Hahn, *The Soong Sisters* (Doubleday, 1941), plate opposite p. 308.
13. Francesca Dal Lago, 'Crossed Legs in 1930s Shanghai: How "Modern" the Modern Woman?', *East Asian History* (June 2000), 103–44.
14. *Liangyou huabao* (December 1930), p. 14, for the Native Products Fashion Show held at the Majestic Hotel, Shanghai, in 1930, which included a Chinese-made wedding dress with a flounced skirt and ties at the neck.
15. T. Christopher Jespersen, *American Images of China: 1913–1949* (Stanford University Press, 1996), pp. 82, 97 and 99, for accounts from the *Washington Post*, *New York Times* and *Los Angeles Times*.

16. The National Archives, Washington, DC and published in T. Christopher Jespersen, *American Images of China*, between pp. 44 and 45; *Vogue*, 15 April 1943, pp. 33–7.

17. Lung-kee Sun, 'The Politics of Hair and the Issue of the Bob in Modern China', *Fashion Theory*, 1 (1997), pp. 353–65.

18. W. H. Auden and Christopher Isherwood, *Journey to a War* (Faber and Faber, 1939), pp. 65, 68.

19. Sven Hedin, *Chiang Kai-shek, Marshal of China*, trans. Bernard Norbelie (John Day and Co., 1940), plate opposite p. 57.

20. *President Chiang Kai-shek: His Life in Pictures* (Government Information Office, Taipei, 1971), pp. 55, 120–21, for examples of Chiang in a long gown; *Liangyou huabao* (November 1928), p. 8, shows Chiang Kai-shek wearing a Sun Yat-sen suit, not a silk gown, to the inauguration of the Native Products Exposition.

21. *A Pictorial History of the Republic of China*, vol. 1, p. 294, pl. 2, p. 484, pl. 2, vol. 2, p. 33, pl. 1, p. 52, pl. 3, p. 63, pl. 1, p. 392, pl. 4; *A Glimpse of Old China* (China Pictorial Publishing House, 1995), p. 88; *President Chiang Kai-shek*, frontispiece, pp. iv and v; Helen and Frank Schreider, 'Taiwan, the Watchful Dragon', *National Geographic*, 1 (1969), pp. 1–45 (p. 12).

22. Andrew Higgins, 'The Man Who Cuts the Emperor's New Clothes', *The Independent*, 16 December 1989.

23. Verity Wilson, 'Dress and the Cultural Revolution', in *China Chic: East Meets West*, pp. 166–86 (pp. 169–70).

24. Sheng Yonghua and Bai Lang (eds), *Lishi de jiaoyin: Tong Xipeng sheying ziliao xuanji* (Footprint of History: Selected Photographs of Tong Xipeng) (*Wenwu chubanshe*, 1990).

25. Ross Terrill, *Madame Mao: The White-Boned Demon* (Stanford University Press, rev. edn, 1999), pp. 45, 111, 218; Claire Roberts (ed.), *Evolution and Revolution: Chinese Dress, 1700–1900s*, Powerhouse Museum exhibition catalogue (Powerhouse Publishing, 1997), p. 24.

26. Roderick MacFarquhar, 'On Photographs', *China Quarterly*, 46 (1971), 289–307 (pp. 300–301). Jiang Qing and Wang Guangmei did, however, appear on the same page of the English-language propaganda magazine *China Pictorial* at this time.

27. Roxane Witke, *Comrade Chiang Ch'ing* (Weidenfeld and Nicolson, 1977), plates between pp. 220 and 221, between pp. 334 and 335; Roberts (ed.), *Evolution and Revolution*, p. 24.

28. In 1975 the Museum of Revolutionary History at Yan'an still displayed pictures of the youthful Jiang Qing with Mao; see David E. Apter and Tony Saich, *Revolutionary Discourse in Mao's Republic* (Harvard University Press, 1994), pp. 170, 188–9, for a flavour of their life at Yan'an; Roxane Witke, *Comrade Chiang Ch'ing*, plate between pp. 220 and 221 (photograph by Roman Karmen).

29. Delia Davin, *'Women-Work': Women and the Party in Revolutionary China* (Clarendon Press, 1976).

30. Henrietta Harrison, *The Making of the Republican Citizen*, p. 208; Rudolf G. Wagner, 'Reading the Chairman Mao Memorial Hall', in *Pilgrims and Sacred Sites in China,* ed. Susan Naquin and Chün-fang Yü (University of California Press, 1992), pp. 378–423 (p. 420, n. 5).

31. See Sterling Seagrave, *The Soong Dynasty* (1985; repr. Corgi Books, 1997), pp. 218–82, for the diamond story; Verity Wilson, 'Dress and the Cultural Revolution', p. 173, for hearsay regarding Jiang Qing's clothes; Roxane Witke, *Comrade Chiang Ch'ing*, plates between pp. 334 and 335, and Ross Terrill, *Madame Mao*, plates on pp. 104 and 105, for cartoons.

Index